To Doug & Deb

Thanks for everything

Heidi & Jim

HUGH
JOHNSON'S

POCKET ENCYCLOPEDIA OF
WINE 1995

ISBN 0-671-88635-6

A Fireside Book
Published by Simon & Schuster Inc.
New York London Toronto
Sydney Tokyo Singapore

Key to Symbols

r	red
p	rosé
w	white
br	brown
(r)	denotes less important wine
dr	dry (assume wine is dry when **dr** or **sw** not indicate
sw	sweet
s/sw	semi-sweet
sp	sparkling
★	plain, everyday quality
★★	above average
★★★	well known, highly reputed
★★★★	grand, prestigious, expensive
▬	usually particularly good value in its class
91 92 etc	recommended years which may be currently available
88' etc	vintage regarded as particularly successful for the property in question
87 etc	Years in **bold** should be ready for drinking (the others should be kept). Where both reds and whites are indicated the red is intended unless otherwise stated.
89	Vintages in colour are the ones to choose first for drinking in '95. They should be à point. **NB** German vintages are codified by a different system. See note on page 103.
(93)	provisional rating
DYA	drink the youngest available
NV	Vintage not normally shown on label. In Champagne, means a blend of several vintages for continuity.
SMALL CAPS	properties, areas or terms cross-referred within the section.

See page 5 for extra explanation.
A quick-reference vintage chart appears on page 216.

Fireside
Simon & Schuster Inc
Rockefeller Center
1230 Avenue of the Americas
New York, New York 10020

© Mitchell Beazley International Ltd 1977–1994
Text © Hugh Johnson 1977–1994
Maps © Mitchell Beazley International Ltd 1977–1994
First edition published 1977
Revised editions published 1978, 1979, 1980, 1981, 1982, 1983, 1984, 1985, 1986, 1987, 1988, 1989, 1990, 1991, 1992, 1993, 1994

ISBN 0-671-88635-5
ISSN 0893-259X

The author and publishers will be grateful for any information which will assist them in keeping future editions up to date. Although all reasonable care has been taken in the preparation of this book, neither the publishers nor the author can accept any liability for any consequences arising from the use thereof, or from the information contained herein.

Editors Susan Keevil, Anthea Snow
Executive Editor Anne Ryland
Production Michelle Thomas
Map origination by Lovell Johns
Produced by Mandarin Offset
Printed in Malaysia

Contents

Foreword

This little book comes of age with its 18th edition. It is irresistible to compare the world it surveys with the one it sketched in 1977. I look back in wonder at the simplicity of the first edition: unhurried little notes rather elegantly laid out on 144 pages with handsome wide margins. Today's book is hugger-mugger in comparison: 216 pages carrying so much information that not only space but grammar and vocabulary are under severe stress.

Of course all it has done is to reflect changing times, improving standards, and burgeoning choice. Wine lists 18 years ago were usually simple, scarcely straying outside Europe's classic regions except for local interest and a touch of colour. Today the world is the wine-drinker's oyster, and very confusing it all is: too complicated, in fact, for any but near-fanatics to want to master it.

Hence the paradox that at the same time as the choice is wider than ever before, more wine-drinkers than ever are tempted to shrug their shoulders and say 'So long as it's Chardonnay...'. On this basis professional wine-buyers are free to concentrate on 'price-points' and let the most precious attribute of wine, the vitality that comes with variety, go hang.

It is all too easy these days for winemakers to follow the fruit-juice formula: maximum control, virtual sterility – and then add a bit of oak flavour for 'style'. But oenological correctness is as stultifying and anti-life as political correctness.

Wine is almost the last food we are allowed to consume that can bring us the authentic taste of local fruit, a singular soil and its unique ecology. This is what the French mean when they talk of 'terroir'. Even if only half of it is true it is still something to fight for. Wine should be as exhilarating as a deep breath on a spring morning; as full of nature's scents, as elusive to analysis.

Who is winning then: the individualist or the Great Homogenizer? Happily the evidence of this book says diversity is well ahead. It is your job and mine, as lovers of the spice of life, to back the individualist every time.

As before, my aim in this book is to squeeze the essence of this ever-changing world of wine into your pocket.

To new readers I must explain that my information is gathered from many sources through innumerable visits and tastings and a perpetual spate of correspondence. The revision process never stops, with constant pressure for inclusion from new producers. Newness itself, however, is not a qualification for entry.

The book is designed to take the panic out of buying. You are faced with a long restaurant wine list or shelf upon mind-numbing shelf of bottles in a store. Your mind goes blank. You fumble for your little book. All you need to establish is what country a wine comes from. Look up the principal words on the label in that country's section. You will find enough potted information to let you judge whether this is the wine you want.

Specifically, you will find the type and colour of wine, its status, whether it is good value, which vintages are recommendable, which are ready to drink – often considerably more. Thousands of cross-references help you delve further. I can browse for hours...

How to use this book

The top line of most entries consists of the following information:

1 Which part of the country in question the wine comes from.
2 Whether it is red, rosé or white (or brown/amber), dry, sweet or sparkling, or several of these (and which is most important).
3 Its general standing as to quality: a necessarily rough and ready guide based on its current reputation as reflected in its prices.

    *   plain, everyday quality

    **   above average

   ***   well-known, highly reputed

  ****   grand, prestigious, expensive

So much is more or less objective. Additionally there is a subjective rating: shading around the stars of any wine which in my experience is usually particularly good within its price range. There are good everyday wines as well as good luxury wines. The shading system helps you find them.

4 Vintage information: which of the recent vintages that *may* still be available can be recommended; of these, which are ready to drink this year, and which will probably improve with keeping. Your first choice for current drinking should be one of the vintage years printed in **bold** type. Buy light-type years for further maturing.

This edition introduces a new short-cut vintage category. Vintages printed in colour are the ones you should choose first for drinking in 1995. Consult the Bordeaux introduction (page 56) for more on this.

German vintages works on a different principle again: see page 103.

...and my thanks

This store of detailed recommendations comes partly from my own notes and partly from those of a great number of kind friends. Without the generous help and cooperation of innumerable winemakers, merchants and critics, I could not attempt it. I particularly want to thank the following for help with research or in the areas of their special knowledge.

Burton Anderson
Colin Anderson MW
Fritz Ascher
Martyn Assirati
Jean-Claude Berrouet
Michael Broadbent MW
Stelios Damianou
Marc Dubernet
Len Evans
Dereck Foster
François Gaignet
Howard Goldberg
Grahame Haggart
James Halliday
Russell Hone
Stephanie Horner
Susan Keevil
Andreas Keller
Gabriel Lachmann
Tony Laithwaite
David Lake MW
Miles Lambert-Gócs
Christopher Lindlar
Giles MacDonogh
Andreas März
Eszter Molnár

Jasper Morris
Vladimir Moskvan
Christian Moueix
Douglas Murray
Nobuko Nishioka
David Orr
Judy Peterson-Nedry
Stuart Pigott
John and Erica Platter
Carlos Read
Jan and Maite Read
Dr Bernard Rhodes
Anne Ryland
Michael, Prinz zu Salm
Peter A Sichel
Stephen Skelton
Domingo de Soares Franco
Steven Spurrier
Charles and Philippa Sydney
Paul Symington
Bob Thompson
Peter Vinding-Diers
Rebecca Wassermann-Hone
Julia Wilkinson
David Wolfe

Grape Varieties

As more and more wine is sold under its grape-variety name, especially in regions and countries with no 'classic' traditions, a knowledge of the flavours and qualities of the most-planted (or rather most-sold) varieties becomes the first weapon in the wine buyer's armoury. Centuries of selection have resulted in each of Europe's traditional wine areas having its favourite variety, or group of varieties. Red burgundy is made of one grape, the Pinot Noir; red Bordeaux of three or four (the proportions at the discretion of the grower). The laws say which grapes must be used, so the labels do not (indeed may not) mention them.

But in newer regions the choice of grapes is the growers' first decision. Where they are proud of it, and intend the wine to have the flavour of a particular grape, its variety is the first thing they put on the label. Hence the originally Californian term 'varietal wine' – meaning, in principle, one grape variety.

At least seven varieties – Cabernet, Pinot Noir, Riesling, Sauvignon Blanc, Chardonnay, Gewürztraminer and Muscat – have tastes and smells distinct and memorable enough to form international categories of wine. To these you can add Merlot, Syrah, Sémillon, Chenin Blanc, Pinots Blanc and Gris, Sylvaner, Nebbiolo, Sangiovese, Tempranillo.... The following are the best and/or commonest wine grapes. Abbreviations used in the text are in brackets.

Grapes for white wine

Albariño The Spanish name for N Portugal's Alvarinho, newly emerging as excellently fresh and fragrant wine in Galicia.

Aligoté Burgundy's second-rank white grape. Crisp (often sharp) wine, needs drinking in 1–3 years. Perfect for mixing with cassis (blackcurrant liqueur) to make a 'Kir'. Widely planted in E Europe, esp Russia.

Blanc Fumé Alias of SAUV BL, referring to its reputedly 'smoky' smell, particularly from the upper Loire (Sancerre and Pouilly). In California often used for oak-aged Sauv Bl and reversed to 'Fumé Blanc'.

Bual Makes top quality sweet madeira wines.

Chardonnay (Chard) The white burgundy grape, the white grape of Champagne, and the best white grape of the New World, partly because it is one of the easiest and most forgiving to grow and vinify. All regions are now trying it, mostly aged (or fermented) in oak to reproduce the flavours of burgundy. Australia and California make classics. Those of Italy, Spain, New Zealand, South Africa, New York State, Bulgaria, Chile, Hungary and the Midi are all coming on strong.

Chasselas A prolific early-ripening grape with little aroma, also grown for eating. Best known as Fendant in Switzerland (where it is supreme), Gutedel in Germany.

Chenin Blanc (Chenin Bl) The great white grape of the middle Loire (Vouvray, Layon etc). Wine can be dry or sweet (or very sweet), but always retains plenty of acidity – hence its long life and use in California, where it can make fine wine, but is rarely so used. See also Steen.

Clairette A dull neutral grape formerly widely used in the S of France.

Colombard Slightly fruity, nicely sharp grape, hugely popular in California, now gaining ground in SW France, South Africa etc.

Fendant See Chasselas.

Folle Blanche High acid/little flavour make this ideal for brandy. Called Gros Plant in Brittany, Picpoul in Armagnac. Respectable in California.

Fumé Blanc (Fumé Bl) See Blanc Fumé.

Furmint A grape of great character: the trademark of Hungary both as the principal grape in Tokay and as vivid vigorous table wine with an appley flavour. Called Sipon in Slovenia. Some grown in Austria.

Grechetto or Greco Ancient grape of central and S Italy: vitality and style.

Gewürztraminer, alias Traminer (Gewürz) One of the most pungent grapes, distinctively spicy with aromas like rose petals and grapefruit. Wines are often rich and soft, even when fully dry. Best in Alsace; also good in Germany, E Europe, Australia, California, Pacific NW, New Zealand.

Grauburgunder See Pinot Gris.

Grüner Veltliner Austria's favourite. Around Vienna and in the Wachau and Weinviertel (also in Moravia) it can be delicious: light but dry and lively. The best age 5 years or so.

Italian Riesling Grown in N Italy and all over E Europe. Much inferior to Rhine RIES, with lower acidity, best in sweet wines. Alias Welschriesling, Olaszrizling (but can no longer legally be labelled simply 'Riesling').

Kerner The most successful of many recent German varieties, mostly made by crossing RIES and SILVANER (but in this case RIES x (red) Trollinger). Early-ripening flowery (but often too blatant) wine with good acidity. Popular in Pfalz, Rheinhessen etc.

Macabeo The workhorse white grape of N Spain, widespread in Rioja (alias Viura) and in Catalan cava country.

Malvasia Known as Malmsey in Madeira, Malvasia in Italy, Malvoisie in France. Alias Vermentino (esp in Corsica). Also grown in Greece, Spain, W Australia, E Europe. Makes rich brown wines or soft whites, ageing magnificently with superb potential not often realized.

Marsanne Principal white grape (with Roussanne) of the N Rhône (eg Crozes-Hermitage, St-Joseph, St-Péray). Also used to effect in Victoria, California and (as Ermitage Blanc) in the Valais. Soft full wines age v well.

Müller-Thurgau (Müller-T) Dominant in Germany's Rheinhessen and Pfalz and too common on the Mosel; a cross between RIESLING and SILVANER. Ripens early to make soft aromatic wines for drinking young. Makes good sweet wines but usually dull, often coarse, dry ones.

Muscadelle Adds aroma to many white Bordeaux.

Muscadet, alias Melon de Bourgogne Makes light, very dry wines with a seaside tang round Nantes in Brittany. They should not be sharp, but faintly salty and very refreshing. (California 'Pinot Bl' is this grape.)

Muscat (Many varieties; the best is Muscat Blanc à Petits Grains). Universally grown, easily recognized, pungent grapes, mostly made into perfumed sweet wines, often fortified (as in France's vins doux naturels). Superb in Australia. Muscat d'Alsace is an unusual manifestation in that it is dry.

Palomino, alias Listan Makes all the best sherry but poor table wine.

Pedro Ximénez, alias PX Makes very strong wine in Montilla and Málaga. Used in blending sweet sherries. Also grown in Argentina, the Canaries, Australia, California, South Africa.

Pinot Blanc (Pinot Bl) A cousin of PINOT N; not related to CHARD, but with a similar, milder character: light, fresh, fruity, not aromatic, to drink young; good for eg Italian spumante. Grown in Alsace, N Italy, S Germany, E Europe. Weissburgunder in Germany. See also Muscadet.

Pinot Gris (Pinot Gr) At best makes rather heavy, even 'thick', full-bodied whites with a certain spicy style. Known (formerly) as Tokay in Alsace; Ruländer or Grauburgunder in Germany; Tocai or Pinot Grigio in Italy and Slovenia (but much thinner wine).

Pinot Noir (Pinot N) Superlative black grape (See Grapes for red wine) used in Champagne and occasionally elsewhere (eg California, Australia) for making white, sparkling, or very pale pink 'vin gris'.

Riesling (Ries) Germany's great grape, and at present the world's most underrated. Wine of brilliant sweet/acid balance, either dry or sweet, flowery in youth but maturing to subtle oily scents and flavours. Very good (usually dry) in Alsace, Austria, parts of E Europe, Australia (widely grown), Pacific NW, California, South Africa. Often called White-, Johannisberg- or Rhine Riesling. Subject to 'noble rot'. Due for a major revival, since (unlike CHARD) it does not need high alcohol for character.

Ruländer German name for PINOT GRIS used for sweeter wines.

Sauvignon Blanc (Sauv Bl) Makes v distinctive aromatic grassy sometimes smoky-scented wine; can be austere (eg upper Loire) or buxom (in Sauternes blended with SEM, and in parts of California). Brilliant success in New Zealand, vg in NE Italy. Also called Fumé Bl or vice versa.

Scheurebe Spicy-flavoured German RIES x SYLVANER, very successful in Pfalz, esp for Auslesen. Can be weedy in dry wines.

Sémillon (Sém) The grape contributing the lusciousness to great Sauternes; subject to 'noble rot' in the right conditions but increasingly important for Graves and dry white Bordeaux too. Makes soft dry wine of great potential. Traditionally called 'Riesling' in parts of Australia. Old Hunter Valley Sém can be great wine.

Sercial Makes the driest madeira; (where myth says it is really RIESLING!).

Seyval Blanc (Seyval Bl) French-made hybrid of French and American vines. V hardy and attractively fruity. Popular and reasonably successful in eastern States and England but banned by EC from 'quality' wines.

Steen South Africa's most popular white grape: good lively fruity wine. Said to be the CHENIN BL of the Loire.

Silvaner, alias Sylvaner Germany's former workhorse grape: wine rarely fine except in Franken where it is savoury and ages admirably, and in Rheinhessen and Baden, where it is enjoying a renaissance. Good in the Italian Tyrol and useful in Alsace. Very good (and powerful) as 'Johannisberg' in the Valais, Switzerland.

Tokay See Pinot Gris. Also a table grape in California and a supposedly Hungarian grape in Australia. The wine Tokay is made of FURMINT.

Traminer See Gewürztraminer.

Trebbiano Important but mediocre grape of central Italy, used in Orvieto, Chianti, Soave, etc. Also grown in S France as Ugni Bl, and Cognac as St-Emilion. Thin, neutral wine; really needs blending.

Ugni Blanc (Ugni Bl) See Trebbiano.

Verdejo The grape of Rueda in Castile, potentially fine and long-lived.

Verdelho Madeira grape making excellent medium-sweet wine; in Australia, fresh soft dry wine of great character.

Verdicchio Gives its name to good dry wine in central-eastern Italy.

Vermentino See Malvasia.

Vernaccia Grape grown in central and S Italy and Sardinia for strong smooth lively wine, sometimes inclining towards sherry.

Viognier Rare grape of the Rhône, grown at Condrieu for v fine fragrant wine. Much in vogue in the Midi, California, etc, but still only a trickle.

Viura See Macabeo.

Weissburgunder See Pinot Blanc.

Welschriesling See Italian Riesling.

Grapes for red wine

Aleatico Dark Muscat variety, alias Aglianico, used the length of W Italy for fragrant sweet wines.

Barbera Most popular of many productive grapes of N Italy, esp Piedmont, giving dark, fruity, often sharp wine. Gaining prestige in California.

Brunello S Tuscan form of SANGIOVESE, splendid at Montalcino.

Cabernet Franc, alias Bouchet (Cab F) The lesser of two sorts of Cab grown in Bordeaux but dominant (as 'Bouchet') in St-Emilion. The Cab of the Loire making Chinon, etc, and rosé.

Cabernet Sauvignon (Cab S) Grape of great character: spicy, herby and tannic, with a characteristic 'blackcurrant' aroma. The first grape of the Médoc, also makes most of the best Californian, Australian, S American and E European reds. Its red wine almost always needs ageing and usually benefits from blending with eg MERLOT, CAB F or SYRAH. Makes very aromatic rosé.

Carignan By far the commonest grape of France, covering hundreds of thousands of acres. Prolific with dull but harmless wine. Best from old vines in Corbières. Also common in N Africa, Spain, California.

Cinsaut Common bulk-producing grape of S France; in S Africa crossed with PINOT N to make PINOTAGE.

Dolcetto Source of soft seductive dry red in Piedmont. Now high fashion (though low budget).

Gamay The Beaujolais grape: light, very fragrant wines, at their best young. Makes even lighter wine on the Loire, in central France, and in Switzerland and Savoie. Known as 'Napa Gamay' in California.

Gamay Beaujolais Not GAMAY but a poor variety of PINOT N in California.

Grenache, alias Garnacha, Alicante, Cannonau Useful grape for strong fruity but pale wine: good rosé and vin doux naturel. Grown in S France, Spain, California. Usually blended (eg Châteauneuf-du-Pape).

Grignolino Makes one of the good everyday table wines of Piedmont.

Kadarka, alias Gamza Makes healthy sound agreeable reds in Hungary, Bulgaria etc.

Lambrusco Productive grape of the lower Po Valley, giving quintessentially Italian, cheerful sweet and fizzy red.

Malbec, alias Cot Minor in Bordeaux, major in Cahors and Argentina. Dark, dense and tannic wine capable of real quality.

Merlot Adaptable grape making the great fragrant and plummy wines of Pomerol and (with CAB F) St-Emilion, an important element in Médoc reds, soft and strong in California, Washington and Australia, lighter but often good in N Italy, Italian Switzerland, Slovenia, Argentina, etc.

Montepulciano Confusingly, a major central-eastern Italian grape of good quality, as well as a town in Tuscany.

Mourvèdre, alias Mataro Excellent dark aromatic tannic grape used mainly for blending in Provence (especially in Bandol) and the Midi.

Nebbiolo, alias Spanna and Chiavennasca One of Italy's best red grapes; makes Barolo, Barbaresco, Gattinara, Valtellina. Intense, nobly fruity and perfumed wine but very tannic, taking years to mature.

Petit Verdot Excellent but awkward Médoc grape now largely superseded.

Pinot Noir (Pinot N) The glory of Burgundy's Côte d'Or, with scent, flavour, and texture unmatched anywhere. Less happy elsewhere; makes light wines rarely of much distinction in Germany, Switzerland, Austria, Hungary. The great challenge to California and Australia (and recently S Africa). Shows exciting promise in California's Carneros and Central Coast, Oregon, the Yarra Valley, Australia, Tasmania and NZ.

Pinotage Singular S African grape (PINOT N x CINSAUT). Can be very fruity and age interestingly, but often jammy.

Sangiovese (or Sangioveto) The main red grape of Chianti and much of central Italy. BRUNELLO is the Sangiovese Grosso.

Saperavi Makes good sharp very long-lived wine in Georgia, Ukraine etc. Blends very well with CABERNET (eg in Moldova).

Spätburgunder German for PINOT N, but a very pale shadow of burgundy.

Syrah, alias Shiraz The great Rhône red grape, with tannic purple peppery wine which can mature superbly. Very important as Shiraz in Australia, increasingly successful in the Midi and California.

Tempranillo The pale aromatic fine Rioja grape, called Ull de Lebre in Catalonia, Cencibel in La Mancha. Early ripening.

Zinfandel (Zin) Fruity adaptable grape peculiar to California with blackberry-like, and sometimes metallic, flavour. Can be gloriously lush, but also makes 'blush' white wine.

Wine & Food

Attitudes to pairing wine and food range from the slapdash to the near-neurotic. Oddly, it is a subject that has attracted very little ink until only recently: it is fertile ground for experiment. Few combinations should be dismissed outright as 'wrong', but generations of experience have produced certain working conventions that can help and certainly do no harm. The following are ideas intended to help you make quick decisions. Any of the groups of recommended wines could be extended at will. In general I have stuck to wines that are widely available, at the same time trying to ring the changes so that the same wines don't come up time and time again – as they tend to do in real life. Remember that in a restaurant that is truly regional (Provençal, Basque, Tuscan, Catalan, Austrian...) there is a ready-made answer – the wine of the region in question.

References to the wines will be found in national sections. The stars refer to the rating system used throughout the book.

Before the meal – aperitifs

The conventional aperitif wines are either sparkling (epitomized by champagne) or fortified (epitomized by sherry). They are still the best, but avoid peanuts, which destroy wine flavours. Olives are also too piquant for most wines; they need sherry or a Martini. Eat almonds, walnuts, crisps or cheese straws instead. A glass of white or rosé table wine before eating is presently in vogue. It calls for something light and stimulating, fairly dry but not acid, with a degree of character, such as:

from France Alsace Pinot Bl, Sylvaner, Ries; Chablis or a good Aligoté; Muscadet; Sauv de Touraine; Graves (or Bordeaux) Blanc; Mâcon (or Bourgogne) Bl; Crépy; Bugey; Haut-Poitou; Côtes de Gascogne. In B'x the fashion is for a glass of sweet Sauternes, Loupiac or Monbazillac.

from Italy Pinot Bianco; Pinot Grigio; Soave; Orvieto Secco; Frascati; Montecarlo; Greco di Tufo; Vernaccia; Verdicchio; Tocai; Lugana; Sauvignon Blanc from NE; Marsala Vergine.

from Germany Any Kabinett wine or QbA. Choose a halbtrocken or open a mature Spätlese (5–12 yrs). A great old Auslese can be the finest of all.

from Spain Fino or manzanilla sherry, or Montilla (with tapas). Albariño.

from Portugal Any vinho verde or, better, Alvarinho; Bucelas.

from Eastern Europe Grüner Veltliner; Welschriesling; Riesling; Leanyka; Müller-Thurgau. Tokay Szamarodni is Hungary's esp tasty contribution.

from the USA (California) Riesling; Chenin Blanc; Colombard; Fumé Blanc; Gewürztraminer; or a good 'house blend'. (New York, Oregon) Riesling. (Washington) Sémillon. Please not Chardonnay.

from Australia Barossa, Clare or Coonawarra Riesling; West Australian Verdelho; or a Marsanne from Victoria.

from South Africa Steen is ideal (the KWV labels it Chenin Blanc).

from England Almost any English wine makes a good talking point as an aperitif, especially in the garden in summer. So does New Zealand Riesling – but above all its Sauvignon Blanc.

First courses

Aïoli A thirst-quencher is needed for its garlic heat. Rhône (★→★★), Provence rosé, Frascati, Verdicchio. And marc, too, for courage.

Antipasto in Italy Dry or medium white (★★): Italian (Arneis, Soave, Pinot Gr, Greco di Tufo); light red (Dolcetto, Franciacorta, young ★★ Chianti).

Artichoke vinaigrette Young red (*): Bordeaux, Côtes du Rhône; or acidic white: Sauvignon de Touraine (or anywhere else).

hollandaise Full-bodied dry or medium white (* or **): Mâcon Blanc, Pfalz, or a California 'house blend'.

Asparagus A difficult flavour for wine, so the wine needs plenty of its own. Sémillon beats Chardonnay, esp from Australia. Alsace Pinot Gris, even dry Muscat can be good, or Jurançon Sec.

Avocado with prawns, crab, etc Dry to medium or slightly sharp white (**→****): Rheingau or Pfalz Kabinett, Sancerre, Pinot Bianco; California or Australian Chard or Sauvignon, Cape Steen, or dry rosé.

vinaigrette Light red (*), or manzanilla sherry.

Bisques Dry white with plenty of body (**): Pinot Gris, Chardonnay. Fino or dry amontillado sherry, or Montilla. Australian Semillon-Sauv Bl.

Boudin (blood sausage) Local Sauvignon or Chenin – esp in the Loire.

Bouillabaisse Very dry white (*→***): Dry rosé of Provence or Corsica, or Cassis, Verdicchio, California Blanc Fumé.

Carpaccio beef Seems to work well with the flavour of most wines, including *** reds. Top Tuscan vino da tavola is appropriate.

salmon Chardonnay (**→****), or champagne.

Caviar Iced vodka. Champagne, if you must, must be full-bodied (eg Clicquot, Krug).

Ceviche California or Australian Chardonnay (**), NZ Sauvignon Blanc.

Cheese fondue Dry white (**): Fendant or Johannisberg du Valais, Grüner Veltliner, Alsace Riesling, NZ Sauvignon Blanc.

Chowders Big-scale white (**), not necessarily bone dry: Pinot Gris, Rhine Spätlese. Or fino sherry, dry madeira or Marsala.

Clams As for oysters.

Consommé Medium-dry sherry (**→****), dry madeira, Marsala Vergine.

Crostini Rustic Tuscan red, Montepulciano d'Abruzzo, Valpolicella.

Crudités Light red or rosé (*→**, no more): Côtes du Rhône, Minervois, Chianti, Zinfandel; or fino sherry.

Dim-Sum Classically, tea: Oolong or Bo-Li. For fun: Sauv Blanc or Riesling with fried Dim-Sum, light red (Chianti, Bardolino) with steamed.

Eggs (See also Soufflés.) These present difficulties: they clash with most wines and spoil good ones. So *→** of whatever is going. As a last resort I can bring myself to drink champagne with scrambled eggs.

Escargots White Mâcon-Villages or young Beaujolais-Villages. In the Midi, vg Petits-Gris go with local white or red. In Alsace, Pinot Bl or Gewurz.

Fish terrine Rheingau Riesling Spätlese Trocken, Chablis, Washington or Australian Semillon, Sonoma Chardonnay; or fino sherry.

Foie gras White (***→****). In Bordeaux they drink Sauternes. Others prefer a late-harvest Riesling (incl New World) or Gewürztraminer, or Alsace Pinot Gris. Old dry amontillado can be sublime. But not Chard.

Gazpacho A glass of fino before and after.

Goat's cheese, grilled or fried (warm salad) Chilled Chinon or Saumur-Champigny, Provence rosé. Or strong red: Ch Musar, Greek or Turkish.

Grapefruit If you must start a meal with grapefruit try port, madeira or sweet sherry with (or in) it.

Gravlax Akvavit or iced sake. Or Grand Cru Chablis, or *** California or Australian Chardonnay.

Guacamole California Chardonnay (**) or Mexican beer.

Haddock, smoked, mousse of A wonderful dish for showing off any stylish full-bodied white, incl Grand Cru Chablis.

Hangtown Fry (oysters, bacon and eggs) NV champagne.

Ham, raw or cured (See also Prosciutto.) Alsace Grand Cru Pinot Gris.

Herrings, raw or pickled Dutch gin (young, not aged) or Scandinavian akvavit, and cold beer.

Hors d'oeuvres (See also Antipasto.) Clean, fruity, sharp white (*→**): Sancerre or any Sauvignon, Grüner Veltliner, Muscadet, Cape Steen; or young light red Bordeaux, Rhône or equivalent. Or fino sherry.

11

Mackerel, smoked An oily wine-destroyer. Manzanilla sherry, or schnapps, peppered or bison-grass vodka. Or good lager.

Mayonnaise Adds richness that calls for a contrasting bite in the wine. Côte Chalonnaise whites (eg Rully) are good. Try NZ Sauvignon Blanc, Verdicchio or a Spätlese trocken from the Pfalz.

Melon Needs a strong sweet wine (if any): port (★★), Bual madeira, Muscat, oloroso sherry or vin doux naturel.

Minestrone Red (★): Grignolino, Chianti, Zinfandel, Shiraz, etc. Or fino.

Mushrooms à la Grecque Greek Verdea or Mantinia, or any hefty dry white, or fresh young red.

Omelettes See Eggs.

Oyster stew California or Australian Chardonnay.

Oysters White (★★→★★★): NV champagne, Chablis or (better) Chablis Premier Cru, Muscadet, white Graves, Sancerre. Guinness or Scotch and water.

Pasta Red or white (★→★★) according to the sauce or trimmings:
    cream sauce Orvieto, Frascati, Italian Chardonnay.
    meat sauce Montepulciano d'Abruzzo, Montefalco d'Arquata, Merlot.
    pesto (basil) sauce Barbera, NZ Sauvignon Blanc.
    seafood sauce (vongole, eg) Verdicchio, Soave, Pomino, Sauv Bl.
    tomato sauce Barbera, Sicilian or S Italian red, Zinfandel.

Pâté According to constituents and quality:
    chicken livers call for pungent white, a smooth red like a light Pomerol, or even amontillado sherry.
    with simple pâté a ★★ dry white: Mâcon-Villages, Graves, Fumé Blanc.
    with duck pâté Chianti Classico or Franciacorta.

Pizza Any ★★ dry Italian red or ★★ Rioja, Australian Shiraz or California Zinfandel. Corbières or Roussillon or red Bairrada.

Prawns or shrimps Dry white (★★→★★★): burgundy, Bordeaux, Chard, Riesling – even fine mature champagne.
    Indian-, Thai- or Chinese-style rich Australian Chardonnay. ('Cocktail sauce' kills wine, and I suspect, in time, people.)

Prosciutto with melon Full-bodied dry or medium white (★★→★★★): Orvieto, Frascati, Pomino, Fendant, Grüner Veltliner, Alsace or California Gewürztraminer, Australian Riesling, Jurançon Sec.

Quiches Dry white with body (★→★★★): Alsace, Graves, Sauvignon, Rheingau dry; or young red (Beaujolais-Villages), according to the ingredients. Never a fine-wine dish.

Salade niçoise Very dry, ★★, not too light or flowery white or rosé: Provençal, Rhône or Corsican; Catalan white; Dâo; California Sauv Bl.

Salads As a first course, especially with blue cheese dressing, any dry and appetizing white wine. After a main course: no wine.
    NB Vinegar in salad dressings destroys the flavour of wine. If you want salad at a meal with fine wine, dress the salad with wine or a little lemon juice instead of vinegar.

Salami Very tasty red or rosé (★→★★): Barbera, young Zinfandel, Tavel or Ajaccio rosé, young Bordeaux, Toro, or Chilean Cabernet.

Salmon, smoked A dry but pungent white: fino sherry, Alsace Pinot Gris, Chablis Grand Cru, Pfalz Riesling Spätlese, vintage champagne. Or vodka, schnapps or akvavit.

Seafood salad Fresh N Italian Chardonnay or Pinot Grigio. Or Italian or Australian Malvasia.

Shark's fin soup Add a teaspoon of cognac. Sip amontillado.

Soufflés As show dishes these deserve ★★→★★★ wines.
    fish Dry white: burgundy, Bordeaux, Alsace, Chardonnay, etc.
    cheese Red burgundy or Bordeaux, Cabernet Sauvignon, etc.
    spinach (tougher on wine) Mâcon-Villages, St-Véran.

Taramasalata A rustic southern white with personality; not necessarily Retsina. Fino sherry works well. Try Australian Chard or Semillon.

Terrine As for pâté, or equivalent red: Mercurey, Beaujolais-Villages, fairly young St-Emilion (★★), California Cab or Zin, Bulgarian or Chilean Cab.

Tomato sauce (on anything) The acidity of tomato sauce is no friend to fine wines. Red (∗∗) will do. Try Chianti. Try skipping tomatoes.

Trout, smoked Sancerre, California or NZ Fumé Blanc. Or Rully.

Vegetable terrine Not a great help to fine wine, but California and Australian Chardonnays make a fashionable marriage.

Fish

Abalone Dry or medium white (∗∗→∗∗∗): Sauvignon Blanc, Chardonnay, Pinot Grigio, Muscadet sur Lie.

Bass, striped or sea Weissburgunder from Baden or Pfalz. Vg for any fine/delicate white.

Beurre blanc, fish with A top-notch Muscadet sur Lie, a Sauvignon/Sémillon blend, or a German Charta wine.

Carpaccio of salmon or tuna Puligny-Montrachet or (∗∗∗) Australian Chardonnay. (See also First courses.)

Cod A good neutral background for fine dry or medium whites: ∗∗→∗∗∗ Chablis, Meursault, cru classé Graves or dryish Vouvray; German Kabinett, or dry Spätlesen and their equivalents.

Coquilles St Jacques See Scallops.

Crab, cioppino Sauvignon Blanc; but West Coast friends say Zinfandel.
   cold, with salad Pfalz Riesling Kabinett or Spätlese, dry California or Australian Riesling, or Viognier from Condrieu.
   softshell ∗∗∗ Chardonnay or top quality German Riesling.
   Chinese, baked with ginger and onion Hungarian Furmint.
   with Black Bean sauce a big Shiraz or Syrah.

Eel, jellied NV champagne or a nice cup of (Ceylon) tea.
   smoked Strong/sharp wine: fino sherry, Bourgogne Aligoté. Schnapps.

Fish and chips, fritto misto (or tempura) Chablis, ∗∗ white Bordeaux, Sauvignon Blanc, Alsace Riesling, Fiano, Montilla, Koshu, tea...

Fish pie (with creamy sauce) Napa Chardonnay, Pinot Gris d'Alsace.

Haddock Rich dry white (∗∗→∗∗∗): Meursault, California or Australian Chard.

Hake Sauv Bl or any freshly fruity white: Pacherenc, Tursan, white Navarra.

Halibut As for Turbot.

Herrings Need a white with some acidity to cut their richness. Bourgogne Aligoté, Gros Plant from Brittany, dry Sauvignon Blanc. Or cider.

Kippers A good cup of tea, preferably Ceylon (milk, no sugar). Scotch?

Lamproie à la Bordelaise 5-yr-old St-Emilion or Fronsac: ∗∗→∗∗∗.

Lobster, richly sauced Vintage champagne, fine white burgundy, cru classé Graves, California or Australian Chard, Pfalz Spätlese, Hermitage Bl.
   salad white (∗∗→∗∗∗∗): NV champagne, Alsace Riesling, Chablis Premier Cru, Condrieu, Mosel Spätlese.

Mackerel Hard or sharp white (∗∗): Sauvignon Blanc from Bergerac or Touraine, Gros Plant, vinho verde, white Rioja. Or Guinness.

Mullet, red A chameleon, adaptable to gd white or red (but avoid the liver).

Mussels Gros Plant (∗→∗∗∗), Muscadet, California 'Chablis'.
   stuffed, with garlic See Escargots.

Perch, Sandre Exquisite fishes for finest wines: Puligny-Montrachet Premiers Crus or noble Mosels. Top Swiss Fendant or Johannisberg.

Salmon, fresh Fine white burgundy (∗∗∗): Puligny- or Chassagne-Montrachet, Meursault, Corton-Charlemagne, Chablis Grand Cru; Condrieu, California, Idaho or Australian Chard, Rheingau Kabinett/Spätlese, California Riesling or equivalent. Young Pinot Noir can be perfect, too.

Sardines, fresh grilled Very dry white (∗→∗∗∗): vinho verde, Dão, Muscadet.

Sashimi If you are prepared to forego the wasabi, sparkling wines, incl California's; or California or Australian Chardonnay, Chablis Grand Cru, Rheingau Riesling Halbtrocken. Otherwise, iced sake or beer.

For key to grape variety abbreviations, see pages 6–9.

Scallops An inherently slightly sweet dish, best with medium-dry whites.
   in cream sauces German Spätlese (★★★) or a -Montrachet.
   grilled or fried Hermitage Blanc, Gewürztraminer, Grüner Veltliner, Bergerac Blanc, Australian Riesling or champagne.
Shad White Graves (★★→★★★) or Meursault or Hunter Semillon.
Shellfish Dry white with plain boiled shellfish, richer wines with richer sauces.
Shrimps, potted Fino sherry, (★★★) Chablis, Gavi or New York Chardonnay.
Skate with black butter White (★★) with some pungency (eg Alsace Pinot Gr) or a clean straightforward one like Muscadet or Entre-Deux-Mers.
Snapper Serious Sauvignon Blanc country.
Sole, plaice, etc – plain, grilled or fried An ideal accompaniment for fine wines: ★★★→★★★★ white burgundy, or its equivalent.
   with sauce Depending on the ingredients: sharp dry wine for tomato sauce, fairly rich for sole véronique, etc.
Sushi Hot wasabi is usually hidden in every piece. German QbA trocken wines or simple Chablis are good enough. Or of course sake.
Swordfish Dry white (★★) of whatever country you are in. Nothing grand.
Trout Delicate white wine, eg ★★★ Mosel (esp from Saar), Alsace Pinot Bl.
   smoked A full-flavoured ★★→★★★ white: Gewürztraminer, Alsace Pinot Gr, Rhine Spätlese, Pinot Bl from Italy or Australian Hunter white.
Tuna, grilled White, red or rosé (★★) of fairly fruity character. NZ Sauvignon Blanc or a top Côtes du Rhône would be fine.
Turbot Fine rich dry white: ★★★ Meursault or Chassagne-Montrachet or its California, Australian or NZ equivalent. Condrieu. Mature Rheingau, Mosel or Nahe Spätlese or Auslese (not trocken).

Meat, poultry etc

Barbecues Red (★★) with a slight rasp, therefore young: Shiraz, Chianti, Zinfandel, Turkish Buzbag. Bandol for a real treat.
Beef, boiled Red (★★): Bordeaux (Bourg or Fronsac), Roussillon, Australian Shiraz. Or good Mâcon-Villages. Or top-notch beer.
   roast An ideal partner for fine red wine: ★★→★★★★ red of any kind.
Beef stew Sturdy red (★★→★★★): Pomerol or St-Emilion, Hermitage, Cornas, Barbera, Shiraz, California/Oregon Pinot Noir, Torres Gran Coronas.
Beef Stroganoff Dramatic red (★★→★★★): Barolo, Brunello, Valpolicella Amarone, Hermitage, late-harvest Zin – even Moldovan Negru de Purkar.
Cabbage, stuffed Hungarian Cabernet Franc/Kadarka, Bulgarian Cabernet.
Cajun food Côtes de Brouilly. With gumbo: amontillado or Mexican beer.
Cassoulet Red (★★) from SW France (Madiran, Cahors, Corbières), or Barbera or Zinfandel or Shiraz.
Chicken casserole Lirac, St-Joseph, Crozes-Hermitage.
   Kiev Alsace Riesling, Bergerac Rouge.
Chicken/turkey/guinea fowl, roast Virtually any wine, incl very best bottles of dry/medium white and finest old reds (esp burgundy). The meat of fowl can be adapted with sauces to match almost any fine wine (eg coq au vin: red burgundy). Avoid sauces which include tomato if you want to taste any good bottles.
Chilli con carne Young red (★→★★★): Barbera, Beaujolais, Navarra, Zinfandel.
Chinese food, Canton or Peking style Dry to medium-dry white (★★→★★★) – Sauvignon Blanc or (better) Riesling – can be good throughout a Chinese banquet. Dry sparkling (esp cava) is good for cutting the oil. Eschew sweet/sour dishes but try an 89/90 St-Emilion ★★ or St-Estèphe cru bourgeois, or Châteauneuf-du-Pape with duck. I often serve both white and red wines concurrently through Chinese meals.
   Szechuan style Muscadet, Alsace Pinot Blanc or v cold beer.
Choucroute garni Alsace, Pinot Blanc, Pinot Gris or Riesling.
Cold meats Generally taste better with full-flavoured white wine than red. Mosel Spätlese or Hochheimer are very good. And so is Beaujolais.

Confit d'oie Young tannic red Bordeaux Cru Bourgeois (★★→★★★) helps cut the richness. Alsace Tokay-Pinot Gris or Gewurztraminer matches it.

Coq au vin Red burgundy (★★→★★★★). In an ideal world one bottle of Chambertin in the dish, two on the table.

Corned beef hash Zinfandel, Chianti, Côtes du Rhône red: (★★).

Curry Medium-sweet white (★→★★), very cold: Orvieto abboccato, California Chenin Bl, Slovenian Traminer, Indian sparkling. Or emphasize the heat with a tannic Barolo or Barbaresco, or deep-flavoured reds such as St-Emilion, Cornas, Shiraz-Cabernet and Valpolicella Amarone.

Duck or goose Rather rich white (★★★): Pfalz Spätlese or Alsace réserve exceptionelle; or ★★★ Bordeaux or burgundy. With oranges or peaches, the Sauternais propose Sauternes, others a top Loire red.
    Peking See Chinese food.
    wild duck Big-scale red (★★★): Hermitage, Châteauneuf-du-Pape, Cornas, Bandol, California or S African Cabernet, Australian Shiraz.

Frankfurters German (★→★★), New York Riesling, Beaujolais. Or Budweiser.

Game birds, young birds plain roasted The best red wine you can afford.
    older birds in casseroles ★★→★★★★ red (Gevrey-Chambertin, Pommard, Grand Cru St-Emilion, Napa Cabernet).
    well-hung game Vega Sicilia, great red Rhône, Château Musar.
    cold game Mature vintage champagne. See page 18 for more.

Game pie, hot Red wine (★★★); **cold** equivalent white or champagne.

Goulash Strong young red (★★): Zinfandel, Bulgarian Cabernet or Mavrud, Hungarian Kadarka, young Australian Shiraz.

Grouse See Game birds – but push the boat right out.

Ham Fairly fresh red burgundy (★★→★★★): Volnay, Savigny, Beaune; Chinon or Bourgueil; slightly sweet German white (Rhine Spätlese); Czech Müller-Thurgau; Tuscan red; lightish Cabernet (eg Chilean).

Hamburger Young red (★→★★): Beaujolais, Corbières or Minervois, Chianti, Zinfandel, Kadarka from Hungary.

Hare Jugged hare calls for ★★→★★★★ flavourful red: not-too-old burgundy or Bordeaux, Rhône (eg Gigondas), Bandol, or a fine Rioja reserva. The same for saddle. Australia's Grange Hermitage would be an experience.

Kebabs Vigorous red (★★): Greek Nemea or Naoussa, Turkish Buzbag, Bulgarian or Chilean Cabernet, Zinfandel.

Kidneys Red (★★→★★★): St-Emilion, Cornas, Barbaresco, Rioja, California, Spanish or Australian Cabernet, Portuguese Bairrada.

Lamb, cutlets or chops As for roast lamb, but a little less grand.
    roast One of the traditional and best partners for very good red Bordeaux – or its Cabernet equivalents from the New World. In Castile, the partner of the finest old Rioja reservas. See page 18.

Liver Young (★★) red: Beaujolais-Villages, St-Joseph, Médoc, Italian Merlot, Breganze Cabernet, Zinfandel, Oregon Pinot Noir.

Meatballs Red (★★→★★★): Mercurey, Crozes-Hermitage, Madiran, Rubesco, Dão, Bairrada, Zinfandel or Cabernet.

Mixed grill A fairly light, easily swallowable red: ★★ Bordeaux from Bourg, Fronsac or Premières Côtes; Côtes de Buzet; Coteaux du Languedoc; Chianti; Chilean Cabernet; or a Cru Beaujolais such as Juliénas.

Moussaka Red or rosé (★→★★): Naoussa from Greece, Chianti, Corbières, Côtes de Provence, Ajaccio or Patrimonio, California 'Burgundy'.

Oxtail or osso bucco Rather rich red (★★→★★★): St-Emilion or Pomerol, Nuits-St-Georges, Barolo or Chianti Classico, Rioja reserva, California or Coonawarra Cabernet; or a dry Riesling Spätlese.

Paella Young (★★) Spanish red, dry white or rosé: Penedès or Rioja.

Partridge, pheasant See Game birds.

Pigeons or squab Red Burgundy (★★→★★★): Beaune, Savigny; Chianti Classico, California/Australian Pinot. Silvaner Spätlese from Franken.

Pork, roast A good rich neutral background to a fairly light red or rich white. It deserves ★★★ treatment – Médoc is fine. Portugal's famous sucking pig is eaten with Bairrada garrafeira, Chinese is good with Beaujolais.

Quail As for pigeon. But does not harm finer reds.

Rabbit Young Italian red (*→★★★★), Chinon, Saumur-Champigny, Rhône rosé.

Ris de veau See Sweetbreads.

Risotto Pinot Gr from Friuli, Gavi, youngish Sém, Dolcetto, or Barbera d'Alba.

    with mushrooms Cahors, Madiran, Barbera.

    with Fungi porcini finest mature Barolo or Barbaresco.

Satay Australian Cabernet-Shiraz or Alsace Pinot Gris or Gewurztraminer.

Sauerkraut Lager or stout. (But see also Choucroute garni.)

Sausages The British banger requires a 2½-yr-old NE Italian Merlot (or a red wine, anyway). See also Frankfurters, Salami.

Shepherd's Pie Rough and ready red (*→★★) seems most appropriate, but beer or dry cider is the real McCoy.

Spare Ribs Gigondas or St-Joseph, or Australian Shiraz, or Zinfandel.

Steak and kidney pie or pudding Red Rioja reserva or mature ★★→★★★ B'x.

Steak, au poivre A fairly young ★★★ Rhône red or Cabernet.

    tartare Vodka or ★★ light young red: Beaujolais, Bergerac, Valpolicella.

    Korean Yuk Whe (the world's best steak tartare) Sake.

    filet or tournedos any ★★★ red (but not old wines with béarnaise sauce).

    T-bone reds of similar bone structure (★★→★★★★): Barolo, Hermitage, Australian Cabernet or Shiraz.

    fiorentina (bistecca) Chianti Classico Riserva or Brunello.

Stews and casseroles A lusty full-flavoured red: young Côtes du Rhône, Corbières, Barbera, Shiraz, Zinfandel, etc.

Sweetbreads A grand dish, so grand wine: Rhine Riesling (★★★) or Franken Silvaner Spätlese, well-matured B'x or burgundy, depending on sauce.

Tandoori chicken Sauvignon Blanc, or young ★★ red Bordeaux.

Thai food Ginger and lemon grass call for Gewürztraminer; coconut curries, Hunter Valley Chard. Alsace Pinot Blanc for refreshment.

Tongue Good for any red or white of abundant character, esp Italian.

Tripe Red (*→★★), eg Corbières, Roussillon or rather sweet white (eg Liebfraumilch). Better: W Australian 'White Burgundy'.

Veal, roast A good neutral background dish for any fine old red which may have faded with age (eg a Rioja reserva) or a ★★★ German white.

Venison Big-scale red (★★★): Rhône, Bordeaux or California Cab of a mature vintage; or rather rich white (Pfalz Spätlese or Alsace Tokay-Pinot Gr).

Vitello tonnato Light red (Valpolicella, Beaujolais) served cool.

Wiener Schnitzel Light red (★★→★★★★) from the Italian Tyrol (Alto Adige) or the Médoc; Austrian Ries, Grüner Veltliner or Gumpoldskirchener.

Vegetarian dishes

Bean salad Red Rioja reserva.

Bean stew Bairrada from Portugal, Toro from Spain.

Cabbage (including 'bubble-and-squeak') Beer or stout.

Choucroute (See also Sauerkraut.) Alsace Pinot Gris or Sylvaner.

Couscous Young red with a bite: Shiraz, Corbières, Minervois, etc.

Fennel-based dishes Pouilly-Fumé, Beaujolais.

'Meaty' aubergine, lentil or mushroom bakes Corbières, Zinfandel.

Mushrooms (in most contexts) Fleshy red; eg ★★★ Pomerol, California Merlot, Australian Shiraz.

    on toast Your best claret.

    wild mushrooms (cèpes best for wine) Barbaresco, Pauillac, St-Estèphe.

Onion/leek tart Fruity dry white (*→★★★): Alsace Pinot Gr or Gewurz. Mâcon-Villages, Jurançon, California/Australian Ries. Or Beaujolais or Loire red.

Peppers or aubergines (eggplant), stuffed Vigorous red (★★): Chianti, Dolcetto, Zinfandel, Bandol, Vacqueyras.

Ratatouille Vigorous young red (★★): Chianti, Zinfandel, Bulgarian, young red Bordeaux or young Côtes du Rhône.

Spinach/pasta bakes Valpolicella (its bitterness helps); Greco di Molise, or Sicilian/Sardinian white.

Cheese

Very strong cheese completely masks the flavour of wine. Only serve fine wine with mild cheeses in peak condition.

Bleu de Bresse, Dolcelatte, Gorgonzola Need emphatic accompaniment: young ★★→★★★ red wine (Barbera, Dolcetto, Moulin-à-Vent, etc).

Cream cheeses: Brie, Camembert, Pont-l'Evêque, Bel Paese, etc In their mild state marry with any good white. When ripe, resort to Gewürz.

Danish Blue Old amontillado/oloroso sherries have necessary horse-power.

English (Scottish, Welsh, Irish) cheeses Can be either mild or strong and acidic. The latter need sweet or strong wine.

> **Cheddar, Cheshire, Wensleydale, Gloucester, etc** Mild: fine burgundy or claret. Mature: gd ruby or vintage character (not vintage) port, old dry oloroso sherry, or v big red (Hermitage, Châteauneuf, Barolo etc).
> **Stilton** Vintage port.

Goat's cheeses White wine (★★→★★★) of marked character, either dry (Sancerre) or sweet (Monbazillac, Sauternes).

Hard Cheese, Parmesan, Gruyère, Emmenthal, Comté, Cantal, old Gouda, Jarlsberg Full-bodied dry whites: Alsace Pinot Gr or Vernaccia, or fino or amontillado sherry. Alternatively old Gouda ('Mimolette') and Jarlsberg have a sweetness that encourages fine old Bordeaux etc.

Roquefort So salty only the sweetest stand a chance. Sauternes is traditional.

Desserts

Apple pie or strudel Sweet (★★→★★★) German, Austrian, Hungarian white.

Apples, Cox's Orange Pippins Vintage port (55 60 63 66 70 75 82).

Bread and butter pudding 10-yr-old Barsac from a good château.

Cakes Bual or Malmsey madeira, oloroso or cream sherry.

Cheesecake Sweet white from Vouvray or Anjou, but nothing special.

Chocolate cake, mousse, soufflés Bual madeira, Huxelrebe Auslese, California orange Muscat, Beaumes-de-Venise. Or a tot of good rum.

Christmas pudding, mince pies Tawny port, cream sherry, Asti or Vinsanto.

Creams, custards, fools Sauternes, Loupiac, Ste-Croix-du-Mont, Monbazillac.

Crème brûlée ★★★→★★★★ Sauternes or Rhine Beerenauslese, best madeira or Tokay. (With concealed fruit, a more modest sweet wine.)

Crêpes Suzette Sweet champagne or Asti Spumante.

Fruit, fresh Sweet Coteaux du Layon, light sweet or liqueur Muscat.
> **stewed, ie apricots, pears, etc** Sweet Muscatel: Muscat de Beaumes-de-Venise, Moscato di Pantelleria or dessert Tarragona.

Fruit flans Sauternes, Monbazillac or sweet Vouvray or Anjou: ★★★.

Fruit salads, orange salad A fine sweet sherry.

Nuts Oloroso sherry, Bual madeira, vintage or tawny port, Vin Santo.

Oranges, caramelized Experiment with old Sauternes.

Pears in red wine A pause before the port.

Raspberries (no cream, little sugar) Excellent with fine reds that themselves taste of raspberries: young Juliénas, Regnié.

Rice Pudding Liqueur Muscat, Moscatel de Valencia, or Loupiac.

Sorbets, ice-creams Asti, or (better) Moscato d'Asti Naturale. Amaretto liqueur with vanilla; rum with chocolate.

Strawberries and cream Sauternes (★★★) or similar sweet Bordeaux, or Vouvray Moelleux (1990).

Strawberries, wild (no cream) Serve with ★★★ red B'x poured over them.

Summer pudding Fairly young Sauternes of a good vintage (82 83 85 86).

Sweet soufflés Sauternes or Vouvray moelleux. Sweet champagne.

Tiramisu Vin Santo, young tawny port, Beaumes-de-Venise.

Trifle Should be sufficiently vibrant with its internal sherry.

Walnuts Nature's match for finest port, madeira, oloroso sherry.

Zabaglione Light gold Marsala.

Food with Finest Wine

With very special bottles the wine sometimes guides the choice of
food rather than the usual way round. The following suggestions
are largely based on the gastronomic conventions of the wine
regions producing these treasures, plus diligent research. They
should help bring out the best in your best wines.

Red wines

**Red Bordeaux and other Cabernet-based wines (very old, light and
delicate: eg pre-59, with exceptions such as 45)** Leg or rack of
young lamb, roast with a hint of herbs (not garlic); entrecôte;
sweetbreads; or cheese soufflé after the meat.

Fully mature great vintages (eg Bordeaux 61 45) Shoulder or saddle of
lamb, roast with a touch of garlic, roast ribs or grilled rump of beef.

Mature but still vigorous (eg 70 66) Shoulder or saddle of lamb (incl kidneys)
with rich sauce, eg béarnaise. Fillet of beef marchand de vin (with
wine and bone-marrow). Avoid Beef Wellington: pastry dulls the palate.

Merlot-based Bordeaux (Pomerol, St-Emilion) Beef as above (fillet is
richest) or venison.

**Côte d'Or red burgundy (Consider the weight and texture, which grow
lighter/more velvet with age. Also the character: Nuits earthy,
Musigny flowery, great Romanées exotic, Pommard foursquare, etc.)**
Roast chicken, or better, capon, is safe standard; guinea-fowl slightly
stronger, then partridge, grouse or woodcock, progressively more
rich/pungent. Hare and venison (chevreuil) are alternatives.

Great old reds The classic burgundian formula is cheese: Epoisses
(unfermented). It is a terrible waste of fine old wines.

Vigorous younger burgundy Duck or goose roasted to minimize fat.

**Great Syrahs: Hermitage, Côte Rôtie, Grange Hermitage, (also Vega
Sicilia)** Beef, venison; bone-marrow on toast; English cheese (esp
best farm Cheddar).

Rioja Gran Reserva, Pesquera... Richly flavoured roasts: wild boar, mutton.

Barolo, Barbaresco Cheese risotto with white truffles; pasta with game
sauce (eg pappardelle alle lepre); porcini mushrooms; Parmesan.

White wines

Very Good Chablis/White burgundy/Chardonnay White fish simply
grilled or meunière with Doria garnish of sautéed cucumber. Dover
sole, turbot, Rex sole are best. (Seabass is too delicate; salmon passes
but does little for fine wine.)

**Supreme white burgundy (Le Montrachet, Corton-Charlemagne) or
equivalent Graves** Roast veal, capon or sweetbreads; richly sauced
white fish as above. Or lobster.

Hermitage Blanc, Condrieu, Châteauneuf Blanc Very light pasta scented
with herbs and tiny peas or broad beans.

Grand Cru Alsace, Riesling Truite au bleu, smoked salmon or choucroute
garni. **Pinot Gris** Roast or grilled veal. **Gewurztraminer** Cheese
soufflé (Munster cheese). **Vendange Tardive** Tarte Tatin.

Sauternes Simple crisp buttery biscuits (eg Langue-de-Chat), white
peaches, nectarines, strawberries (without cream). Not tropical fruit.
Experiment with cheeses.

Supreme Vouvray moelleux etc Buttery biscuits, apples, apple tart.

Beerenauslese/TBA Biscuits, peaches, greengages.

Finest old amontillado/oloroso Pecan nuts.

Great vintage port or madeira Walnuts or pecans.

Old vintage champagne (not blanc de blancs) As aperitif, or with cold
partridge, grouse or woodcock.

The 1993 Vintage

No vintage year is easy to summarize in brief. 1993 is slipperier than most, with the only general truth about it that while hardly anybody is crowing, a great number are feeling relieved. Northern Europe was swept by almost constant rain in September, drenching a crop that in August looked close to perfect. There was no need to make bad wine, therefore, but a serious risk that good wine would be diluted, losing vital balance.

For once, early prognostications for Bordeaux and Burgundy are not dissimilar. The grapes were healthy and evenly ripe; time to harvest, and the rain came down. Early pickers (eg Merlot in Pomerol and St-Emilion) made some lovely wine. There will be excellent red burgundies. Médocs may have a 'stretched' feeling. Neither region is overjoyed with its white, although they will be good easy-drinking – and Sauternes is distinctly morose.

The Loire Valley missed the worst rains and made good wines, especially reds and some fine Chenin Blancs. Sancerre and Pouilly were rained on, though, so will be ripe and easy to drink soon. Champagne made plenty of wine, but not of vintage quality.

Further east the rain came later and less persistently. Alsace made very good wines with its early grapes; possibly less good with the later Rieslings. And few late-harvest wines.

The Rhône Valley was unlucky. From north to south the rain washed away hopes of a great vintage. In contrast further south in the Midi conditions were almost ideal.

Northern Italy and northern Spain were both caught by the rain belt – not catastrophically, but enough to dilute high quality from Piedmont to the Veneto, also in Rioja, Navarra, Catalonia and the Duero. In the high Douro in Portugal nothing went right from springtime onwards. There will be no 1993 vintage port.

The centre and south of Italy and Spain came below the broad band of rain. Any rain there was welcome to relieve drought. Tuscany, especially Montalcino, made fine wines. Umbria and the Adriatic coast, the Roman region and the south, and in Spain Valdepeñas and Andalucia are all well content.

East again in Germany, north did best. Rain interrupted picking, but botrytis developed and there are excellent sweet wines in the Mosel-Saar-Ruwer and the Rheingau. Franken claims its best vintage for years. Austria is very happy with its 1993s and eastern Europe happier still. Hungary, Bulgaria and Romania all had first-class harvests. In Tokaji the botrytis was phenomenal and the Aszú wines should be excellent in time.

California's weather can be as awkward as anybody's. In the north May and June were wet; flowering was messy and regularity never took over until a late heat-wave harvest. The Central Coast had the best weather and a fine vintage. Oregon's was predictably variable; Washington's predictably steady.

Much of southeast Australia had a wet summer and rot problems exacerbated grape shortages. But vintage conditions were good, as usual, and there will be fine wines from careful producers. New Zealand demonstrated its affinity with northern Europe: overall rain made winemaking a wet business.

France

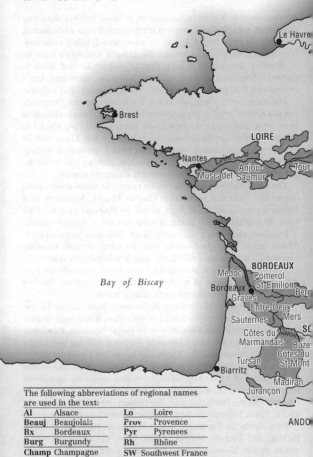

Le Havre

Brest

LOIRE

Nantes   Loire
Muscadet   Anjou-
            Saumur   Tour

Bay of Biscay

BORDEAUX
Médoc   Pomerol
Bordeaux   St-Emilion   Berg
        Graves
        Entre-Deux-
        Sauternes   Mers
            Côtes du Garonne
        Marmandais   Buze
                Côtes du
        Tursan   St-Mont
                        Madiran
                Jurançon
    Biarritz

ANDO

The following abbreviations of regional names
are used in the text:

Al	Alsace	**Lo**	Loire
Beauj	Beaujolais	**Prov**	Provence
Bx	Bordeaux	**Pyr**	Pyrenees
Burg	Burgundy	**Rh**	Rhône
Champ	Champagne	**SW**	Southwest France

Every year sees fresh challenges to France's pole position in the
wine world. Yet no-one has displaced her by definitively bettering
even one of her many kinds of wine. Tens of thousands of properties make wine of all complexions over a large part of her surface.
This is a guide to their names, types, producers and vintages.

All France's best wine regions have appellations contrôlées,
which may apply to a single small vineyard or to a large district.
The system varies with region, Burgundy on the whole having
the smallest and most precise appellations, and Bordeaux the
widest, most general. In between lies an infinity of variations.

An appellation contrôlée is a guarantee of origin, production
method, grape varieties and quantities produced, but only
partially one of quality. All AC wines are officially tasted, but many

of shoddy quality get through the net. The AC therefore is the first thing to look for on a label. But the next is the name of the maker. The best names are a vital ingredient of the pages that follow. Regions without the overall quality and traditions required for an appellation can be ranked as vins délimités de qualité supérieure (VDQS), a shrinking category. Government policy is to promote these to AC status, and develop the relatively new and highly successful vins de pays. Vins de pays are increasingly worth trying. They include some brilliant originals and often offer France's best value for money – which means the world's.

Recent vintages of the French classics

Red burgundy

Côte d'Or Côte de Beaune reds generally mature sooner than the bigger wines of the Côte de Nuits. Earliest drinking dates are for lighter commune wines, eg Volnay, Beaune; latest for the biggest wines of eg Chambertin, Romanée. But even the best burgundies are much more attractive young than the equivalent red Bordeaux.

1993 Thoroughly satisfactory; some v fine. 1998–2010.
1992 Ripe, plump, pleasing. No great concentration. 1996–2005.
1991 Very good to poor. Depends on date of harvest: before/after rain. Best like 89s.
1990 A great vintage to rival 88: perfect weather compromised only by drought on some slopes and over-production in some v'yds. Long life ahead.
1989 A yr of great charm, not necessarily for v long maturing, but will age. Now–2015.
1988 Exceptional quality; a great vintage. 1996–2020?
1987 Small crop with promising ripe fruit flavours esp in Côte de Beaune. Now–2010.
1986 A v mixed bag – aromatic but rather dry: generally lacks flesh. Now–2000.
1985 At best a great vintage. Concentrated wines will be splendid. Now–2010.
1984 Lacks natural ripeness; tends to be dry and/or watery. Now – if at all.
1983 Powerful, vigorous, tannic and attractive vintage, compromised by rot. The best are splendid, but be careful. Now–2000.
1982 Big vintage, pale but round and charming. Best in Côte de Beaune. Drink up.
1981 A small crop, ripe but picked in rain.
1980 A wet yr, but v attractive wines from best growers who avoided rot. Côte de Nuits best. Drink.
1979 Big, generally good, ripe vintage with weak spots. Drink up.
1978 A small vintage of outstanding quality. The best will live to 2000+.
1976 Hot summer, excellent vintage. As usual great variations, but the best (esp Côte de Beaune) tannic, rich and long-lived – to 2000.
1972 Firm and full of character, the best have aged v well. Drink soon.
1971 V powerful and impressive wines, not as long-lasting as they first appeared. Drink.
Older fine vintages: 69, 66, 64, 62, 61, 59 (all mature).

Beaujolais 93: Crus to keep. 92: good primeur wines; not keepers. 91: small crop of outstanding wines, Crus excellent. 90 was a lusciously ripe vintage; top Crus will keep. 89 was v fine, drink soon. 88 is entirely ready. 87 and 86 wines should be finished. 85 was a wonderful vintage, but generally avoid older wines except possibly some Moulin-à-Vent.

White burgundy

Côte de Beaune Well-made wines of good vintages with plenty of acidity as well as fruit will improve and gain depth and richness for some years – anything up to 10. Lesser wines from lighter vintages are ready for drinking after 2 or 3 years.

1993 Less good than reds; early drinking.
1992 Ripe, aromatic and charming. Will develop beautifully. Now–2005.
1991 Mostly lack substance. Frost problems. For early drinking. Now–97.
1990 Very good, even great, but with a tendency to fatness. Now–2000+.
1989 Revealing itself as a model. At best ripe, tense, structured and long. Now–2005.
1988 Extremely good, some great wines but others rather dilute. Now–2000.
1987 Mainly disappointing, though a few exceptions have emerged. Now.
1986 Powerful wines; most with better acidity and balance than 85. Now–97.
1985 V ripe; those that still have balance are ageing v well. Now–2000.
1984 Most lean or hollow. Avoid.
1983 Potent wines; some exaggerated, some faulty, but the best splendid. Drink soon.
1982 Fat, tasty but delicate whites of low acidity. Drink up.
1981 A sadly depleted crop with great promise. But time to drink up.
1980 A weak, but not bad, vintage. Should be finished.
1979 Big vintage. Overall good and useful, not great. Drink up.
1978 Vg wines, firm and well-balanced. Keep only the best.
1971 Great power and style. Top wines are now wonderful. Drink up.

The white wines of the Mâconnais (Pouilly-Fuissé, St-Véran, Mâcon-Villages) follow a similar pattern, but do not last as long. They are more appreciated for their freshness than their richness.

Alsace 93 was good, fruity, not for long keeping. 92 was splendid; 91 admirable. 90 was the third outstanding vintage in succession. 89 and 88 both made wines of top quality (though rain spoiled some 88s). 87s should be drunk soon and 86s finished. Top 85s and 83s may be drunk or kept even longer.

FRANCE

Chablis Grand Cru Chablis of vintages with both strength and acidity can age superbly for up to 10 years; Premiers Crus proportionately less.

1993 Fair quality; nothing great. Now–99.
1992 Ripe and charming wines. Now–99.
1991 Generally better than Côte d'Or. Useful wines. Now–97.
1990 Grands Crus will be magnificent; other wines may lack intensity and acidity. Now–2000.
1989 Excellent vintage of potent character. Now–2000.
1988 Almost a model: great pleasure now in store. Now–98.
1987 Rain at harvest. Wines for the short term. Drink up.
1986 A splendid big vintage. Now or soon.
1985 Good but often low-acid wines. The best Grands Crus are ready.
1983 Superb vintage if not over-strong. Wonderful Grands Crus now.

Red Bordeaux

Médoc/red Graves For some wines bottle-age is optional: for these it is indispensable. Minor châteaux from light vintages need only 2 or 3 yrs, but even modest wines of great years can improve for 15 or so, and the great châteaux of these years need double that time.

1993 Ripe grapes but a drenching vintage. Under the circumstances, remarkably good.
1992 Rain at flowering, in August and at vintage. A huge crop; some good early drinking.
1991 Frost in April halved crop and rain interrupted vintage. Yet top wines may turn out to be classics.
1990 A paradox: a drought year with a threat of over-production. Self-discipline was essential. Its results are magnificent. To 2020.
1989 Early spring and splendid summer. The top wines will be classics of the ripe dark kind with elegance and length. Small ch's are uneven. To 2020.
1988 Generally excellent; ripe, balanced, for long keeping. To 2020.
1987 Much more enjoyable than seemed likely. Not for long keeping. Now or soon.
1986 Another splendid, huge, heatwave harvest. Superior to 85 in Pauillac and St-Julien. Now–2020.
1985 Very good vintage, in a heatwave. V fine wines already accessible. Now–2010.
1984 Poor. Little Merlot but good ripe Cabernet. No charm. Originally overpriced. To 98?
1983 A classic vintage, esp in Margaux: abundant tannin with fruit to balance it. To 2010.
1982 Made in a heatwave. Huge, rich, strong wines which promise a long life but are developing unevenly. Most châteaux are now ready. Now–2010.
1981 Admirable despite rain. Not rich, but balanced and fine. Now–2000.
1980 Small late harvest ripe but rained-on. Some delicious light wines. Drink up.
1979 Abundant harvest of above average quality. Now–2000.
1978 A miracle vintage: magnificent long warm autumn. Some excellent wines. Now–97.
1976 Excessively hot, dry summer; rain just before vintage. Generally vg; now ready.
1975 A v fine vintage. For long keeping, but some may not improve now; many have lost their fruit.
1973 A huge vintage, attractive young but fading fast.
1971 Small crop. Less fruity than 70 and less consistent. Most have faded away.
1970 Big, excellent vintage with scarcely a failure. Now–2000.
1966 A v fine vintage with depth, fruit and tannin. Now.
Older fine vintages: 62, 61, 59, 55, 53, 52, 50, 49, 48, 47, 45, 29, 28.

St-Emilion/Pomerol
1993 As in the Médoc, but probably better; good despite terrible vintage weather.
1992 Exceptionally dilute but some charming wines to drink quickly.
1991 A sad story. Terrible frost and little chance to recover. Many wines not released.
1990 Another chance to make great wine or a lot of wine. Now–2020.
1989 Large, ripe, early harvest; an overall triumph. To 2020.
1988 Generally excellent; ideal conditions. But some overproduced. Now–2000+.
1987 Some v adequate wines (esp in Pomerol) but for drinking soon.
1986 A prolific vintage; but top St-Emilions have long life ahead.
1985 One of the great yrs, with a long future. To 2010.
1984 A sad story. Most of the crop wiped out in spring. Avoid.
1983 Less impressive than it seemed. Drink soon.
1982 Enormously rich and concentrated wines, most excellent. Now–2000+.
1981 A vg vintage, if not as great as it first seemed. Now or soon.
1980 A poor Merlot yr; v variable quality. Too late.
1979 A rival to 78, but not developing as well as hoped. Now or soon.
1978 Fine wines, but some lack flesh. Drink soon.
1976 V hot, dry summer, but vintage rain. Some excellent. Drink soon.
1975 Most St-Emilions good, the best superb. Pomerol made splendid wine. Now–2000.
1971 On the whole better than Médocs, but now ready.
1970 Beautiful wines with great fruit and strength. V big crop. Now.
Older fine vintages: 67, 66, 64, 61, 59, 53, 52, 49, 47, 45.

23

France entries also cross-refer to Châteaux of Bordeaux section, pages 56–77.

Abel-Lepitre Brut NV; Brut **85 86 88**; Cuvée 134 Bl de Blancs NV; Réserve Crémant Bl de Blancs Cuvée 'C' **83 85 86 88**; Rosé **83 85 86 88** CHAMPAGNE house, also owning GOULET and St-Marceaux. Luxury Cuvée: Cuvée Reserve Abel-Lepitre **85**.

Abymes Savoie w ✭ DYA Hilly little area nr Chambéry; light mild Vin de Savoie AC from the Jacquère grape.

Ackerman-Laurance Vg classic method sparkling house of the Loire, at SAUMUR, said to be the oldest in the region. Fine CREMANT DE LOIRE.

Ajaccio Corsica r p w ✭→✭✭✭ 89' 90' **91 92 93** The capital of CORSICA. AC for some vg SCIACARELLO reds. Top grower: Peraldi.

Aligoté Second-rank burgundy white grape and its wine. Should be pleasantly tart and fruity with local character when young. BOUZERON is the one commune to have an all-Aligoté appellation, but try others from good growers. NB PERNAND-VERGELESSES. Value.

Aloxe-Corton Burg r w ✭✭→✭✭✭ 78' **85' 87 88' 89' 90' 91 92** Village at N end of COTE DE BEAUNE famous for its two GRANDS CRUS: CORTON (red), CORTON-CHARLEMAGNE (white). Village wines much lighter but can be good value.

Alsace Al w (r sp) ✭✭→✭✭✭ **85' 86 87 88 89 90' 91 92 93** Aromatic, fruity, often strong, rather Germanic dry white from eastern foothills of Vosges Mountains, bordering the River Rhine. Generally dry but increasingly made sweet (see Vendange Tardive and Sélection des Grains Nobles). Sold by grape variety (Pinot Bl, Ries, GEWURZ, etc). Matures well up to 5, even 10 yrs; GRAND CRU even longer. Also good quality and value CREMANT, but red wines (Pinot N) should be avoided.

Alsace Grand Cru w ✭✭✭→✭✭✭✭ 76 83 85 86 87 88 89' 90 **91 92 93** AC restricted to 50 of the best named v'yds (1,400 acres) and noble grapes (Riesling, Pinot Gr ('Tokay'), GEWURZ and MUSCAT). Not without controversy.

Ampeau, Robert Exceptional grower and specialist in MEURSAULT; also POMMARD, etc. Perhaps unique in only releasing long matured bottles.

André, Pierre Négociant at Ch Corton-André, ALOXE-CORTON; v'yds in CORTON, SAVIGNY, GEVREY-CHAMBERTIN etc. Also owns down-market REINE PEDAUQUE.

d'Angerville, Marquis Famous burgundy grower with immaculate 30-acre estate in VOLNAY. Top wines: Champans and Clos des Ducs.

Anjou Lo r p w (sw dr sp) ✭→✭✭✭ Loire AC embracing wide spectrum of styles. Esp good red (Cab) ANJOU-VILLAGES, strong dry SAVENNIERES, luscious COTEAUX DU LAYON Chenin Bl whites.

Anjou-Coteaux de la Loire Lo w dr sw ✭✭→✭✭✭ AC for some forceful Chenin Bl whites. Only 100 acres; mostly sweet or v sweet.

Anjou-Villages Lo r ✭→✭✭✭ AC for reds (mainly Cab F) from less limited zone than SAUMUR-CHAMPIGNY. Potentially juicy and good value.

Appellation Contrôlée (AC or AOC) Government control of origin and production of all the best French wines (see France Introduction).

Apremont Savoie w ✭✭ DYA One of the best villages of SAVOIE, for pale delicate whites, mainly from Jacquère grapes, recently incl CHARD.

Arbin Savoie r ✭✭ Deep-coloured lively red from MONDEUSE grapes, rather like a good Loire Cabernet. Ideal après-ski wine. Drink at 1–2 yrs.

Arbois Jura r p w (sp) ✭✭→✭✭✭ Various good and original light but tasty wines; speciality is VIN JAUNE. On the whole DYA.

l'Ardèche, Coteaux de Central France r p (w) ✭→✭✭✭ DYA Bargain country reds; best from Syrah, Gamay and recently Cab. Also powerful, almost burgundy-like CHARD 'Grand Ardèche' from LOUIS LATOUR.

l'Arlot, Domaine de Outstanding producer of supreme NUITS ST GEORGES, esp Clos de l'Arlot, red and white.

Armagnac Region of SW France and its often excellent brandy, a fiery spirit of rustic character. The outstanding red of the area is MADIRAN.

Aube Southern extension of CHAMPAGNE region. See Bar-sur-Aube.

Aujoux, J-M Substantial grower/merchant of BEAUJOLAIS. Swiss-owned.

Auxey-Duresses Burg r w ✱✱→✱✱✱✱ 78 83 85 87 88 89 90' 91 92 93 Second-rank (but v pretty) CÔTE DE BEAUNE village: affinities with VOLNAY, MEURSAULT. Best estates: Diconne, HOSPICES DE BEAUNE (Cuvée Boillot), LEROY, M Prunier, R Thévenin. Drink whites in 4–5 yrs; top: Leroy's Les Boutonniers.

Avize Champ ✱✱✱✱ One of the top Côte des Blancs villages. All CHARDONNAY.

Ay Champ ✱✱✱✱ One of the best Pinot N-growing villages of CHAMPAGNE.

Ayala NV; Demi-Sec NV; Brut 89; Château d'Ay 82 83 85; Grande Cuvée 82 83 85 88; Bl de Blancs 82 83 88; Brut Rosé NV Once-famous Ay-based old-style CHAMPAGNE concern. Deserves notice for fresh appley wines.

Bachelet, Denis Brilliant young grower of GEVREY-CHAMBERTIN. Top wine: CHARMES-CHAMBERTIN.

Bahuaut, Donatien Leading Loire-wine merchants and distributors of Ch de la Cassemichère, MUSCADET.

Bandol Prov r p (w) ✱✱✱ 82 83 85' 86 87' 88 89 90 91 92 93 Little region near Toulon producing Provence's best wines; vigorous tannic reds from the Mourvèdre grape; esp DOM OTT, Dom de Pibarnon, Ch Pradeaux, Mas de la Rouvière, DOM TEMPIER, Ch Vannières.

Banyuls Pyr br sw ✱✱ One of the best VINS DOUX NATURELS, made chiefly of Grenache (a Banyuls GRAND CRU is over 75% Grenache, aged for 2 yrs+). Technically a distant relation of port. Best wines are RANCIOS eg from Domaine des Masses, Dom du Mas Blanc (✱✱✱), Dom Vial Magnères (Blanc), at 10–15 yrs old. Also cheap NV wines.

Bar-sur-Aube Champ w (p) ✱✱ Important secondary CHAMPAGNE region 100 miles SE of R Marne, Epernay etc. Some good lighter wines and excellent ROSÉ DES RICEYS.

Barancourt Brut Réserve NV; Rosé NV; Bouzy Grand Cru 81 83 85; Rosé GC 85 Grower at Bouzy making full-bodied CHAMPAGNE. New owners Champagne Vranken; now esp Bouzy Rouge and Rosé Grand Cru.

Barrique The Bordeaux (and Cognac) term for an oak barrel holding 225 litres (eventually 300 bottles). Barrique-ageing to flavour almost any wine with oak was the craze of the late '80s, with some sad results.

Barsac Bx w sw ✱✱→✱✱✱✱ 70 71' 75 76' 78 79' 80' 81 82 83' 85 86' 88' 89' 90' 91 93 Neighbour of SAUTERNES with similar superb golden wines, generally less rich and more racy. Richly repays ageing. Top ch'x: CLIMENS, COUTET, DOISY-DAENE, DOISY-VEDRINES.

Barton & Guestier BORDEAUX shipper since 18th C, now owned by Seagram.

Bâtard-Montrachet Burg w ✱✱✱✱ 78 79 83 85 86' 87 88 89' 90' 91 92 93 Larger (55-acre) neighbour of MONTRACHET. Should be v long-lived with intense flavours and rich texture. Bienvenues-Bâtard-M is a separate adjacent 9-acre GRAND CRU with 15 owners, thus no substantial bottlings and v rare. Top growers incl BOUCHARD PÈRE, DROUHIN, Gagnard, LOUIS LATOUR, LEFLAIVE, Lequin-Roussot, MOREY, Niellon, RAMONET, SAUZET.

Baumard, Domaine des Leading grower of ANJOU wine, esp SAVENNIÈRES and COTEAUX DU LAYON (Clos Ste-Catherine).

Baur, Léon Small but vigorous ALSACE family firm at Eguisheim. Esp for Ries: Elisabeth Stumpf; also oaked Pinot. Don't confuse with LÉON BEYER.

Béarn SW France r p w ✱→✱✱ Wide-spread low-key AC of growing local (Basque) interest, esp wines of coop Sallies de Béarn-Bellocq.

Beaujolais Beauj r (p w) ✱ DYA The simple AC of the v big Beaujolais region: light short-lived fruity red from Gamay grapes. Beaujolais Supérieur means little different.

Confusingly, the best wines of the Beaujolais region are not identified as Beaujolais at all on their labels. They are known simply by the names of their 'crus': Brouilly, Chénas, Chiroubles, Côte de Brouilly, Fleurie, Juliénas, Morgon, Moulin-à-Vent, Regnié, Saint-Amour. See entries for each of these. The Confrérie des Compagnons du Beaujolais offers a 'Beaujolais Grumé' label to selected wines from the region with ageing potential.

Beaujolais de l'année The BEAUJOLAIS of the latest vintage, until the next.

Beaujolais Primeur (or Nouveau) Same as above, made in a hurry (often only 4–5 days fermenting) for release at midnight on the third Wednesday in November. Ideally soft, pungent, fruity and tempting; often crude, sharp, too alcoholic. BEAUJ-VILLAGES should be a better bet.

Beaujolais-Villages Beauj r ✹✹ 92 93 Wines from better (N) half of BEAUJOLAIS; should be much tastier than plain BEAUJOLAIS. The 10 (easily) best 'villages' are the 'CRUS': FLEURIE etc (see note on page 25). Of the 30 others the best lie around Beaujeu. Crus cannot be released EN PRIMEUR before December 15th. Best kept until spring (or longer).

NB This edition introduces a new short-cut vintage category. Vintages in colour are the ones you should choose first for drinking in 1995.

Beaumes-de-Venise Rh br (r p) ✹✹→✹✹✹ DYA Generally France's best dessert MUSCAT, from S COTES DU RHONE; can be high-flavoured, subtle, lingering (eg CHAPOUTIER, Dom de Coyeux, Dom Durban, JABOULET, VIDAL-FLEURY). Red and rosé from Ch Redortier and the coop also good.

Beaune Burg r (w) ✹✹✹ 78' 83 85' 87 88 89' 90' 91 92 93 Middle-rank classic burgundy. Many fine growers. Négociants' CLOS wines (usually PREMIER CRU) are often best; eg DROUHIN's superb Clos des Mouches, JADOT's Clos des Ursules. Beaune du Château is a (good) BOUCHARD PERE brand. Best v'yds: Bressandes, Fèves, Grèves, Marconnets, Teurons.

Becker, Caves J Proud old family firm at Zellenberg, ALSACE. Classic Ries Hagenschlauf and GRAND CRU Froehn MUSCAT. Second label: Gaston Beck.

Bellet Prov p r w ✹✹✹ Fashionable much above average local wines from nr Nice. Serious producers: Ch'x de Bellet and Crémat. Pricey.

Bergerac Dordogne r w dr sw ✹✹ 90 92' 93' Lightweight, often tasty, BORDEAUX-style. Drink young, the white v young. See also Monbazillac, Montravel, Pécharmant. Growers incl Courts-les-Muts, JAUBERTIE, Michel de Montaigne, Ch de Panisseau, Tiregand.

Besserat de Bellefon Grande Tradition NV; Cuvée des Moines Brut and Rosé NV; Grande Cuvée NV; Brut and Rosé 82 85 Reims CHAMPAGNE house for light wines, esp CREMANT. Owned by MARNE et CHAMPAGNE.

Beyer, Léon Ancient ALSACE family firm at Eguisheim making forceful dry wines that need ageing at least 3–5 yrs. Comtes d'Eguisheim Gewurz is renowned, but lately inconsistent. 'Cuvée Particulière' Ries of GRAND CRU Pfersigberg esp fine. Beyer is militant against GC restrictions.

Bichot, Maison Albert One of BEAUNE's biggest growers and merchants. V'yds (Domaine du Clos Frantin is excellent) in CHAMBERTIN, RICHEBOURG, CLOS DE VOUGEOT, etc, and Domaine Long-Depaquit in CHABLIS; also many other brand names.

Billecart-Salmon NV; Rosé NV; Brut 85 86; Bl de Blancs 83 85 86; Grande Cuvée 82 One of the best small CHAMPAGNE houses, founded in 1818, still family-owned. Fresh-flavoured wines incl a v tasty rosé. New CUVEE: Elisabeth Salmon Rosé (88).

Bize, Simon Admirable red burgundy grower with 35 acres in SAVIGNY-LES-BEAUNE. Usually model wines, racy and elegant.

Blagny Burg r w ✹✹→✹✹✹ (w) 78 83 85 86' 87 88 89 90' 91 92 93 Hamlet between MEURSAULT and PULIGNY-MONTRACHET: whites have affinities with both (sold under each AC), reds with VOLNAY (sold as AC Blagny). Good ones need age; esp AMPEAU, Jobard, LATOUR, LEFLAIVE, Matrot, G Thomas.

Blanc de Blancs Any white wine made from white grapes only, esp CHAMPAGNE (usually both red and white). Not an indication of quality.

Blanc de Noirs White (or slightly pink or 'blush') wine from red grapes.

Blanck, Marcel Versatile ALSACE grower at Kientzheim. Good Pinot Bl, and GRANDS CRUS Furstentum (GEWURZ, Pinot Gr, esp Ries), Schlossberg (Ries).

Blanquette de Limoux Midi w sp ✹✹ Good bargain sparkler from nr Carcassonne with long local history. V dry and clean; increasingly tasty as more CHARD and Chenin Bl is added. Normally NV.

Blaye Bx r w ✴ 88 89 90 92 93 Your daily BORDEAUX from E of the Gironde. PREMIERES COTES DE BLAYE is the AC of the better wines.

Boisset, Jean-Claude Dynamic burgundy merchant/grower at NUITS-ST-GEORGES, owns BOUCHARD-AINE, Lionel Bruck, Delaunay, JAFFELIN, Morin Père et Fils, de Marcilly, Pierre Ponnelle, Thomas-Bassot, VIENOT. Generally high commercial standards.

Bollinger NV 'Special Cuvée'; Grande Année 69 70 73 75 76 79 82 83 85 88; Rosé 81 82 83 85 Top CHAMPAGNE house, at AY. Dry, very full-flavoured style, needs ageing. Luxury wines: RD (73 75 76 79 81 82), Vieilles Vignes Françaises (69 70 75 79 80 81 82 85 88) from ungrafted Pinot vines. Pioneered Charter of Quality ('91). Investor in Petaluma, Australia.

Bonneau du Martray, Domaine Biggest grower (with 27 acres) of CORTON-CHARLEMAGNE of the highest quality; also red GRAND CRU CORTON. Cellars at PERNAND-VERGELESSES. Whites often outlive reds.

Bonnes-Mares Burg r ✴✴✴–✴✴✴✴✴ 69 71 76 78' 79 80 83 85' 86 87 88 89 90' 91 92 93 37-acre GRAND CRU between CHAMBOLLE-MUSIGNY and MOREY-ST-DENIS. V sturdy long-lived wines, less fragrant than MUSIGNY; can rival CHAMBERTIN. Top growers: DUJAC, Groffier, JADOT, MUGNIER, ROUMIER, DOM DES VAROILLES, DE VOGUE.

Bonnezeaux Lo w sw ✴✴✴ 76' 78 81 83 85' 86 88' 89' 90' 91 92 93' Unusual rich tangy wine from Chenin Bl grapes, the best of COTEAUX DU LAYON. Esp Ch de Fesles, Dom du Petit Val. Ages well – but v tempting young.

Bordeaux Bx r w (p) ✴ 88 89 90 92 93 (for ch'x see pages 56–77) Catch-all AC for low-strength B'x wine. Not to be despised: it may be light but its flavour cannot be imitated. There is no more satisfactory daily drink.

Bordeaux Sup**érieur** ✴–✴✴✴ As above, with slightly more alcohol.

Borie-Manoux Admirable BORDEAUX shippers and château-owners, owned by the Castéja family. Ch'x incl BATAILLEY, BEAU-SITE, DOMAINE DE L'EGLISE, HAUT-BAGES-MONPELOU, TROTTEVIEILLE.

Bouchard Aîné Long-est (1750) burgundy shipper/grower with 62 acres in BEAUNE, MERCUREY, etc. Good, not top quality. Bought in '93 by BOISSET.

Bouchard Père et Fils Important burgundy shipper (est 1731) and grower with 209 acres of excellent v'yds, mainly in the COTE DE BEAUNE, and cellars at the Château de Beaune. Vg, if not quite top quality.

Bouches-du-Rhône Prov r p w ✴ VINS DE PAYS from Marseille environs. Robust reds from southern varieties, Cab S, Syrah and Merlot.

Bourg Bx r (w) ✴✴ 83 85' 86' 88' 89' 90' 92 93 Un-fancy claret from E of the Gironde. For châteaux see Côtes de Bourg.

Bourgogne Burg r w (p) ✴✴ 88' 89 90' 91 92 Catch-all Burgundy AC, with higher standards than basic BORDEAUX. Light, often good flavour, best at 2–4 yrs. Top growers make bargain beauties from fringes of Côte d'Or villages; do not despise. BEAUJOLAIS CRUS can also be labelled Bourgogne.

Bourgogne Grand Ordinaire Burg r w (p) ✴ DYA Lowest Burg AC, also allowing GAMAY. Rare. White may incl ALIGOTE, Pinot Bl, Melon de Bourgogne.

Bourgogne Passe-Tout-Grains Burg r (p) ✴ Age 1–2 yrs Junior burgundy: minimum 33% Pinot N, the balance GAMAY, mixed in the vat. Often enjoyable. Not as 'heady' as BEAUJOLAIS.

Bourgueil Lo r ✴✴✴ 76' 83' 85 86' 88 89' 90' 91 92 93' Normally delicate fruity Cab red from TOURAINE. Deep-flavoured, long-lasting in best yrs, ageing like Bordeaux. ST-NICOLAS-DE-BOURGUEIL often lighter. Esp from Audebert, Billet, Caslot, Cognard, Druet, Jamet, Lamé-Delille-Boucard.

Bouvet-Ladubay The major producer of sparkling SAUMUR, controlled by TAITTINGER. Excellent CREMANT DE LOIRE. 'Saphir' is vintage wine. Deluxe 'Trésor' is oak-fermented, with 2 yrs age.

Bouzeron Village of the COTE CHALONNAISE distinguished for the only single-village AC ALIGOTE. Top grower: de Villaine.

Bouzy Rouge Champ r ✴✴✴ 85 86 88 89 90 91 Still red of famous red-grape CHAMPAGNE village. Like light burgundy, ageing early but can last well.

Brédif, Marc One of the most important growers and traders of VOUVRAY, owned by LADOUCETTE.

Bricout Brut NV (Réserve, Prestige, Cuvée Spéciale Arthur Bricout, C S Charles Koch); Rosé NV; Brut **82 85 86** Small CHAMPAGNE house at AVIZE making light wines. Owned by Kupferberg of Mainz.

Brouilly Beauj r ** **91 92 93** Biggest of the 10 CRUS of BEAUJOLAIS: fruity, round, refreshing wine, can age 3–4 yrs. CH DE LA CHAIZE is largest estate. Top growers: Michaud, Dom de Combillaty, Dom des Grandes Vignes.

Brut Champ Term for the driest wines of CHAMPAGNE.

Bugey Savoie r p w sp *→** DYA VDQS district for light sparkling, still or half-sparkling wines. Grapes incl Roussette (or Roussanne) and good CHARD. Best from Cerdon and Montagnieu.

Buxy Burg w ** Village in AC MONTAGNY with good coop for CHARD.

Buzet SW France r w ** **86 88 89' 90' 92' 93** Good BORDEAUX-style wines from just SE of Bordeaux. Good value area with well-run cooperative. Best wines are barrel-aged: Ch de Gueyze, Cuvée Napoléon (now Cuvée Baron d'Ardeuil). Also Ch'x de Padère and Sauvagnères.

Cabardès Midi r (p w) *→** **85 86 88 89 90 91 92** Newcomer VDQS region north of Carcassonne, CORBIÈRES, etc. MIDI and BORDEAUX grapes show promise in Ch Rivals, Ch Ventenac, Coops de Conques sur Orbiel.

Cabernet See Grapes for red wine (pages 8–9).

Cabernet d'Anjou Lo p *→** DYA Delicate, grapey, often rather sweet rosé.

Cabrières Midi p (r) ** DYA COTEAUX DU LANGUEDOC vintage best for fragrant rosé from eg Domaine du Temple.

Cahors SW France *→** **82 83 85 86' 88 89' 90' 92' 93** Historically 'black' and tannic from Malbec grapes, now made like BORDEAUX: full-bodied and distinct or much lighter. Top growers: Baldès (esp 'Prince Probus'), Ch'x de Caix, de Chambert, Lagrezette, Latuc, St-Didier; Clos la Coutale, Dom Eugénie, Clos de Gamot, Jouffreau, Dom de Paillas, Vigouroux (esp Ch de Haute-Serre). Lighter wines from coop, Caves d'Olt.

Cairanne Rh r p w ** **86 88 89 90 91 92** Good solid COTES DU RHONE-VILLAGES, esp from Doms Brusset, l'Oratoire St-Martin, Rabasse-Charavin.

Calvet Famous old shippers of BORDEAUX and burgundy, now owned by Allied-Hiram Walker. Some reliable standard wines, esp from Bordeaux.

Canard-Duchêne Brut NV; Demi-Sec NV; Rosé NV; Charles VII NV; Brut **83 85 88** Quality CHAMPAGNE house owned by VEUVE-CLICQUOT, hence the Moët-Hennessy group. Fair prices for tasty, Pinot N-tasting wines.

Canon-Fronsac Bx r **→*** **78 82 83' 85' 86 88 89' 90' 92 93** Full tannic reds of increasing quality from small area W of POMEROL. Need less age than formerly (89s and even 90s vg now). Eg Ch'x: CANON, CANON DE BREM, CANON-MOUEIX, Coustolle, Junayme, Mazeris-Bellevue, Moulin-Pey-Labrie, Toumalin, La Truffière, Vraye-Canon-Boyer. See also Fronsac.

Cantenac Bx r *** Village of HAUT-MEDOC entitled to the AC MARGAUX. Top châteaux include BRANE-CANTENAC, PALMER, etc.

Cap Corse Corsica w br **→*** CORSICA's wild N cape. Splendid Muscat from Clos Nicrosi, Rogliano, and rare soft dry Vermentino white. Vaut le détour, if not le voyage.

Caramany Pyr r (w) * **88 89 90 91 92** Notionally superior new AC for part of COTES DU ROUSSILLON-VILLAGES.

Cassis Prov w (r p) ** DYA Seaside village E of Marseille known for lively dry white wine, one of the best in PROVENCE (eg Domaine du Paternel). Not to be confused with cassis, a blackcurrant liqueur made in Dijon.

Cave Cellar, or any wine establishment.

Cave coopérative Wine-growers' cooperative winery. Coops now account for 55% of all French production (4 out of 10 growers are members). Almost all are now well-run, well-equipped and make good value wine.

Cellier des Samsons BEAUJOLAIS/MACONNAIS coop at Quincié with 2,000 grower-members. Widely distributed.

Cépage Variety of vine, eg CHARDONNAY, Merlot.

Cérons Bx w dr sw ** **81 83' 85' 86' 88' 89' 90 91 92 93** Neighbour of SAUTERNES with some good sweet wine châteaux, eg de Cérons et de Calvimont, Grand Enclos, Haura. Ch Archambeau makes vg dry GRAVES.

Chablis Burg w ·**→**** 89 90 91 92 93   Unique full-flavoured dry minerally wine of N Burgundy, CHARD only, from 10,000 acres (doubled since '85). Top growers incl J-M Brocard, J Collet, R Dauvissat, J Defaix, Droin, DURUP, FEVRE, Geoffroy, J-P Grossot, LAROCHE, LONG-DEPAQUIT, MICHEL, PIC, Raveneau, G Robin, Vocoret. Simple unqualified 'Chablis' may be thin; best is PREMIER or GRAND CRU (see below). The coop, La Chablisienne, has v high standards and many different labels.

Chablis Grand Cru Burg w ***→**** 78 83 85 86 88 89 90 91 92 93   In maturity a match for greatest white burgundy: forceful but often dumb in youth, at best almost SAUTERNES-like with age. 7 v'yds: Blanchots, Bougros, Clos, Grenouilles, Preuses, Valmur, Vaudésir. See Moutonne.

Chablis Premier Cru Burg w *** 85 86 88 89 90 91 92 93   Technically second-rank but at best excellent, more typical of CHABLIS than its GRANDS CRUS. Often outclasses more expensive MEURSAULT and other CHARDS. Best v'yds incl Côte de Lechet, Fourchaume, Mont de Milieu, Montée de Tonnerre, Montmains, Vaillons. See Chablis for producers.

Chai Building for storing and maturing wine, esp in BORDEAUX.

Chambertin Burg r **** 69 71 76 78' 79 80 82 83 85' 87 88 89 90' 91 92 93   32-acre GRAND CRU producing some of the meatiest, most enduring and best red burgundy, 15 growers, incl BOUCHARD PERE, Camus, Damoy, DROUHIN, MORTET, PONSOT, Rebourseau, Rossignol-Trapet, ROUSSEAU, Tortochot, Trapet.

Chambertin-Clos de Bèze Burg r **** 69 71 76 78' 79 80 82 83 85 87 88 89 90' 91 92 93   37-acre neighbour of CHAMBERTIN. Similarly splendid wines. May legally be sold as Chambertin. 10 growers incl B CLAIR, CLAIR-DAU, Damoy, DROUHIN, Drouhin-Laroze, FAIVELEY, JADOT, ROUSSEAU.

Chambolle-Musigny Burg r (w) ***→**** 78' 82 83 85' 87 88 89 90' 91 92 93   420-acre COTE DE NUITS village with fabulously fragrant, complex, never heavy wine. Best v'yds: Les Amoureuses, part of BONNES-MARES, Les Charmes, MUSIGNY. Growers to note: Barthod, DROUHIN, FAIVELEY, Hudelot-Noëllat, JADOT, Moine-Hudelot, Mugneret, MUGNIER, RION, ROUMIER, Serveau, DE VOGUE.

Champagne Sparkling wine of Pinots N and Meunier and/or CHARD, and its region (70,000+ acres 90 miles E of Paris); made by METHODE CHAMPENOISE. Wines from elsewhere, however good, cannot be champagne.

Champigny See Saumur.

Chandon de Briailles, Domaine Small burgundy estate at SAVIGNY. Makes wonderful CORTON (and Corton Blanc) and vg PERNAND-VERGELESSES.

Chanson Père et Fils Growers (with 110 acres) and négociants at BEAUNE.

Chantovent Major brand of VIN DE TABLE, largely from MINERVOIS.

Chapelle-Chambertin Burg r *** 78' 82 83 85 87 88 89' 90' 91 92 93   13-acre neighbour of CHAMBERTIN. Wine more 'nervous', not so meaty. Top producers: JADOT, LEROY, Rossignol-Trapet, Trapet.

Chapoutier Long-est'd growers and traders of top-quality Rhône wines.

Charbaut, A et Fils Brut NV; Bl de Blancs Brut NV; Brut Rosé NV; Brut 79 82 85 87 88; Certificate Bl de Blancs 82 85; Certificate Rosé 79 82 85   Substantial Epernay CHAMPAGNE house. Clean light wines. Good rosé. New CUVEE launched '93: Grand Evénement Brut NV.

Chardonnay See Grapes for white wine (pages 6–8). Also the name of a MACON-VILLAGES commune. Hence Mâcon-Chardonnay.

Charmes-Chambertin Burg r *** 71 76 78' 79 83 85' 87 88 89' 90' 91 92 93   76-acre neighbour of CHAMBERTIN, includes the AC MAZOYERES-CHAMBERTIN. Wine more 'supple', rounder. Growers incl BACHELET, Castagnier, DROUHIN, DUJAC, LEROY, ROTY, ROUSSEAU.

Chartron & Trebuchet Young co (founded '84): some delicate harmonious white burgundies, esp Dom Chartron's PULIGNY-MONTRACHET, Clos de la Pucelle, and BATARD- and CHEVALIER-MONTRACHET. Also good ALIGOTE.

For key to grape variety abbreviations, see pages 6–9.

Chassagne-Montrachet Burg r w ***→***** r (***) 78' **82 83** 85 **87** 88 89' 90' 91 92 93; w 78' **83 85** 86 88 89' 90 **91** 92 93   750-acre COTE DE BEAUNE village with excellent rich dry whites and sterling hefty reds. Whites rarely have the extreme finesse of PULIGNY-MONT next door but often cost less. Best v'yds incl part of MONTRACHET, BATARD-MONTRACHET, Boudriottes (r w), Caillerets, CRIOTS-BATARD-MONTRACHET, Morgeot (r w), Ruchottes, CLOS ST-JEAN (r). Growers incl Amiot-Bonfils, Colin-Deleger, Delagrange-Bachelet, DROUHIN, J-N Gagnard, GAGNARD-DELAGRANGE, Lamy-Pillot, MAGENTA, Ch de la Maltroye, MOREY, Niellon, RAMONET-PRUDHON.

Chasseloir, Dom du HQ of the firm of Chéreau-Carré: makers of several excellent AC-leading domaine MUSCADETS (esp Ch du Chasseloir).

Château An estate, big or small, good or indifferent, particularly in BORDEAUX (see pages 56–77). In Burgundy the term 'domaine' is used.

Château d'Arlay Major JURA estate; 160 acres in skilful hands with wines incl vg VIN JAUNE, VIN DE PAILLE, Pinot N and MACVIN.

Château de Beaucastel Rh r w *** 78 79 81 **83** 85 86' **87** 88 89 90 91 92 One of the biggest (173 acres), best-run CHATEAUNEUF-DU-PAPE estates. Deep-hued wines for at least 10 yrs ageing. Small amount of wonderful Roussanne white to keep 5–10 yrs. Second label: Coudoulet de Beaucastel (vg white). New interest: Beaucastel Estate, California.

Château de la Chaize Beauj r *** **91 92 93**   Best-known BROUILLY estate.

Château-Chalon Jura w ***   Unique strong dry yellow wine, like sharpish fino sherry. Usually ready when bottled (at about 6 yrs). A curiosity.

Château Corton-Grancey Burg r *** 78 82 83 85 88 89 90 91 92 93   Famous ALOXE-CORTON estate; property of LOUIS LATOUR: benchmark wines.

Château Fortia Rh r (w) *** 78 81 83 85 86 88 89 90 91 92   Traditional CHATEAUNEUF property. Owner's father, Baron Le Roy, also fathered the APPELLATION CONTROLEE system in the '20s. Good, but not at the v top today.

Château Fuissé Burg w ***   The ultimate POUILLY-FUISSE estate. Its PF VIEILLES VIGNES is ****, sumptuous with age.

Château-Grillet Rh w **** 89 90 91 92   7.5-acre v'yd: one of France's smallest ACs. Intense fragrant absurdly over-expensive. Drink young.

Château de Meursault Burg r w ***   100-acre estate owned by PATRIARCHE with good v'yds and wines in BEAUNE, MEURSAULT, POMMARD, VOLNAY. Splendid cellars open to the public for tasting.

Château de Mille Prov r p w **   Leading star of advancing COTES DU LUBERON.

Château du Nozet Lo w *** 89 90 91' 92' 93'   Biggest best-known estate of POUILLY (FUME) -SUR-LOIRE. Esp, Baron de L, can be wonderful (at a price).

Château Rayas Rh r (w) *** 78' 79 81 85 86 88 89 90 91 92   Famous old-style property of only 38 acres in CHATEAUNEUF-DU-PAPE. Concentrated wines are entirely Grenache, yet can age superbly. Pignan is second label. Also vg Ch Fonsalette, COTES DU RHONE (NB Cuvée Syrah).

Château de Selle Prov r p w **→***   100-acre estate of OTT family nr Cotignac, Var. Pace-setters for PROVENCE. Cuvée Spéciale is largely Cab.

Château Simone Prov r p w **   Age 2–6 yrs   Famous old property in Palette; the only one with a name in this AC nr Aix-en-Provence. The red is best: smooth but herby and spicy. White is catching up.

Château Val-Joanis Prov r p w **→***   Impressive estate making vg COTES DU LUBERON wines. To try.

Château Vignelaure Prov r **→*** 82' 83' 85 **86 87** 88 89 90 91 92   135-acre Provençal estate nr Aix, making exceptional more-or-less BORDEAUX-style wine with Cab, Syrah and Grenache grapes.

Châteaumeillant Lo r p w *   DYA   Tiny VDQS area nr SANCERRE. Light Gamay and Pinot N. Good pale rosé.

Châteauneuf-du-Pape Rh r (w) *** 78' 79 81 83 85 86 88 89 90 91 92 7,400 acres nr Avignon with v mixed standards but many fine wines. Best are dark, strong, exceptionally long-lived. Others light and/or disappointing. White can be heavy: mostly now 'DYA'. Top growers incl ch'x DE BEAUCASTEL, FORTIA, La Nerthe, RAYAS; Doms de Beaurenard, les Cailloux; Les Cèdres, Clos des Papes, VIEUX TELEGRAPHE, etc.

Châtillon-en-Diois Rh r p w ∗ DYA Small AC of mid Rhône. Adequate largely Gamay reds; white (some ALIGOTE) mostly made into CLAIRETTE DE DIE.

Chauvenet, F Substantial modern firm in NUITS; buys grapes on contract from good growers for wide range of much-appreciated COTE D'OR wines, incl CORTON-CHARLEMAGNE, CHARMES-CHAMBERTIN, etc. Assoc with J-C BOISSET.

Chave, Gérard To many the superstar grower of HERMITAGE, red and white.

Chavignol Village of SANCERRE with famous v'yd, Les Monts Damnés. Chalky soil gives vivid wines that age 4–5 yrs. Also fromage de chèvre.

Chénas Beauj r ✱✱✱ 90 91 92 93 Smallest BEAUJOLAIS CRU and one of the weightiest; neighbour to MOULIN-A-VENT and JULIENAS. Growers incl Benon, Braillon, Champagnon, Charvet, Ch Chèvres, DUBOEUF, Robin, coop.

Chenin Blanc See Grapes for white wine (pages 6–8).

Chenonceau, Ch de Lo ∗∗ Architectural jewel of the Loire recently for excellent AC Touraine Sauv Bl, Cab, Cot (Malbec) and ✱✱✱ Chenin.

Chevalier-Montrachet Burg w ✱✱✱✱ 78 83 85' 86 88 89' 90 91 92 93 17-acre neighbour of MONTRACHET: similar luxurious wine, perhaps less powerful. Incl 2.5-acre Les Demoiselles. Growers incl LATOUR, JADOT, BOUCHARD PERE, CHARTRON & TREBUCHET, Deleger, LEFLAIVE, Niellon, PRIEUR.

Cheverny Lo r p w (sp) ✱→✱✱ DYA Loire AC nr Chambord. Dry crisp whites from Sauv Bl. Also Gamay, Pinot N or Cab reds; generally light but tasty. 'Cour Cheverny' uses the local Romorantin grape.

Chevigny, Pascal Producer of fine VOSNE-ROMANEE: neighbour to LA TACHE.

Chevillon, R 21-acre estate at NUITS-ST-GEORGES; outstanding winemaking.

Chignin Savoie w ∗ DYA Light soft white from Jacquère grapes for Alpine summers. Chignin-Bergeron is best and liveliest.

Chinon Lo r ✱✱✱ 76 83' 85 86' 88 89' 90' 91' 92 93' Juicy, variably rich Cab F from TOURAINE. Drink cool, young; treat exceptional vintages like BORDEAUX. Top growers: Baudry, Couly-Dutheil (esp Clos de l'Echo), Druet, Joguet, Mabileau, Raffault, Dom de Roncée.

Chiroubles Beauj r ✱✱✱ 91 92 93 Good but tiny BEAUJOLAIS CRU next to FLEURIE; freshly fruity silky wine for early drinking (1–3 yrs). Growers incl Bouillard, Cheysson, DUBOEUF, Fourneau, Passot, Raousset, coop.

Chorey-lès-Beaune Burg r (w) ✱✱ 85 87 88 89 90' 91 92 93 Minor AC on flat land N of BEAUNE: 2 fine growers: Germain (Ch de Chorey), TOLLOT-BEAUT.

Chusclan Rh r p w ∗→✱✱ 88 89 90 91 92 Village of COTE DU RHONE-VILLAGES. Middle-weight wines (rosé best) from the coop. Labels incl Cuvée des Monticaud, Seigneurie de Gicon.

Cissac HAUT-MEDOC village just west of PAUILLAC.

Clair, Bruno Recent little domaine at MARSANNAY. Vg wines from there and GEVREY-CHAMBERTIN (esp CLOS DE BEZE), FIXIN, MOREY-ST-DENIS, SAVIGNY.

Clairet Very light red wine, almost rosé.

Clairette Traditional white grape of the MIDI. Can give soft pretty wine.

Clairette de Bellegarde Midi w ∗ DYA AC nr Nîmes: plain neutral white.

Clairette de Die Rh w dr s/sw sp ✱✱ NV Popular dry or (better) semi-sweet MUSCAT-flavoured sparkling wine from E Rhône; or straight dry CLAIRETTE white, surprisingly ageing well 3–4 yrs. Worth trying.

Clairette du Languedoc Midi w ∗ DYA Plain neutral white from nr Montpellier, but watch for improvements.

Clape, La Midi r p w ✱→✱✱ AC to note of COTEAUX DU LANGUEDOC. Full-bodied wines from limestone hills between Narbonne and the sea. Red gains character after 2–3 yrs, Malvasia white after even longer. Vg rosé.

Claret Traditional English term for red BORDEAUX.

Climat Burgundian word for individual named v'yd, eg BEAUNE Grèves.

Clos A term carrying some prestige, reserved for distinct, usually walled, v'yds, often in one ownership. Frequent in Burgundy and ALSACE. Les Clos is CHABLIS' Grandest Cru.

Clos de Bèze See Chambertin-Clos de Bèze.

Clos des Lambrays Burg r ✱✱✱ 83 85' 87 88 89' 90' 91 92 93 15-acre GRAND CRU v'yd at MOREY-ST-DENIS. Changed hands in '79 after a shaky period. Now, after replanting, looking good (for a v long life).

Clos des Mouches Burg r w *** Splendid PREMIER CRU BEAUNE v'yd, largely owned by DROUHIN. White and red, spicy and memorable – and consistent.

Clos de la Roche Burg r *** 72 78' 82 83 85' 86 87 88 89' 90 91 92 93 38-acre MOREY-ST-DENIS GRAND CRU. Powerful complex wine like CHAMBERTIN. Esp BOUCHARD P, BOUREE, CASTAGNIER, DUJAC, Lignier, PONSOT, REMY, ROUSSEAU.

Clos du Roi Burg r *** Part of GRAND CRU CORTON. Also a BEAUNE PREMIER CRU.

Clos St-Denis Burg r *** 76 78 79 82 83 85' 87 88 89' 90' 91 92 93 16-acre GRAND CRU at MOREY-ST-DENIS. Splendid sturdy wine growing silky with age. Growers incl DUJAC, Lignier, PONSOT.

Clos Ste Hune Al w V fine austere Ries from TRIMBACH; perhaps ALSACE's best. Needs 5 yrs age to reveal potential; doesn't need GRAND CRU status.

Clos St-Jacques Burg r *** 78' 80 82 83 85' 86 87 88 89' 90' 91 92 93 17-acre GEVREY-CHAMBERTIN PREMIER CRU. Excellent powerful velvety, often better (and dearer) than some of GRANDS CRUS. Main grower: ROUSSEAU.

Clos St-Jean Burg r *** 78 83 85' 87 88 89' 90' 91 92 93 36-acre PREMIER CRU of CHASSAGNE-MONTRACHET. Vg red, more solid than subtle, from eg Ch de la Maltroye. NB Domaine RAMONET.

Clos de Tart Burg r *** 85' 87 88' 89' 90' 92 93 GRAND CRU at MOREY-ST-DENIS, owned by MOMMESSIN. At best wonderfully fragrant, whether young or old.

Clos de Vougeot Burg r *** 78 83 85' 87 88 89' 90' 91 92 93 124-acre COTE DE NUITS GRAND CRU with many owners. Variable, occasionally sublime. Maturity depends on the grower's philosophy, technique and position on hill. Top growers incl CLAIR-DAU, DROUHIN, Drouhin-Laroze, ENGEL, FAIVELEY, GRIVOT, Gros, Hudelot-Noëllat, JADOT, LEROY, Chantal Lescure, MEO-CAMUZET, Mugneret, Rebourseau, ROUMIER.

Coche-Dury 16-acre MEURSAULT domaine (and 1 acre+ of CORTON-CHARLEMAGNE) with sky-high reputation for oak-perfumed wines. Also vg ALIGOTE.

Cognac Town and region of the Charentes, W France, and its brandy.

Collines Rhodaniennes Rh r w p * Popular Rhône VIN DE PAYS. Mainly reds: Merlot, Syrah, Gamay.

Collioure Pyr r ** 82 83 85 86 88 89 90 91 92 Strong dry red from BANYULS area. Tiny production. Top growers include de Baillaury, Guy de Barlande, Dom du Mas Blanc, Dom de la Rectorie, La Tour Vieille.

Comté Tolosan SW r w p Regional VIN DE PAYS for Midi and Pyrenees v'yds. Predominantly red from traditional SW varieties.

Condrieu Rh w **** DYA Outstanding soft fragrant white of great character (and price) from the VIOGNIER grape, planted on only 40+ acres. Top growers: DELAS, Dumazet, GUIGAL, Pinchon, Ch du Rozay, Vernay. CHATEAU-GRILLET is similar. Don't try ageing it.

Corbières Midi r (p w) *→*** 88 89 90 91 92 Good vigorous bargain reds, rarely disappointing at their price. Best growers incl Ch'x Aiguilloux, de Cabriac, des Ollieux, Les Palais, de Quéribus, de la Voulte Gasparet, Dom de Villemajou; Coops de Embrès et Castelmaur, Paziols, St-Laurent-Cabrerisse, etc.

Cordier, Ets D Important BORDEAUX shipper and château-owner: wonderful track-record but troubled present. Incl Ch'x CANTEMERLE, GRUAUD-LAROSE, LAFAURIE-PEYRAGUEY, MEYNEY, TALBOT, and also SANCERRE, Clos de la Poussie.

Cornas Rh r **→*** 78' 79 80 81 83' 85' 86 88 89 90 91 92 Expanding district S of HERMITAGE. Sturdy v dark Syrah wine of unique quality. Needs 5–15 yrs' ageing. Top are de Barjac, Clape, DELAS, JABOULET, Verset.

Corsica (Corse) Strong wines of all colours. Better ACs incl AJACCIO, CAP CORSE, PATRIMONIO, Sartène. VIN DE PAYS: ILE DE BEAUTE!

Corton Burg r ***→**** 78' 83 85' 86 87 88 89' 90' 91 92 93 The only GRAND CRU red of the COTE DE BEAUNE. 200 acres in ALOXE-CORTON incl CLOS DU ROI, Les Bressandes. Rich powerful, should age well. Many good growers.

Corton-Charlemagne Burg w **** 78' 79 82 83 85' 86' 87 88 89' 90' 91 92 93 The white section (one-third) of CORTON. Rich spicy lingering wine, behaves like a red and ages magnificently. Top growers: BONNEAU DU MARTRAY, Chapuis, COCHE-DURY, Delarche, Dubreuil-Fontaine, FAIVELEY, HOSPICES DE BEAUNE, JADOT, LATOUR, Rapet.

Costières de Nîmes Midi r p w *→*** DYA   Large new AC of improving
quality from the Rhône delta. Formerly Costières du Gard. NB Ch de
Nages, Ch de la Tuilerie ('Dinettes et Croustilles').

Côte(s) Means hillside; generally a superior v'yd to those on the plain.
Many ACs are prefixed by either 'Côtes' or 'Coteaux', meaning the
same. In ST-EMILION distinguishes valley slopes from higher plateau.

Côte de Beaune Burg r w **→****   Used geographically: the southern half
of the COTE D'OR. Applies as an AC only to parts of BEAUNE itself.

Côte de Beaune-Villages Burg r w ** 85 88 89' 90' 91 92 93   Regional
APPELLATION for secondary wines of classic area. Cannot be labelled
'Côte de Beaune' without either '-Villages' or village name appended.

Côte de Brouilly Beauj *** 90 91 92 93   Fruity rich vigorous BEAUJOLAIS
CRU. One of best. Esp from: Dom de Chavanne, G Cotton, Ch Delachanel,
J-C Nesme, Ch Thivin.

Côte Chalonnaise Burg r w sp **→***   V'yd area between BEAUNE and
MACON. See Givry, Mercurey, Montagny, Rully. Alias 'Région de Mercurey'.

Côte de la Malepère Midi r *   Recent and v promising VDQS for reds half-
way in style between BORDEAUX and Midi.

Côte de Nuits Burg r (w) **→****   N half of COTE D'OR. Mostly red wine.

Côte de Nuits-Villages Burg r (w) ** 88 89 90 91 92 93   A junior AC for
extreme N and S ends of Côte; well worth investigating for bargains.

Côte d'Or Département name applied to the central and principal
Burgundy v'yd slopes, consisting of the COTE DE BEAUNE and COTE DE
NUITS. The name is not used on labels.

Côte Rôtie Rh r ***→**** 78 79 80 82 83' 84 85' 86 87 88 89 90 91 92
Potentially the finest Rhône red, from just S of Vienne; can achieve
complex, almost BORDEAUX-like delicacy with age. Top growers include
Barge, Champet, CHAPOUTIER, DELAS, Gentaz-Dervieux, GUIGAL, JABOULET,
Jamet, Jasmin, Rostaing, VIDAL-FLEURY.

Coteaux d'Aix-en-Provence Prov r p w *→***   AC on the move. Est'd CH
VIGNELAURE challenged by Ch'x Commanderie de la Bargemone,
Fonscolombe and Dom de Trévallon. See COTEAUX DES BAUX-EN-PROVENCE.

Coteaux d'Ancenis Lo r p w * DYA   Light Cab and Gamay reds and rosés,
sharpish whites, from MUSCADET country.

Coteaux de l'Ardèche See l'Ardèche.

Coteaux de l'Aubance Lo p w sw ** DYA   Light ANJOU wines: sweet, and
only from Chenin Bl. Best are MOELLEUX; demi-sec in lesser yrs. Esp
from Dom Richou, Dom des Rochettes (to age, not DYA).

Coteaux des Baronnies Rh r p w *   Rhône VIN DE PAYS. Syrah, Merlot, Cab S
and CHARD, plus traditional grapes. Promising.

Coteaux des Baux-en-Provence Prov r p w *→***   Neighbour of COTEAUX
D'AIX, also gathering speed. NB the excellent Domaine de Trévallon
(Cab and Syrah) and Mas de Gourgonnier.

Coteaux Champenois Champ r w (p) *** DYA (whites)   The AC for non-
sparkling CHAMPAGNE. Vintages (if mentioned) follow those for
Champagne. Do not pay inflated prices.

Coteaux du Giennois Lo r p w * DYA   Up-and-coming Loire VDQS area
north of SANCERRE. Light Gamay and Pinot N, Sauvignon à la SANCERRE.
Top grower: Balland-Chapuis.

Coteaux du Languedoc Midi r p w *→***   Scattered well-above-ordinary
MIDI AC areas. Best reds (eg CABRIERES, LA CLAPE, FAUGERES, St-Georges-
d'Orques, Quatourze, ST-CHINIAN, St-Saturnin) age for 2–3 yrs. Now
also some good whites. Follow with increasing interest.

Coteaux du Layon Lo w s/sw sw ** 79 82 85' 86 88' 89 90' 91 92 93'   The
heart of ANJOU, centred on Rochefort, S of Angers: sweet Chenin with
admirable acidity, ageing almost forever, excellent aperitif or dessert.
Since '93 new AC Selection des Grains Nobles (cf ALSACE). Top ACs:
BONNEZEAUX, C du L-Chaume. Incl: J-C Dom d'Ambinos, Douet, TOUCHAIS.

Coteaux du Loir Lo r p w dr sw ★★ 78 82 83 85 86 88' 89' 90' 91 92 93' Small region N of Tours. Occasionally excellent wines of Chenin Bl, Gamay, Cab, etc. Best v'yd: JASNIERES. Loir is a tributary of the Loire.

Coteaux de la Loire See Anjou-Coteaux de la Loire.

Coteaux du Lyonnais Rh r p (w) ★ DYA Junior BEAUJOLAIS. Best EN PRIMEUR.

Coteaux de Peyriac Midi r p ★ DYA One of the most-used VIN DE PAYS names of the Aude département. Huge quantities.

Coteaux de Pierrevert Rh r p w sp ★ DYA Minor southern VDQS nr Manosque. Well-made coop wine, mostly rosé, with fresh whites.

Coteaux de Saumur Lo w dr sw ★★→★★★ DYA Potentially fine semi-sweet Chenin. Creamy-sweet (MOELLEUX) at best.

Coteaux du Tricastin Rh r p w ★ 85 86 88 89 90 91 92 Fringe COTES DU RHONE of increasing quality. Attractive PRIMEUR red. Dom de Grangeneuve best.

Coteaux Varois Prov r p w ★→★★★ Substantial new AC zone: California-style Dom de St-Jean de Villecroze makes vg red.

Coteaux du Vendômois Lo r p w ★ DYA Fringe Loire from N of Blois with VDQS rank. Mainly Gamay and Pineau d'Aunis (for rosé).

Côtes d'Auvergne Central France r p (w) ★ DYA Flourishing small VDQS. Red (at best) like light BEAUJOLAIS. Chanturgues is best known. Corent is rosé.

Côtes de Blaye Bx w ★ DYA Run-of-the-mill BORDEAUX white from BLAYE.

Côtes de Bordeaux Saint-Macaire Bx w dr sw ★ DYA Every-day BORDEAUX white from E of SAUTERNES.

Côtes de Bourg Bx r ★→★★★ 82' 83 85' 86' 88' 89' 90 92 93 Appellation used for many of the better reds of BOURG. Ch'x incl DE BARBE, La Barde, DU BOUSQUET, Brûlesécaille, La Croix de Millorit, Falfas, Font Guilhem, Grand-Jour, de la Grave, La Grolet, Guerry, Haut-Maco, Lalibarde, Lamothe, Mendoce, Peychaud, Rousset, Tayac, de Thau.

Côtes de Castillon Bx r ★→★★★ 82 85 86' 88' 89' 90' 92 93 Flourishing region just E of ST-EMILION. Similar but lighter wines. Ch'x incl Beauséjour, La Clarière-Laithwaite, Fonds-Rondes, Haut-Tuquet, Lartigue, Moulin-Rouge, PITRAY, Rocher-Bellevue, Ste-Colombe, Thibaud-Bellevue.

Côtes de Duras Dordogne r w ★ 89' 90' 92' 93 Neighbour to BERGERAC, dominated by its v competent coop. Similar light wines.

Côtes du Forez Central France r p ★ DYA Fashionable light Beaujolais-style Gamay red, can be good in warm yrs. VDQS status.

Côtes-de-Francs Bx r w ★★ 85 86' 88' 89' 90' 92' 93 Fringe BORDEAUX from E of ST-EMILION. Increasingly attractive tasty wines, esp from Ch'x de Belcier, La Claverie, de Francs, Lauriol, PUYGUERAUD, La Prade.

Côtes du Frontonnais SW France r p →★★ DYA Local wine of Toulouse, gaining admirers everywhere. Ch Bellevue-la-Forêt (250 acres) makes outstanding silky red and rosé l'Allégresse'.

Côtes de Gascogne SW w (r) ★→★★★ DYA VIN DE PAYS esp deliciously floral Sauv whites, Ugni Bl, Colombard and Gros Manseng blends, all in bountiful supply. Top growers: Dom de Biau, Grassa, Coop de Plaimont.

Côtes du Haut-Roussillon SW France br sw ★→★★ NV Area for VINS DOUX NATURELS N of Perpignan.

Côtes du Jura Jura r p w (sp) ★ DYA Various light tints/tastes. ARBOIS is better.

Côtes du Lubéron Rh r p w sp ★→★★★ 88 89 90 Spectacularly improving country wines from N PROVENCE. The stars are CH DE MILLE and CH VAL-JOANIS, with vg largely Syrah red, and whites as well. Others incl a good coop and Ch de la Canorgue.

Côtes de la Malpère Midi r (w) ✳ DYA   Rising star on frontier of MIDI and SW, nr Limoux. Watch for fresh eager reds.

Côtes du Marmandais Dordogne r p w ✳ DYA   Light wines from southeast of BORDEAUX. The coop at Cocumont makes most of the best.

Côtes de Montravel Dordogne w dr sw ✳ DYA   Part of BERGERAC; traditionally medium-sweet wine, now often dry.

Côtes de Provence Prov r p w ✳→✳✳✳   Wines of Provence; revolutionized by new attitudes and investment. Commanderie de Peyrassol, Dom Gavoty, DOM OTT, Dom Richeaume are leaders. 60% is rosé, 30% red. See also Coteaux d'Aix, Bandol, etc.

Côtes du Rhône Rh r p w ✳→✳✳ 89 90 91 92   Basic AC of the Rhône Valley. Best drunk young – even as PRIMEUR. Wide variations of quality due to grape ripeness: tending to rise with alcohol %. See C du R -Villages.

Côtes du Rhône-Villages Rh r p w ✳→✳✳ 88 89 90 91 92   Wine of 17 best S Rhône villages. Substantial and on the whole reliable. S'times delicious. See Beaumes-de-Venise, Cairanne, Chusclan, Laudun, Rasteau, etc.

Côtes Roannaises Central France r ✳ DYA   Minor Gamay region between Lyon and the Loire.

Côtes du Roussillon Pyr r p w ✳→✳✳ 88 89 90 91 92   E Pyrenees AC. Hefty CARIGNAN reds best, can be v tasty. Some whites are sharp VINS VERTS.

Côtes du Roussillon-Villages Pyr r ✳✳ 85 86 88 89 90 91 92   The region's best reds, from 28 communes incl CARAMANY, LATOUR DE FRANCE. Best labels: Cuvée Blanes, Cazes Frères, Ch de Corneilla, Gauby, Ch de Jau, Coop Lesquerde, Coop Les Vignerons Catalans. Some producers now choose to renounce AC status and make single variety VINS DE PAYS.

Côtes de St-Mont SW France r w p ✳   Promising VDQS from the Gers, not unlike MADIRAN. The same coop as COTES DE GASCOGNE.

Côtes de Thongue Midi r w ✳ DYA   Above average VIN DE PAYS from the HERAULT. Some good wines coming.

Côtes de Toul E France p r w ✳ DYA   Very light VDQS wines from Lorraine; mainly VIN GRIS (rosé).

Côtes du Ventoux Prov r (w) ✳✳ 89' 90' 91 92 93   Booming AC for tasty reds between the Rhône and PROVENCE. La Vieille Ferme, owned by J-P Perrin of CH DE BEAUCASTEL, is top producer.

Côtes du Vivarais Prov r p w ✳ DYA   Pleasant country wines from south Massif Central VDQS. Like light COTES DU RHONE: eg Dom de Belvezet.

Coulée de Serrant Lo w dr sw ✳✳✳ 73 76' 78 79' 81 82 83' 85' 86 88 89' 90' 91 92 93   10-acre Chenin Bl v'yd on Loire's N bank at SAVENNIERES. Intense strong fruity/sharp wine, good aperitif. Ages almost for ever.

Coussergues, Domaine de Midi r w p ✳ DYA   Large estate in notorious territory nr Beziers. Experiments with CHARD etc producing bargains.

Crémant In CHAMPAGNE means 'creaming' (half-sparkling). Since '75 an AC for quality classic method sparkling from ALSACE, Loire, BOURGOGNE and most recently LIMOUX – often a bargain. Term phasing out in Champagne.

Crémant de Loire w sp ✳✳→✳✳✳ NV   High quality sparkling wine from ANJOU, TOURAINE and Pays Nantais.

Crépy Savoie w ✳✳ DYA   Light soft Swiss-style white from S shore of Lake Geneva. 'Crépitant' has been coined for its faint fizz.

Criots-Bâtard-Montrachet Burg w ✳✳✳ 78' 79 83 85 86 88 89 90 91 92 93   4-acre neighbour to BATARD-M. Similar wine without extreme pungency.

Crozes-Hermitage Rh r (w) ✳✳ 83 85 86 88 89 90 91 92   Nr HERMITAGE: larger, less distinguished. Often excellent but much lighter reds, but choose carefully: eg Fayolle et Fils, Alain Graillot, Dom de Thalabert of JABOULET, GAEC de la Syrah. Jaboulet's Mule Blanche is good white.

Cru Growth, as in first growth/classed growth – meaning v'yd. Also, in BEAUJOLAIS, one of the top 10 villages.

Cru Bourgeois General term for MEDOC châteaux below CRU CLASSE. There are 250-odd in the Syndicat, covering 7,000 acres, with an annual competition. Others who use the term are prosecuted. In '94 a Paris merchant was jailed for a year.

Cru Bourgeois Supérieur (Cru Grand Bourgeois) One rank better than the last – must be barrel-aged. Being phased out by typically unhelpful Brussels decree from '93.

Cru Classé Classed growth. One of the first five official quality classes of the MEDOC, classified in 1855. Also any growth of another district (eg GRAVES, ST-EMILION, SAUTERNES) named in its local classification.

Cru Exceptionnel Rank above CRU BOURGEOIS SUPERIEUR, immediately below CRU CLASSE. Cru Bourgeois divisions are being phased out as of '93. Now officially suppressed by Brussels – but memories are long.

Cruse et Fils Frères Senior BORDEAUX shipper. Owned by Société des Vins de France. The Cruse family (not the company) owns CH D'ISSAN.

Cussac Village S of ST-JULIEN. (AC HAUT-MEDOC). Top ch'x: BEAUMONT, LANESSAN.

Cuve Short-cut method of making sparkling wine in a tank. Sparkle dies away in glass much quicker than with METHODE CHAMPENOISE wine.

Cuvée Wine contained in a cuve or vat. A word of many uses: 'blend' (as in CHAMPAGNE); in Burgundy interchangeable with 'CRU'. Often just refers to a 'lot' of wine.

De Castellane Brut NV; Brut 85 89; Cuvée Royale 82 88; Prestige Florens de Castellane 82 86; Cuvée Commodore Brut 85 88 Long-established Epernay CHAMPAGNE house, now part-owned by LAURENT-PERRIER. Good rather light wines incl Maxim's house champagne.

De Luze, A & Fils BORDEAUX shipper owned by Rémy-Martin of COGNAC.

Degré alcoolique Degrees of alcohol, ie percent by volume.

Deiss, Marcel Fine ALSACE grower at Bergheim with 50 acres, wide range incl splendid Ries (GRAND CRU Schoenenberg), GEWURZ (Altenburg at Bergheim), good Sélection des Grains Nobles and vin de paille.

Delamotte Brut, Bl de Bls, Cuvée Nicolas Delamotte Small CHARD-dominated CHAMPAGNE house at Le Mesnil, owned by LAURENT-PERRIER. Fine wines.

Delas Frères Old and worthy firm of Rhône wine specialists with v'yds at CONDRIEU, CORNAS, COTE ROTIE, HERMITAGE. Top wines: Condrieu, Marquise de Tourette Hermitage (red and white). Owned by DEUTZ.

Delbeck Small fine CHAMPAGNE house reborn '91. Plenty of Pinot N.

Delorme, André Leading COTE CHALONNAISE merchants and growers. Specialists in CREMANT DE BOURGOGNE and excellent RULLY.

Demi-Sec Half-dry: in practice more than half sweet. (Eg of CHAMPAGNE.)

Deutz Deutz Brut Classic NV; Rosé NV; Brut 79 81 82 85 88; Rosé 82 85 88; Bl de Bls 81 82 85 88 One of better small CHAMPAGNE houses. Full-flavoured wines. Luxury brands: Cuvée William Deutz (79 82 85), Rosé (85). V successful branches in California and NZ. Also Sekt in Germany.

Dirler, Jean-Pierre ALSACE producer of Kessler, Saering and Spiegel GRAND CRUS: each esp for Ries.

Dom Pérignon, Cuvée 71 73 75 76 78 82 83 85 87; Rosé 78 80 82 83 85 Luxury CUVEE of MOET & CHANDON (launched 1936), named after the legendary Abbey cellarmaster who 'invented' CHAMPAGNE. Astonishing consistent quality, esp with 10–12 yrs bottle-age.

Domaine Property, particularly in Burgundy and the south.

Dopff & Irion Another excellent Riquewihr (ALSACE) business. Esp MUSCAT les Amandiers, Ries de Riquewihr, Ries Les Murailles, Gewurz Les Sorcières, Pinot Gr Les Maquisards: long-lived. Good Crémant d'Alsace.

Dopff au Moulin Ancient top-class family wine house at Riquewihr, ALSACE. Best: GEWURZ Eichberg, Ries Schoenenberg, Sylvaner de Riquewihr. Pioneers of sparkling wine in Alsace; good CUVEES: Bartholdi and Julien.

Doudet-Naudin SAVIGNY-LES-BEAUNE burgundy merchant and grower. V'yds incl BEAUNE-CLOS DU ROI, Redrescul. Unfashionably dark long-lived wines, supplied by Berry Bros & Rudd of London, eventually come good.

Dourthe Frères BORDEAUX merchant with wide range of ch'x, mainly good CRUS BOURGEOIS, incl BELGRAVE, MAUCAILLOU, TRONQUOY-LALANDE. Beau-Mayne is their well-made brand.

Doux Sweet.

Drappier, André Leading Aube region CHAMPAGNE house, esp Bl de Noirs.

DRC See Romanée-Conti, Domaine de la.

Drouhin, J & Cie Deservedly prestigious Burgundy grower (130 acres) and merchant with highest standards. Cellars in BEAUNE; v'yds in Beaune, CHABLIS, CLOS DE VOUGEOT, MUSIGNY, etc. and Oregon, USA. Top wines incl BEAUNE-CLOS DES MOUCHES, CHABLIS LES CLOS, CORTON-CHARLEMAGNE, GRIOTTE-CHAMBERTIN, PULIGNY-MONTRACHET Les Folatières.

Duboeuf, Georges The grand fromage of BEAUJOLAIS. Top-class merchant at Romanèche-Thorin. Leader of the region in every sense, with a huge range of admirable wines. Also MOULIN-A-VENT untypically aged in new oak, and white MACONNAIS.

Dubos High-level BORDEAUX négociant.

Duclot BORDEAUX négociant; top-growth specialist. Linked with J-P MOUEIX.

Dujac, Domaine Burgundy grower (Jacques Seysses) at MOREY-ST-DENIS with v'yds in that village, BONNES-MARES, ECHEZEAUX, GEVREY-CHAMBERTIN, etc. Splendidly vivid and long-lived wines. Now also in MEURSAULT, and planting Cab in COTEAUX VAROIS.

Dulong Highly competent BORDEAUX merchant. Breaks all the rules with unorthodox Rebelle blends.

Durup, Jean One of the biggest CHABLIS growers with 140 acres, including DOMAINE DE L'EGLANTIERE and admirable Ch de Maligny.

Duval-Leroy Coteaux Champenois r p w; Tradition NV; Bl de Blancs Brut NV; Fleur de Champagne Brut NV and Rosé NV; Cuvée des Rois Rosé NV; Fleur de Champagne Brut 88; Cuvée des Rois Brut **86** Large progressive Vertus producer with high standards.

Echézeaux Burg r ∗∗∗ 78' **82 83** 85' **87** 88 89' **90' 91 92 93** 74-acre GRAND CRU between VOSNE-ROMANEE and CLOS DE VOUGEOT. Can be superlative, fragrant, without great weight, eg Confuron-Cotetidot, ENGEL, Gouroux, A F Gros, Jacqueline Jayer-Gilles, MONGEARD-MUGNERET, Mugneret, DOM DE LA ROMANEE-CONTI.

The Confrérie des Chevaliers du Tastevin is the wine fraternity of Burgundy: the world's most famous of its kind. It was founded in 1933 by a group of Burgundian patriots, led by Camille Rodier and Georges Faiveley, to rescue their beloved region from a period of slump by promoting its inimitable wines. Today it regularly holds banquets, with elaborate and sprightly ceremonies, for 600 guests, at its headquarters, the Cistercian château in the Clos de Vougeot. The Confrérie has branches in many countries and members among lovers of wine all over the world. See also Tastevin, page 53.

Edelzwicker Alsace w ∗ DYA Modest blended light white: often fruity, good.

Eguisheim, Cave Vinicole d' Vg ALSACE coop: fine GRAND CRUS Hatchbourg, Hengst, Ollwiller and Spiegel. Owns WILLM. Top label: Wolfberger (65% of production). Grande Réserve and Sigillé ranges best. Good CREMANT.

En Primeur See Primeur.

Engel, R Top-class grower of CLOS DE VOUGEOT, ECHEZEAUX, VOSNE-ROMANEE.

Entre-Deux-Mers Bx w ∗→∗∗∗ DYA Improving standard dry white from BORDEAUX from between the Garonne and Dordogne rivers. Often a good buy, as techniques improve. Esp ch'x BONNET, Gournin, Latour-Laguens, Moulin de Launay, Séguin, Thieuley, Turcaud etc.

L'Estandon The everyday wine of Nice (AC COTES DE PROVENCE).

l'Etoile Jura w dr sp (sw) ∗∗ Subregion of the Jura known for stylish whites, incl VIN JAUNE, similar to CHATEAU-CHALON; good sparkling.

Faiveley, J Family-owned growers (with 182 acres) and merchants at NUITS-ST-GEORGES, with v'yds in CHAMBERTIN-CLOS DE BEZE, CHAMBOLLE-MUSIGNY, CORTON, MERCUREY, NUITS (150 acres). Consistent high quality recently. Wines for serious ageing.

Faller, Théo Top ALSACE grower at Domaine Weinbach, Kaysersberg. Concentrated firm dry wines needing unusually long ageing, up to 10 yrs. Esp GRAND CRUS Geisburg (Ries), Kirchberg de Ribeauvillé (Gewurz).

Faugères Midi r (p w) ★→★★★ 88 89 90 **91** 92 Isolated COTEAUX DU LANGUEDOC village with above-average wine. Gained AC status in '82. Best growers: Dom Alquier, Dom des Estanilles, Ch La Liquière.

Fessy, Sylvain Dynamic BEAUJOLAIS merchant with wide range.

Fèvre, William Excellent CHABLIS grower with the biggest GRAND CRU holding (40 acres). But spoils some of his top wines with new oak. One whimsy wine he calls Napa Vallée de France. His label is Dom de la Maladière.

Fiefs Vendéens Lo r p w ★ DYA Up-and-coming VDQS for light wines from the Vendée, just S of MUSCADET on the Atlantic coast.

Fitou Midi r ★★ 85 **86** 88 89 90 **91** 92 Superior CORBIERES red; powerful, ages well. Best from coops at Cascastel, Paziols and Tuchan. Interesting experiments with Mourvèdre in Leucate.

Fixin Burg r ★★ 78' 83 85' 88' 89' 90 91 92 93 Worthy and under-valued northern neighbour of GEVREY-CHAMBERTIN. Often splendid reds. Best v'yds: Clos du Chapitre, Les Hervelets, Clos Napoléon. Growers incl Bertheau, CLAIR, FAIVELEY, Gelin, Gelin-Moulin, Guyard.

Fleurie Beauj r ★★★ 90 91 92 93 The epitome of a BEAUJOLAIS CRU: fruity, scented, silky, racy. Top wines from Chapelle des Bois, Chignard, DUBOEUF, Ch de Fleurie, the coop.

Fortant de France Midi r p w ★→★★ Brand (dressed to kill) of fair quality single-grape wines from the neighbourhood of Sète. See Skalli.

Frais Fresh or cool.

Frappé Ice-cold.

Froid Cold.

Fronsac Bx r ★→★★★ 82 83 85' 86' 88' 89' 90' **92** 93 Picturesque area of increasingly fine tannic reds just W of ST-EMILION. Ch'x incl de Carles, DALEM, LA DAUPHINE, Fontenil, Mayne-Vieil, Moulin-Haut-Laroque, LA RIVIERE, La Rousselle, La Valade, La Vieille Cure, Villars. Give them time. See also smaller Canon-Fronsac.

Frontignan Midi br sw ★ NV Strong sweet liquorous MUSCAT of ancient repute.

Gagnard-Delagrange, Jacques Estimable small (13-acre) grower of CHASSAGNE-MONTRACHET, including some Montrachet.

Gaillac SW France r p w dr sw sp ★→★★ mostly DYA Ancient area coming to life. Ch Larroze is the quality leader, others incl Jean Cros, Dom d'Escausses, Dom des Hourtets, Dom de Labarthe and Robert Plageoles. Important coops: Labastide de Lévis (with fruity wines from local Mauzac grapes), La Cave Tecou (esp wood-aged 'Passion'). Slightly fizzy Perlé is value. Reds can age well.

Gamay See Grapes for red wine (pages 8–9).

Gard, Vin de Pays du The Gard département at the mouth of the Rhône is a centre of good VINS DE PAYS; incl Coteaux Flaviens, Pont du Gard, SABLES DU GOLFE DU LION, Salaves, Uzège and Vaunage. Watch this area.

Geisweiler et Fils Big Burgundy merchant and grower. Now owned by the Rehs of the Mosel. Cellars and 50 acres at NUITS-ST-GEORGES, also 150 acres at Bevy in HAUTES-COTES DE NUITS and 30 in the COTE CHALONNAISE.

Gevrey-Chambertin Burg r ★★★ 83 85' 87 88 89' 90' 91 92 93 The village containing the great CHAMBERTIN and its Grand Cru cousins and many other noble v'yds (eg PREMIERS CRUS Cazetiers, Combe aux Moines, CLOS ST-JACQUES, Clos des Varoilles), as well as much more commonplace land. Growers incl BACHELET, Boillot, Damoy, DROUHIN, FAIVELEY, JADOT, Leclerc, LEROY, MORTET, ROUSSEAU, ROTY, Roumier, TRAPET, DOM DES VAROILLES.

Gewürztraminer Speciality grape of ALSACE: one of 4 allowed for specified GRAND CRU wines. Perfumed like old roses, often tasting like grapefruit.

Gigondas Rh r p ★★ 78 79 83 85 86 **88** 89' **90** 91 92 Worthy neighbour to CHATEAUNEUF-DU-PAPE. Strong, full-bodied, sometimes peppery wine, eg Dom du Cayron, Dom les Pallières, Dom du Pesquier, Dom Raspail-Ay, Dom St-Gayan, Ch du Trignon.

Ginestet Long-established B'x négociant now owned by Jacques Merlaut, said to be second in turnover. Merlaut's empire incl Ch'x CHASSE-SPLEEN, HAUT-BAGES-LIBERAL, LA GURGUE, FERRIERE.

Gisselbrecht, Louis High quality ALSACE shippers at Dambach-la-Ville. Ries and Gewurz best. Cousin Willy Gisselbrecht's wines are v competitive.

Givry Burg r w ✷✷ 85' 88' 89' 90' 91 92 93   Underrated COTE CHALONNAISE village: light but tasty and typical burgundy from eg Dom Joblot, L Latour, T Lespinasse, Clos Salomon, BARON THENARD.

Gosset Brut NV; Rosé NV; Brut 81 82 83 85 86 88; Grande Réserve; Grand Millésime Brut 79 82 83 85 88; Grand Rosé 85 88   Small, v old CHAMPAGNE house at AY. Excellent full-bodied wine (esp Grand Millésime). Now linked with PHILIPPONNAT.

Goulaine, Château de The ceremonial showplace of MUSCADET; a noble family estate and its appropriate wine.

Goulet, George NV; Rosé 85; Crémant Bl de Blancs 83 85   High quality Reims CHAMPAGNE house linked with ABEL LEPITRE. Luxury brand: Cuvée du Centenaire (79 82 83 85).

Goût Taste, eg goût anglais – as the English like it (ie dry).

Grand Cru One of top Burgundy v'yds with its own appellation contrôlée. Similar meaning in recent ALSACE law, but more vague elsewhere. In ST-EMILION the third rank of ch'x, incl about 200 properties.

Grand Roussillon Midi br sw ✷✷ NV   Broad AC for MUSCAT and other sweet fortified wines (VINS DOUX NATURELS) of E Pyrenees.

Grande Champagne The AC of the best area of COGNAC.

Grande Rue, La Burg r ✷✷✷ 89' 90' 91 92 93   Recently-promoted GRAND CRU in VOSNE-ROMANEE, neighbour to ROMANEE-CONTI. Owners, the Lamarche family, are trying harder.

Grands-Echézeaux Burg r ✷✷✷✷ 69' 76 78' 82 83 85' 86 87 88' 89' 90' 91' 92 93   Superlative 22-acre GRAND CRU next to CLOS DE VOUGEOT. Wines not weighty but aromatic. Viz: DROUHIN, ENGEL, MONGEARD-MUGNERET, DOM DE LA ROMANEE-CONTI.

Gratien, Alfred and Gratien & Meyer Brut NV; Cuvée Paradis Brut; Cuvée Paradis Rosé; Brut 79 82 83 85   Excellent smaller family CHAMPAGNE house with top traditional standards. (Fine v dry long-lasting wine). Also its counterpart at SAUMUR. (Vg Cuvée Flamme.)

Graves Bx r w ✷✷→✷✷✷✷   Large region S of Bordeaux city with excellent soft earthy reds, and dry whites (Sauv Bl-Sém) reasserting star status.

Graves de Vayres Bx r w ✷ DYA   Part of ENTRE-DEUX-MERS; no special character.

Griotte-Chambertin Burg r ✷✷✷✷ 78' 83 85' 87 88' 89' 90' 91 92 93   14-acre GRAND CRU adjoining CHAMBERTIN. Similar wine, but less masculine, more 'tender'. Growers incl DROUHIN, PONSOT.

Grivot, Jean 25-acre COTE DE NUITS domaine, in 5 ACs incl RICHEBOURG, NUITS PREMIERS CRUS, VOSNE-ROMANEE, CLOS DE VOUGEOT, etc. Top quality.

Gros Plant du Pays Nantais Lo w ✷ DYA   Junior VDQS cousin of MUSCADET, sharper, lighter; from the COGNAC grape, aka Folle Blanche, Ugni Bl, etc.

Guigal, E and M Celebrated growers and merchants of CONDRIEU, COTE ROTIE and HERMITAGE. Since '85 owners of VIDAL-FLEURY. By ageing single-v'yd Côte Rôtie (La Landonne, La Mouline, La Turque) in new oak Guigal breaks local tradition. His standard wines are good value.

Guyon, Antonin Considerable domaine at ALOXE-CORTON with adequate wines from CHAMBOLLE-MUSIGNY, CORTON, etc, and HAUTES-COTES DE NUITS.

Haut-Benauge Bx w ✷ DYA   AC for a limited area in ENTRE-DEUX-MERS.

Haut-Médoc Bx r ✷✷→✷✷✷ 70 75 78 81' 82' 83' 85' 86' 87 88' 89' 90' 91 92 93   Big AC including all the best parts of the MEDOC. Most of the zone has communal ACs (eg MARGAUX, PAUILLAC). Some excellent châteaux (eg LA LAGUNE) are simply AC HAUT-MEDOC.

Haut-Montravel Dordogne w dr sw ✷ 90' 93   Medium-sweet BERGERAC.

Haut Poitou Lo w (r) ✷→✷✷ DYA   Up-and-coming young VDQS S of ANJOU. Vg whites (CHARD, Sauv) from coop. Has rejected restrictions of AC status. Current financial problems.

Hautes-Côtes de Beaune Burg r w ✷✷ 85 88 89' 90' 91 92 93   Appellation for a dozen villages in the hills behind the COTE DE BEAUNE. Light wines, worth investigating. Top growers: Cornu, Mazilly.

Hautes-Côtes de Nuits Burg r w ✹✹ 85 88 89' 90' 91 92 93 As above, for COTE DE NUITS. An area on the way up. Top growers: C Cornu, Jayer-Gilles, M Gros. Also has large BEAUNE coop; good esp from GEISWEILER.

Heidsieck, Charles Brut Réserve NV; Brut 79 81 83 85; Rosé 81 83 85 Major Reims CHAMPAGNE house, now controlled by Rémy Martin; also incl Trouillard, de Venoge. Luxury brands: Cuvée Champagne Charlie (81 82 83), Bl des Millénaires (83). Fine quality recently; NV a bargain.

Heidsieck, Monopole Brut NV; Rosé NV; Brut 79 82 83 85 87 88; Rosé 79 82 83 85 88 Important CHAMPAGNE merchant and Reims grower now owned by Seagram and made by MUMM. Luxury brands with note: Diamant Bleu (76 79 82 85), Diamant Rosé (82 85 88).

Henriot Brut Souverain NV; Bl de Bls de Chard NV; Brut 79 82 85 88; Brut Rosé 81 83 85 88; Cuvée Baccarat 79 82 83 85 Old family CHAMPAGNE house linked with VEUVE CLICQUOT in the Möet Hennessy group. Fresh fine style: luxury CUVÉES (eg Baron Philippe de Rothschild) withdrawn.

Hérault Midi Biggest v'yd département in France with 980,000 acres of vines. Chiefly VIN DE TABLE but some good AC COTEAUX DU LANGUEDOC, and, more interestingly, pioneering Vins de Pays de l'Hérault.

Hermitage Rh r w ✹✹✹→✹✹✹✹✹ 61 66 70 72 78' 79 80 82 83' 84 85 86 87 88 89 90 91 92 'Manliest' wine of France: dark powerful and profound. Needs long ageing. White is heady and golden; now usually made for early drinking, though best wines mature for up to 25 yrs. Top makers: CHAPOUTIER, CHAVE, DELAS, Faurie, Grippat, GUIGAL, JABOULET, Sorrel.

Hospices de Beaune Historic hospital in BEAUNE, with excellent v'yds (known by 'CUVÉE' names) in BEAUNE, CORTON, MEURSAULT, POMMARD, VOLNAY. Wines are auctioned on the third Sunday of each November.

Hugel et Fils The best-known ALSACE growers and merchants; founded at Riquewihr in 1639 and still in the family. 'Johnny' H is the region's beloved spokesman. Quality escalates with Cuvée Tradition and then Jubilée Réserve ranges. SELECTIONS DES GRAINS NOBLES vg: Hugel pioneered this style in Alsace. Many are sweet, but not all.

Ile de Beauté Name given to VINS DU PAYS from CORSICA. Mostly red.

Impériale BORDEAUX bottle holding 8.5 normal bottles (6.4 litres).

Irancy ('Bourgogne Irancy') Burg r (p) ✹✹ 85 88 89 90 91 92 93 Good light red made nr CHABLIS from Pinot N and the local César. The best vintages are long-lived and mature well. To watch.

Irouléguy SW France r p (w) ✹✹ DYA Agreeable local wines, mainly Tannat reds, of the Basque country.

Jaboulet, Paul Old family firm at Tain, leading growers of HERMITAGE (esp La Chapelle ✹✹✹✹) and merchants of other Rhône wines.

Jaboulet-Vercherre & Cie Burgundy merchant house with v'yds (34 acres) in POMMARD, etc, and cellars in BEAUNE. Should try harder.

Jacquart Brut NV (Tradition and Selection); Brut Rosé NV; Brut 85 87 Relatively new ('62) coop-based CHAMPAGNE marque; in quantity the sixth largest. Fair quality. Luxury brands: Cuvée Nominée Blanc 85, CN Rosé 85. Vg Mosaïque Bl de Blancs 86, Mosaïque Rosé 86.

Jacquesson Small quality Epernay CHAMPAGNE house. Several gd luxury CUVÉES.

Jadot, Louis Much-respected top quality Burgundy merchant house with v'yds (150 acres) in BEAUNE, CORTON etc. Incl former estate of CLAIR-DAU. Wines to bank on.

Jaffelin Independently run quality négociant, bought in '92 from DROUHIN by BOISSET.

Jardin de la France Lo r w p One of the four regional VINS DE PAYS. Covers Loire Valley: Gamay and Sauv Bl wines (slightly more red than white), mostly single grape. Top vin de pays de zone: Marches de Bretagne.

Jasnières Lo w (r p) ✹✹✹ 76 78 79 83 85 86 88' 89' 90' 91 92 93 V rare dry rather VOUVRAY-like wine of N TOURAINE.

Jaubertie, Domaine de la English-owned top BERGERAC estate (114 acres). Sumptuous luxury Sauv Bl, Cuvée Mirabelle. Equally fine Réserve red.

Jayer, Henri See Rouget, Emmanuel.

Jeroboam In BORDEAUX a 6-bottle bottle (holding 4.5 litres) or triple magnum; in CHAMPAGNE a double magnum.

JosMeyer Family house at Wintzenheim, ALSACE. Vg long-ageing wines, esp GEWURZ and Pinot Bl. Fine Ries from Hengst GRAND CRU. Wide range of grape varieties, labels and locations.

Juliénas Beauj r ✱✱✱ **90** 91 92 93 Leading CRU of BEAUJOLAIS: vigorous fruity wine to keep 2–3 yrs. Growers incl Ch du Bois de la Salle, Dom Bottière, Ch des Capitans, Ch de Juliénas, Dom R Monnet, Ch des Vignes and coop.

Jura See Côtes de Jura.

Jurançon SW France w sw dr ✱✱–✱✱✱✱ 82 83 85 86 88 89 90 91 92 93 Rare high-flavoured long-lived speciality of Pau in Pyrenean foothills, at best like wild-flower SAUTERNES. Not to be missed. Both sweet and dry should age. Top growers: Barrère, Chigné, Gaillot, Guirouilh, Lamouroux, Larredya, Ramonteu (Dom Cauhapé). Also coop's Grain Sauvage.

Kaefferkopf Alsace w dr sw ✱✱✱ Ammerschwihr v'yd famous for blends rather than single-grape wines; growers not happy with restrictions of GRAND CRU status.

Kientzheim-Kayserberg Important ALSACE coop for quality as well as style. Esp for GEWURZ, Ries (Schlossburg GRAND CRU) and Crémant d'Alsace.

Kientzler, André Fine ALSACE Ries specialist in Geisburg GRAND CRU, esp VENDANGE TARDIVE and SELECTION DES GRAINS NOBLES. Equally good from GCs Kirchberg de Ribeauvillé for Gewurz and Osterberg for occasional 'vins de glaces' (Eisweins).

Kreydenweiss Fine ALSACE grower with 24 acres at Andlau, esp for Pinot Gr (vg from Moenchberg GRAND CRU), Pinot Bl and Ries. Top wine: Kastelberg (Ries ages 20 yrs plus); also fine Auxerrois 'Kritt Klevner' and good VENDANGE TARDIVE. One of first in Alsace to use new oak. Good Ries-Pinot Gr blend 'Clos du Val d'Eléon'.

Kriter Popular sparkler processed in Burgundy by PATRIARCHE.

Krug Grande Cuvée; **64 66 69 71 73 75 76 79 81 82 85**; Rosé; Clos du Mesnil (Bl de Blancs) 79 80 81 82 83; Krug Collection 62 64 66 69 71 73 76 Small but supremely prestigious CHAMPAGNE house. Dense full-bodied v dry wines of superlative quality. Owned by Rémy Martin (but no-one would know).

Kuentz-Bas Top-quality ALSACE grower and merchant at Husseren-les-Châteaux, esp for Pinot Gr (Tokay d'Alsace) and GEWURZ. Also good VENDANGES TARDIVES.

Labouré-Roi Outstandingly reliable merchant at NUITS. Mostly whites. Many fine domaine wines, esp René Manuel's MEURSAULT, Chantal Lescure's Nuits, CLOS DE VOUGEOT. Vg CHABLIS. Also VOLNAY-SANTENOTS.

Ladoix-Serrigny Burg r (w) ✱✱ Northernmost village of COTE DE BEAUNE below hills of CORTON. To watch for bargains.

Ladoucette, de Leading producer of POUILLY-FUME, based at CH DE NOZET. Luxury brand: Baron de L. Also SANCERRE Comte Lafond (and PIC CHABLIS).

Lafarge, Michel 23-acre COTE DE BEAUNE estate, with outstanding VOLNAYS.

Lafon, Domaine des Comtes 32-acre quality Burgundy estate in MEURSAULT, LE MONTRACHET and VOLNAY. Glorious intense wines; extraordinary dark reds.

Laguiche, Marquis de Largest owner of LE MONTRACHET. Magnificent wines made by DROUHIN.

Lalande de Pomerol Bx r ✱✱ 82 83 85 86' 88' 89' 90' 92 93 Neighbour to POMEROL. Wines similar but less mellow. Top ch'x: Les Annereaux, DE BELAIR, Belles-Graves, Bertineau-St-Vincent, La Croix Bellevue, La Croix-St-André, Les Hauts-Conseillants, Les Hauts-Tuileries, Moncets, SIAURAC, TOURNEFEUILLE.

Langlois-Château Producer of sparkling SAUMUR, controlled by BOLLINGER.

To decipher codes, please refer to symbols key at front of book, and to 'How to use this book' on page 5.

Lanson Père & Fils Black Label NV; Rosé NV; Brut 88   Important CHAMPAGNE house with cellars at Reims. Luxury brand: Noble Cuvée (81 85). Black Label is a reliable fresh (sometimes thin) NV. New CUVEE: Bl de Blancs 83.

Laroche Important grower (238 acres) and dynamic CHABLIS merchant, incl Domaines La Jouchère and Laroche. Top wines: Blanchots and Clos. Also blends good non-regional CHARD.

Latour, Louis Famous Burgundy merchant and grower with v'yds (120 acres) in BEAUNE, CORTON, etc. Among the v best for white: CHEVALIER-MONTRACHET, CORTON-CHARLEMAGNE, Les Demoiselles, MONTRACHET, gd value MONTAGNY and ARDECHE CHARD, etc. Developing Pinot N in the Var.

Latour de France r (w) *→*** 88 89 90 **91** 92   New AC in COTES DE ROUSSILLON-VILLAGES.

Latricières-Chambertin Burg r *** 78' **83** 85' 88' 89' 90' 91 92 93   17-acre GRAND CRU neighbour of CHAMBERTIN. Similar wine but lighter and 'prettier' eg from FAIVELEY, LEROY, PONSOT, TRAPET.

Laudun Rh r p w *   Village of COTES DU RHONE-VILLAGES. Attractive wines from the coop incl fresh whites. But Dom Palaquié is better.

Laugel, Michel One of the biggest ALSACE merchant houses at Marlenheim: esp good Cuvée Jubilaire range and CREMANT.

Laurent-Perrier Brut NV; Rosé NV; Brut 78 79 81 82 85 88   Excellent dynamic highly successful family-owned CHAMPAGNE house at Tours-sur-Marne. Luxury brands: Cuvée Grande Siècle (NV and 81-82-85 blend), CGS Exceptionnellement Millésimée 85, CGS Alexandra Brut Rosé (82 85). Ultra Brut is bone dry. Owns SALON, DELAMOTTE, DE CASTELLANE.

Leflaive, Domaine Sometimes considered the best of all white burgundy growers, at PULIGNY-MONTRACHET. Best v'yds: Bienvenue- and Chevalier-Montrachet, Clavoillons, Pucelles. Now some wines lack staying power.

Leflaive, Olivier Négociant at PULIGNY-MONTRACHET since '84, now with 22 acres of his own, nephew of the above. Reliable whites and reds, incl less famous ACs, have upgraded seriously since '90.

Léognan Bx r w ***→*****   Top village of GRAVES with its own AC: PESSAC-LEOGNAN. Best ch'x: DOM DE CHEVALIER, HAUT-BAILLY, MALARTIC-LAGRAVIERE.

Leroy Important NEGOCIANT-ELEVEUR at AUXEY-DURESSES with a growing domaine and the finest stocks of old wines in Burgundy. Part-owners of DOM DE LA ROMANEE-CONTI. In '88 bought the 35-acre Noëllat estate in CLOS VOUGEOT, NUITS, ROMANEE-ST-VIVANT, SAVIGNY, etc. Leroy's range, from AUXEY whites to CHAMBERTIN and neighbours, is simply magnificent.

Lichine, Alexis & Cie BORDEAUX merchants (once of the late Alexis Lichine), proprietors of CH LASCOMBES. No connection with CH PRIEURE LICHINE.

Lie, sur On the lees. MUSCADET is often bottled straight from the vat, without racking or filtering, for maximum freshness and character.

Limoux Pyr r w ** NV   Austerely dry non-sparkling version of BLANQUETTE DE LIMOUX (sometimes labelled Limoux Nature) and a good claret-like red from the coop: Anne des Joyeuses. Vinavius (89 90) is oak-aged and even better. Recently also 'Grand Chardonnay'.

Lirac Rh r p (w) ** 85 86 **88** 89 90 91 92   Next to TAVEL. Similar wine (red overtaking rosé), esp Doms Maby, de la Mordorée, St-Roch, Ch de Segriés.

Listel Midi r p w *→*** DYA   Vast (4,000-acre+) historic estate on sandy beaches of the Golfe du Lion. Owned by giant Salins du Midi salt co. Pleasant light 'vins des sables' incl sparkling. Dom du Bosquet-Canet is a fruity Cab, and Dom de Villeroy makes a fresh BLANC DE BLANCS SUR LIE and CHARD since '89. Also fruity almost non-alcoholic PETILLANT, Ch de Malijay, COTES DU RHONE, and Abbaye de Ste-Hilaire COTEAUX VAROIS.

Listrac-Médoc Bx r **→***   Village of HAUT-MEDOC next to MOULIS. Best ch'x: CLARKE, FONREAUD, FOURCAS-DUPRE, FOURCAS-HOSTEN.

Long-Depaquit Vg CHABLIS domaine (esp MOUTONNE), owned by BICHOT.

Lorentz Two small quality ALSACE houses at Bergheim: Gustave L and Jerome L, have same management. Esp GEWURZ and Ries from Altenberg de Bergheim and Kanzlerberg.

Loron & Fils Big-scale Burgundy grower and merchant at Pontanevaux; specialist in BEAUJOLAIS and sound VINS DE TABLE.

Loupiac Bx w sw ★★ 76 79' 80 83 85 86' 88' 89 90 91 93 Across the River Garonne from SAUTERNES. Top châteaux: Clos-Jean, Haut-Loupiac, LOUPIAC-GAUDIET, RICAUD, Rondillon.

Lugny ('Mâcon-Lugny') Burg r w sp ★★ 89 90 91 92 93 Village next to VIRE with good active coop. Les Genevrières is sold by LOUIS LATOUR.

Lupé-Cholet & Cie Once famous merchants/growers at NUITS-ST-GEORGES, now controlled by BICHOT. Estate wines: Clos de Lupé and Ch Gris.

Lussac-St-Emilion Bx r ★★ 82 85 86' 88' 89' 90' 92 93 NE neighbour to ST-EMILION. Top ch'x incl Barbe Blanche, Bel Air, DU LYONNAT, Tour de Grenat, Villadière. Coop (at PUISSEGUIN) makes pleasant Roc de Lussac.

Macération carbonique Traditional technique of fermentation with whole bunches of unbroken grapes in a closed vat. Fermentation inside each grape eventually bursts it, giving vivid fruity mild wine, not for ageing. Esp in BEAUJOLAIS; now much used in the MIDI and elsewhere.

Machard de Gramont BURGUNDY family estate: cellars in NUITS and v'yds in BEAUNE, Nuits, POMMARD, SAVIGNY. Extremely well-made reds.

Mâcon Burg r w (p) ★★ 89' 90' 91 92 93 Sound, usually unremarkable reds, tasty dry (CHARD) whites. Wine with village name (eg Mâcon-Prissé) is better; POUILLY-FUISSE best AC, ST-VERAN also vg. See also Mâcon-Villages.

Mâcon-Lugny See Lugny.

Mâcon Supérieur The same but in theory slightly better, from riper grapes.

Mâcon-Villages Burg w ★★→★★★ 89 90 91 92 93 Increasingly well-made typical white burgundies (when not over-produced). Eg Mâcon-Clessé, MACON-LUGNY, Mâcon-Prissé, MACON-VIRE, La Roche-Vineuse. Best coop is probably Chaintré. Best grower: Thevenet of Clessé. Should terrify most New World CHARD growers.

Mâcon-Viré See Mâcon-Villages and Viré.

Macvin Jura w sw ★★ AC for 'traditional' MARC and grape juice aperitif.

Madiran SW France r ★★★ 82 85' 86' 88 89' 90' 92 93 Dark vigorous red from ARMAGNAC, like hard but fruity MEDOC with a fluid elegance of its own. Ages 5–10 yrs, but 'barriques' are changing it, not necessarily for the better. Top growers: Ch'x d'Arricau-Bordes, d'Aydie, Barréjat, Dom de Bouscassé, Dom Capmartin, Laplace, Montus, Peyros.

Magenta, Duc de Recently revamped Burgundy estate (30 acres) based at CHASSAGNE-MONTRACHET, managed by JADOT.

Magnum A double bottle (1.5 litres).

Mähler-Besse First-class Dutch wine merchants in BORDEAUX, with a share in CH PALMER. Brands incl Cheval Noir.

Mailly-Champagne Top CHAMPAGNE coop. Luxury wine: Cuvée des Echansons.

Maire, Henri The biggest grower/merchant of JURA wines. Not the best.

Maranges Burg r ★★ New ('89) AC for 600-odd acres of S COTE DE BEAUNE, beyond SANTENAY, one-third PREMIER CRU. Top/first négociant: JAFFELIN.

Marc Grape skins after pressing; also the strong-smelling brandy made from them (see Italian 'Grappa').

Marcillac SW France r p ★ DYA Promoted to AC (too hastily?) in '90. Good wines from coop Cave de Valady (rustic reds) and Dom du Cros.

Margaux Bx r ★★→★★★★ 66 70 75 78 79 81 82' 83' 85 86' 87 88' 89 90' 91 92 93 Village of the HAUT-MEDOC making some of the most 'elegant' red BORDEAUX. AC incl CANTENAC and several other villages. Top ch'x incl MARGAUX, LASCOMBES, RAUSAN-SEGLA, etc.

Margnat Major producer of everyday VIN DE TABLE.

Marne et Champagne, Ste Recent but huge-scale CHAMPAGNE house, owner (since '91) of LANSON and many smaller brands, incl BESSERAT DE BELLEFON.

Marque déposée Trademark.

France entries also cross-refer to Châteaux of Bordeaux section, pages 56–77.

Marquis de Chasse Branded Bordeaux (red and white) from the négociant GINESTET, named for the related CH CHASSE-SPLEEN (not its second wine).

Marsannay Burg p w (r) ✹✹✹ 85 88' 89' 90' 91 92 93 (rosé DYA) Village with fine light red and delicate Pinot N rosé. Incl villages of Chenôve, Conchey, Growers incl Charlopin, CLAIR, Dijon University, JADOT, Quillardet, TRAPET.

Mas de Daumas Gassac Midi r w p ✹✹✹ 80 81 82 83 85 86 87 88 89 90 91 92 The one 'first-growth' estate of the LANGUEDOC, producing potent largely Cab wines on apparently unique soil. Also Rosé Frisant and a sumptuous white of blended CHARD, Viognier, Petit Manseng, etc. Now also a vg quick-drinking red, Les Terrasses de Guilhem, from a nearby coop. Sensational quality. VIN DE PAYS status.

Maufoux, Prosper Family firm of burgundy merchants at SANTENAY. Reliable wines, esp whites, that keep well. Alias Marcel Amance.

Maury Pyr r sw ✶→✹✹ NV Red VIN DOUX NATUREL from ROUSSILLON.

Mazis (or Mazy) Chambertin Burg r ✹✹✹ 78' 83 85' 87 88' 89' 90' 91 92 93 30-acre GRAND CRU neighbour of CHAMBERTIN, sometimes equally potent. Best from FAIVELEY, HOSPICES DE BEAUNE, LEROY, ROTY.

Mazoyères-Chambertin See Charmes-Chambertin.

Médoc Bx r ✹✹ 78 82' 83 85 86' 87 88' 89' 90' 92 93 AC for reds of the less good (northern) part of BORDEAUX's biggest and best district. Flavours tend to slight earthiness. HAUT-MEDOC is better. Top châteaux incl LA CARDONNE, GREYSAC, LOUDENNE, LES ORMES-SORBET, POTENSAC, LA TOUR-DE-BY.

Meffre, Gabriel Perhaps the biggest S Rhône estate, based at GIGONDAS. Includes Ch de Vaudieu, CHATEAUNEUF-DU-PAPE. Variable quality.

Ménétou-Salon Lo r p w ✹✹ DYA Attractive light wines from W of SANCERRE: Sauv Bl white, Pinot N red.

Méo-Camuzet V fine domaine in CLOS DE VOUGEOT, NUITS, RICHEBOURG, VOSNE-ROMANEE. HENRI JAYER oversees winemaking. Esp: V-R Cros Parantoux.

Mercier & Cie, Champagne Brut NV; Brut Rosé NV; Brut 81 82 83 85 86 88 One of the biggest CHAMPAGNE houses at Epernay. Controlled by MOET & CHANDON. Good commercial quality, sold mainly in France. Bulle d'Or is premium NV CUVEE, as is Reserve de l'Empereur NV.

Mercurey Burg r w ✹✹→✹✹✹✹ 85 88' 89' 90' 91 92 93 Leading red wine village of COTE CHALONNAISE. Good middle-rank burgundy incl more and improving whites. Growers incl Ch de Chamirey, Chanzy, FAIVELEY, M Juillot, Dom de Suremain.

Mercurey, Région de The up-to-date name for the COTE CHALONNAISE.

Métaireau, Louis The ringleader of a group of top MUSCADET growers. Expensive well-finished wines.

Méthode champenoise The traditional laborious method of putting bubbles into CHAMPAGNE by refermenting the wine in its bottle. Must be referred to as 'classic method' or 'méthode traditionelle' when used outside the region. Not mentioned on champagne labels.

Méthode traditionelle See entry above.

Meursault Burg w (r) ✹✹✹→✹✹✹✹✹ 78' 83 85 86 88 89' 90' 91 92 93 COTE DE BEAUNE village with some of the world's greatest whites: savoury, dry but nutty and mellow. Best v'yds: Charmes, Genevrières, Perrières; also: Goutte d'Or, Meursault-Blagny, Poruzots, Narvaux, Tillets. Growers incl AMPEAU, CH DE MEURSAULT, COCHE-DURY, Delagrange, P Javillier, Jobard, LAFON, LATOUR, LEROY, MAGENTA, Manuel, Matrot, Michelot-Buisson, P MOREY, G ROULOT. See also Blagny.

Meursault-Blagny See Blagny.

Michel, Louis CHABLIS domaine with model, unoaked, v long-lived wines, incl superb LES CLOS.

Midi General term for the south of France west of the Rhône delta. Improving reputation, brilliant promise.

Minervois Midi r (p w) br sw ✹→✹✹✹ 85 86 88 89 90 91 92 Hilly AC region for good MIDI wines: lively, full of flavour, esp from Dom de Ste-Eulalie, Ch de Gourgazaud and La Livinère. See also St-Jean de Minervois.

Mis en bouteille au château/domaine Bottled at the château, property or estate. NB dans nos caves (in our cellars) or dans la région de production (in the area of production) are often used but mean little.

Moelleux Creamy sweet. Used of the sweet wines of VOUVRAY, etc.

Moët & Chandon Brut NV; Rosé 81 82 85 86 88; Brut Imperial 76 78 81 82 83 85 86 88 Much the biggest CHAMPAGNE merchant and grower, with cellars in Epernay, and branches in Argentina, Australia, Brazil, California, Germany and Spain. Consistent quality, esp in Vintage wines. Coteaux Champenois 'Saran' can be disappointing. Prestige CUVEE: DOM PERIGNON. Links with CLICQUOT, HENRIOT, MERCIER, POMMERY, RUINART, etc.

Moillard Big family firm (Domaine Thomas-Moillard) of growers and merchants in NUITS-ST-GEORGES, making full range incl dark and v tasty wines, eg CLOS DU ROI, CLOS DE VOUGEOT, CORTON, etc.

Mommessin, J Major BEAUJOLAIS merchant, merged with THORIN. Owner of CLOS DE TART. White wines less successful than red.

Monbazillac Dordogne w sw ** 75 76 79 80 83' 85 86' 88' 89' 90' 91 92 93 Golden SAUTERNES-style wine from BERGERAC. Can age well. Ch Monbazillac and Ch Septy are best known.

Mondeuse Savoie r ** DYA Red grape of SAVOIE. Good vigorous deep-coloured wine. Perhaps NE Italy's Refosco.

Mongeard-Mugneret 50+-acre VOSNE-ROMANEE estate. Fine ECHEZEAUX, RICHEBOURG, SAVIGNY, VOSNE PREMIER CRU, VOUGEOT, etc.

Monopole V'yd under single ownership.

Mont-Redon, Dom de Rh r (w) *** 83 85 86 88 89 90 91 92 Outstanding 235-acre CHATEAUNEUF-DU-PAPE estate. Reliable early-maturing wines.

Montagne-St-Emilion Bx r ** 82' 83 85 86' 88' 89' 90' 92 93 NE neighbour and largest 'satellite' of ST-EMILION: similar wines and AC regulations; becoming more important each year. Top ch'x: St-André-Corbin, Calon, Faizeau, Haut-Gillet, ROUDIER, Teyssier, DES TOURS, VIEUX-CH-ST-ANDRE.

Montagny Burg w (r) ** 89' 90 91 92 93 COTE CHALONNAISE village. Between MACON and MEURSAULT, both geographically and gastronomically. Top producers: Cave Coop de Buxy, LOUIS LATOUR, Michel, Ch de la Saule.

Montée de Tonnerre Burg w *** 86 88 89 90 91 92 93 Famous excellent PREMIER CRU of CHABLIS. Growers incl Duplessis, Raveneau, Robin.

Monthélie Burg r (w) **→*** 78 83 85 87 88' 89' 90' 91 92 93 Little-known neighbour, s'times almost equal of VOLNAY. Excellent fragrant reds. Growers incl BOUCHARD PERE, COCHE-DURY, COMTE LAFON, DROUHIN, Garaudet, Ch de Monthélie (de Suremain), Monthélie-Douhairet.

Montlouis Lo w dr sw (sp) **→*** 75 76 78 82 83' 85' 86 88' 89' 90' 91 92 93' Neighbour of VOUVRAY. Similar sweet or dry long-lived wine. Top growers: Berger, Deletang, Levasseur, Taille aux Loups.

Montrachet Burg w **** 69' 71 78 79 82 83 85' 86' 88 89' 90 91 92 93 (Both 't's in the name are silent.) 19-acre GRAND CRU v'yd in both PULIGNY- and CHASSAGNE-MONTRACHET. Potentially the greatest white burgundy: strong, perfumed, intense, dry yet luscious. Top wines from LAFON, LAGUICHE (DROUHIN), RAMONET, DOM DE LA ROMANEE-CONTI, THENARD.

Montravel See Côtes de Montravel.

Moreau & Fils CHABLIS merchant and grower with 187 acres. Also major table wine producer. Best wine: Clos des Hospices (GRAND CRU).

Morey, Domaines 50 acres in CHASSAGNE-MONTRACHET. Vg wines made by family members, incl BATARD-MONTRACHET.

Morey-St-Denis Burg r *** 78 82 83 85' 86 87 88 89' 90' 91 92 93 Small village with four GRANDS CRUS between GEVREY-CHAMBERTIN and CHAMBOLLE-MUSIGNY. Glorious wine often overlooked. Growers incl Amiot, Bryczek, Castagnier, DUJAC, Groffier, Lignier, Moillard-Grivot, PONSOT, ROUSSEAU, Serveau.

Morgon Beauj r *** 85 88 89 90 91 92 93 The 'firmest' CRU of BEAUJOLAIS, needing time to develop its rich and savoury flavour. Growers incl Aucoeur, Ch de Bellevue, Desvignes, Janodet, Lapierre, Ch de Pizay. Excellent from DUBOEUF.

Moueix, J-P et Cie Legendary leading proprietor and merchant of ST-EMILION, POMEROL and FRONSAC. Châteaux incl LA FLEUR-PETRUS, MAGDELAINE and part of PETRUS. Now also has a venture in California: see Dominus.

Moulin-à-Vent Beauj r *** 85 88 89 90 91 92 93 The 'biggest' and best wine of BEAUJOLAIS; powerful, meaty and long-lived, eventually can even taste like fine Rhône or burgundy. Many good growers, esp Ch du Moulin-à-Vent, Ch La Tour du Bief.

Moulis Bx r **→*** Village of the HAUT-MEDOC with its own AC and several CRUS EXCEPTIONNELS: CHASSE-SPLEEN, MAUCAILLOU, POUJEAUX (THEIL), etc. Good hunting ground.

Mousseux Sparkling.

Mouton Cadet Popular brand of blended red and white BORDEAUX.

Moutonne CHABLIS GRAND CRU honoris causa (between Vaudésir and Preuses), owned by BICHOT.

Mugnier, J-F 10-acre Ch de Chambolle estate with first-class CHAMBOLLE-MUSIGNY Les Amoureuses and MUSIGNY. Also BONNES-MARES.

Mumm, G H & Cie Cordon Rouge NV; Crémant de Cramant NV (called Mumm de Cramant NV since '92); Cordon Rouge 79 82 85 88; Rosé 82 85 88 Major CHAMPAGNE grower and merchant owned by Seagram. Luxury brands: René Lalou (79 82 85), Grand Cordon (85; launched '91). The Cramant can be superb, Cordon Rouge pretty tasteless. Also in Napa, California.

Muré, Clos St-Landelin ALSACE merchant at Rouffach with v'yds in GRAND CRU Vorbourg. Full-bodied wines: ripe (unusual) Pinot N, big Ries and Muscat VENDANGES TARDIVES.

Muscadet Lo w ** DYA Popular, good value, often delicious dry wine from around Nantes. Should never be sharp but should have an iodine tang. Perfect with fish. The best are bottled SUR LIE – on their lees.

Muscadet de Sèvre-et-Maine Wine from the central (best) part of the area.

Muscat Distinctively perfumed grape and its (usually sweet) wine, often fortified as VIN DOUX NATUREL. Made dry in ALSACE.

Muscat de Beaumes-de-Venise See Beaumes-de-Venise.

Muscat de Frontignan Midi br sw ** DYA Sweet MIDI MUSCAT. Quality improving.

Muscat de Lunel Midi br sw ** NV Ditto. A small area but good.

Muscat de Mireval Midi br sw ** NV Ditto, from nr Montpellier.

Muscat de Rivesaltes Midi br sw * NV Sweet MUSCAT from large zone near Perpignan.

Musigny Burg r (w) **** 69 72 76 78 79 82 83 85' 86 87 88' 89' 90' 91 92 93 25-acre GRAND CRU in CHAMBOLLE-MUSIGNY. Can be the most beautiful, if not the most powerful, of all red burgundies (and a little white). Best growers: DROUHIN, JADOT, LEROY, MUGNIER, ROUMIER, DE VOGUE.

Nature Natural or unprocessed – esp of still CHAMPAGNE.

Néac Village N of POMEROL. Wines sold as LALANDE DE POMEROL.

Négociant-éleveur Merchant who 'brings up' (ie matures) the wine.

Nicolas, Ets Paris-based wholesale and retail wine merchants controlled by Castel Frères. One of the biggest in France and one of the best.

Nuits-St-Georges r **→*** 69 71 76 78' 82 83 85' 86 87 88' 89' 90' 91 92 93 Important wine town: wines of all qualities, typically sturdy and full-flavoured. Name often shortened to 'Nuits'. Best v'yds incl Les Cailles, Clos des Corvées, Les Pruliers, Les St-Georges, Vaucrains, etc. Many growers and merchants esp DOM DE L'ARLOT, CHAUVENET, Chevillon, FAIVELEY, Gouges, GRIVOT, LEROY, MACHARD DE GRAMONT, Michelot, RION.

d'Oc Midi r p w Regional VIN DE PAYS for Languedoc and ROUSSILLON. Esp single-grape wines and VINS DE PAYS PRIMEURS.

Oisly & Thesée, Vignerons de Go-ahead coop in E TOURAINE (Loire), with good Sauv Bl, Cab and CHARD. Blended wines labelled Baronnie d'Aignan. Good value.

Orléanais, Vin de l' Lo r p w ✳ DYA Small VDQS for light but fruity wines.

Ostertag Little ALSACE domaine at Epfig. Uses new oak for good Pinot N and makes the best Ries and Pinot Gr of GRAND CRU Muenchberg. Gewurz from lieu-dit Frönholz is worth ageing.

Ott, Domaines Top high-quality producer of PROVENCE, incl CH DE SELLE (rosé, red), Clos Mireille (white), BANDOL and Ch de Romassan.

Pacherenc du Vic-Bilh SW France w sw ★ NV Rare minor speciality of the ARMAGNAC region. Domaine Capmartin's are some of the best.

Paillard, Bruno Brut Première Cuvée NV; Rosé Première Cuvée NV; Chard Réserve Privée NV, Brut 79 81 83 85 Small but prestigious young CHAMPAGNE house: excellent silky vintage and NV; fair prices.

Palette Prov r p w ✳✳ Near Aix-en-Provence. Aromatic reds and good rosés from CH SIMONE.

Parigot-Richard Producer of vg CREMANT DE BOURGOGNE at SAVIGNY.

Pasquier-Desvignes V old firm of BEAUJOLAIS merchants nr BROUILLY.

Patriarche One of the bigger firms of burgundy merchants. Cellars in BEAUNE; also owns CH DE MEURSAULT (100 acres), sparkling KRITER, etc.

Patrimonio Corsica r w p ✳✳→✳✳✳ 90 91 92 93 Wide range from dramatic chalk hills in N CORSICA. Fragrant reds, crisp whites, fine VINS DOUX NATURELS. Top grower: Gentile.

Pauillac Bx r ✳✳→✳✳✳✳ 66' 70' 75 78' 79 81' 82' 83' 85' 86' 87 88' 89' 90' 91 92 93 The only BORDEAUX (HAUT-MEDOC) village with 3 first-growths (CHATEAUX LAFITE, LATOUR, MOUTON) and many other fine ones, famous for high flavour; v varied in style.

Pécharmant Dordogne r ✳✳ 89 90 92 93 Usually better-than-typical light BERGERAC: more 'meat'. Best: Dom du Haut-Pécharmant, Ch de Tiregand.

Pelure d'oignon 'Onion skin' – tawny tint of certain rosés.

Perlant or Perlé Very slightly sparkling.

Pernand-Vergelesses Burg r (w) ✳✳✳ 78' 83 85 87 88' 89' 90 91 92 93 Village next to ALOXE-CORTON containing part of the great CORTON and CORTON-CHARLEMAGNE v'yds and one other top v'yd: Ile des Vergelesses. Growers incl BONNEAU DU MARTRAY, CHANDON DE BRIAILLES, Delarche, Dubreuil-Fontaine, JADOT, LATOUR, Rapet.

Perrier, Joseph Cuvée Royale Brut NV; Cuvée Royale Bl de Blancs NV; Cuvée Royale Rosé NV; Brut 76 79 82 83 85 Family-run CHAMPAGNE house with considerable v'yds at Châlons-sur-Marne. Light fruity style, best in prestige CUVEE (since '89) Cuvée Joséphine 82 85.

Perrier-Jouët Brut NV; Blason de France NV; Blason de France Rosé NV; Brut 76 79 82 85 86 88 Excellent CHAMPAGNE-growers and makers at Epernay, the first makers of dry CHAMPAGNE and once the smartest name of all, now owned by Seagram. Luxury brands: Belle Epoque (79 82 83 85 86 88) in a painted bottle, Blason de France Rosé (NV). Also Belle Epoque Rosé (79 82 85 86).

Pessac-Léognan Recent AC for part of N GRAVES, incl the area of most of the GRANDS CRUS.

Pétillant Slightly sparkling.

Petit Chablis Burg w ✳✳ DYA Wine from 4th-rank CHABLIS v'yds. Not much character but can be pleasantly fresh. Best from coop La Chablisienne.

Pfaffenheim Top ALSACE coop with 500 acres. Strongly individual wines of all varieties incl good Sylvaner and vg Pinots (N, Gr, Bl). GRANDS CRUS: Goldert, Steinert. Hartenberger Crémant d'Alsace is vg.

Philipponnat NV; Rosé NV; Réserve Spéciale 82 85 88; Grand Blanc Vintage 76 81 82 85 86 88; Clos des Goisses 76 78 79 82 85 86 Small family-run CHAMPAGNE house: well-structured, wines, esp remarkable single v'yd Clos des Goisses, charming rosé. Owners: Marie Brizard. Since '92 also Le Reflet Brut NV.

Piat Père & Fils Important merchants of BEAUJOLAIS and MACON wines at Mâcon, now controlled by Grand Metropolitan. V'yds in MOULIN-A-VENT, also CLOS DE VOUGEOT. BEAUJOLAIS, MACON-VIRE in special Piat bottles maintain a fair standard. But Piat d'Or is dreadful.

Pic, Albert Fine CHABLIS producer, controlled by DE LADOUCETTE.

Picard, Michel Dynamic young négociant firm at Chagny making waves. Moderate quality.

Picpoul de Pinet Midi w *→** AC exclusively for the old variety Picpoul. Best growers: Dom Gaujal, Coop Pomérols.

Pineau de Charente Strong sweet aperitif of white grape juice and COGNAC.

Pinot See Grapes for white and red wine (pages 6–9).

Piper-Heidsieck Brut NV; Brut Rosé NV; Brut 76 79 82 85 CHAMPAGNE-makers of old repute at Reims, now owned by Rémy-Cointreau. Rare (76 79 85 88) and Brut Sauvage (79 82 85) are far ahead of their other, rather light wines. See also Piper Sonoma, California.

Pol Roger Brut White Foil NV; Brut 73 75 76 79 82 85 86 88; Rosé 75 79 82 85 86; Blanc de Chardonnay 79 82 85 86 Top-ranking family-owned CHAMPAGNE house at Epernay. Esp good NV White Foil, Rosé, Réserve PR (86) and CHARD. Sumptuous luxury CUVÉE: 'Sir Winston Churchill' (75 79 82 85).

Pomerol Bx r **→**** 70 71' 75' 76 78 79 81' 82' 83' 85 86 88 89 90 92 93 Next village to ST-EMILION: similar but more plummy and creamy wines, maturing sooner, reliable and delicious. Top châteaux: CERTAN-DE-MAY, L'EVANGILE, LA FLEUR, LA FLEUR-PETRUS, LATOUR-A-POMEROL, PETRUS, TROTANOY, VIEUX CH CERTAN, etc.

Pommard Burg r *** 69 71 72 78' 82 83 85' 86 87 88' 89' 90 91 92 93 The biggest COTE D'OR village. Few superlative wines, but many potent and distinguished ones to age 10 yrs+. Best v'yds: Epenots, HOSPICES DE BEAUNE CUVÉES, Rugiens. Growers incl Comte Armand, G Billard, Billard-Gonnet, J-M Boillot, de Courcel, Gaunoux, LEROY, MACHARD DE GRAMONT, de Montille, Mussy, Ch de Pommard, Pothier-Rieusset.

Pommery Brut NV; Rosé NV; Brut 82 83 85 87 88 89 Very big CHAMPAGNE growers and merchants at Reims, bought by Möet-Hennessy in '91. Wines are much improved. The luxury brand, Louise Pommery (81 82 83 85 87 88), is outstanding. Louise Pommery Rosé (82 83 85 88 89).

Ponsot, J M 25-acre MOREY-ST-DENIS estate. Many GRANDS CRUS: CHAMBERTIN, CHAPELLE-C, LATRICIERES-C, CLOS DE LA ROCHE, CLOS ST-DENIS. V high quality.

Pouilly-Fuissé Burg w **→**** 89' 90' 91 92 93 The best white of the MACON area. At its best (eg Ch Fuissé VIEILLES VIGNES) outstanding, but almost always over-priced compared with (eg) CHABLIS.

Pouilly-Fumé Lo w **→**** 89 90' 91' 92' 93' 'Gun-flinty', fruity, often sharp white from upper Loire, nr SANCERRE. Grapes must be Sauv Bl. Good vintages improve for 2–3 yrs. Top growers incl Bailly, Blondelet, Dagueneau, Figeat, LADOUCETTE, Redde, Renaud, Saget, Tirel, Ch de Tracy.

Pouilly-Loché Burg w ** POUILLY-FUISSE's neighbour. Similar, much cheaper, but scarce.

Pouilly-sur-Loire Lo w * DYA Inferior wine from the same v'yds as POUILLY-FUME but different grapes (Chasselas). Rarely seen today.

Pouilly-Vinzelles Burg w ** 88 89 90 91 92 Neighbour of POUILLY-FUISSE. Similar wine, worth looking for. Value.

Pousse d'Or, Domaine de la 32-acre estate in POMMARD, SANTENAY and esp VOLNAY, where its MONOPOLES Bousse d'Or and Clos des 60 Ouvrées are tannic, powerful and justly famous.

Premier Cru First-growth in BORDEAUX, but the second rank of v'yds (after GRAND CRU) in Burgundy.

Premières Côtes de Blaye Bx r w *→** 82 85 86 88' 89' 90' 92 93 Restricted AC for better wines of BLAYE, greater emphasis on reds. Ch'x include Barbé, LE BOURDIEU, Charron, l'Escadre, Haut-Sociondo, Le Menaudat, La Rose-Bellevue, Segonzac, La Tonnelle.

Premières Côtes de Bordeaux Bx r w (p) dr sw *→** Large hilly area E of GRAVES across the R Garonne: a good bet for quality and value, though never brilliant. Largely Merlot. Châteaux incl Carsin, La Croix de Roche, Fayau, Fontenil, Gardera, HAUT-BRIGNON, du Juge, Laffitte (sic), Lamothe, Peyrat, Plaisance, REYNON, Tanesse. An area to watch.

Prieur, Domaine Jacques Splendid 35-acre estate all in top Burgundy sites, incl PREMIER CRU MEURSAULT, VOLNAY, PULIGNY- and even LE MONTRACHET. Now 50% owned by RODET and quality rejuvenated, esp since '89.

Primeur 'Early' wine for refreshment and uplift; esp BEAUJOLAIS; VINS DE PAYS too. Wine sold 'En Primeur' is offered still in barrel for future delivery.

Prissé See Mâcon-Villages.

Propriétaire-récoltant Owner-manager.

Provence See Côtes de Provence.

Puisseguin St-Emilion Bx r *** 82 85 86 88' 89' 90' 92 93 Eastern neighbour of ST-EMILION, its smallest 'satellite'; wines similar – not so fine or weighty but often good value. Ch'x incl La Croix de Berny, LAURETS, Puisseguin, Soleil, Teyssier, Vieux-Ch-Guibeau. Also Roc de Puisseguin from coop.

Puligny-Montrachet Burg w (r) ****78' 82 83' 85' 86' 88 89' 90' 91 92 93 Bigger neighbour of CHASSAGNE-MONTRACHET with potentially even finer, more vital and complex rich dry whites. Apparent finesse can also be the result of over-production. Best v'yds: BATARD-MONTRACHET, Bienvenues-Bâtard-Montrachet, Champ-Canet, CHEVALIER-MONTRACHET, Clavoillon, Les Combettes, MONTRACHET, Pucelles, etc. Top growers incl Amiot-Bonfils, AMPEAU, J-M Boillot, BOUCHARD PERE, L Carillon, CHARTRON, H Clerc, DROUHIN, JADOT, LATOUR, DOM LEFLAIVE, O LEFLAIVE, Pernot, SAUZET.

Quarts de Chaume Lo w sw *** 75 76 78' 79' 82 85' 86 88' 89' 90' 91 92 93' Famous 120-acre plot in COTEAUX DU LAYON. Chenin Bl grapes. Immensely long-lived intense rich golden wine, esp Dom des Beaumard, Ch de Bellerive, Ch La Suronde.

Quatourze Midi r w (p) *89 90 91 92 Minor AC area nr Narbonne.

Quincy Lo w ** 90' 91 92 93' Small area: v dry SANCERRE-style wine of Sauv Bl. Worth trying. Growers: Domaine Mardon, Meunier-Lapha, Sorbe.

Ramonet, Domaine Leading estate in CHASSAGNE-MONTRACHET with 34 acres, incl some MONTRACHET. Vg whites, and red CLOS ST-JEAN.

Rancio Term for the much-appreciated tang of brown wood-aged fortified wine, esp BANYULS and other VDN. A fault in table wines.

Rasteau Rh r br sw (p w dr) *** 85' 86 88 89 90 91 92 Village of S Rhône Valley. V sound reds from the Cave des Vignerons. Good strong sweet dessert wine is the (declining) local speciality.

Ratafia de Champagne Sweet aperitif made in CHAMPAGNE of 67% grape juice and 33% brandy. Not unlike PINEAU DE CHARENTE.

Récolte Crop or vintage.

Regnié Beauj r *** 91 92 93 BEAUJOLAIS village between MORGON and BROUILLY, promoted to CRU in '88. About 1,800 acres. Try DUBOEUF's.

Reine Pédauque, La Burgundy growers and merchants at ALOXE-CORTON. See André, Pierre.

Remoissenet Père & Fils Fine burgundy merchant (esp for white wines) with a tiny BEAUNE estate. Give his reds time. Also broker for NICOLAS wine shops. Some of his best wines are from DOM THENARD.

Rémy Pannier Important Loire wine merchant at SAUMUR.

Resplandy Value range of MIDI AC wines from Val d'Orbieu.

Reuilly Lo w (r p) ** 90' 91 92 93' Neighbour of QUINCY with similar wine gaining in reputation. NB New Chai de Reuilly. Also good Pinot Gr.

Riceys, Rosé des Champ p *** DYA Minute AC in S CHAMPAGNE for a notable Pinot N rosé. Principal producer: A Bonnet.

Richebourg Burg r ****69' 71 72 7678' 80' 82 8385' 86 87 88' 89' 90' 91 92 93 19-acre VOSNE-ROMANEE GRAND CRU. Powerful perfumed fabulously expensive wine, among Burgundy's very best. Top growers: BICHOT, GRIVOT, J Gros, LEROY, MEO-CAMUZET, DOM DE LA ROMANEE-CONTI.

Riesling See Grapes for white wine (pages 6–8).

Rion, Daniel et Fils 36-acre domaine in Prémeaux (NUITS). Excellent VOSNE-ROMANEE (Les Vignes Rondes, Les Beaumonts), Nuits PREMIERS CRUS and CHAMBOLLE-MUSIGNY-Les Charmes. NB Also Patrice Rion.

Rivesaltes Midi r w br dr sw ✱✱ NV   Fortified wine of E Pyrenees. A tradition v much alive, if struggling these days. Top producers: Doms Boudau, Cazes, Château de Calce, Château de Jau.

Roche-aux-Moines, La Lo w sw ✱✱✱ 75 76' 78 79 82 83 85' 86 88' 89' 90' 91 92' 93'   60-acre v'yd in SAVENNIERES, ANJOU. Intense strong fruity/sharp wine, needs long ageing or drinking fresh.

Rodet, Antonin Substantial quality burgundy merchant with large (375-acre) estate, esp in MERCUREY (Ch de Chamirey). See also Prieur. Now owned by LAURENT-PERRIER.

Roederer, Louis Brut Premier NV; Rich NV; Brut 71 73 75 76 78 79 81 83 85 86 88; Bl de Blancs 88; Brut Rosé 75 83 85 86 88   One of best CHAMPAGNE-growers and merchants at Reims. Reliable NV, plenty of flavour. Luxury brand: velvety Cristal Brut (79 82 83 85 86 88), in white glass bottles, needs time. See California, Australia (Tasmania).

Romanée, La Burg r ✱✱✱✱ 78' 82 83 85' 86 87' 88' 89' 90' 91 92 93   2-acre GRAND CRU in VOSNE-ROMANEE, just uphill from ROMANEE-CONTI. Monopole of Liger-Belair, sold by BOUCHARD PERE.

Romanée-Conti Burg r ✱✱✱✱ 66' 76 78' 80' 82 83 84 85' 86 87' 88' 89' 90' 91 92   4.3-acre MONOPOLE GRAND CRU in VOSNE-ROMANEE; 450 cases pa. The most celebrated and expensive red wine in the world, with reserves of flavour beyond imagination. 85 88 90 are astonishing. See next entry.

Romanée-Conti, Domaine de la (DRC)   The grandest estate in Burgundy. Includes the whole of ROMANEE-CONTI and LA TACHE and major parts of ECHEZEAUX, GRANDS ECHEZEAUX, RICHEBOURG and ROMANEE-ST-VIVANT. Also a v small part of MONTRACHET and VOSNE-ROMANEE. Crown-jewel prices. Keep top DRC wines for decades.

Romanée-St-Vivant Burg r ✱✱✱✱ 76 78' 80' 82 83 85' 86 87 88' 89' 90' 91 92   23-acre GRAND CRU in VOSNE-ROMANEE. Similar to ROMANEE-CONTI but lighter and less sumptuous. Top growers: DRC and LEROY.

Ropiteau Burgundy wine-growers and merchants at MEURSAULT. Specialists in Meursault and COTE DE BEAUNE wines.

Rosé d'Anjou Lo p ✱ DYA   Pale slightly sw rosé. CAB D'ANJOU should be better.

Rosé de Loire Lo p ✱→✱✱ DYA   AC for dry Loire rosé (ANJOU is sweet).

Roty, Joseph Small grower of classic GEVREY-CHAMBERTIN, esp CHARMES- and MAZIS-CHAMBERTIN. Long-lived wines.

Rouget, Emmanuel Inheritor (nephew) of the legendary 13-acre estate of Henri Jayer in ECHEZEAUX, NUITS, VOSNE-ROMANEE. Top wine: V-R Cros Parantoux. Jayer (ret'd '88) still consults here and at DOM MEO-CAMUZET.

Roumier, Georges 35-acre domaine with exceptional BONNES-MARES, CLOS DE VOUGEOT, MUSIGNY, etc. High standards. Long-lasting reds.

Rousseau, Domaine A Major burgundy grower famous for CHAMBERTIN, etc, of v highest quality. Wines are intense, long-lived and mostly GRAND CRU.

Roussette de Savoie Savoie w ✱✱ DYA   Tastiest of the fresh whites from S of Lake Geneva.

Roussillon Largest producer of VDNS (often 'Grands Roussillons'), lighter MUSCATS now taking over from darker heavier wines. See Côtes du R.

Ruchottes-Chambertin Burg r ✱✱✱ 78' 80 83 85' 86 87 88' 89' 90' 91 92 93   7.5-acre GRAND CRU neighbour of CHAMBERTIN. Similar splendid lasting wine of great finesse. Top growers: LEROY, Mugneret, ROUMIER, ROUSSEAU.

Ruinart Père & Fils 'R' de Ruinart Brut NV; 'R' de Ruinart Rosé NV; 'R' de Ruinart Brut 86 88 90   The oldest CHAMPAGNE house, now owned by Moët-Hennessy, with notably fine crisp wines, esp the luxury brands: Dom Ruinart Blanc de Blancs (81 82 83 85 86 88), Dom Ruinart Rosé (81 82 83 85 86). NB the vg mature Rosé. Good value.

Rully Burg r w (sp) ✱✱ 88' 89' 90' 91 92 93   COTE CHALONNAISE village famous for CREMANT. Still white and red are light but tasty, gd value, esp whites. Growers incl DELORME, FAIVELEY, Dom de la Folie, Jacquesson, A RODET.

Sables du Golfe du Lion Midi p r w ✱ DYA   VIN DE PAYS from Mediterranean sand-dunes: esp GRIS DE GRIS from Carignan, Grenache and Cinsaut. Dominated by LISTEL.

Sablet Rh r w (p) ✱✱ 89 90 **91 92**   Admirable COTES DU RHONE village, esp Dom de Boissan, Ch du Trignon, Dom de Verquière.

St-Amour Beauj r ✱✱ **91 92** 93   Northernmost CRU of BEAUJOLAIS: light, fruity, irresistible. Growers to try: Janin, Patissier, Revillon.

St-André-de-Cubzac Bx r w ✱→✱✱ 85 86 88' 89' 90' 92' 93   Town 15 miles NE of BORDEAUX, centre of the minor Cubzaguais region. Sound reds have AC BORDEAUX SUPERIEUR. Incl: Domaine de Beychevelle, Ch du Bouilh, CH DE TERREFORT-QUANCARD, CH TIMBERLAY.

St-Aubin Burg w (r) ✱✱ 85′ 86' 88 89' 90 91 92 93   Little-known neighbour of CHASSAGNE-MONTRACHET, up a side-valley. Several PREMIERS CRUS: light firm quite stylish wines at fair prices. Also sold as COTE DE BEAUNE-VILLAGES. Top growers: Clerget, JADOT, J Lamy, LAMY-PILLOT, H Prudhon, Roux, Thomas.

St-Bris Burg w (r) ✱ DYA   Village west of CHABLIS known for fruity ALIGOTE, but chiefly for SAUVIGNON DE ST-BRIS. Also good CREMANT.

St-Chinian Midi r ✱→✱✱ 88 89 90 **91 92**   Hilly area of growing reputation in COTEAUX DU LANGUEDOC. AC since '82. Tasty southern reds, esp at Berlou.

St-Emilion Bx r ✱✱→✱✱✱✱ 70' **71 75** 79' 81 82' 83' 85' 86' 88 89' 90' 92 93   The biggest top-quality BORDEAUX district (13,000 acres); solid rich tasty wines from hundreds of châteaux, incl AUSONE, CANON, CHEVAL BLANC, FIGEAC, MAGDELAINE, etc. Also a good coop.

St-Estèphe Bx r ✱✱→✱✱✱✱ 75 76 78' 79 81 82' 83' 85' 86 87 88' 89' 90' 91 92 93   Northern village of HAUT-MEDOC. Solid, structured, occasionally superlative wines. Top châteaux: CALON-SEGUR, COS D'ESTOURNEL, MONTROSE, etc, and more notable CRUS BOURGEOIS than any other HAUT-MEDOC commune.

St-Gall Brut NV; Extra Brut NV; Brut Blanc de Blancs NV; Brut Rosé NV; Brut Bl de Blancs 88   Brand name used by Union-Champagne, the vg CHAMPAGNE-growers' coop at AVIZE. Style is usually softer than true BRUT.

St-Georges-St-Emilion Bx r ✱✱ 82 83' 85' 86' 88' 89' 90' 92 93   Part of MONTAGNE-ST-EMILION with high standards. Best châteaux: Belair-Montaiguillon, Marquis-St-G, ST-GEORGES, Tour du Pas-St-G.

St-Jean de Minervois Sweet fine MINERVOIS MUSCAT. Vg recent progress.

St-Joseph Rh r (p w) ✱✱ 83 85 86 88 89 **90 91 92**   N Rhône AC of second rank but reasonable price. Vigorous but variable wine often better than CROZES-HERMITAGE, esp from CHAPOUTIER, CHAVE, Grippat, JABOULET.

St-Julien Bx r ✱✱✱→✱✱✱✱ 70' **75** 78' **79** 81' 82' 83' 85' 86 87' **88**' 89' 90' 91 92 93   Mid-MEDOC village with a dozen of BORDEAUX's best châteaux, incl BEYCHEVELLE, DUCRU-BEAUCAILLOU, GRUAUD-LAROSE, and three LEOVILLES, etc. The epitome of well-balanced, fragrant and savoury red wine.

St-Nicolas-de-Bourgueil Lo r ✱✱ 82 83 85' 86 88 89' 90' 91 92 93'   The next village to BOURGUEIL: the same lively and fruity Cab F red. Top growers: Amirault, Cognard, Jamet, Mabilleau, Taluau.

St-Péray Rh w sp ✱✱ NV   Rather heavy white from the northern Rhône, much of it made sparkling. A curiosity worth trying once.

St-Pourçain-sur-Sioule Central France r p w ✱→✱✱ DYA   Light but venerable local wine of Vichy. Red and rosé made from Gamay and/or Pinot N, white from Tressalier and/or CHARD or Sauv Bl. Recent vintages vastly improved but still pricey. AC on the way? Top growers: Dom de Bellevue, Ray and good coop.

St-Romain Burg r w ✱✱ (w) 86' 88 89' 90' **91** 92 93   Overlooked village just behind the COTE DE BEAUNE. Value, esp for firm fresh whites. Reds have a clean 'cut'. Top growers: FEVRE, Jean Germain, Gras, LATOUR, LEROY, Thévenin-Monthélie.

St-Véran Burg w ✱✱ 90 **91** 92 93   Next-door AC to POUILLY-FUISSE. Similar but better value: real character from the best slopes of MACON-VILLAGES. Try DUBOEUF's, Dom des Deux Roches, CH FUISSE and Dom des Valanges.

For key to grape variety abbreviations, see pages 6–9.

Ste-Croix-du-Mont Bx w sw ✹✹ 75 76' 82 83 86' 88' 89 90 91 92 93
Neighbour to SAUTERNES with similar golden wine. No superlatives but well worth trying, esp Clos des Coulinats, Ch Loubens, Ch Lousteau Vieil, Ch du Mont. Often a bargain, esp with age.

Dull technical stuff

Botrytis cinerea (French pourriture noble, German Edelfäule, English noble rot) is a form of mould that attacks the skins of ripe grapes in certain vineyards in warm and misty autumn weather.

Its effect, instead of rotting the grapes, is to wither them. The skin grows soft and flaccid, the juice evaporates through it, and what is left is a super-sweet concentration of everything in the grape except its water content.

The world's best sweet table wines are all made of 'nobly rotten' grapes. They occur in good vintages in Sauternes, the Rhine and the Mosel (where wine made from them is called Trockenbeerenauslese), in Tokaji in Hungary, in Burgenland in Austria, and elsewhere – California and Australia included. The danger is rain on pulpy grapes already far gone in botrytis. All too often the growers' hopes are dashed by the weather.

Salon 71 73 76 79 82   The original Blanc de Blancs CHAMPAGNE, from Le Mesnil in the Côte de Blancs. Superlative intense v dry wine with long keeping qualities in tiny quantities. Bought in '88 by LAURENT-PERRIER.

Sancerre Lo w (r p) ✸✸✸ 86 88 89 90' 91 92' 93'   Very fragrant and fresh Sauv Bl, almost indistinguishable from POUILLY-FUMÉ, its neighbour across the Loire. Top wines can age 5 yrs. Also light Pinot N red (best drunk at 2–3 yrs) and rosé. Occasional vg VENDANGES TARDIVES. Top growers incl Bailly, Bonnard, Bourgeois, CORDIER, Cotat, Crochet, Gitton, Jolivet, Pinard and Reverdy.

Santenay Burg r (w) ✹✹✹ 78' 82 83 85' 87 88' 89' 90 91 92 93   Sturdy reds from village S of CHASSAGNE. Best v'yds: La Comme, Les Gravières, Clos de Tavannes. Top growers: Lequin-Roussot, MOREY, POUSSE D'OR.

Saumur Lo r p w sp ✱→✹✹   Versatile district in ANJOU. Fresh fruity whites, vg CRÉMANT (producers incl BOUVET-LADUBAY), pale rosés and increasingly good Cab F (see next entry).

Saumur-Champigny Lo r 82 85 86' 88 89' 90' 91 92 93'   Flourishing 10-village AC for fresh Cab F ageing remarkably in sunny years. Look for Ch'x de Chaintres, du Hureau, Doms Filliatreau, Ruault, coop St-Cyr.

Sauternes Bx w sw ✹✹→✹✹✹✹ 67' 71 75 76' 78 79' 80' 81 82 83' 85 86' 88' 89' 90' 91 92   District of 5 villages (incl BARSAC) which make France's best sweet wine, strong (14%+ alcohol), luscious and golden, demanding to be aged. Top châteaux are D'YQUEM, CLIMENS, COUTET, GUIRAUD, SUDUIRAUT, etc. Dry wines cannot be sold as Sauternes.

Sauvignon Blanc See Grapes for white wine (pages 6–8).

Sauvignon de St-Bris Burg w ✹✹ DYA   A baby VDQS cousin of SANCERRE, from nr CHABLIS. To try. 'Dom Saint Prix' from Dom Bersan is good.

Sauvion & Fils Ambitious and well-run MUSCADET house, based at the Ch de Cléray. Top wine: Cardinal Richard.

Sauzet, Etienne Top-quality white burgundy estate at PULIGNY-MONTRACHET. Clearly-defined, well-bred wines, at best superb.

Savennières Lo w dr sw ✹✹✹ 75 76' 78 82 83 85 86' 88 89' 90' 93   Small ANJOU district of pungent long-lived whites, incl Clos du Papillon, COULÉE DE SERRANT, Ch d'Épiré, ROCHE-AUX-MOINES.

Savigny-lès-Beaune Burg r (w) ✹✹✹ 78' 85' 87 88' 89' 90' 91 92 93   Important village next to BEAUNE, similar balanced mid-weight wines, often deliciously lively, fruity. Top v'yds: Dominode, Les Guettes, Marconnets, Serpentières, Vergelesses; growers: BIZE, Camus, CHANDON DE BRIAILLES, CLAIR, Ecard, Girard-Vollot, LEROY, Pavelot, TOLLOT-BEAUT.

Savoie E France r w sp ✹✹ DYA   Alpine area with light dry wines like some Swiss or minor Loires. APREMONT, CRÉPY and SEYSSEL are best-known whites, ROUSSETTE is more interesting. Also good MONDEUSE red.

Schaller, Edgard ALSACE grower (dry style wines) in Mandelburg GRAND CRU, Mittelwihr; esp for Ries 'Mambourg Vieilles Vignes' (needs time) and 'Les Amandiers' (younger-drinking).

Schlumberger ALSACE grower-merchants at Guebwiller. Unusually rich wines incl luscious Kessler and Kitterlé GRAND CRU GEWURZ (also SGN and VT). Fine Kitterlé and Saering Ries. Also good Pinot Gr.

Schröder & Schÿler Old BORDEAUX merchants, owners of CH KIRWAN.

Sciacarello Red grape of CORSICA's best red and rosé, eg AJACCIO, Sartène.

Sec Literally means dry, though CHAMPAGNE so-called is medium-sweet (and better at breakfast, tea-time and weddings than BRUT).

Sélection des Grains Nobles (SGN) Description coined by HUGEL for ALSACE equivalent to German Beerenauslese. Grains nobles are individual grapes with 'noble rot' (see page 52).

Sèvre-et-Maine The département containing the best v'yds of MUSCADET.

Seyssel Savoie w sp ✷✷ NV   Delicate pale dry Alpine white, making very pleasant sparkling wine.

Sichel & Co Two famous merchant houses. In BORDEAUX Peter A Sichel runs Maison Sichel and owns CH D'ANGLUDET and part of CH PALMER. In Germany, Peter M F Sichel (of New York) runs Sichel Söhne, makers of BLUE NUN and respected merchants.

Silvaner See Grapes for white wine (pages 6–8).

Sipp, Jean and Louis Ribeauvillé GRAND CRU ALSACE producers competing to make finest Ries (in Kirchberg): Jean's with youthful elegance (smaller v'yd, own vines only), Louis' finer when mature.

Sirius Serious oak-aged blended BORDEAUX from Maison SICHEL.

Skalli Dynamic producer of good wines from Cab, Merlot, CHARD, etc, at Sète in the Languedoc. FORTANT DE FRANCE is standard brand. Experimental wines extraordinary.

Sur Lie See Lie and Muscadet.

Syrah See Grapes for red wine (pages 8–9).

Tâche, La Burg r ✷✷✷✷ 69' 70 76 78' 80' 82 83 85' 86 87 88' 89' 90' 91 92 15-acre (1,500 case) GRAND CRU of VOSNE-ROMANEE and one of best v'yds on earth: dark perfumed luxurious wine. See DOM DE LA ROMANEE-CONTI.

Taittinger Brut NV; Rosé NV; Brut 73 75 76 78 79 80 82 83 85 86 89; Collection Brut 78 81 82 83 85 86   Fashionable Reims CHAMPAGNE growers and merchants with a light flowery touch. Luxury brand: Comtes de Champagne Blanc de Blancs (79 81 82 83 85 86), also vg Rosé (79 83 85 86). Also owns Champagne Irroy. See also Domaine Carneros, California.

Tastevin, Confrérie des Chevaliers du   Burgundy's colourful successful promotion society. Wine with their Tastevinage label has been approved by them and is usually of a fair standard. A tastevin is the traditional shallow silver wine-tasting cup of Burgundy. See also page 37.

Tavel Rh p ✷✷✷ DYA   France's most famous, though not her best, rosé: strong and dry. Best growers: Ch d'Aquéria, Bernard, Maby, Dom de la Mordorée, Ch de Trinquevedel. Drink v young.

Tempier, Domaine Top grower of BANDOL, with noble reds and rosé.

Thénard, Domaine The major grower of GIVRY, but best known for his substantial portion (4+ acres) of LE MONTRACHET. Could still try harder with this jewel.

Thorin, J Grower and major merchant of BEAUJOLAIS, owner of the Château des Jacques, MOULIN-A-VENT.

Thouarsais, Vin de Lo r w ✷ DYA   Light Gamay and Sauv VDQS S of SAUMUR.

Tokay d'Alsace See under Pinot Gris (Grapes for white wine – pages 6–8).

Tollot-Beaut Stylish burgundy grower with 50+ acres in the COTE DE BEAUNE, incl Beaune Grèves, CORTON, SAVIGNY- (Les Champs Chevrey) and at his CHOREY-LES-BEAUNE base.

Touchais, Moulin Extraordinary luscious COTEAUX DU LAYON from spectacular old stocks of the Touchais family. Vintages back to the '20s are like creamy honey and not over-priced.

Touraine Lo r p w dr sw sp ✶→✶✶✶✶ Big mid-Loire province with immense range of wines, incl dry white Sauv, dry and sweet Chenin Bl (eg VOUVRAY), red CHINON and BOURGUEIL, light red Cabs, Gamays and rosés; often bargains. Amboise, Azay-le-Rideau and Mesland are subsections of the AC.

Trapet Two domaines in GEVREY-CHAMBERTIN, both good; esp R Trapet.

Trévallon, Domaine de Provence r ✶✶✶ Estate at Les Baux with rich intense Cab-Syrah blend.

Trimbach, F E Distinguished ALSACE grower and merchant at Ribeauvillé. Best wines include the austere Ries CLOS STE-HUNE, GRAND CRU Geisberg and Cuvée Frédéric-Emile (Ries from GC Osterberg). Also Gewurz.

Turckheim, Cave Vinicole de Perhaps the best coop in ALSACE. Many fine wines incl GRANDS CRUS from 900+ acres, eg vg Pinot Gr from GC Hengst.

Tursan SW France r p w ✶ Emerging VDQS in the Landes. Sound reds. Ch de Bachen (✶✶✶), owned by the ✶✶✶ chef Michel Gérard, guarantees notoriety and suggests an AC on the way.

Vacqueyras Rh r ✶✶ 85 86 88 89 90 91 92 Neighbour to GIGONDAS and often better value. Try JABOULET's version or Ch de Montmirail.

Val d'Orbieu, Vignerons du Association of some 200 top growers and coops in CORBIERES, COTEAUX DU LANGUEDOC, MINERVOIS, ROUSSILLON etc with Maison SICHEL, marketing a first-class range of selected MIDI AC wines.

Valençay Lo w ✶ DYA VDQS neighbour of CHEVERNY: similar pleasant sharpish.

Vallée du Paradis Midi r w p ✶ Popular VINS DE PAYS of local red varieties.

Valréas Rh r (p w) ✶✶ 88 89 90 **91 92** COTES DU RHONE village with big coop and good mid-weight reds.

Varichon & Clerc Principal makers and shippers of SAVOIE sparkling wines.

Varoilles, Domaine des Burgundy estate of 30 acres, principally in GEVREY-CHAMBERTIN. Tannic wines with great keeping qualities.

Vaudésir Burg w ✶✶✶✶ 78' 83' 85' 86 88 89' **90 91 92** 93 Arguably the best of 7 CHABLIS GRANDS CRUS (but then so are the others).

VDQS Vin Délimité de Qualité Supérieure (see page 21).

Vendange Harvest.

Vendange Tardive Late harvest. In ALSACE equivalent to German Auslese, but stronger and frequently less fine.

Veuve Clicquot Yellow label NV; White Label Demi-Sec NV; Gold Label 76 78 79 82 83 (since '85 called Vintage Réserve: 85 88); Rosé Reserve 83 85 Historic CHAMPAGNE house of highest standing, now owned by LVMH. Full-bodied, almost rich: one of CHAMPAGNE's surest things. Cellars at Reims. Luxury brand: La Grande Dame (**79 83 85 88**).

Vidal-Fleury, J Long-established shippers and growers of top Rhône wines, esp HERMITAGE and COTE ROTIE. Bought in '85 by GUIGAL.

Vieilles Vignes Old vines – therefore the best wine. Used by many, especially by BOLLINGER, DE VOGUE and CH FUISSE.

Viénot, Charles Grower-merchant of good burgundy, owned by BOISSET at NUITS. 70 acres in CORTON, Nuits, RICHEBOURG, etc.

Vieux Télégraphe, Domaine du Rh r (w) ✶✶✶ 78' 79 81 82 83 85 86 88 89 90 91 92 A leader in fine, vigorous, modern CHATEAUNEUF-DU-PAPE.

Vignoble Area of vineyards.

Vin de l'année This year's wine. See Beaujolais, Beaujolais-Villages.

Vin Doux Naturel (VDN) Sweet wine, fortified with wine alcohol, so the sweetness is 'natural', not the strength. The speciality of ROUSSILLON. A vin doux liquoreux is several degrees stronger.

Vin de garde Wine that will improve with keeping. The serious stuff.

Vin Gris 'Grey' wine is v pale pink, made of red grapes pressed before fermentation begins, unlike rosé which ferments briefly before pressing. Oeil de Perdrix means much the same; so does 'blush'.

NB This edition introduces a new short-cut vintage category. Vintages in colour are the ones you should choose first for drinking in 1995.

Vin Jaune Jura w ★★★ Speciality of ARBOIS: odd yellow wine like fino sherry. Normally ready when bottled (at at least 7 yrs old). Best is CH-CHALON.

Vin nouveau See Beaujolais Nouveau.

Vin de paille Wine from grapes dried on straw mats, consequently v sweet, like Italian passito. Esp in the JURA.

Vin de Pays The junior rank of country wines. No one should overlook this category, the most dynamic in France today. More than 140 vins de pays names have come into active use recently, mainly in the Midi. They fall into three categories: regional (eg Vin de Pays d'Oc for the whole Midi); departmental (eg Vin de Pays du Gard for the Gard département near the mouth of the Rhône), and vins de pays de zone, the most precise, usually with the highest standards. Single-grape vins de pays and vins de pays primeurs (reds and whites, all released on the third Thursday in November) are especially popular. Well-known zonal vins de pays include Coteaux de l'Uzège, Côtes de Gascogne, Val d'Orbieu. Don't hesitate. There are some gems among them, and many charming trinkets.

Vin de Table Standard everyday table wine, not subject to particular regulations about grapes and origin. Choose VINS DE PAYS instead.

Vin Vert Very light acidic refreshing white wine, a speciality of ROUSSILLON (and v necessary in summer in those torrid parts).

Vinsobres Rh r (p w) ★★ 85 86 88 89 90 91 92 Contradictory name of good S Rhône village. Potentially substantial reds, but many ordinary.

Viré Burg w ★★ 90 91 92 93 One of the best white wine villages of MACON. Good wines from Clos du Chapitre, JADOT, Ch de Viré, coop.

Visan Rh r p w ★★ 88 89 90 91 92 One of the better southern Rhône villages. Reds much better than whites.

Viticulteur Wine-grower.

Vogüé, Comte Georges de ('Dom les Musigny') First-class 30-acre domaine at CHAMBOLLE-MUSIGNY. At best the ultimate BONNES-MARES and MUSIGNY.

Volnay Burg r ★★★ 78 80 83 85' 87 88' 89' 90' 91 92 93 Village between POMMARD and MEURSAULT: often the best reds of the COTE DE BEAUNE, not strong or heavy but structured and silky. Best v'yds: Caillerets, Champans, Clos des Chênes, Clos des Ducs, etc. Best growers: D'ANGERVILLE, J Boillot, HOSPICES DE BEAUNE, LAFARGE, LAFON, de Montille, POUSSE D'OR, M ROSSIGNOL.

Volnay-Santenots Burg r ★★★ Excellent red wine from MEURSAULT is sold under this name. Indistinguishable from Premier Cru VOLNAY.

Vosne-Romanée Burg r ★★★→★★★★ 78' 83 85' 86 87 88' 89' 90' 91 92 93 Village with Burgundy's grandest CRUS (ROMANEE-CONTI, LA TACHE, etc). There are (or should be) no common wines in Vosne. Many good growers incl Arnoux, Castagnier, CHEVIGNY, ENGEL, GRIVOT, Gros, JAYER, LATOUR, LEROY, MEO-CAMUZET, MONGEARD-MUGNERET, Mugneret, RION, DRC.

Vougeot See Clos de Vougeot.

Vouvray Lo w dr sw sp ★★→★★★★ 76' 78' 79 82 83 85' 86 88 89' 90' 91 92 93 Small district of TOURAINE with v variable wines, at their best intensely sweet and almost immortal. Good dry sparkling. Best producers: Allias, BREDIF, Brisebarre, Champalou, Foreau, Fouquet, Ch Gaudrelle, Huet, Ch Moncontour, Poniatowski.

Willm, A N ALSACE grower at Barr, with vg GEWURZ Clos Gaensbronnel.

'Y' (pronounced 'ygrec') 78' 79' 80' 84 85 86 87 88 89 Dry wine produced occasionally at CH D'YQUEM. Most interesting with age.

Ziltener, André Swiss burgundy grower/mail-order merchant based at Ch Ziltener, CHAMBOLLE MUSIGNY. Wide range; sound wines.

Zind-Humbrecht 64-acre ALSACE estate in Thann, Turckheim, Wintzenheim. First-rate single-v'yd wines (esp Clos St-Urbain Ries), and v fine from GRANDS CRUS Goldert (GEWURZ and MUSCAT), Hengst and Rangen.

Châteaux of Bordeaux

The seven fat years of the 1980s in Bordeaux were followed in biblical style by three lean ones. Some customers used to rich dark vintages have resented being shown the other side of the Bordeaux coin. But as one château-owner said: 'After these unnatural Mediterranean summers, at last a fresh breeze from the Atlantic'. We may never love the mean-spirited '91s, but well-made '92s and '93s are what claret is all about: fresh, fragrant, clean-cut drinking, and at much more modest prices. Meanwhile the great maturing stocks of the 'Mediterranean' decade are not going to disappear overnight.

The 1993 crop came in under incessant rain: picked in oilskins by disheartened workers. But August sun had already given the grapes thick skins and sweet juice, making excellent raw material. We shall enjoy the '93s – some of them very much indeed.

In this edition I have introduced a new indicator for choosing between vintages, this time coloured type picks out certain years. These have been chosen, in the great majority of cases by their châteaux-owners or managers, as the wines from each particular property to enjoy in 1995. Thus they reflect personal taste as well as judgement: some like their wines well-hung; others fresh and very fruity. It is yet another aspect of the glorious diversity which is Bordeaux.

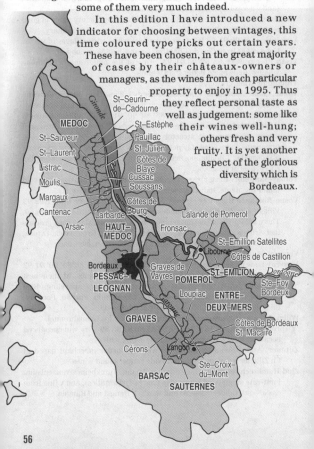

Vintages shown in light type should only be opened now out of curiosity to gauge their future. Vintages shown in bold type are deemed (usually by their makers) to be ready for drinking. Remember though that the French tend to enjoy the vigour of young wines, and that many 82s, 83s, 85s and most good 86s have at least another decade of development in front of them. Vintages marked thus ' are regarded as particularly successful for the property in question. Vintages in colour are the best for '95 drinking.

d'Agassac H-Méd r ** 82' 83' 85' 86 88 89' 90' 91 92 93 Sleeping Beauty 14th-C moated fort. 86 acres v nr Bordeaux suburbs. Same owners as ch'x CALON-SEGUR and DU TERTRE. Lively wine much drunk in Holland.

d'Alesme Mar r ** 78 79 81 82 83 85 86 87 88' 89 90 Tiny (17-acre) third-growth, formerly 'Marquis-d'Alesme'. Better than its reputation.

Andron-Blanquet St-Est r ** 82 83 85' 86 88 89' 90 Sister château to COS-LABORY. 40 acres. Wines lack charm.

L'Angélus St-Em r *** 79' 81 82 83' 85' 86 87' 88 89' 90' 92 93' Well-sited 57-acre classed-growth on ST-EMILION CÔTES. A star of recent vintages.

d'Angludet Cant-Mar r **→*** 61 66 70' 76' 78' 79 80 81' 82 83 85 86 87 88' 89' 90 91 92 93 75-acre CRU EXCEPTIONNEL of classed-growth quality owned by Peter A Sichel. Close to MARGAUX of great style. Value.

d'Archambeau Graves r w dr (sw) ** (r) 82 83 85 86 88 89 90 91 92 (w) 88 90' 91 92 93 Up-to-date 54-acre property at Illats. Vg fruity dry white; since '85 fragrant barrel-aged reds.

d'Arche Saut w sw ** 79 80 81 82 83' 85 86' 88' 89' 90 Classed-growth of 88 acres rejuvenated since '80. Rich juicy wines.

d'Arcins Central Méd r ** 185-acre Castel family property (Castelvin is a well-known VIN DE TABLE). Sister to next-door Barreyres (160 acres).

Arnauld H-Méd r ** 85 88 90 45 acres of old vines in Arcins, esp since '85.

l'Arrosée St-Em r *** 79 81 82 83 85' 86' 87 88 89' 90' 24-acre CÔTES estate. Name means watered, but wine is top-flight: opulent, structured.

Ausone St-Em r **** 75 76' 78 79 81 82' 83' 85 86' 87 88 89 90 91 92 93 First-growth with 17 acres (about 2,500 cases) in the best position on the CÔTES. Famous rock-hewn cellars under the v'yd. At best the firmest, most elegant and subtle St-Emilion. See also Ch Belair.

Bahans-Haut-Brion Graves r *** NV and 82 83 85 86' 87 88 89' 90 91 92 93 The second-quality wine of CH HAUT-BRION. Worthy of its noble origin.

Balestard-la-Tonnelle St-Em r ** 83 85 86' 87 88' 89 90' 92 93 Historic 30-acre classed-growth on plateau. Big flavour; more finesse since '85.

de Barbe Côtes de Bourg r (w) ** 82' 83 85 86 87 88 89 90 92 93 The biggest (148 acres) and best-known château of BOURG. Tasty light but fruity Merlot.

Baret Pessac-L r w ** (r) 83 85 86 88 89' 90' Famous name recovered from a lull. Now run by BORIE-MANOUX. White well-made, too.

Bastor-Lamontagne Saut w sw ** 71 76 79 81 82 83 85 86 87 88' 89' 90' Large Bourgeois Preignac property of classed-growth quality. Excellent rich wines. Second label: Les Remparts de Bastor (92). NB also their Ch St-Robert at Pujols for red and white GRAVES. 10,000 cases.

The following abbreviations of regional names are used in the text:

Bx	Bordeaux	Méd	Médoc	St-Em	St-Emilion
E-Deux-Mers	Entre-Deux-Mers	Pau	Pauillac	St-Est	St-Estèphe
		Pessac-L	Pessac-Léognan	St-Jul	St-Julien
H-Méd	Haut-Médoc			Saut	Sauternes
Mar	Margaux	Pom	Pomerol		

Batailley Pau r ✱✱✱ 70 75' 78' 79' 81 82' 83' 85' 86 87 88' 89' 90' 91 92 93
The bigger of the famous pair of fifth-growths (with HAUT-BATAILLEY) on the borders of PAUILLAC and ST-JULIEN. 110 acres. Fine, firm, strong-flavoured wine. Home of the Castéja family of BORIE-MANOUX.

Beaumont Cussac (H-Méd) r ✱✱ 82 85 86' 87 88 89' 90' 91 92 93   200-acre+ CRU BOURGEOIS, well-known in France for easily enjoyable and improving wines from maturing vines. Second label: Ch Moulin d'Arvigny. 35,000 cases. In the same hands as CH BEYCHEVELLE since '87.

Beauregard Pom r ✱✱✱ 82' 83 85 86 87 88 89' 90' 92 93   42-acre v'yd; pretty 17th-C château nr LA CONSEILLANTE owned by a bank. Well-made rather delicate wines to drink young. Second label: Benjamin de Beauregard.

Beauséjour-Duffau-Lagarosse St-Em r ✱✱✱ 82 83 85 86 88 89' 90'   Part of the old Beau-Séjour Premier Grand Cru estate on the W slope of the CÔTES. 17 acres in old family hands; firm-structured, concentrated, fine.

Beau-Séjour-Bécot St-Em r ✱✱ 75 81 82' 83 85 86' 87 88' 89' 90' 91 92 93
The other half of the above; 45 acres. Controversially demoted in class in '85 but much revved-up since. The Bécots also own CH GRAND-PONTET.

Beau-Site St-Est r ✱✱ 75' 78' 79 81 82 83 85 86' 87 88 89' 90 92 93   55-acre CRU BOURGEOIS EXCEPTIONNEL in same hands as CH BATAILLEY etc. Quality and substance typical of ST-ESTÈPHE.

Belair St-Em r ✱✱✱ 71 75' 78 79 82' 83' 85' 86' 88' 89' 90' 91 92 93   Sister château/neighbour of AUSONE. Wine a shade softer, less complex. V high standard recently. Makes a NV, Roc-Blanquant, in magnums only.

de Bel-Air Lalande de Pom r ✱✱ 82' 83 85 86 87 88' 89' 90 92 93   The best-known estate of L de P, just N of POMEROL. Pomerol-style wine. 37 acres.

Bel-Air-Marquis-d'Aligre Soussans-Mar r ✱✱ 79' 81 82' 85 86 88 89 90 Organically-run CRU EXCEPTIONNEL with 42 acres of old vines giving only 3,500 cases. The owner likes gutsy wine.

Belgrave St-Laurent r ✱✱ 81 82 83 85 86' 87 88 89 90'   Obscure fifth growth in ST-JULIEN's back-country. 107 acres. Managed by DOURTHE since '79. Second label: Diane de Belgrave – since '87.

Bellegrave Listrac r ✱✱ 82 83 85 86 88 89 90 92 93   38-acre CRU BOURGEOIS making full-flavoured wine with advice from PICHON-LALANDE.

Bel-Orme-Tronquoy-de-Lalande St-Seurin-de-Cadourne (H-Méd) r ✱✱ 75' 79' 81 82 83 85 86 87 88 89 90 91 92 93   60-acre CRU BOURGEOIS N of ST-ESTÈPHE. Old v'yd producing tannic wines. More effort now.

Berliquet St-Em r ✱✱ 78 81 82 83 85 86 87 88 89' 90 91 92 93   23-acre Grand Cru Classé recently v well-run (sold by the ST-ÉMILION coop).

Bertineau St-Vincent Lalande de Pom r ✱✱   10 acres owned by top oenologist Michel Rolland (see also Le Bon Pasteur).

Beychevelle St-Jul r ✱✱✱→✱✱✱✱ 70' 75' 78 81 82' 83 85 86' 87 88 89' 90 91 92 93   170-acre fourth growth with MEDOC's finest mansion. New owners (an insurance company) since '85. Wine of elegance and power, just below top flight ST-JULIEN. Second wine: Amiral de Beychevelle.

Biston-Brillette Moulis r ✱✱   Another attractive MOULIS. 7,000 cases.

Bonalgue Pom r ✱✱   Ambitious 2,500-case estate to watch. Les Hautes-Tuileries is sister château. Wines built to age.

Bonnet E-Deux-Mers r w ✱✱ (r) 90 91 92 93 (w) DYA   Big-scale producer (600 acres!) of some of the best ENTRE-DEUX-MERS.

Le Bon Pasteur Pom r ✱✱✱ 70 75 76 79 81 82 83 85 86' 87 88 89' 90' 92 93 Excellent small property on ST-EM boundary, owned by consultant oenologist Michel Rolland. Concentrated, s'times even creamy wines.

Le Boscq St-Est r ✱✱ 82 83 85 86 87 88 89' 90 92 93   Leading CRU BOURGEOIS giving excellent value in tasty ST-ESTÈPHE ('Vieilles Vignes').

Le Bourdieu-Vertheuil H-Méd r ✱✱ 81 82 83 85 86 88 89 90' 92 93   Vertheuil CRU BOURGEOIS with sister château, Victoria, (134 acres in all); well-made ST-ESTÈPHE-style wines. New owners, equipment and effort since '90.

Châteaux entries also cross-refer to France section, pages 20–55.

Bourgneuf Pom r ** 81 82 83 85' **86** 88 89' 90 92 93   22-acre v'yd on chalky clay soil, making fairly rich wines with typically plummy POMEROL perfume. 5,000 cases. Aka Bourgneuf-Vayron.

Bouscaut Graves r w ** 81 82' 83 85 86' **88 89** 90 92 93   Classed-growth at Cadaujac bought in '80 by Lucien Lurton of CH BRANE-CANTENAC etc. 75 acres red (largely Merlot); 15 acres white. Never yet brilliant, but slowly getting there.

du Bousquet Côtes de Bourg r ** 82 83 85 86 88 89 90' 92 93   Reliable estate with 148 acres making attractive solid wine.

Boyd-Cantenac Mar r *** 78' 79 81 82' 83' 85 86' 87 **88** 89 90 91 92 93   44-acre third growth often producing attractive wine, full of flavour, if not of third growth class. See also Ch Pouget.

Branaire-Ducru St-Jul r *** 75' 79' 81 82' 83 85 86 87 88 89' 90' 91 92 93   Fourth growth of 125 acres, producing notably spicy and flavoury wine in the '70s. The late '80s saw a full-scale revival. New owners in '88. Second label: Duluc.

Brane-Cantenac Cantenac-Mar r *** 75' 78' **79 81 82'** 83 85 86' 87 88 89 90   Big (211-acre) second growth. Rich, even gamey wines of strong character. Same owners as CH'X BOUSCAUT, CLIMENS, DURFORT-VIVENS, VILLEGEORGE, etc. Second labels: Ch'x Baron de Brane, Notton.

du Breuil Cissac r ** 88 89 90 92 93   Abandoned historic château bought by owners of CISSAC and restored. To follow.

Brillette Moulis r ** 81' 82 83 85' 86 88 89' 90 91 92 93   70-acre CRU BOURGEOIS. Reliable and attractive. Second label: Berthault Brillette.

La Cabanne Pom r ** 79 81 82' 83 85 86 87 88' 89' 90' 91 92 93   Well regarded 25-acre property nr the great TROTANOY. Recently modernized. Second wine: Dom de Compostelle. See also CH HAUT-MAILLET.

Cadet-Piola St-Em r *** 75' 78 79 81 82 83' 85' 86 87 88 89' 90 91 92 93'   Distinguished little property just N of the town of ST-EMILION. 3,000 cases of tannic wine. CH FAURIE-DE-SOUCHARD has same owner; less robust wine.

Caillou Saut w sw ** 75 76 78 81 **82 83 85 86 87** 88' 89' 90' 91 92   Well-run second-rank 37-acre BARSAC v'yd for firm fruity wine. Private Cuvée (**81 83 85 86 88** 89') is a top selection.

Calon-Ségur St-Est r *** 78' 79' 81 82' 83 85' **86' 87** 88' 89 90 91 92 93   Big (123-acre) third growth of great reputation for fruity hearty wines; less stylish than very top ST-ESTEPHES but currently on good form. Second label: Marquis de Ségur.

Cambon-la-Pelouse H-Méd r ** 82 85 86 87 88 89 90 92 93   Big (145-acre) accessible CRU BOURGEOIS. A sure bet for fresh typical MEDOC without wood-ageing.

Camensac St-Laurent r ** 81 82' 85 86' 87 **88 89** 90 91 **92** 93   149-acre fifth growth, previously with the same expert direction as LAROSE-TRINTAUDON. Good lively if not exactly classic wines. Second label: La Closerie de Camensac.

Canon Canon-Fronsac r **▷▶▷▶▶ 82 83 85 86' 88 89' 90 92   Tiny property of Christian MOUEIX. Long-ageing wine.

Canon St-Em r *** 79' 81 82' 83 85' **86 87** 88' 89' 90' 92 93   Famous first-classed-growth with 44+ acres on the plateau W of the town. Conservative methods; v impressive wine, among ST-EMILION's best. Second label (in '91): Clos J Kanon.

Canon-de-Brem Canon-Fronsac r ** 81 82' 83 **85 86** 88 89' 90 **92** 93   One of the top FRONSAC v'yds for vigorous wine. MOUEIX property.

Canon-la-Gaffelière St-Em r *** 82 83 85 86' 87 88' 89 90' 92 93   47-acre classed-growth on the lower slopes of the COTES, under German ownership. Total renovation in '85. Now stylish, meaty and impressive.

Canon-Moueix Canon-Fronsac r ** 83 85 86 87 88 89' 90 92 93   The latest MOUEIX investment in this rising AC. V stylish wine.

Cantegril Graves r ** 88 89 90   Good earthy red from CH DOISY-DAENE.

Cantemerle Macau r *** 61 78 81 82 83' 85 87 88 89' 90 91 92 93
Romantic S MEDOC estate, a château in a wood with 150 acres of vines. Officially fifth growth; potentially much higher for its harmony of flavours. Problems in late '70s, but a new broom (CORDIER) since '81 has restored to potential. New cellars and oak vats in '90. Second label: Villeneuve de Cantemerle.

Cantenac-Brown Cantenac-Mar r *** 70 78 79 81 82 83 85 86' 87 88 89 90' 91 92 93 Formerly old-fashioned 77-acre third growth. New owners (same as PICHON-LONGUEVILLE) investing heavily; direction from J-M Cazes and v promising recent vintages. Big wines. Second label: Canuet.

Capbern-Gasqueton St-Est r ** 81 82 83 85 86 88 89 90 92 93 Good 85-acre CRU BOURGEOIS; same owner as CALON-SEGUR.

Cap-de-Mourlin St-Em r ** 79' 81 82' 83 85 86 87 88 89 90 92 93 Well-known 37-acre property of the Cap-de-Mourlin family, owners of CH BALESTARD and CH ROUDIER, MONTAGNE-ST-EM. Rich tasty ST-EMILION.

Carbonnieux Graves r w ** 82 83 85 86' 87 88 89' 90' 91 92 93 Historic estate at LEOGNAN making rather light reds (since '85 much better). The whites, 50% Sémillon (eg 87 88 89 90 91 92'), have the structure to age 10 yrs. Ch'x Le Pape and Le Sartre are also in the family. Second label: La Tour-Léognan.

Cardaillan Graves r ** The trusty red wine of the distinguished (SAUTERNES) CH DE MALLE.

La Cardonne Blaignan (Méd) r ** 88 89 90 91 92 93 Large (300-acre+) CRU BOURGEOIS of the northern MEDOC, bought in '73 by the Rothschilds of LAFITE and sold in '90. Big changes since. Fairly simple fruity Médoc, best when young.

Les Carmes-Haut-Brion Graves r ** 81' 82' 83 85 86 87 88' 89 90' 91 92 93' Small (9-acre) neighbour of HAUT-BRION with higher than Bourgeois standards. Old vintages show its potential. Only 1,500 cases.

Caronne-Ste-Gemme St-Laurent r **→*** 81 82' 83 85 86 87 88 89' 90 91 92 93' CRU BOURGEOIS EXCEPTIONNEL of 100 acres. Steady stylish quality repays patience. At minor CRU CLASSE level.

Carteau-Côtes-Daugay St-Em ** Emerging 5,000-case GRAND CRU; to follow for full-flavoured wines maturing fairly early.

du Castéra Méd r ** 85 86 87 88 89 90' 91 92 93 Historic property at St-Germain (N MEDOC). Recent investment; tasty but not tannic wine.

Certan-Giraud Pom r ** 75 79 81 82 83' 85 86 88 89' 90' 92 93 Small (17-acre) property next to PETRUS. Good, but one expects more.

Certan-de-May Pom r *** 70 75 78 79 81 82' 83' 85' 86 87 88' 89' 90' 91 92 93 Neighbour of VIEUX CHATEAU CERTAN. Tiny property (1,800 cases) with full-bodied, rich and tannic wine, consistently flying v high.

Chambert-Marbuzet St-Est r ** 70 76 78 79 81 82 83 85 86 87 88 89' 90' 91 92 93 Tiny (20-acre) sister château of HAUT-MARBUZET. Vg predominantly Cab wine, aged v tastily in new oak. The owner, M Duboscq, likes it well hung.

Chantegrive Graves r w ** 215-acre estate, half white, half red; modern GRAVES of high quality. Cuvée Caroline is top white selection (89 90 92 93), Cuvée Edouard top red (82 83 85). Other labels incl Mayne-Lévêque, Bon-Dieu-des-Vignes.

Chasse-Spleen Moulis r *** 75' 76 78' 79 81' 82' 83' 85 86 87 88 89' 90' 91 92 93 180-acre CRU EXCEPTIONNEL of classed-growth quality. Consistently good, usually outstanding, long-maturing wine. Second label: Ermitage de C-S. One of the surest things in Bordeaux. See also La Gurgue.

Chéret-Pitres Graves r w *→** Substantial estate in the up-and-coming village of Portets. Drink young or keep.

Cheval Blanc St-Em r **** 64 66 70 71 75' 76 78 79 80 81' 82' 83' 84 85' 86 87 88 89 90' 91 92 93 This and AUSONE are the 'first growths' of ST-EMILION. Cheval Blanc is richer, more full-blooded, intensely vigorous and perfumed, from 100 acres. Delicious young and lasts a generation. Second wine: Le Petit Cheval.

Chevalier, Domaine de Graves r w **** 66 70' 76 78 79' 81' **82** 83' 84 85 86' 87 88' 89' 90' 91 92 93 Superb small estate of 36 acres at LEOGNAN. The red is stern at first, richly subtle with age. The white is delicate but matures to rich flavours (**79'** 81 **82 83' 85' 87'** 88 89' 90 91 92 93').

Chicane Graves r ** 85 86 88 89 90' **91** 92 93 Satisfying and reliable product of the Langon merchant Pierre Coste. (Domaine de Gaillat is another.) Drink at 2–6 yrs (the Gaillat a little later).

Cissac Cissac r ** 70' 71 75' 76 78' 79 81 82' 83' 83' 85 86' 87 88 89 90 91 92 Pillar of the bourgeoisie. 80-acre CRU GRAND BOURGEOIS EXCEPTIONNEL: steady record for tasty, v long-lived wine. Second wine: Les Reflets du Ch Cissac. Also, since '87, CH DU BREUIL.

Citran Avensan (H-Méd) r ** 78' 82 83 85 86 87 88 89' 90 91 92 93 CRU GRAND BOURGEOIS EXCEPTIONNEL of 178 acres, bought by Japanese in '87. Major works. 89 is turbo-charged. Second label: Moulins de Citran. To watch.

Clarke Listrac r (p w) ** 82 83 85' 86' **87** 88 89' 90 91 92 93 Huge (350-acre) CRU BOURGEOIS Rothschild development, incl visitor facilities and neighbouring Ch'x Malmaison and Peyrelebade. Also a unique sweet white 'Le Merle Blanc du Ch Clarke'.

Clerc-Milon Pau r *** 78' 79 81 **82'** 83 85 86' 87 88 89' 90' 91 92 93 Once-forgotten little fifth growth bought by the late Baron Philippe de Rothschild in '70. Now 73 acres with MOUTON input. Not thrilling in the '70s (except 70), but vg 85, 86 (esp), and now 88, 89 and 90.

Climens Saut w sw **** 71' 75' **76 78 79** 80' 81 **82** 83' **85' 86'** 88' 89 90' 74-acre BARSAC classed-growth making some of the world's most stylish wine (but not the v sweetest) for a good 10 yrs' maturing. (Occasional) second label: Les Cyprès. Same owner as CH BRANE-CANTENAC etc.

Clinet Pom r *** 81 82 83 85 86 87 88' 89' 90' 91 92 93 17-acre property in central POMEROL making intense wines from old vines. Since '86 one of the models for POMEROL.

Clos l'Eglise Pom r *** 75 78 79' 81 83 85 86 88 89 90' 92 93 14-acre v'yd on one of the best sites in POMEROL. Fine wine without great muscle or flesh. The same family owns CH PLINCE.

Clos Floridène Graves r w *** (r) 90' 91 92 93' (w) 86 87' 88 89' Tour de force by one of the best white-wine-makers of Bordeaux, Denis Dubourdieu. Oak-fermented Sauv-Sém to keep 5 yrs. Also fruity red (86 88 89 90 91 92 93). See also Ch Reynon.

Clos Fourtet St-Em r *** 78 79 81 82' 83 85 86 88 89 90 Well-placed 42-acre first growth on the plateau, cellars almost in town. Back on form in '90 after a middling patch. Same owners as BRANE-CANTENAC, CLIMENS etc. Second label: Dom de Martialis.

Clos Haut-Peyraguey Saut w sw ** 83 85 86' 87 88' 89 90' Tiny production of good medium-rich wine. Haut-Bommes is the second label.

Clos des Jacobins St-Em r *** 75' 78 79 81 82' 83' 85 86 87 88' 89' 90' 92 93 Well-known and well-run little (18-acre) classed-growth owned by the shipper CORDIER. Wines of notable depth and style.

Clos du Marquis St-Jul r ** 81 82 83 85 86' 87 88 89' 90 91 92 The second wine of LEOVILLE-LAS-CASES, cut from the same cloth.

Clos René Pom r *** 75 81 82' 83 85 86 87 88 89 90 Leading château W of POMEROL. 38 acres. Increasingly concentrated. Aka Ch Moulinet-Lasserre.

Clos St-Martin St-Em r *** 88 89 90' 9 acres in prime spot co-owned with Grandes-Murailles and Côte Baleau; the other two were demoted in the '85 reclassification. A muddle, but taste the wines.

La Closerie-Grand-Poujeaux Moulis r ** 85 86 88 89 90 91 92 93' Small but respected middle-MEDOC property modernized in '92/'93. Also owners of neighbouring ch'x Bel-Air-Lagrave and Haut-Franquet.

La Clotte St-Em r ∗∗ 82 83' 85 86 88 89 90' 92 93 Tiny COTES GRAND CRU: pungent supple wine. Drink at owners' restaurant, La Cadène, in ST-EM. Winemaker change in '90. Second label: Clos Berger Bosson (**91**).

Colombier-Monpelou Pau r ∗∗ 81 82 83 85 86' 87 88 89 90' **91** 92 93 Reliable small CRU BOURGEOIS made to a fair standard.

La Conseillante Pom r ∗∗∗∗ 70' 75 76 79 81' 82' 83 84 85 86 87 88 89 90' 91 92 93 29-acre historic property on the plateau between PETRUS and CHEVAL BLANC. Some of the noblest and most fragrant POMEROL, worthy of its superb position; drinks well, young or old.

Corbin (Giraud) St-Em r ∗∗ 75 79 81 82' 83 85 86 88 89 90' 92 93 28-acre classed-growth in N ST-EMILION where a cluster of Corbins occupy the plateau edge. Top vintages are v rich. Same owner as CERTAN-GIRAUD.

Corbin-Michotte St-Em r ∗∗ 75 81 82 83 85 86 88 89' 90 Well-run 19-acre property; 'generous' POMEROL-like wine.

Cordeillan-Bages Pau r ∗∗ A mere 1,000 cases of full-blooded PAUILLAC from the château-hotel of J-M Cazes (see Lynch-Bages).

Cos-d'Estournel St-Est r ∗∗∗∗ 61 66 70 75' 76' 78' 79 81' 82' 83' 84 85' 86' 87 88' 89' 90' 91 92 93' 140-acre second growth with eccentric chinoiserie tower overlooking CH LAFITE. Always full-flavoured, often magnificent. Now regularly one of best in the MEDOC. Second label: CH DE MARBUZET.

Cos-Labory St-Est r ∗∗ 82 83 85 86 87 88 89' 90' 91 92 93 Little-known fifth growth neighbour of COS-D'ESTOURNEL with 37 acres. Efforts since '85 have raised it steadily to classed-growth form (esp 90). ANDRON-BLANQUET is in effect its second wine.

Coufran St-Seurin-de-Cadourne (H-Méd) r ∗∗ 81 82' 83 85 86' 87 88 89 90 91 92 93 Coufran and CH VERDIGNAN, on the northernmost hillock of the HAUT-MEDOC are co-owned. Coufran has mainly Merlot vines; soft supple wine. 148 acres. Ch Soudars is another, smaller sister.

Couhins-Lurton Graves w ∗∗ 85 86' 88 89 90 91 92 93 Tiny quantity of v fine oaky Sauv Bl for maturing. Classed-growth château, being restored.

Coutet Saut w sw ∗∗∗ 67' 70' 71' 73 75' 76 79 81 82 83' 85 86' 87 88' 89' 90' Traditional rival to CH CLIMENS; 91 acres in BARSAC. Usually slightly less rich; at its best equally fine. Cuvée Madame is a v rich selection of the best. A dry GRAVES is sold under the same name.

Couvent des Jacobins St-Em r ∗∗ 75 78 79' 81 82' 83 85 86 87 88 89 90 92 93 Well-known 22-acre v'yd on E edge of town. Among the best of its kind. Splendid cellars. Second label: Ch Beau-Mayne.

Le Crock St-Est r ∗∗ 79 81 82 83 85 86 87 88 89 90' 92 93 Outstanding CRU BOURGEOIS of 74 acres in the same family as CH LEOVILLE-POYFERRE. Among the best CRUS BOURGEOIS of the commune.

La Croix Pom r ∗∗ 75' 76 79' 81 82 83 85' 86 87 88 89 90 91 92 93 Well-reputed property of 32 acres. Appealing plummy POMEROL with a spine; matures well. Also La C-St-Georges, La C-Toulifaut, Castelot, Clos des Litanies and HAUT-SARPE (St-Em).

La Croix du Casse Pom r ∗∗ Sister château of CLINET. 22 acres making easy-drinking POMEROL.

La Croix-de-Gay Pom r ∗∗∗ 81 82' 83' 85 86 88' 89 90 91 92 30 acres in best part of the commune. Recently on fine form. Has underground cellars (rare in POMEROL). LA FLEUR-DE-GAY is the best selection.

Croizet-Bages Pau r ∗∗ 82' 83 85 86 87 88 90' 92 52-acre fifth growth (lacking a château or a reputation) with the same owners as CH RAUZAN-GASSIES. Only a flicker of life.

Croque-Michotte St-Em r ∗∗ 75 81 82' 83 85 86 87 88 89' 90' 35-acre POMEROL-style classed-growth on the Pomerol border.

de Cruzeau Graves r w ∗∗ (r) 86 88 89 90 91 92 93 100-acre GRAVES-LEOGNAN v'yd recently developed by André Lurton of LA LOUVIERE etc. V high standards; to try. Oak-fermented white: keeps 2–3 years.

Curé-Bon-la-Madeleine St-Em r ∗∗ 75 78 81 82' 83 85 86 88 89 90 Tiny little-known (12-acre) property between AUSONE and CANON.

Dalem Fronsac r ✳✳ 82 83 85 86 88 89 90 92 93   Leading full-blooded FRONSAC. 36 acres; 85% Merlot.

Dassault St-Em r ✳✳ 82 83 85 86 88 89 90   Consistent early-maturing middle-weight GRAND CRU. 58 acres.

La Dauphine Fronsac ✳✳ 85 86 87 88 89' 90' 92 93   Old star rejuvenated by J-P MOUEIX.

Dauzac Labarde-Mar r ✳✳→✳✳✳ 82' 83' 85' 86 87 88' 89' 90' 92 93'   Substantial fifth growth nr the river S of MARGAUX, an underachiever for many years. New owner (an insurance company) in '89; direction since '92 by André Lurton. 120 acres. 22,000 cases. Second wine: La Bastide Dauzac.

Desmirail Mar r ✳✳ 82 83' 85 86 87 88 89 90   Third growth, now 45 acres. A long-defunct name revived in '81 by Lucien Lurton of BRANE-CANTENAC. So far wines for drinking fairly young.

Doisy-Daëne Barsac w (r) sw dr ✳✳✳ 76' 78 79 80 81 82 83 85 86 88' 89' 90' 91   Forward-looking 34-acre estate making crisp oaky dry white and red CH CANTEGRIL as well as notably fine (and long-lived) sweet BARSAC. L'Extravagance (90) was a super-cuvée.

Doisy-Dubroca Barsac w sw ✳✳ 75' 76 78 79 81 83 85 86 87 88' 89 90'   Tiny (8.5-acre) BARSAC classed-growth allied to CH CLIMENS.

Doisy-Védrines Saut w sw ✳✳ 71 75' 76' 78 79 80 81 82' 83' 85 86 88' 89' 90 92   50-acre classed-growth at BARSAC, nr CLIMENS and COUTET, recently re-equipped. Delicious, sturdy, rich: for keeping. NB the 89.

La Dominique St-Em r ✳✳✳ 78 79 81 82' 83 86' 87 88' 89' 90' 92 93   45-acre classed-growth next door to CH CHEVAL BLANC; at best almost as arresting. Second label: St Paul de Dominique (91).

Ducluzeau Listrac r ✳✳   Tiny sister property of DUCRU-BEAUCAILLOU. 10 acres, unusually 90% Merlot.

Ducru-Beaucaillou St-Jul r ✳✳✳✳ 61 62 64 66 70' 75' 76 78' 79 80 81 82' 83' 84 85' 86' 87 88 89 90 91 92 93   Outstanding second company; 120 acres overlooking the river. Second label: La Croix-Beaucaillou. The owner, M Borie, makes classic cedar-scented claret for v long ageing. See also Grand-Puy-Lacoste, Haut-Batailley, Lalande-Borie.

Duhart-Milon-Rothschild Pau r ✳✳✳ 78 79 80 81 82' 83 85 86 87 88 89 90 91 92 93   Fourth growth neighbour of LAFITE, under the same management. Maturing vines; increasingly fine quality. 110 acres. Second label: Moulin de Duhart.

Duplessis-Fabre Moulis r ✳✳ 82 83 85 86 87 88' 89 90 92 93   Former sister château of FOURCAS-DUPRE; since '89 owned by DOURTHE. To watch.

Durfort-Vivens Mar r ✳✳✳ 78' 79' 81 82' 83 85' 86 87 88' 89' 90   Relatively small (49-acre) second growth owned by M Lurton of BRANE-CANTENAC. Recent wines have structure (lots of Cab S) and class.

Dûtruch-Grand-Poujeaux Moulis r ✳✳ 81 82' 83 85 86 87 88 89 90 91 92 93   One of the leaders of MOULIS; full-bodied and tannic wines.

de l'Eglise, Domaine Pom r ✳✳ 79' 81 82' 83 85 86 88 89 90 92 93   Small property: stylish resonant wine distributed by BORIE-MANOUX.

L'Eglise-Clinet Pom r ✳✳✳ 70 71 75 76 78 79 81 82' 83' 84 85' 86 87 88' 89 90' 91 92 93'   11 acres. Ranked v nr top; full fleshy wine. Changed hands in '82; 86 90 noble. 1,700 cases. Second label: La Petite Eglise.

L'Enclos Pom r ✳✳ 70 75 79 82' 83 85 86 87 88 89' 90' 91 92 93   Respected 26-acre property on west side of POMEROL, nr CLOS RENE. Big well-made long-flavoured wine.

L'Evangile Pom r ✳✳✳→✳✳✳✳ 75' 78 79 82' 83' 85' 86 87 88' 89' 90' 92 93   33 acres between PETRUS and CHEVAL BLANC. Deep-veined but elegant style. In the same area and class as LA CONSEILLANTE. Bought in '90 by Domaines (Lafite) Rothschild.

To decipher codes, please refer to symbols key at front of book, and to 'How to use this book' on page 5.

de Fargues Saut w sw *** 70' 71' 75' 76' 78 79 80 81 83 85' 86 87 88 89 90 25-acre v'yd by ruined château in same ownership as CH D'YQUEM. Fruity and extremely elegant wines, maturing earlier than Yquem.

Faurie-de-Souchard St-Em r ** 85 86 88 89 90 91 92 Small Grand Cru Classé on the COTES. See also Ch Cadet-Piola.

de Ferrand St-Em **→***→*** 85 86 87 88 89 90 92 93 Big (75-acre) plateau estate. Rich, oaky wines, sometimes too tannic.

Ferrande Graves r (w) ** 81 82 83 85 86 88 89 90 91 92 93 Major estate of Castres: 100+ acres. Easy enjoyable red and good white at 1–4 yrs.

Ferrière Mar r ** 81 82 83 85 86 87 88 89 90 92 93 Phantom third growth; only 10+ acres. Now in same capable hands as CHASSE-SPLEEN.

Feytit-Clinet Pom r **→***→*** 75' 79 81 82' 83 85' 86 87 88' 89' 90' 92 Little property nr LATOUR-A-POMEROL. Fine ripe wines. Managed by J-P MOUEIX.

Why do the Châteaux of Bordeaux have such a large section of this book devoted to them? The reason is simple: collectively they form by far the largest supply of high-quality wine on earth. A single typical Médoc château with 150 acres (some have far more) makes approximately 26,000 dozen bottles of identifiable wine each year – the production of two or three California 'boutique' wineries.

The tendency over the last two decades has been to buy more land. Many classed-growths have expanded very considerably since their classification in 1855. The majority has also raised its sights and invested the good profits of the past decade in better technology.

Fieuzal Graves r (w) *** 75 78' 79 81 82' 83 85' 86' 87 88 89 90' 91 92 75-acre classed-growth at LEOGNAN. Finely made, memorable wines of both colours esp since '84. Classic whites since '85 are 4–10-yr keepers (esp 85 90 92). Second label: Ch le Bonnat.

Figeac St-Em r **** 64 70' 75' 76' 78 80 81 82' 83 84 85' 86' 87 88 89' 90' Famous first growth neighbour of CHEVAL BLANC. 98-acre gravelly v'yd gives one of Bordeaux's most stylish, rich but elegant wines, often maturing relatively quickly but lasting almost indefinitely. Second label: Grangeneuve.

Filhot Saut w sw dr ** 75 76' 79' 82' 83' 85 86' 87 88 89 90' 91 92 Second-rank classed-growth with splendid château, 148-acre v'yd. Lightish rather simple (Sauv) sweet wines for fairly early drinking, a little dry, and red. Vg 'Crème de Tête' (90 extremely rich).

La Fleur St-Em r ** 75 78 79 81 82' 83 85 86 88 89' 90' 92 93 16-acre COTES estate; increasingly fruity wines. Now managed by J-P MOUEIX.

La Fleur-de-Gay 1,000-case super-cuvée of CH LA CROIX DE GAY.

La Fleur-Pétrus Pom r **** 70 75' 78 79 81 82' 83' 85 86 87 88' 89' 90' 92 18-acre v'yd flanking PETRUS and under same management. Exceedingly fine plummy wines; POMEROL at its most stylish.

Fombrauge St-Em r ** 79 81 82' 83 85 86 87 88' 89 90 92 93 120-acres at St-Christophe-des-Bardes, E of ST-EMILION; Danish connections. Reliable mainstream St-Emilion making great efforts. Second label: Ch Maurens.

Fonbadet Pau r ** 70 76 78 79 81' 82' 83 84 85 86 87 88 89 90' 91 92 93 CRU BOURGEOIS of solid reputation. 38 acres next to PONTET-CANET. Old vines; wine needs long bottle-age. Value.

Fonplégade St-Em r ** 75 78 79 81 82' 83 85 86 87 88 89 90' 48-acre Grand Cru Classé on the COTES W of ST-EMILION in the Armand Moueix group. Firm and long-lasting.

Fonréaud Listrac r ** 78' 79 81 82' 83 85' 86' 87 88 89 90 91 92 93 One of the bigger (96 acres) and better CRUS BOURGEOIS of its area. New broom (and barrels) since '83. Now also 5 acres of white: Le Cygne, barrel-fermented. See also Ch Lestage.

Fonroque St-Em r ** 70 75' 78 79 81 82 83' 85' 86 87 88 89' 90' 92 48 acres on the plateau N of ST-EMILION. J-P MOUEIX property. Big deep dark wine that nonetheless opens up quite young.

Les Forts de Latour Pau r *** 70' 75 78' **79 80** 81 82' **83 84** 85 86' 87 90 91 92 93   The second wine of CH LATOUR; well worthy of its big brother. For long unique in being bottle-aged at least 3 yrs before release; since '90 offered EN PRIMEUR as well. Specially fine 82 and 90.

Fourcas-Dupré Listrac r ** 70' 75 78' 79 81 82' 83' 85' 86' **87 88 89'** 90 91 92 93   Top-class 100-acre CRU BOURGEOIS EXCEPTIONNEL making consistent and elegant wine. To follow. Second label: Ch Bellevue-Laffont.

Fourcas-Hosten Listrac r **→**** 70 75 78' 79 81 82' 83' 85 86' **87** 88 89 90 91 92 93   96-acre CRU BOURGEOIS currently considered the best of its (underestimated) commune. Firm wine with a long life.

Franc-Mayne St-Em r ** 85 86 87 88 89' 90' 92 93   '89 acquisition of AXA Insurance. 18 acres run by J-M Cazes (LYNCH-BAGES). High standards. Ch'x La Fleur-Pourret and Petit-Figeac (19 acres) are in same stable.

de France Pessac-L r w **   Well-known GRAVES, 65 acres red, 10 white recently replanted. Recent reds notable.

La Gaffelière St-Em r *** 70 79 82' 83' 85 86' **87** 88' 89' 90' 92   61-acre first growth at the foot of the COTES below CH BEL-AIR. Elegant, not rich wines; worth its rank since '82, after a bad patch.

La Garde Graves r (w) ** 81 82' 83' 84 85 86 88 89 **90** 91 92 93   Substantial property making reliably sound red.

Le Gay Pom r *** 70 75' 76 78 79 82' 83' 85 86 88 89' 90' 92   Fine 14-acre v'yd on N edge of POMEROL. Same owner as CH LAFLEUR; under J-P MOUEIX management since '85. Impressive tannic wines.

Gazin Pom r *** 81 82 83 85 86 87' 88 89' 90' 91 92 93   Large property (for POMEROL) with 58 acres next to PETRUS. Inconsistent up to '85; now back on top form. Distributed (except tiny '91 crop) by J-P MOUEIX. Second label: Ch l'Hospitalet.

Gilette Saut w sw *** 37 49 53 55 59 61 62   Extraordinary small Preignac château which stores its sumptuous wines in cask to a great age. Only about 5,000 bottles of each. Ch Les Justices is the sister château.

Giscours Labarde-Mar r *** 70 71' 75' **76** 78' 79' **81'** 82' **83'** 85 86 87 88 89' 90 91 92 93   Splendid 182-acre third growth S of CANTENAC. Dynamically run with excellent vigorous wine in '70s; '80s less sure-footed. Second labels: Ch'x Cantelaude, Grand Goucsirs (!). Ch La Houringue is baby sister.

du Glana St-Jul r ** 81 82' 83 85 86 88 89 90 91 92 93   Big CRU BOURGEOIS in centre of ST-JULIEN. Undemanding; undramatic; value.

Gloria St-Jul r **→*** 70' 75' 76 78' 79 81 82' 83 85 86 87 88 89 90 92 93   Outstanding CRU BOURGEOIS making wine of vigour and finesse, up to classed-growths in quality. 110 acres. In '82 the owner, the late Henri Martin, bought CH ST-PIERRE. Recent return to long-maturing style. Second label: Peymartin.

Grand-Barrail-Lamarzelle-Figeac St-Em r ** 78 79 82' 83 85 86 87 88 89 90 91 **92 93**   48-acre property S of FIGEAC, incl Ch La Marzelle. Well-reputed and popular, if scarcely exciting.

Grand-Corbin-Despagne St-Em r **→*** 70 75 76 78 79 81 82' 83 85 86 88 89 90' 91 92 93   One of biggest and best GRANDS CRUS on CORBIN plateau. A new generation (of the founding Despagne family, since 1812) in '93. Also owns Ch Maison Blanche, Montagne St-Emilion.

Grand-Mayne St Em ** 82 83 85 **86** 87 88 89' 90'   40-acre Grand Cru Classé on W COTES. To watch for rich tasty wines.

Grand-Pontet St-Em r ** 82' 83 85 86' 88 89 90' 91 92 93   35 acres beside CH BEAU-SEJOUR-BECOT; both revitalized since '85.

Grand-Puy-Ducasse Pau r *** 78 79 81 82' 83 85 86 **87** 88 89' 90 91 92 93   Well-known fifth growth enlarged to 90 acres under expert management. Recent wines less steady. Second label: Ch Artigues-Arnaud.

Grand-Puy-Lacoste Pau r *** 70' 75 76 78' 79' 81' 82' 83 85' 86' 87 88' 89' 90' 91 92 93   Leading fifth growth famous for excellent full-bodied vigorous PAUILLAC. 110 acres among the 'Bages' châteaux, owned by the Borie family of DUCRU-BEAUCAILLOU. Second label: Lacoste-Borie.

Gravas Saut w sw ★★ 83' **85 86** 88 89' 90' 92 93 Small BARSAC property; impressive firm sweet wine. NB Cuvée Spéciale.

La Grave, Domaine Graves r w ★★ 85 86 88 89' 90' 91 92 93 Innovative little estate with lively reds; delicious oak-aged whites (w 87 90 93) Made at CH DE LANDIRAS by Peter Vinding-Diers.

La Grave-Trigant-de-Boisset Pom r ★★★ 75' 76' 78 79 81' 82' 83 85 86' 87 88 89' 90 92 93 Verdant château with small but first-class v'yd owned by CHRISTIAN MOUEIX. Elegant beautifully structured POMEROL.

Gressier-Grand-Poujeaux Moulis r ★★→★★★ 70 75' 78 79' 81 82 83' 85 86 87 88 89 90 91 92 93 Good CRU BOURGEOIS, neighbour of CHASSE-SPLEEN. Fine firm wine with good track record for repaying patient cellaring.

Greysac Méd r ★★ 81' 82 83 85 86 88 **89** 90 91 92 93 Elegant 140-acre property. Easy early-maturing wines popular in US.

Gruaud-Larose St-Jul r ★★★ 70' 75' 76 78' 79 81 82' 83 85 86 87 88' 89' 90' 91 92 93 One of the biggest and best-loved second growths. 189 acres. Smooth, rich, stylish claret, year after year. Owned by CORDIER. Excellent second wine: Sarget de Gruaud-Larose.

Guadet-St-Julien St-Em ★★ 75 81 82 83 85 86 87 88 89 90' 92 93 Extremely well-made wines from v small Grand Cru Classé.

Guiraud Saut w (r) sw (dr) ★★★ 76 78' 79' 80 **81 82** 83' 84 85 86' **87** 88 89' 90' 92 Restored classed-growth of top quality. 250+ acres. At best excellent sweet wine of great finesse, and a small amount of red and dry white. The 86, 88, 89 and 90 will be superb in time.

Guiteronde du Hayot Saut ★★ 75-acres in BARSAC; known for finesse and value.

La Gurgue Mar r ★★ 81 82 83' 85' 86 87 88 89' 90 91 92 93 Small, well-placed 30-acre property, for MARGAUX of the fruitiest sort. From owners of CHASSE-SPLEEN and HAUT-BAGES-LIBERAL. Alas, the inspired winemaker, Mme Villars, died in '93. To watch.

Hanteillan Cissac r ★★ 81 82' 83 85' 86 87 88' 89 90' 91 92 93 Large v'yd renovated since '73. V fair Bourgeois wine. Ch Laborde is second quality.

Haut-Bages-Averous Pau r ★★ 82' 83 85 86 87 88 89' 90 91 92 93 The second wine of CH LYNCH BAGES. Delicious easy drinking.

Haut-Bages-Libéral Pau r ★★ 78 80 82' 83 85 86' 87 88 89 90' 91 92 93 Lesser-known fifth growth of 64 acres (next to Latour) in same stable as CHASSE-SPLEEN. Results are excellent, full of PAUILLAC vitality.

Haut-Bages-Monpelou Pau r ★★ 81 82' 83 85 86 87 88 89' 90 91 92 93 25-acre CRU BOURGEOIS stable-mate of CH BATAILLEY on former DUHART-MILON land. Good minor PAUILLAC.

Haut-Bailly Graves r ★★★ 70' 78 79' 80 81' 82 83 85 86' 87 88' 89' 90' 92 93' 70-acres+ at LEOGNAN, esp for some of the best ripe, round, intelligently-made red GRAVES since '79. Second label: La Parde de Haut-Bailly.

Haut-Batailley Pau r ★★★ 66 70' 75' 78' 79 81 82' 83 85 86 87 88 89' 90' 91 92 93 Smaller part of fifth growth BATAILLEY: 49 acres. Often gentler than sister château, GRAND-PUY-LACOSTE. Second wine: La Tour-d'Aspic.

Haut-Bergey Pessac-L r ★★ 40 acres, largely Cab; fragrant delicate GRAVES.

Haut-Bommes See Clos Haut-Peyraguey.

Haut-Brignon Premières Côtes r w ★ Big producer of standard wines at Cénac, owned by major CHAMPAGNE coop. Do not confuse with the next!

Haut-Brion Pessac (Graves) r (w) ★★★★ 61 64 **70'** 71' 75' 76 78' 79' 80 81 82' 83' **84** 85' 86' **87** 88' 89' 90' 91 92 93 The oldest great château of BORDEAUX and only non-MEDOC first growth of 1855. 108 acres. Beautifully harmonious, never aggressive wine. Particularly good (and modestly priced) since '75. A little full dry white in 78 79 81 83 85 86 87 **88** 89' 90 91 92 93. See Bahans-Haut-Brion, La Mission-Haut-Brion.

Haut-Maillet Pom ★★ 82 83 85 86 88 89 90 91 92 93 12-acre sister château of LA CABANNE. Well-made gentle wines.

Haut-Marbuzet St-Est r ★★→★★★ 70 75' 76 78' 79 80 **81 82'** 83' 85' 86' 87 88 89' 90' 91 92 93' The best of many good ST-ESTEPHE CRUS BOURGEOIS. 100 acres, 60% Merlot. Second ch'x CHAMBERT-MARBUZET, MacCARTHY, MacCarthy-Moula, Tour de Marbuzet. New oak gives them classic style.

Haut-Pontet St-Em r ✱✱ Consistent 12-acre v'yd of the COTES well deserving its GRAND CRU status. 2,500 cases.

Haut-Quercus St-Em r ✱✱ 83 85 **86** 88 89' 90 92 93 Oak-aged coop wine to a v high standard.

Haut-Sarpe St-Em r ✱✱ **79 81 82 83'** 85 **86 87** 88 89 90' 91 92 93 Grand Cru Classé (6,000 cases) with elegant château and park. Same owner as CH LA CROIX, POMEROL.

Hortevie St-Jul r ✱✱ **81** 82 83 85' 86' **87** 88 89' 90' 91 92 93 One of the few ST-JULIEN CRUS BOURGEOIS. This tiny v'yd and its bigger sister TERREY-GROS-CAILLOU are shining examples.

Houissant St-Est r ✱✱ 82 83 85 **86 87** 88 89' 90' 91 92 93 Typical robust well-balanced ST-ESTEPHE CRU BOURGEOIS also called Ch Leyssac; well-known in Denmark.

d'Issan Cantenac-Mar r ✱✱✱ 70 **75'** 78 79 81 82' 83' 85 86 **87** 88 89 90' 91 92 93 Beautifully restored moated château with 75-acre third growth v'yd; fragrant, virile, delicate wine. Second label: Ch de Candale.

Kirwan Cantenac-Mar r ✱✱✱ 78 81 **82' 83'** 85 86 87 88 89' 90' 91 92 93' Well-run 86-acre third growth owned by SCHRODER & SCHYLER. Mature v'yds giving ever tastier wines. New consultant (M Rolland) since '92.

Labégorce Mar r ✱✱ 75' **78 79** 81 82' 83' 85 **86 87** 88 89' 90' 91 92 93 Substantial 69-acre property N of MARGAUX producing long-lived wines of true Margaux quality. New owner since '89.

Labégorce-Zédé Mar r ✱✱→✱✱✱ 75' 78 79 81' 82' 83' 85 86' 87 88 89' 90' 91 92 93 Outstanding CRU BOURGEOIS on road N from MARGAUX. 62 acres. Typically delicate, fragrant; truly classic since '81. Same family as VIEUX CH CERTAN. Second label: Dom Zédé. Also 23 acres of AC Bordeaux: 'Z'.

Lacoste-Borie The second wine of CH GRAND-PUY-LACOSTE.

Lafaurie-Peyraguey Saut w sw ✱✱✱ 78 80 81' **82** 83' **85** 86' **87 88** 89' 90' Fine classed-growth of only 49 acres at Bommes, belonging to CORDIER. After a lean patch, good, rich and racy wines in late '80s.

Lafite-Rothschild Pau r ✱✱✱✱ 59 75' 76' **78 79** 81' 82' 83 84 85 86' 87 88' 89' 90' 91 92 93 First growth of fabulous style and perfume in its great vintages, which keep for decades. Resplendent since '76. Amazing circular cellars opened '87; joint ventures in Chile ('88), California ('89), Portugal ('92). Second wine: CARRUADES DE LAFITE. 225 acres. Also owns CH'X LA CARDONNE, DUHART-MILON, L'EVANGILE, RIEUSSEC.

Lafleur Pom r ✱✱✱✱ 70' 75' 78 79 **81 82'** 83 85' 86' 88' 89' 90' Superb 12-acre property just N of PETRUS. Resounding wine of the tannic, less 'fleshy' kind. Same owner as LE GAY. Second wine: Pensées de Lafleur.

NB This edition introduces a new short-cut vintage category. Vintages in colour are the ones you should choose first for drinking in 1995.

Lafleur-Gazin Pom r ✱✱ 70 75' **78 79** 81 82' 83 85' 86 87 88' 89 90 92 Distinguished small J-P MOUEIX estate on the NE border of POMEROL.

Lafon-Rochet St-Est r ✱✱ **70' 79** 81 82 83' 85 86 87 88' 89' 90' 91 92 93 Fourth growth neighbour of COS D'ESTOURNEL, restored in '60s and again recently. 110 acres. Rather hard dark full-bodied ST-ESTEPHE reluctant to 'give'. Same owner as CH PONTET-CANET. Second label: Numéro 2.

Lagrange Pom r ✱✱ 70' 75' **78 81** 82' 83 85' **86** 87 88 89' 90' 92 93 20-acre v'yd in the centre of POMEROL run by the ubiquitous house of J-P MOUEIX. Rising profile for flavour/value.

Lagrange St-Jul r ✱✱✱ 70 75 79 81 82 83 84 85' 86' 87 88' 89' 90' 91 92 93 Formerly run-down third growth inland from ST-JULIEN, bought by Suntory ('83). 280 acres now in tiptop condition. A property to follow. Second wine: Les Fiefs de Lagrange (83' 85 86 87 88 **89** 90 91 92 93).

La Lagune Ludon r ✱✱✱ 70' 75' 76' 78' 79 81 82' 83' 85 86' 87 88' 89' 90' 91 92 93 Well-run ultra-modern 160-acre third growth in the extreme S of the MEDOC. Attractively rich wines with marked oak; steadily v high quality. Owned by CHAMPAGNE AYALA.

Lalande-Borie St-Jul r ** 79 81 82 83 85 86 87 88 89 90' 91 92 93   A baby brother of the great DUCRU-BEAUCAILLOU created from part of the former v'yd of CH LAGRANGE.

Lamarque Lamarque (H-Méd) r ** 82 83' 85 86' 87 88 89 90' 91 92 93   Splendid medieval fortress of the central MEDOC with 113 acres giving admirable and improving wine of high Bourgeois standard.

Lamothe Bergeron H-Méd r **   150 acres at CUSSAC making 25,000 cases of reliable claret. Run by GRAND-PUY-DUCASSE.

Landiras Graves w r ** (w) 88' 90 91 92 93   Medieval ruin in S GRAVES replanted in '80s by Peter Vinding Diers. 50 acres Sém, 15 red (88 89 90' 91 92 93). See also Domaine La Grave. Second label: Notre Dame de Landiras (B'x AC).

Lanessan Cussac (H-Méd) r **→**** 78' 79 81 82 83 85 86' 87 88' 89' 90' 91 92 93   Distinguished 108-acre CRU BOURGEOIS EXCEPTIONNEL just S of ST-JULIEN. Can be classed-growth quality. Fine rather than burly but ages v well. Same family owns châteaux de Ste-Gemme, Lachesnaye, La Providence.

Langoa-Barton St-Jul r *** 70' 75' 76 78' 79 81 82' 83 85 86' 87 88' 89' 90' 91 92 93   49-acre third growth sister château to LEOVILLE-BARTON. V old family property with impeccable standards, and value. Second wine: Lady Langoa.

Larcis-Ducasse St-Em r ** 66 78 79 81 82' 83 84 85 86 87 88' 89' 90' 91 92 93   Top property of St-Laurent, E neighbour of ST-EMILION, on CÔTES next to CH PAVIE. 30 acres in fine situation. Long-lived wines in keeping.

Larmande St-Em r ** 75' 78 79 81 82 83 85 86 87 88' 89' 90' 91 92 93   Substantial 54-acre property related to CAP-DE-MOURLIN. Replanted, re-equipped and now making rich strikingly scented wine. Second label: Ch des Templiers.

Laroque St-Em r ** 75' 78 79 81 82' 83 85 86 88 89 90 91 92 93   Important 108-acre v'yd on the ST-EMILION CÔTES in St-Christophe.

Larose-Trintaudon St-Laurent r ** 82 83 85 86 87 88 89 90' 91 92 93   The biggest v'yd in the MEDOC: 425 acres. Modern methods make reliable fruity and charming CRU BOURGEOIS wine to drink young. New management in '89 and second label Larose St-Laurent.

Laroze St-Em r ** 81 82 83 85 86 87 88' 89' 90' 91 92 93   Big v'yd (74 acres) on W CÔTES. Fine lightish wines from sandy soil; soon enjoyable.

Larrivet-Haut-Brion Graves r (w) ** 75' 76 79' 81 82' 83 85 86 87 88 89 90 91 92   Little property at LEOGNAN with perfectionist standards. Also 500 cases of barrel-fermented white to age up to 10 yrs.

Lascombes Mar r (p) *** 70' 75' 82 83 85 86 87 88' 89' 90' 91 92 93   240-acre second growth owned by British brewers Bass-Charrington, lavishly restored. After a poor patch, new vigour since '82. A second growth needs the severest standards. Second wine: Ch Segonnes.

Latour Pau r **** 61 62 64 66 67 70' 73 75' 76 78' 79 80 81 82' 83 84 85 86' 87 88' 89' 90' 91 92 93   First growth considered the grandest statement of the MEDOC. Rich, intense, almost immortal wines in great years; classical and pleasing even in weak ones. 150 acres sloping to the R Gironde. Some controversy over style in early '80s but Latour always needs time to show its hand. British-owned from '63 to '93. Now again in (private) French hands. Second wine: LES FORTS DE LATOUR.

Latour-Martillac Graves r w ** (r) 82' 83 85' 86 87 88' 89 90 91 92   Small but serious property at Martillac. 10 acres of white grapes; 37 of black. The white can age admirably (86 87 88 **89 90** 91 **92** 93'). The owner is resurrecting the neighbouring Ch Lespault.

Latour-à-Pomerol Pom r **** 70' 76 79 81 82 83 85' 86 87 88' 89' 90' 92 93   Top growth of 19 acres under MOUEIX management. POMEROL of great power and perfume, yet also ravishing finesse.

Châteaux entries also cross-refer to France section, pages 20–55.

des Laurets St-Em r ✱✱ 82 83 85 86 88 89' 90' 92 93   Major property in PUISSEGUIN-ST-EMILION and MONTAGNE-ST-EMILION (to the E) with 160 acres of v'yd on the COTES (40,000 cases). Sterling wines sold by J-P MOUEIX.

Laville-Haut-Brion Graves w ✱✱✱✱ 79 81 82 83 85' 86 87' 88 89' 90 91 92   A tiny production of one of the v best white GRAVES for long succulent maturing, made at CH LA MISSION-HAUT-BRION.

Léoville-Barton St-Jul r ✱✱✱ 61' 70' 75' 76 78' 81 82' 83 85' 86' 87 88' 89' 90' 91 92 93   90-acre portion of the great second growth Léoville v'yd in Anglo-Irish hands of the Barton family for over 150 years. Powerful classic claret; traditional methods, v fair prices. Major investment has raised already v high standards. See also Langoa-Barton.

Médoc: the class system

The Médoc has 60 crus classés, ranked in 1855 in five classes. In a separate classification it has 18 Crus Grands Bourgeois Exceptionnels and 41 Crus Grands Bourgeois (which must age their wine in barrels), and 68 Crus Bourgeois. (The terms Grand Bourgeois and Exceptionnel are not acceptable to the EC, and are therefore no longer used on labels.)

Apart from the first growths, the five classes of 1855 are now considerably jumbled in quality, with some second growths at fifth growth level and vice versa. They also overlap in quality with the Crus Exceptionnels. (Besides the official 18, another 13 châteaux are unofficially acknowledged as belonging to this category.) The French are famous for logic.

Léoville-Las-Cases St-Jul r ✱✱✱✱ 61 66' 75' 76 78' 79 81' 82' 83' 84 85' 86' 87 88 89' 90' 91 92 93'   Largest of Léovilles, next to LATOUR; 210 acres. One of highest reputations in Bordeaux. Elegant complex powerful austere wines, for immortality. Second label CLOS DU MARQUIS also outstanding.

Léoville-Poyferré St-Jul r ✱✱✱ 79 81 82' 83' 85 86' 87 88 89' 90' 91 92 93   For years the least outstanding of the Léovilles; since '80 again living up to the great name. 156 acres. Second label: Ch Moulin-Riche.

Lestage Listrac r ✱✱ 82' 83 85 86' 87 88 89' 90' 91 92 93   130-acre CRU BOURGEOIS in same hands as CH FONREAUD. Light, quite stylish wine aged in oak since '85. Second wine: Ch Caroline. Also white: La Mouette.

Lilian-Ladouys St-Est ✱✱ 89 90 91 92 93   Recent creation: a 50-acre CRU BOURGEOIS with high ambitions and real early promise. To watch.

Liot Barsac w sw ✱✱ 75' 76 82 83 85 86 88 89' 90' 92 93   Consistent fairly light golden wines from 50 acres.

Liversan St-Sauveur r ✱✱ 82' 83 85 86' 87 88' 89' 90' 91 92 93   116-acre Grand Cru Bourgeois inland from PAUILLAC. Since '84 the Polignac family has greatly improved standards. Second wine: Ch Fonpiqueyre.

Livran Méd r ✱✱ 82' 83 85 86 88' 89' 90' 91 92 93   Big CRU BOURGEOIS at St-Germain in the N MEDOC. Consistent round wines (half Merlot).

Loudenne St-Yzans (Méd) r ✱✱ 82' 83 85 86' 87' 88 89' 90 91 92 93   Beautiful riverside château owned by Gilbeys since 1875. Well-made CRU BOURGEOIS red and an increasingly delicious dry white from 120 acres. The white is best at 2–4 yrs (90 91 92' 93).

Loupiac-Gaudiet Loupiac w sw ✱✱ 85 86 87 88 89 90 91 92 93   Reliable source of value almost-SAUTERNES, just across R Garonne. 7,500 cases.

La Louvière Graves r w ✱✱✱ (r) 81 82' 83 85 86' 87 88' 89' 90' 91 92 93' (w) 86 88 89' 90' 91 92 93   Noble 135-acre LEOGNAN estate restored by the ubiquitous Lurtons. Excellent white, and classed-growth standard red.

de Lussac St-Em r ✱✱ 82 83 85 86 88 89' 90 91 92 93   One of the best estates in LUSSAC-ST-EMILION (to the NE).

Lynch-Bages Pau r (w) ✱✱✱→✱✱✱✱ 61' 66 70 75' 78' 79 81 82' 83' 84 85' 86' 87 88' 89' 90' 91 92 93'   Always popular, now a regular star. 200 acres. Rich robust wine: deliciously dense, brambly; aspiring to greatness. Second wine: HAUT-BAGES-AVEROUS. From '90, intense oaky white. Owner, J-M Cazes, also directs PICHON-LONGUEVILLE etc for AXA Insurance.

Lynch-Moussas Pau r ✱✱ 81 82 83 85 86 87 88 89 90' 91 92 93 Fifth growth restored by the director of CH BATAILLEY since '69. Now 60+ acres are making serious wine, gaining depth as the young vines age.

du Lyonnat Lussac-St-Em r ✱✱ 82 83 85 86' 88 89 90' 91 92 93 120-acre estate with well-distributed reliable wine.

MacCarthy St-Est r ✱✱ The second label of CHAMBERT-MARBUZET.

Macquin-St-Georges St-Em r ✱✱ 85 86' 88 89 90' 91 92 93 Steady producer of delicious 'satellite' ST-EMILION at ST-GEORGES.

Magdelaine St-Em r ✱✱✱ 70' 71' 73 75 76 78 82' 83' 85 86 88 89' 90' 92 93 Leading CÔTES first growth: 28 acres next to AUSONE owned by J-P MOUEIX. Beautifully balanced subtle wine: not normally the richest. Substantial new investment ('92) promises even better things.

Magence Graves r w ✱✱ Go-ahead 45-acre property in S GRAVES. Sauv Bl-flavoured dry white and fruity red. Both age well 2–6 yrs.

Malartic-Lagravière Graves r (w) ✱✱✱ (r) 82' 83 85 86' 87 88 89 90' 91 92 93' (w) 87' 88 89 90 91 92 93 Well-known LEOGNAN classed-growth of 53 acres. Well-structured rather hard red and a v little long-ageing Sauvignon white. Austere wines that need cellaring. Perhaps the style will change with new owners: LAURENT-PERRIER ('90).

Malescasse Lamarque (H-Méd) r ✱✱ 82 83 85 86 87 88 89 90 91 92 93 Renovated CRU BOURGEOIS with 100 acres in good situation. Second label: Le Tana de Malescasse. New (corporate) owners in '92. To watch.

Malescot-St-Exupéry Mar r ✱✱✱ 79 82' 83' 85 86 87 88 89 90' 91 92 93 Third growth of 84 acres. Often tough when young, eventually fragrant and stylish MARGAUX. New consultant from '90 augurs well.

de Malle Saut w r sw dr ✱✱✱ (w sw) 75 76 75 78 79 80 81' 82' 83 85 86' 87 88 89' 90' 91 93 Beautiful château with Italian gardens at Preignac. 124 acres. Vg SAUTERNES (second label: Ste Hélène); also dry white (90) and red (GRAVES) CH DU CARDAILLAN (✱✱) (88).

de Malleret H-Méd r ✱✱ 82 83 85 86 88 89' 90 92 93 An aristocrat's domaine. The Marquis du Vivier makes 25,000 cases of fine gentlemanly claret at Le Pian, among forests just N of Bordeaux.

de Marbuzet St-Est r ✱✱ Second label of COS-D'ESTOURNEL: equally reliable.

Margaux Mar r (w) ✱✱✱✱ 61' 78' 79 80 81' 82' 83' 85 86' 87 88' 89' 90' 91 92 93' First growth (209 acres), the most penetrating and fabulously perfumed of all in its (v frequent) best vintages. Pavillon Rouge (81 82' 83 84 85 86' 87 88 89 90' 91 92 93) is second wine. Pavillon Blanc is best white (Sauv) of MEDOC (79 80 81 82 83 84 85 86 87 88 89 90 91 92).

Marquis-d'Alesme See d'Alesme.

Marquis-de-Terme Mar r ✱✱→✱✱✱ 81' 82 83 85 86' 87 88' 89' 90' 91 92 93 Renovated fourth growth of 84 acres. Fragrant, fairly lean style has developed since '85, with more Cab S and more flesh.

Martinens Mar r ✱✱ 81 82 83 85 86 88 89 90 91 92 93 Worthy 75-acre CRU BOURGEOIS of the mayor of CANTENAC; new barrels since '89.

Maucaillou Moulis r ✱✱ 75' 78 79 81 82 83' 85' 86' 87 88' 89' 90' 91 92 93 130-acre CRU BOURGEOIS with CRU CLASSE standards, property of DOURTHE family. Richly fruity Cap de Haut-Maucaillou is second wine.

Mazeyres Pom r ✱✱ Consistent, useful lesser POMEROL. 5,000 cases.

Méaume Bx Supérieur r ✱✱ Englishman's domaine, N of POMEROL. Since '80 has built solid reputation for vg daily claret to age 4–5 yrs. 7,500 cases.

Meyney St-Est r ✱✱→✱✱✱ 75' 78' 79 81 82' 83 85 86 87 88' 89' 90 91 92 93 Big (125-acre) riverside property next door to CH MONTROSE with a superb situation; one of the best of many steady CRUS BOURGEOIS in ST-ESTEPHE. Owned by CORDIER. Second label: Prieur de Meyney.

Millet Graves r w (p) ✱✱ (r) 82 83 85 86 88 89 90' 92 Useful GRAVES. Second label, Clos Renon: drink young. Cuvée Henri is new oak-aged white.

La Mission-Haut-Brion Graves r ✱✱✱✱ 61 64 66 71' 74 75' 76 78' 79 80 81 82' 83 84 85' 86 87 88 89' 90' 91 92 Neighbour and long-time rival to CH HAUT-BRION; since '84 in same hands. New equipment in '87. Serious grand old-style for long maturing; 'bigger' wine than H-B. 30 acres.

Monbousquet St-Em r ✶✶ 78' 79' 81 82 83 85' 86 88' **89'** 90' 93   Attractive early-maturing wine from deep gravel soil: lasts well. Second label: Ch Caperot 91 92'.

Monbrison Arsac-Mar r ✶✶ 81 82 83 **84 85** 86 87 88' 89' 90 91 92 93   A new name to watch. Top Bourgeois standards. 4,000 cases plus 2,000 of second label, Ch Cordet. Sadly an inspired winemaker died in 92.

Montrose St-Est r ✶✶✶ 61 66 70' 75' 76 78' 79 81 82' 83 84 85 86' 87 88 89' 90' 91 92 93   158-acre family-run second growth well-known for deeply coloured forceful old-style claret. Vintages 79–85 (except 82) were lighter, but recent Montrose is almost ST-ESTEPHE's answer to CH LATOUR. Second wine: La Dame de Montrose.

Moulin du Cadet St-Em ✶✶ 75' 81 82' 83 85 **86** 88 89' 90' 92 93   Little v'yd on the COTES, owned by J-P MOUEIX. Fragrant medium-bodied wines.

Moulin-à-Vent Moulis r ✶✶ 81 82' 83 85' 86 **87** 88 89' 90' 91 92 93   60-acre property in the forefront of this booming AC. Lively forceful wine. LA TOUR-BLANCHE (MEDOC) has same owners.

Moulinet Pom r ✶✶✶ 82 83 85 86 87 88 89' **90** 92 93   One of POMEROL's bigger châteaux, 45 acres on lightish soil; wine lightish too.

Mouton-Baronne-Philippe See d'Armailhac.

Mouton-Rothschild Pau r ✶✶✶✶ 61 62' 66' 70' 71 75' 76 78 81 82' 83' 85' 86' 87 88' 89' 90' 91 92 93   Officially a first growth since '73, though for 40 yrs worthy of the title. 175 acres (87% Cab S) make majestic rich wine (also, from '91, white Aile d'Argent). Also the world's greatest museum of art relating to wine. Baron Philippe, the foremost champion of the MEDOC, died in '88. His daughter Philippine now reigns. See also Opus One, California.

Nairac Saut w sw ✶✶ 73 75 76' **78** 79 **80** 81 82 83' 85 86' 87 88 89 90' 92 93   Perfectionist BARSAC classed-growth. Wines to lay down for a decade.

Nenin Pom r ✶✶✶ 70' 75' 76 78 82 83 85' 86 87 88' 89 90 93   Well-known 66-acre estate; on a (v necessary) but slow upswing since '85.

d'Olivier Graves r w ✶✶ (r) 82 83 **84 85** 86 87 88 89' 90' 91 92 93 (w) 90 91 92 93   90-acre classed-growth, surrounding a moated castle at LEOGNAN. 9,000 cases red, 12,000 white. New broom in '89 has not upgraded quality as drastically as necessary.

Les Ormes-de-Pez St-Est r ✶✶✶→✶✶✶✶ 75' 78' 79 81 82' 83' 85 86' 87 88 89' 90' 91 92   Outstanding 72-acre CRU BOURGEOIS owned by CH LYNCH-BAGES. Increasingly notable full-flavoured ST-ESTEPHE.

Les Ormes-Sorbet Méd r ✶✶ 78 79 81 82' 83 85' 86' 87 88 89 90' 91 92 93   Emerging 10,000-case producer of good stylish red aged in new oak at Couquèques. A leader of the N MEDOC. Second label: Ch de Conques.

Palmer Cantenac-Mar r ✶✶✶✶ 61' 66' 70 71' 75' 76 78' 79' 81 82 83' 84 85 86' 87 88' 89 90 91 92 93   The star of CANTENAC: a third growth often of nearly first growth quality. Wine of power, flesh, delicacy and much Merlot. 110 acres with Dutch, British (Peter A Sichel) and French owners. Second wine: Réserve du Général.

Pape-Clément Graves r (w) ✶✶✶ 75' 83 85' 86' 87 88' 89' 90' 92 93'   Ancient v'yd with record of seductive, scented, not ponderous reds. Early '80s poor: dramatic new resolve (and more white) since '85.

de Parenchère r (w) ✶✶ 89 90   Steady supply of useful AC Ste-Foy Bordeaux from handsome château with 125 acres.

Patache d'Aux Bégadan (Méd) r ✶✶ 82' 83' 85 86 88 89' 90' 91 92 93   90-acre CRU BOURGEOIS of the N MEDOC. Fragrant largely Cab wine with the earthy quality of its area.

Paveil (de Luze) Mar r ✶✶ 81 82' 83' 85 86' 87 88' 89' 90 91 92 93   Old family estate at SOUSSANS. Small but highly regarded.

Pavie St-Em r ✶✶✶ 78 79' 81 82' 83' 85 86' 87 88' 89' 90' 92 93'   Splendidly-sited first growth; 92 acres mid-slope on the COTES. Rich and tasty and on top form since '82. PAVIE-DECESSE and La Clusière in same family.

Pavie-Decesse St-Em r ✶✶→✶✶✶   24 acres seriously challenging their big brother (above).

Pavie-Macquin St-Em r ****→***** 82 83 85' 86 87 88 89 90 91 92 Another Pavie challenge; this time the neighbours up the hill. 25-acre COTES v'yd E of ST-EMILION. Fine organic winemaking. Second label: Les Chênes.

Pavillon Rouge (Blanc) du Château Margaux See Ch Margaux.

Pedesclaux Pau r ****** 82' 83 85 86 87 88 89 90' 91 92 93 50-acre fifth growth on the level of a good CRU BOURGEOIS. Solid strong wines that Belgians love. Second labels: Bellerose, Grand-Duroc-Milon.

Petit-Village Pom r ******* 75' 78 79 81 82' 83 85' 86 87 88 89' 90' 91 92 Top property revived. 26 acres next to VIEUX CHATEAU CERTAN, same owner (AXA) as CH PICHON-LONGUEVILLE since '89. Powerful plummy wine.

Pétrus Pom r ******** 61 64 66 67 70' 71' 75' 78 79' 80 81 82' 83 84 85' 86 87 88' 89' 90 92 93 The great name of POMEROL. 28 acres of gravelly clay giving massively rich and concentrated wine. 95% Merlot vines. Each vintage adds lustre (NB no 91). The price too is legendary.

Peyrabon St-Sauveur r ****** 82' 83 85 86' 87 88 89' 90' 91 92 93 Serious 132-acre CRU BOURGEOIS popular in the Low Countries. Also La Fleur-Peyrabon (only 12 acres).

Peyre-Labade Listrac ****** Second label of CH CLARKE.

Peyreau St-Em r ****** Sister château of Clos l'Oratoire.

de Pez St-Est r ******* 70' 75' 76 78' 79 81 82' 83 85 86' 87 88 89 90' 91 92 93' Outstanding CRU BOURGEOIS of 60 acres. As reliable as any of the classed-growths of the village if not as fine.

Phélan-Ségur St-Est r ****** 75' 81 82' 85 86 87 88' 89' 90' 91 92 93 Big and important CRU BOURGEOIS (125 acres): some fine old vintages. 83 84 had to be withdrawn, but from '86 has gone from strength to strength.

Pibran Pau r ****** 88 89' 90' 91 92 93 Small CRU BOURGEOIS allied to PICHON-LONGUEVILLE. V classy wine with real PAUILLAC drive.

Pichon-Lalande (formerly Pichon-Longueville, Comtesse de Lalande) Pau r ******** 61 66 70' 75' 76 78' 79' 81 82' 83' 84 85' 86' 87 88 89' 90' 91 92 93 'Super-second' growth neighbour to CH LATOUR. 148 acres. Consistently among v top performers; long-lived wine of fabulous breed for those who like it luscious, even in lesser yrs. Second wine: Réserve de la Comtesse. Rivalry across the road (next entry) is worth watching.

Pichon-Longueville (formerly Baron de Pichon-Longueville) Pau r *****→****** 78 79' 81 82' 83 85 86' 87 88 89' 90' 91 92 77-acre second growth: wines have varied widely. Since '87 owned by AXA Insurance, run by J-M Cazes (LYNCH-BAGES). Revitalized winemaking matches aggressive building works. Second label: Les Tourelles de Longueville.

Le Pin Pom r ******** 82 83 85 86 87 88 89 90' A mere 500 cases of Merlot, with same owners as VIEUX CHATEAU CERTAN. A perfectionist miniature.

Pindefleurs St-Em r ****** 79 81 82' 83 85 86 88 89 90' 92 93' Steady 23-acre v'yd on light soil. Second label: Clos Lescure.

St-Emilion: the class system

St-Emilion has its own class system, revised in 1985. At the top are 2 Premiers Grands Crus Classés 'A': Châteaux Ausone and Cheval Blanc. Then come 9 Premiers Grands Crus Classés 'B'. 63 châteaux were elected as Grands Crus Classés (seeking re-election in 1994). Another 170-odd are classed simply as Grands Crus, a rank renewable each year after official tastings. St-Emilion Grand Cru is therefore the very approximate equivalent of Médoc Crus Bourgeois and Grand Bourgeois.

Pique-Caillou Graves r ****** 85' 86 88' 89 90' 91 92 93 Nr Bordeaux airport. Refurbished; ripe seductive GRAVES. Also next-door Ch Chênevert.

de Pitray Castillon r ****** 82 83 85 86 87 88 89 90 91 92 93 Large (62-acre) v'yd on COTES DE CASTILLON E of ST-EM. Good flavoursome chewy wines.

Plagnac Méd r ****** 82 83 85 86 88 89' 90' 91 92 93 CRU BOURGEOIS at Bégadan restored by CORDIER. To follow.

Plince Pom r ****** 75 79 81 82 83 85 86 88 89' 90 92 Reputable 20-acre property nr Libourne. Attractive lightish wine from sandy soil.

La Pointe Pom r ★★→★★★ 82 83' 85 86 **87** 88 89' 90' 92 Prominent 63-acre estate; well-made wines, but relatively spare of flesh. New consultant in '86. LA SERRE is in the same hands.

Pontac-Monplaisir Graves r (w) ★★ 87 89 90 91 92 93 Another GRAVES property offering delicious white and fragrant light red.

Pontet-Canet Pau r ★★★ 81 82' 83 85 86' 87 88 89' 90' 91 92 93 182-acre neighbour to MOUTON-R. Dragged its feet for many yrs. Owners (same as LAFON-ROCHET) have done better since '85. Should make v fine wines: tannin has been the problem. Second label: Les Hauts de Pontet.

Pontoise-Cabarrus H-Méd r ★★ Useful and improving 60-acre CRU BOURGEOIS at ST-SEURIN. Wines need 5–6 yrs.

Potensac Méd r ★★ 78' 79 81' 82' 83 85' 86 87 88 89' 90' 91 92 93 Best-known CRU BOURGEOIS of N MEDOC. Neighbouring ch'x Lassalle and Gallais-Bellevue and LEOVILLE-LAS-CASES all owned by Delon family. Class shows.

Pouget Mar ★★ 78 81 82' 83 85 86 87 88 89 90 91 92 93 19-acres attached to BOYD-CANTENAC. Same owners since 1906. Similar, rather lighter wines.

Poujeaux (Theil) Moulis r ★★ 70' 75' **76** 78 79' 81 82' 83' 85' 86 87 88' 89' 90' 91 92 93' Family-run CRU EXCEPTIONNEL of 120 acres. 20,000-odd cases of characterful tannic and concentrated wine for a long life. Second label: La Salle de Poujeaux. Also Ch Arnauld.

Prieuré-Lichine Cantenac-Mar r ★★★ 70 75 78' 82' 83' 85 86' 87 88 89' 90' 91 92 93 143-acre fourth growth brought to the fore by the late Alexis Lichine. Excellent full fragrant MARGAUX. Second wine: Clairefont.

Puy-Blanquet St-Em r ★★ 75' 82' 83 85 86 88 89' 90' 92 93 The major property of St-Etienne-de-Lisse, E of ST-EMILION, with over 50 acres. Early-maturing St-Em in early '80s; now firming up well.

Puygueraud Côte de Francs r ★★ 85 86 88 89' 90 92 93 Leading château of this rising district. Wood-aged wines of surprising class. Ch Laclaverie and Les Charmes-Godard follow the same lines.

Rabaud-Promis Saut w sw ★★ 83' 85 86' 88' 89' 90 74-acre classed-growth at Bommes. To follow since '86.

Rahoul Graves r w ★★ (r) 82 83 85 86 88 89' 90' 91 92 37-acre v'yd at Portets making particularly good wine in the '80s from maturing vines; 80% red. White also oak-aged.

Ramage-la-Bâtisse H-Méd r ★★ 82 83' 85 86 88 **89'** 90 91 92 93 Potentially outstanding CRU BOURGEOIS of 130 acres at ST-SAUVEUR, N of PAUILLAC. Increasingly good since '85. Ch Tourteran is second wine.

Rausan-Ségla Mar r ★★★ 70' 82 83' 84 85 86' 88' 89' 90' 91 92 93 106-acre second growth famous for its fragrance; a great MEDOC name trying successfully to regain its rank since '82. New owners in '89 and again in '94. To watch: second wine Ségla.

Rauzan-Gassies Mar r ★★ 75' 78' 82 83 85 86 88 89' 90' 92 93 75-acre second-growth neighbour of the last with little excitement to report for two decades, now perking up – but still far to go.

Raymond-Lafon Saut w sw ★★★ 75' 76 78 79 80' 81 82 83' 85 86' 87 88 89' 90' 91 92 Serious SAUTERNES estate of 44 acres run by the ex-manager of YQUEM. Splendid wines for long ageing. Among the top Sauternes.

de Rayne-Vigneau Saut w sw ★★★ 76' 83 85 86' 88 89 90' 91 92 164-acre classed-growth at Bommes. Standard sweet wine and dry Rayne Sec.

Respide-Médeville Graves w (r) ★★ (w) 86 87 88 89 **90** 91 92' 93 One of the better unclassified white châteaux. Full-flavoured wines for ageing. (NB Cuvée Kauffman.) Drink the reds at 2–4 yrs.

Reynon Premières Côtes r w ★★ 100 acres for fragrant white from old Sauv vines (VIEILLES VIGNES) (90 91 92 93'); serious red (85 **86** 88' **89** 90 91 92 93). Second wine (red): Ch Reynon-Peyrat. See also Clos Floridène.

Reysson Vertheuil (H-Méd) r ★★ 82' 83 85 86 **87** 88 89' 90' Recently replanted 120-acre CRU BOURGEOIS in Japanese hands.

Ricaud Loupiac w sw (r dr) ★★ (w) 81 82 83' 85 86' 88 89 90 91 92 Substantial grower of almost SAUTERNES-like wine just across the river. New owners are working hard. It ages well.

Rieussec Saut w sw ★★★ 71' 75' 80 81 82 83' 85 86' 87 88' 89' 90' 91 92 93
Worthy neighbour of CH D'YQUEM with 136 acres in Fargues, bought in
'84 by the (Lafite) Rothschilds. Not the sweetest; can be exquisitely
fine. Also dry 'R' and super-wine Crème de Tête.

Ripeau St-Em r ★★ 81 82 83 85 86 87 88 89 90 Steady GRAND CRU in the
centre of the plateau. 40 acres.

La Rivière Fronsac r ★★ 82 83 85' 86 87 88' 89 90 The biggest and most
impressive FRONSAC property. Tannic but juicy wines win prizes in
youth and stay young for a decade.

de Rochemorin Graves r (w) ★★ 82 83 85 86 87 88 89' 90' 91 92 93 An
important restoration at Martillac by CH LA LOUVIERE's owner: 165 acres
of maturing vines promise great things. Oaky whites to keep 4–5 yrs.

Romer-du-Hayot Saut w sw ★★ 81 82 83 85 86' 88 89' 90 Classed-growth
with a growing reputation. La Guiteronde (BARSAC) is sister château.

de Roquetaillade-la-Grange Graves r w ★★ 89 90 91 92 93 Substantial
estate: fine red (S) GRAVES and well-made white. See Cap de Mourlin.

Roudier Montagne-St-Em r ★★ 75-acre 'satellite': classic ST-EMILION flavour.

Rouget Pom r ★★ 75' 76' 78 79 81 82 83' 85' 86 88 89' 90 Attractive old
estate on the N edge of POMEROL. Good, without polish; needs age.

Royal St-Emilion Brand name of the important and dynamic growers'
coop. See also Berliquet, Haut-Quercus.

Ruat-Petit-Poujeaux Moulis r ★★ 82 85 86 88 89 90 91 92 93 45-acre v'yd
gaining in reputation for vigorous wine, to drink in 5–6 yrs.

St-André-Corbin St-Em r ★★ 79' 81 82' 83 85' 86 88 89 90 92 54-acre
estate in MONTAGNE- and ST-GEORGES-ST-EMILION: long record of above
average wines.

St-Bonnet Méd r ★★ 82 83 85 86 89 90 91 92 93 Big N MEDOC estate at St-
Christoly. V flavoury wine.

St-Estèphe, Marquis de St-Est r ★ 82 86 88 89 90 93 The growers' coop;
bigger but not as interesting as formerly.

St-Georges St-Georges-St-Em r ★★ 82 85' 86 87 88' 89' 90' 92 93 Noble
18th-C château overlooking the ST-EMILION plateau from the hill to the
north. 125 acres. Vg wine sold direct to the public.

St-Georges-Côte-Pavie St-Em r ★★ 82 83' 85' 86 88' 89' 90' 92 Perfectly
placed little v'yd on the COTES. Run with dedication.

St-Pierre St-Jul r ★★★ 70' 78' 81' 82' 83' 85 86' 87 88' 89' 90' 91 92 93
Small (42-acre) fourth growth bought in '82 by the late Henri Martin of
CH GLORIA. V stylish and consistent classic ST-JULIEN.

de St-Pierre Graves w (r) ★★ Main-line white of notable character and
flavour to drink young or keep. Also red.

de Sales Pom r ★★★ 75' 82' 83 85 86 88 89' 90' 92 Biggest v'yd of POMEROL
(116 acres), attached to grandest château. Rarely poetry, but good
lucid prose. Second labels: ch'x Chantalouette, du Delias.

Saransot-Dupré Listrac r (w) ★★ 86 88 89 90 92 93 Small property
performing well since '86. Also one of Listrac's growing band of whites.

Sénéjac H-Méd r (w) ★★ 78 79 81 82' 83' 85 86' 87 88 89' 90' 91 92 93
60-acre CRU BOURGEOIS in S MEDOC run with zeal by a New Zealander.
All-Sém white to age (89 90 91 92 93). Second label: Dom de l'Artigue.

La Serre St-Em r ★★ 75 81 82 83 85 86 88' 89 90 92 93 Small GRAND CRU,
same owner as LA POINTE. Reliably tasty.

Siaurac Lalande de Pom r ★★ Substantial, consistent; nr POMEROL. 57 acres.

Sigalas-Rabaud Saut w sw ★★★ 75 76' 79 80 82 83' 85 86 87 88' 89' 90'
91 92 The smaller part of the former Rabaud estate: 34 acres in
Bommes making first-class sweet wine in a rich grapey style.

Siran Labarde-Mar r ★★ 70 75' 78' 81 82' 83 85 86 88 89' 90' 74-acre
property approaching CRU CLASSE quality.

Smith-Haut-Lafitte Graves r (w p) ★★ (r) 82' 85 86 89' 90' 91 92 93 (w: age
2–3 yrs) Classed-growth at Martillac: 122 acres (14 of white). New
ambitious owners in '90. Formerly light wines now much more
concentrated. Second label: Les Hauts de Smith.

Sociando-Mallet H-Méd r ✹✹ 70 75 78 79 81 82' 83 85' 86' 88' 89' 90' 91 92
Splendid CRU GRAND BOURGEOIS at ST-SEURIN. 65 acres. Conservative big-
boned wines to lay down for yrs. Second wine: Lartigue-de-Brochon.

Soudars H-Méd r ✹✹ Sister to COUFRAN; new CRU BOURGEOIS doing v well.

Soutard St-Em r ✹✹✹ 70' 71 75' 76 78' 79 81 82' 83 85' 86 87 88' 89' 90' 91
92 93 Excellent 48-acre classed-growth, 60% Merlot. Potent; long-
lived, exciting young to French palates. Second label: Clos de la Tonnelle.

Suduiraut Saut w sw ✹✹✹ 67 70 76' 78 79' 81 82' 83' 84 85 86 88' 89' 90'
One of the best SAUTERNES, in its best vintages supremely luscious. 173
acres potentially of top class. Selection: Cuvée Madame (82 83 86 89).

du Tailhas Pom r ✹✹ 5,000 cases. POMEROL of the lighter kind, near FIGEAC.

Taillefer Pom r ✹✹ 81 82 83 85 86 88' 89 90 92 28-acre property on the
edge of POMEROL owned by the Armand Moueix family (see also
Fonplégade). 10 yrs is plenty.

Talbot St-Jul (w) ✹✹✹ 78' 79 81 82' 83' 85' 86' 87 88' 89' 90 91 92 93
Important 240-acre fourth growth, sister to GRUAUD-LAROSE. Wine
similarly attractive: rich, satisfying, reliable and gd value. Vg second
label: Connétable Talbot. White is 'Caillou Blanc'.

Tayac Soussans-Mar r ✹✹ 82 83 85 86 87 88 89 90 92 93 MARGAUX's biggest
CRU BOURGEOIS. Reliable if not noteworthy.

de Terrefort-Quancard Bx r w ✹✹ Huge producer of good value wines at
ST-ANDRE-DE-CUBZAC on the road to Paris. Rocky subsoil contributes to
surprising quality. 33,000 cases. Drink at 2–5 yrs.

Terrey-Gros-Caillou St-Jul ✹✹ 79 82' 83 85 86' 87 88 89 90 91 92 93
Sister-château to HORTEVIE; at best equally noteworthy and stylish.

du Tertre Arsac-Mar r ✹✹ 70' 79' 81 82' 83' 85 86 87 88' 89' 90' 91 92 93
Fifth growth isolated S of MARGAUX; restored to its proper status by the
owner of CALON-SEGUR. Fragrant and long-lived.

Tertre-Daugay St-Em r ✹✹✹ 82' 83' 85 86 87 88' 89' 90' 92 Small, spectacularly sited GRAND CRU. Restored to proper rank by owner of LA GAFFELIERE.

Le Tertre-Rôteboeuf St-Em ✹✹→✹✹✹✹ 85 86 87 88' 89' 90' 91 92 93 A new
star making concentrated, even dramatic, largely Merlot wine since
'83. The 'roast beef' of the name gives the idea.

Thieuley E-Deux-Mers r p w ✹✹ Substantial supplier esp of clairet (rosé)
and grapey Sauv Bl. But reds are aged in oak.

Timberlay Bx r (w) ✹ 185 acres at ST-ANDRE-DE-CUBZAC. Pleasant light wines
to age 2–5 yrs. Same owners as VILLEMAURINE.

Toumilon Graves r w ✹✹ Little château in St-Pierre-de-Mons to note.
Fresh and charming red and white.

La Tour-Blanche Saut w (r) sw ✹✹✹ 81' 82 83' 85 86 87 88' 89' 90' 91 92 93
Historic leader of SAUTERNES, now a government wine college. Coasted
in '70s; hit historic form again in '88.

La Tour-de-By Bégadan (Méd) r ✹✹ 79' 81 82' 83 85' 86 87 88' 89' 90' 91
92 93 V well-run 144-acre CRU BOURGEOIS in N MEDOC steadily increasing
its reputation for sturdy, impressive yet instantly appealing wine.

La Tour-Carnet St-Laurent r ✹✹ 82 83 85 86 88 89' 90 91 92 93' Fourth
growth with medieval fortress, long neglected. Light wine (bolder
since '86). Second wine: Sire de Comin.

La Tour-Figeac St-Em r ✹✹ 79 81 82' 83 85 86 88 89' 90' 34-acre GRAND
CRU between CH FIGEAC and POMEROL. Wines should be more striking.

La Tour-Haut-Brion Graves r ✹✹✹ 70 75 78 79 81 82' 83 85 86 87 88 89 90 91
92 93 Formerly second label of CH LA MISSION-HAUT-BRION. Up to '83 a
plainer, v tannic wine for long life. Now a separate v'yd: easier wines.

La Tour-Haut-Caussan Méd r ✹✹ Ambitious small (23-acre) estate at
Blaignan attracting admiration.

La Tour-du-Haut-Moulin Cussac (H-Méd) r ✹✹ 81 82' 83 85' 86' 87 88' 89'
90' 91 92 93 Conservative producer of intense wine: top CRUS BOURGEOIS.

For key to grape variety abbreviations, see pages 6–9.

La Tour-de-Mons Soussans-Mar r ✶✶ 70' 82' 83 85 86' 88' 89' 90' 91 92 Famous CRU BOURGEOIS of 87 acres, 3 centuries in the same family. A long dull patch but new wines look better.

Tour du Pas St-Georges St-Em r ✶✶ Wine from 40 acres of ST-GEORGES-ST-EMILION made by AUSONE winemaker. V stylish; to follow.

La Tour-du-Pin-Figeac St-Em r ✶✶ 26-acre GRAND CRU worthy of restoration.

La Tour-du-Pin-Figeac-Moueix St-Em r ✶✶ 81 82 83 85 86 88' 89' 90' 92 Another 26-acre section of the same old property, owned by the Armand Moueix family. Splendid site; powerful wines.

La Tour-St-Bonnet Méd r ✶✶ 82' 83 85 86 87 88 89' 90' 91 92 Consistently well-made potent N MEDOC from St-Christoly. 100 acres.

Tournefeuille Lalande de Pom r ✶✶ 81' 82' 83' 85 86 88 89 90' 91 92 93 Best-known château of NEAC. 43 acres; sound wine. Also Ch de Bourg.

des Tours Montagne-St-Em r ✶✶ 82 85 86 88 89 90 92 93 Spectacular château with modern 170-acre v'yd. Sound easy wine.

Toutigeac, Domaine de E-Deux-Mers r (w) ✶ 89 90 91 92 93 Enormous producer of useful Bordeaux at Targon.

Tronquoy-Lalande St-Est r ✶✶ 70 79 81 82' 83 85 86 88 89 90 92 93 40-acre CRU BOURGEOIS; typical high-coloured, ageable ST-EST. DOURTHE-distributed.

Troplong-Mondot St-Em r ✶✶→✶✶✶✶ 82' 83 85' 86 87 88' 89' 90' 92 93 70 acres well-sited on the COTES above CH PAVIE (and in the same family). Now run with passion. To follow. Second wine: Mondot.

Trotanoy Pom r ✶✶✶✶ 61' 70' 71' 75' 76' 78 79 81 82 83 84 85' 86 87 88 89 90' 92 93 Usually the second POMEROL, after PETRUS, from the same stable. Only 27 acres; but at best a glorious fleshy perfumed wine.

Trottevieille St-Em r ✶✶✶ 79' 81 82' 83 85' 86 87 88 89' 90 92 93 GRAND CRU of 27 acres on the COTES. Dragged its feet for yrs. Same owners as BATAILLEY have raised their sights since '85. To watch.

Le Tuquet Graves r w ✶✶ 89 90 91 92 93 Big estate at Beautiran. Light fruity wines; the white better. (Cuvée Spéciale oak-aged.)

Verdignan Méd r ✶✶ 81 82 83 85 86 87 88 89' 90 91 92 Substantial Bourgeois sister to CH COUFRAN. More Cab than Coufran.

Vieux Château Certan Pom r ✶✶✶ 78 79 81 82' 83' 85 86' 87 88' 89' 90' 92 93 Traditionally rated close to PETRUS in quality, but totally different in style; almost HAUT-BRION build. 34 acres. Same (Belgian) family owns LABEGORCE-ZEDE and tiny POMEROL, Le Pin. See also Puygueraud.

Vieux-Château-St-André St-Em r ✶✶ 79' 81 82' 83 85' 86 87 88' 89' 90' 91 92 93' Small v'yd in MONTAGNE-ST-EMILION owned by the leading winemaker of Libourne. To follow. 2,500 cases.

Villegeorge Avensan r ✶✶ 82 83' 85 86 87' 88 89 90 92 93 24-acre CRU BOURGEOIS N of MARGAUX; same owner as BRANE-CANTENAC. Enjoyable rather tannic wine. Sister château: Duplessis (Hauchecorne).

Villemaurine St-Em r ✶✶ 82' 83 85' 86 87 88 89 90 91 92 93 Small GRAND CRU with splendid cellars well-sited on the COTES by the town. Firm wine with a high proportion of Cab.

Vray-Croix-de-Gay Pom ✶✶ 75' 82' 83 85 86 88 89 90 92 V small ideally situated v'yd in the best part of POMEROL. Needs devotion.

Yon-Figeac St-Em r ✶✶ 81 82 83 85 86 88 89 90 59-acre GRAND CRU to follow for savoury wine.

d'Yquem Saut w sw (dr) ✶✶✶✶ 67' 71' 73 75' 76' 77 78 79 80' 81' 82' 83' 84 85 86' 87 88' 89' (90' 91 93 to come) The world's most famous sweet-wine estate. 250 acres; only 500 bottles per acre of v strong intense luscious wine, kept 4 yrs in barrel. Most vintages improve for 15 yrs+. Also dry Ygrec ('Y') in 78 79 80 84 85 (86 v little) 87 88 89 91 92.

More Bordeaux châteaux are listed under Canon-Fronsac, Côtes de Bourg, Côtes de Castillon, Côtes de Francs, Fronsac, Lalande de Pomerol, Loupiac, Premières Côtes de Blaye, Premières Côtes de Bordeaux, St-André-de-Cubzac, Ste-Croix-du-Mont in the A–Z of France, pages 20–55.

Bordeaux's 'second wines'

Bordeaux's top châteaux have for centuries offered a Grand Vin and a second selection. The practice was revived in the 1960s by Château Latour with its remarkable Les Forts de Latour. Increasing yields and prosperity, especially in the 1980s, made the need for strict selection obvious. Most top châteaux started 'second wines', usually very good value. The following is a list of those worth looking out for (big brothers listed alongside).

Amiral de Beychevelle – CH BEYCHEVELLE

Artiges-Arnaud – CH GRAND-PUY-DUCASSE

Bahans Haut-Brion – CH HAUT-BRION

Baron de Brane/Notton – CH BRANE-CANTENAC

La Bastide Dauzac – CH DAUZAC

Beau-Mayne – CH COUVENT DES JACOBINS

Benjamin de Beauregard – CH BEAUREGARD

Le Bonnat – CH FIEUZAL

de Candale – CH D'ISSAN

Cantelaude – CH GISCOURS

Canuet – CH CANTENAC-BROWN

Cap de Haut-Maucaillou – CH MAUCAILLOU

Caroline – CH LESTAGE

Carruades de Lafite – CH LAFITE-ROTHSCHILD

Chambert-Marbuzet – CH HAUT-MARBUZET

Chantalouette and du Delias – CH DE SALES

Château Caperot – CH MONBOUSQUET

Château Grand Goucsirs – CH GISCOURS

Château Roquefort – CH TERTRE-DAUGAY

Château des Templiers – CH LARMANDE

Les Chênes PAVIE-MACQUIN

Clairefont – CH PRIEURE-LICHINE

Le Clémentin du Pape-Clément – CH P-CLEMENT

Clos de la Gravette VIEUX CHATEAU CERTAN

Clos J Kanon – CH CANON

Clos Labère – CH RIEUSSEC

Clos Lescure – CH PINDEFLEURS

Clos du Marquis CH LEOVILLE-LAS-CASES

Clos de la Tonnelle – CH SOUTARD

La Closerie de Camensac – CH CAMENSAC

Connétable de Talbot – CH TALBOT

de Conques – CH LES ORMES-SORBET

Cordet – CH MONBRISON

La Croix-Beaucaillou – CH DUCRU-BEAUCAILLOU

Les Cyprès – CH CLIMENS

La Dame de Montrose – CH MONTROSE

Diane de Belgrave – CH BELGRAVE

Dom de l'Artigue – CH SENEJAC

Dom de Compostelle – CH LA CABANNE

Dom de Martialis – CH CLOS FOURTET

Dom Zédé – CH LABEGORCE-ZEDE

Duluc – CH BRANAIRE-DUCRU

Ermitage de Chasse-Spleen – CH CH SPLEEN

Les Fiefs de Lagrange – CH LAGRANGE

Fonpiqueyre – CH LIVERSAN

Les Forts de Latour – CH LATOUR

Franck Phélan – CH PHELAN-SEGUR

Grand Parc – CH LEOVILLE-LAS-CASES

Grangeneuve – CH FIGEAC

Haut-Bages-Averous – CH LYNCH-BAGES

Haut-Bommes – CH CLOS HAUT-PEYRAGUEY

Les Hauts de Pontet – CH PONTET-CANET

Les Hauts de Smith – CH SMITH-HAUT-LAFITTE

l'Hospitalet – CH GAZIN

L de Louvière – CH LA LOUVIERE

Lacoste-Borie – CH GRAND-PUY-LACOSTE

Lady Langoa – CH LANGOA-BARTON

Lamouroux – CH RAUSAN-SEGLA

Larose St-Laurent – CH LAROSE-TRINTAUDON

Lartigue-de-Brochon – CH SOCIANDO-MALLET

Ludon-Pomiès-Agassac – CH LA LAGUNE

MacCarthy – CH CHAMBERT-MARBUZET

Mademoiselle de St-Marc – CH LA TOUR BLANCHE

de Marbuzet – CH COS-D'ESTOURNEL

Marquis de Ségur – CH CALON-SEGUR

Maurens – CH FOMBRAUGE

Mayne-Lévêque – CH CHANTEGRIVE

Mondot – CH TROPLONG-MONDOT

Moulin d'Arvigny – CH BEAUMONT

Moulin de Duhart – CH D-MILON-ROTHSCHILD

Moulin-Riche – CH LEOVILLE-POYFERRE

Moulinet-Lasserre – CH CLOS RENE

Moulins de Citran – CH CITRAN

Notre Dame de Landiras – CH LANDIRAS

Numéro 2 – CH LAFON-ROCHET

La Parde de Haut-Bailly – CH HAUT-BAILLY

Pavillon Rouge – CH MARGAUX

Pensées de Lafleur – CH LAFLEUR

Le Petit Cheval – CH CHEVAL BLANC

La Petite Eglise – CH L'EGLISE-CLINET

Peymartin – CH GLORIA

Peyre-Labade – CH CLARKE

Prieur de Meyney – CH MEYNEY

Les Reflets du Ch Cissac – CH CISSAC

Réserve de la Comtesse – CH PICHON-LALANDE

Réserve du Général – CH PALMER

Reynon-Peyrat – CH REYNON

St-Paul de Dominique – CH LA DOMINIQUE

Ste-Hélène – CH DE MALLE

La Salle de Poujeaux – CH POUJEAUX-THEIL

Sarget de Gruaud-Larose – CH G-LAROSE

Ségla – CH RAUSAN-SEGLA

Segonnes – CH LASCOMBES

Sire de Comin – CH TOUR-CARNET

Le Tana de Malescasse – CH MALESCASSE

La Tour-d'Aspic – CH HAUT-BATAILLEY

La Tour-Léognan – CH CARBONNIEUX

Les Tourelles de Longueville – CH PICHON-L

Tourteran – CH RAMAGE-LA-BATISSE

Villeneuve de Cantemerle – CH CANTEMERLE

Italy

1992 was probably the turning point in the reputation and fortunes of the Italian wine industry, whose genial chaos has always tended to mask its real values and qualities. January 23 that year saw the enactment of a completely revised version of the seriously discredited DOC legislation, which for 30 years has caused confusion among consumers and militated against both quality and innovation.

'Law 164' is intended to end all the old anomalies, but especially that by which a vino da tavola, officially the lowest grade of wine classification, was frequently a much better and more expensive) wine than one made within the statutory requirements of a DOC – or even a DOCG, formerly the most elevated appellation available.

Eventually (though this will take many years) the new laws will bring Italian appellations very close in spirit to those of France, where all the stress is on geography – or 'terroir'. They are also intended (like the French laws) to discourage the marketing of high quality wines simply by grape variety name.

Law 164 is most graphically represented by a pyramid, whose base is the humble vino da tavola. No geographical (or varietal) claims can be made at this level: only a brand name. The next level is a new institution, intended to mirror the French vin de pays and known as IGT (Indicazione Geografica Tipica). IGTs use a geographical name and can also use the name of a locally authorized grape. Above IGTs come DOCs and DOCGs. These can label information as specific as a single vineyard (vigna) name – but only by producing less: sacrificing quantity for quality.

Thus the highest rank in the pyramid will be a vigna wine from a DOCG zone. But whereas the rank of DOCG was formerly limited to a dozen famous areas, it will now become the right of any DOC which has performed well enough for five years. Conversely a DOC which functions half-heartedly will lose its rank (some 50 are already threatened). Even more radically, an outstanding proprietorial wine 'which does honour to Italy' may be eligible for its own DOCG status. Some are already well on the way.

A distinct advantage of the pyramid system is that producers in a DOC zone can decide at vintage time how high they are going to pitch their wine. Self-discipline can give them the right to the top appellation; high yields and lower concentration will automatically demote them down the pyramid.

There is very much more detail to the new Law, and much that only experience will finally determine, but it is a convincingly bold attempt to sort out the minestrone of the old system. No doubt the German government will pay due heed.

Meanwhile, as always, the best advice is to be bold. Do not cling limply to familiar names. This edition is packed with new creations: some thrillingly good – some (Italy is Italy) merely cosmetic. But be prepared to pay more for quality.

The following abbreviations are used in the text:

Ab	Abruzzi	**F-VG**	Friuli-Venezia Giulia
Ap	Apulia	**Lat**	Latium
Bas	Basilicata	**Lig**	Liguria
Cal	Calabria	**Lom**	Lombardy
Cam	Campania	**Mar**	Marches
E-R	Emilia-Romagna	**Pie**	Piedmont

Sar	Sardinia
Si	Sicily
T-AA	Trentino-Alto Adige
Tus	Tuscany
Umb	Umbria
VdA	Valle d'Aosta
Ven	Veneto
fz	frizzante
pa	passito

Abbazia di Rosazzo ★★★ Leading estate of COLLI ORIENTALI. White Ronco delle Acacie and R di Corte and red R dei Roseti are vg single-v'yd wines.

Abboccato Semi-sweet.

Adanti ★★ Umbrian maker of good red SAGRANTINO DI MONTEFALCO, VDT BIANCO D'ARQUATA and Rosso d'Arquata (a vg BARBERA-Canaiolo-MERLOT blend). Also good CAB S. Value.

Aglianico del Vulture Bas DOC r dr (s/sw sp) ★★★ 82 85 86 87 88 90 91 92 93 Among the best wines of S Italy. Ages well to rich aromas. Called vecchio after 3 yrs, RISERVA after 5. Top growers: FRATELLI D'ANGELO (also makes vg pure Aglianico VDT Canneto), Paternoster.

Alba Major wine centre of PIEDMONT, on R Tanaro, S of Turin.

Albana di Romagna E-R DOCG w dr s/sw (sp) ★★(★) DYA Italy's first DOCG for white wine, though it is hard to see why. Albana is the grape. Cold fermentation now robs it of what little character it had. FATTORIA PARADISO makes some of the best. AMABILE is often better than dry. FATTORIA ZERBINA's botrytis-sweet PASSITO is outstanding.

Alcamo Si DOC w ★ Soft neutral whites. Rapitalà is the best brand.

Aleatico Excellent red Muscat-flavoured grape, for sweet, aromatic, strong dessert wines, chiefly of the south. Aleatico di Puglia DOC (best grower, Candido) is better and more famous than A di Gradoli (Lat) DOC.

Alezio Ap DOC p (r) ★★ (r) 91 92 93 Recent DOC at Salento, esp for delicate rosé. Top grower: Calò Michele (who also makes good barrel-aged NEGROAMARO VDT, Vigna Spano).

Allegrini ★★★ Top quality producer of Veronese wines, incl fine VALPOLICELLA from prime new v'yds and vg AMARONE.

Altare ★★★ Reputed small producer of modern BAROLO and BARBERA VDT Vigna Larigi.

Altesino ★★ Top estate for BRUNELLO DI MONTALCINO and VDT Palazzo Altesi.

Alto Adige T-AA DOC r p w dr sw sp ★→★★★ DOC covering 20 different wines, usually named after grape varieties, in 33 German-speaking villages around Bolzano. Best are white. Region often called Südtirol.

Ama, Castello di, (or Fattoria di Ama) ★★★★ One of the best, most consistent modern CHIANTI CLASSICO estates, nr Gaiole. San Lorenzo, Bertinga, La Casuccia and Bellavista are top single-v'yd wines. Also vg VDTs, CHARD, SAUV, MERLOT (Vigna L'Apparita), PINOT N (Il Chiuso).

Amabile Semi-sweet, but usually sweeter than ABBOCCATO.

Amaro Bitter. When prominent on label, content is not wine but 'bitters'.

Amarone High-octane version of VALPOLICELLA; potent dry impressive and long-lived, from air-dried grapes. See also Recioto.

Amarone della Valpolicella Ven DOC ★★★→★★★★ 81 83 84 85 86 88 90 93 Best from ALLEGRINI, BERTANI, Brigaldara, Corte Sant Alda, DAL FORNO, GUERRIERI-RIZZARDI, LE RAGOSE, MASI, QUINTARELLI, San Rustico, Serègo Alighieri, Speri.

Anghelu Ruju Port-like version of Sardinian CANNONAU from SELLA & MOSCA.

Anselmi, Roberto ★★★ A leader in SOAVE with his single-v'yd Capitel Foscarino and exceptional sweet dessert RECIOTO dei Capitelli.

Antinori, Marchesi L & P Immensely influential long-established Tuscan house of the highest repute, now wholly owned by Piero A, producing first-rate CHIANTI CLASSICO (esp PEPPOLI, Tenute Marchese Antinori, Villa Antinori and Badia a Passignano), Umbrian (CASTELLO DELLA SALA) and PIEDMONT (PRUNOTTO) wines. Distinguished for pioneering new VDT styles, eg TIGNANELLO, SOLAIA (Tuscany), CERVARO DELLA SALA (Umbria). Marchese Piero A was called the Voice of Italy in world wine circles in the 1970s and '80s. See also Prunotto.

Aquileia F-VG DOC r w ★★ (r) 88 89 90 91 92 93 12 single-grape wines from around town of Aquileia on border of Slovenia. Good REFOSCO.

Argiano ★★★ Top MONTALCINO producer, owned by Noemi Marone Cinzano. Esp for BRUNELLO and ROSSO.

Argiolas, Antonio Important Sardinian producer with astonishing quality. Vg: CANNONAU, NURAGUS, VERMENTINO and red VDT Turriga.

Arneis Pie w ★★→★★★ DYA At last a white worthy of BAROLO country. A revival of an ancient grape to make fragrant light wine. Now DOC under ROERO, a zone N of Alba, and recently as LANGHE. Good from Castello di Neive, CERETTO (Blangé), Correggia, Deltetto, BRUNO GIACOSA, Malabaila, Malvirà, Marengo-Marenda, Angelo Negri, VIETTI, Gianni Voerzio.

Artimino ★★ Ancient hill-town W of Florence. Fattoria di A produces top DOCG CARMIGNANO.

Assisi Umb r (w) ★★ DYA Rosso and Bianco di Assisi are v attractive VDT. Drink cool.

Asti Major wine centre of PIEDMONT.

Asti (Spumante) Pie DOCG w sp ★★→★★★ NV Immensely popular sweet and v fruity Muscat sparkling wine, now updated to DOCG with raised standards. V low in alcohol. Can be delicious at dessert. Top producers: BERA, CINZANO, FONTANAFREDDA, GANCIA, MARTINI & ROSSI.

Attems, Conti Famous old COLLIO estate with range of good typical wines (esp PINOT GRIGIO). Now run by Collavini.

Avignonesi ★★★ MONTEPULCIANO house with range of good wines: VINO NOBILE, blended red Grifi, top CHARD, SAUV, MERLOT and superlative VIN SANTO.

Azienda agricola/agraria A farm producing crops, often incl wine.

Azienda/casa vinicola Wine firm using bought-in grapes and/or wines.

Azienda vitivinicola A (specialized) wine estate.

Badia a Coltibuono ★★→★★★ Fine CHIANTI-maker in an old abbey at Gaiole with a restaurant and collection of old vintages. Also produces VDT SANGIOVETO (82 83 85 86 88 90 93).

Banfi (Castello or Villa) ★★→★★★ The production department of the biggest US importer of Italian wine. Huge plantings at MONTALCINO, mostly SANGIOVESE, but also Syrah, PINOT N, CAB, CHARD, SAUV etc, are part of a drive for quality plus quantity. BRUNELLO is good but 'Poggio all'Oro' is ★★★★. Centine is ROSSO DI MONTALCINO. In PIEDMONT Banfi produces vg sparkling Banfi Brut, Principessa GAVI, BRACCHETTO D'ACQUI, PINOT GR.

Barbacarlo Lom r dr sw sp ★★ Delicate wines with typical bitter-almond taste, from OLTREPO PAVESE.

Barbaresco Pie DOCG r ★★★→★★★★ 85' 86 87 88' 89' 90' 93 Neighbour of BAROLO from the same grapes. Perhaps marginally less sturdy. At best palate-cleansing, deep, subtle and fine. At 4 yrs becomes RISERVA. Producers incl CERETTO, CIGLIUTI, GAJA, BRUNO GIACOSA, Marchesi di Gresy, MOCCAGATTA, Nada, Pelissero, PIO CESARE, Produttori del B, PRUNOTTO, Alfredo Roagna, BRUNO ROCCA, Sottimano.

Barbatella, Cascina La ★★★ Top producer of BARBERA D'ASTI: excellent single-v'yd Sonvico and dell'Angelo.

Barbera Dark acidic red grape, the second most planted in Italy after SANGIOVESE, a speciality of PIEDMONT also used in Lombardy, Emilia-Romagna and other northern provinces. Its best wines follow...

Barbera d'Alba Pie DOC r ★★→★★★ 85' 86 87 88' 89' 90' 91 92 93 Tasty tannic fragrant red. SUPERIORE can age 7 yrs or more. Round ALBA, NEBBIOLO is sometimes added to make a VDT (some barrique-aged 100% BARBERA is also vdt). Top producers incl A CONTERNO, GAJA, GRASSO, G MASCARELLO, PRUNOTTO, Scavino, VIETTI, VOERZIO.

Barbera d'Asti Pie DOC r ★★→★★★ 85' 86 87 88' 89' 90' 91 92 93 For real BARBERA-lovers: solely Barbera grapes, tangy and appetizing, drunk young or aged up to 7 yrs or longer. Top growers incl La Barbatella, Bava, Bertelli, BOFFA, BRAIDA, Brema, Cascina Castlét, Chiarlo, COPPO, SCARPA, Trinchero, Viarengo.

Barbera del Monferrato Pie DOC r ★→★★★ DYA Easy-drinking BARBERA from Alessandria and ASTI. Pleasant, slightly fizzy, s'times sweetish.

Barberani ★★ Leading ORVIETO producer; Calcaia is sweet, botrytis-affected.

Barco Reale Tus DOC r ★★ DOC for junior wine of CARMIGNANO; same grapes.

Bardolino Ven DOC r (p) ★★ DYA Pale light slightly bitter red from E shore of Lake Garda. Bardolino CHIARETTO is even paler and lighter. Top makers: GUERRIERI-RIZZARDI, Fratelli Zeni.

81

Barolo Pie DOCG r ★★★→★★★★★ 79' 82' 85' 86 88' 89' 90' 93 Small area S of ALBA with one of Italy's supreme reds: rich, tannic alcoholic (min 13°), dry but wonderfully deep and fragrant (also crisp and clean) in the mouth. From NEBBIOLO grapes. Ages for up to 15 yrs (RISERVA after 5).

Top Barolo producers incl Altare, Cavallotto, Ceretto, Clerico, Conterno, Conterno-Fantino, Cordero, Gaya, Giacosa, Elio Grasso, Silvio Grasso, G Manzone, Mascarello, A Oberto, Parusso, Pio Cesare, Prunotto, Ratti, Rocche dei Manzoni, Sandrone, Scavino, Fratelli Seghesio, Vietti, Voerzio.

Bellavista ★★★ FRANCIACORTA estate rivalling CA'DEL BOSCO for brisk subtle sparkling. Also notable Crémant. Good VDT reds from CAB and PINOT N.

Bera, Fratelli ★★ Family estate. Vg MOSCATO D'ASTI.

Berlucchi, Guido Italy's biggest producer of sparkling METODO CLASSICO, at FRANCIACORTA. Steady quality.

Bertani ★★ Well-known producers of quality Veronese wines (VALPOLICELLA, AMARONE, SOAVE, etc).

Bertelli ★★★ Good small PIEDMONT producer: BARBERA D'ASTI, VDT CAB, CHARD.

Biancara, La ★★★ FRIULI grapes are used here to make number one quality GAMBELLARAS. (ZONIN makes number one quantity.)

Bianco White.

Bianco d'Arquata Umb w ★★ DYA See Adanti.

Bianco di Custoza Ven DOC w (sp) ★→★★★ DYA Twin of SOAVE from W of Verona.

Bianco di Pitigliano Tus DOC w ★ DYA Soft fruity lively wine from nr Grosseto.

Biancolella ISCHIA's best white. A VDT from D'AMBRA.

Bigi, Luigi & Figlio Famous producers of ORVIETO and other wines of Umbria and Tuscany. Their TORRICELLA v'yd produces vg dry Orvieto.

Biondi-Santi ★★→★★★★★ The original producer of BRUNELLO DI MONTALCINO, from 45-acre Il Greppo v'yd. Prices are v high but old vintages unique.

Boca Pie DOC r ★★ 85 88 90 91 92 93 From same grape as BAROLO (NEBBIOLO) in N of PIEDMONT. Look for Poderi ai Valloni.

Boffa, Alfiero Small estate for top BARBERA D'ASTI. Esp single-v'yd wines.

Bolla Famous Veronese firm producing VALPOLICELLA, SOAVE, etc. Top wines: Castellaro (one of the v best SOAVES), Creso (red and white), Jago.

Bonarda Minor red grape (alias Croatina) widely grown in PIEDMONT, Lombardy, Emilia-Romagna and blended with BARBERA.

Bonarda (Oltrepò Pavese) Lom DOC r ★★ Soft fresh often FRIZZANTE red from S of Pavia.

Borgo del Tiglio ★★★ FRIULI estate for one of NE Italy's top MERLOTS: VDT Rosso della Centa; also good are COLLIO CHARD, TOCAI and BIANCO.

Boscarelli, Poderi ★★★ Small estate with vg VINO NOBILE DI MONTEPULCIANO, barrel-aged VDT Boscarelli and good ROSSO DI M.

Brachetto d'Acqui Pie DOC r sw (sp) ★★ DYA Sweet sparkling red with enticing Muscat scent.

Braida see Bricco dell'Uccellone.

Bramaterra Pie DOC r ★★ 85 88 89 90 91 92 93 Neighbour to GATTINARA. NEBBIOLO grapes predominate in a blend.

Breganze Ven DOC ★→★★★ (r) 85 86 87 88 90 91 92 93 A catch-all for many varieties around Vicenza. CAB and PINOT BL are best. Top producers: B Bartolomeo, MACULAN.

Bricco Term for a high (and by implication vg) ridge v'yd in PIEDMONT.

Bricco del Drago Pie vdt 85 86 88 89 90 93 Original long-lived blend of DOLCETTO and NEBBIOLO from Cascina Drago.

Bricco Manzoni Pie r ★★ 82' 85' 88' 89' 90' 91 92 93 V successful blend of NEBBIOLO and BARBERA from Monforte d'Alba.

Bricco dell'Uccellone Pie r ★★★ 85 86 87 88 89 90 91 92 93 Barrique-aged BARBERA from the firm of the late Giacomo Bologna. Bricco della Bigotta and Ai Suma are others.

Brindisi Ap DOC r ★★ Strong NEGROAMARO. Esp Patriglione (★★★) from Taurino.

Brunello di Montalcino Tus DOCG r ★★★→★★★★ 82' 83' 85' 86 88' 90' 91 92 93 With BAROLO, Italy's most celebrated red: strong, full-bodied, high-flavoured and long-lived. 4 yrs' ageing, after 5 becomes RISERVA. Montalcino is 25 miles S of Siena.

Good Brunello di Montalcino producers include Altesino, Argiano, Banfi, Fattoria dei Barbi, Biondi-Santi, Caparzo, Case Basse, Casanova di Neri, Cerbaiona, La Chiesa di Santa Restituta, Col d'Orcia, Costanti, Eredi Fuligni, Lisini, Pacenti, Ciacci Piccolomini, Poggio Antico, Poggione, Salvioni, Talenti. See also Rosso di Montalcino (value).

Brusco dei Barbi Tus r ★★ 88 89 90 91 92 93 Lively variant on BRUNELLO using old CHIANTI GOVERNO method.

Bukkuram Celebrated Moscato di Pantelleria from De Bartoli.

Cà del Bosco ★★★★ FRANCIACORTA estate making some of Italy's v best sparkling wine, CHARD, and excellent reds (see Zanella).

Cabernet Sauvignon Much used in NE Italy and increasingly (esp in VDT) in Tuscany, PIEDMONT and the south.

Cafaggio, Villa ★★ Solid CHIANTI CLASSICO estate. Good red VDT: Solatio Basilica.

Caldaro or Lago di Caldaro T-AA DOC r ★→★★★ DYA Alias KALTERERSEE. Light soft slightly bitter-almond red from SCHIAVA grapes. CLASSICO from a smaller area is better. From a huge area.

Caluso Passito Pie DOC w sw (fz) ★★ Made from Erbaluce grapes; delicate scent, velvety taste. Tiny production. Best from Bianco, Ferrando.

Candido, Francesco ★★ Top grower of Salento, Puglia; good reds: Duca d'Aragona, Cappello del Prete, SALICE SALENTINO; vg dessert wine: ALEATICO DI PUGLIA.

Cannonau di Sardegna Sar DOC r (p) dr s/sw ★★ 88 89 90 91 92 Cannonau (Grenache) is Sardinia's basic red grape; its wine often formidably strong (min 13.5% alcohol for DOC), but mild in flavour.

Cantalupo, Antichi Vigneti di Top GHEMME wines from the Arlunno family – esp single-v'yd Breclemae and Carellae.

Cantina Cellar or winery.

Cantina Sociale (CS) Growers' coop.

Capannelle ★★★ Good producer of VDT (formerly CHIANTI CLASSICO), nr Gaiole.

Caparzo, Tenuta ★★★ MONTALCINO estate with excellent BRUNELLO La Casa; also CHARD and red blend Ca'del Pazzo.

Capezzana, Tenuta di (or Villa) ★★→★★★ The Tuscan estate (W of Florence) of the Contini Bonacossi family. Excellent CHIANTI Montalbano and CARMIGNANO. Also vg Bordeaux-style red, GHIAIE DELLA FURBA.

Capri Cam DOC r p w ★→★★ Famous island with widely abused name. But some interesting wines from La Caprense.

Carema Pie DOC r ★★→★★★ 85 88 89 90 91 92 93 Old speciality of N PIEDMONT. Best from Luigi Ferrando (or the CANTINA SOCIALE).

Carignano del Sulcis Sar DOC r p ★★→★★★ 85' 86 87' 88' 89 90 91 92 93 Well-structured red with capacity for ageing. Best: Terre Brune from CANTINA SOCIALE di Santadi.

Carmignano Tus DOCG r ★★★ 85 86 88 90 91 92 93 Section of CHIANTI using 10% CAB to make reliably good, and some v fine, wine. Good producers: Ambra, Artimino, CAPEZZANA, Poggiolo.

Carpenè Malvolti Leading producer of classic PROSECCO and other sparkling wines at Conegliano, Veneto.

Carso F-VG DOC r w ★★→★★★ 88 89 90 91 92 93 DOC nr Trieste incl good MALVASIA. Terrano del C is a REFOSCO red. Top grower: Edi Kante.

Casa fondata nel... Firm founded in...

Casalte, Fattoria Le ★★★ Good VINO NOBILE DI MONTEPULCIANO from the Barioffi family; also ROSSO and white VDT Celius.

Casanova di Neri ★★★ BRUNELLO DI MONTALCINO (and vg ROSSO DI M) from the Neri family; better every year.

Cascina Castlet ★★→★★★ Conc BARBERA PASSITO, VDT Passum, vg BARBERA D'ASTI.

Case Basse ✱✱✱ Small estate with v impressive BRUNELLO and VDT Intistieti.

Case Bianche, Le ✱✱ Reliable estate nr Conegliano (Ven) for PROSECCO, SAUV and surprising Wildbacher (from ancient Austrian red grape).

Castel del Monte Ap DOC r p w ✱✱ (r) 88 90 91 92 93 Dry fresh well-balanced southern wines. The red is RISERVA after 3 yrs. Rosé most widely known. RIVERA's Il Falcone stands out.

Castell'in Villa ✱✱✱ Vg CHIANTI CLASSICO estate.

Castellare ✱✱→✱✱✱ Small but admired CHIANTI CLASSICO producer with first-rate SANGIOVESE VDT I Sodi di San Niccoló and sprightly GOVERNO del Castellare, a modern version of old-style CHIANTI.

Castello d'Albola Old CHIANTI CLASSICO estate owned by ZONIN. Average.

Castello di Cacchiano ✱✱✱ First-rate CHIANTI CLASSICO estate at Gaiole. Outstanding RISERVA 'Millenio'.

Castello di Farnetella ✱✱ Estate between CHIANTI CLASSICO and MONTEPULCIANO where Giuseppe Mazzocolin of FELSINA makes vg SAUV and Chianti Colli Senesi.

Castello della Sala ✱✱✱ ANTINORI's estate at ORVIETO. Borro is the regular white. Top wine is Cervaro della Sala: CHARD and GRECHETTO aged in oak. Muffato della S is one of Italy's best botrytis wines.

Castello di San Polo in Rosso ✱✱✱ CHIANTI CLASSICO estate with first-rate red VDT Cetinaia (aged in standard casks, not barriques).

Castello di Uzzano Famous old CHIANTI CLASSICO estate at Greve. Quality declining recently.

Castello di Verrazzano ✱✱ Important CHIANTI CLASSICO estate near Greve.

Castello di Volpaia ✱✱ First-class CHIANTI CLASSICO estate at Radda, with elegant, rather light Chianti and VDT red Balifico, which contains CAB, and all-SANGIOVESE COLTASSALA.

Castelluccio ✱✱✱ Best SANGIOVESE of Emilia-Romagna from Baldi family: VDT Ronco dei Cigliegi and Ronco della Simia.

Cavalleri ✱✱→✱✱✱ FRANCIACORTA's No 3, after CA DEL BOSCO and BELLAVISTA, vg SPUMANTE.

Cavallotto ✱✱→✱✱✱ Reliable BAROLO estate: esp Barolo Vigna San Giuseppe.

Càvit (Cantina Viticoltori) Group of good quality coops near Trento. Wines incl MARZEMINO, CAB, PINOTS N, BL and GR, NOSIOLA. Top wines: Brume di Monte (red and white) and sparkling Graal and Firmato.

Cerasuolo Ab DOC p ✱✱ The ROSATO version of MONTEPULCIANO D'ABRUZZO.

Cerasuolo di Vittoria Si r ✱→✱✱✱ 88 89 90 91 92 93 Cherry-red from southern Sicily: best from COS, Giuseppe Coria's is a fine matured non-DOC version.

Ceretto ✱✱✱ Vg grower of BARBARESCO (Bricco Asili), BAROLO (Bricco Rocche), top BARBERA D'ALBA (Piana), CHARD (La Bernardina), DOLCETTO and ARNEIS.

Cervaro See Castello della Sala.

Chardonnay Has recently joined permitted varieties for several N Italian DOCs (eg T-AA, FRANCIACORTA, F-VG). Some of the best (eg from ANTINORI, FELSINA, GAJA, LUNGAROTTI) are still only VDT.

Chianti Tus DOCG r ✱→✱✱ 90 91 92 93 The lively local wine of Florence and Siena. Fresh fruity and tangy, still sometimes sold in straw-covered flasks. Mostly made to drink young. Of the subdistricts, RUFINA and Colli Fiorentini can make CLASSICO-style RISERVAS. Montalbano, Colli Senesi, Aretini and Pisani make lighter wines.

Chianti Classico Tus DOCG r ✱✱→✱✱✱ 88 89 90 91 92 93 (Riserva) 83 85 86 88 90 93 Senior CHIANTI from the central area. Its old pale astringent style is becoming rarer as top estates opt for either darker tannic wines or softer and fruitier ones. Some are among the best wines of Italy. Members of the Consorzio use the badge of a black rooster, but several top firms do not belong.

To decipher codes, please refer to symbols key at front of book, and to 'How to use this book' on page 5.

Outstanding Chianti Classico producers incl Ama, Bibbiano, Cacchiano, Capaccia, Casa Emma, Castel Ruggero, Castellare, Castell'in Villa, Coltibuono, Felsina, Fonterutoli, Fontodi, Isole e Olena, Querciabella, La Massa, Le Filigare, Le Masse di San Leolino, Lilliano, Palazzino, Paneretta, Poggerino, Rampolla, Riecine, Rocca di Castagnoli, Rodano, San Fabiano Calcinaia, San Giusto, Valtellina, Vecchie Terre di Montefili, Verrazzano, Vignamaggio, Volpaia.

Chianti Putto Tus DOCG r *→*** DYA From a league of producers outside the CLASSICO zone. The neck-label, a pink cherub, is now rarely seen.

Chiaretto Rosé (the word means 'claret') produced esp around Lake Garda. See Bardolino, Riviera del Garda.

Chiesa di Santa Restituta *** Estate for admirable BRUNELLO DI MONTALCINO, vg ROSSO DI M and red VDT Pian de Cerri.

Chionetti **→**** Makes best DOLCETTO DI DOGLIANI (look for Briccolero).

Ciacci Piccolomini *** Vg BRUNELLO DI MONTALCINO (best is Vigna di Pianrosso) and ROSSO DI M.

Cigliuti, Renato *** Small top estate for BARBARESCO.

Cinqueterre Lig DOC w dr sw pa ** Fragrant fruity white from steep coast nr La Spezia. PASSITO is known as SCIACCHETRA (**→***). Good from De Batte, Coop Agricola di Cinqueterre, Forlini & Cappellini, F Giusti.

Cinzano Major Vermouth company also known for its ASTI from PIEDMONT, and Florio MARSALA. Now owned by Grand Met.

Cirò Cal DOC r (p w) ** 87 88 89 90 91 92 93 V strong red from Gaglioppo grapes; fruity white (to drink young). Best are from LIBRANDI (Duca San Felice), San Francesco (Donna Madda and Ronco dei Quattroventi) and Caparra & Siciliani.

Classico Term for wines from a restricted area within the limits of a DOC. By implication, and often in practice, the best of the district. Applied to sparkling wines it denotes the classic method.

Clerico, Domenico Constantly evolving PIEDMONT wines; the aim is for international flavour. Esp good for BAROLO.

Col d'Orcia *** Top estate of MONTALCINO with interesting VDT. Best wine is BRUNELLO (look for Poggio al Vento).

Colle Picchioni ** Estate S of Rome making the best MARINO white; also red (CAB-MERLOT) VDT, Vigna del Vassallo, perhaps Latium's best.

Colli Hills. Occurs in many wine-names.

Colli Berici Ven DOC r p w ** (r) 88 90 91 92 93 Hills S of Vicenza. CAB is the best wine. Top producer is Villa Dal Ferro.

Colli Bolognesi E-R DOC r p w ** (w) DYA (r) 85 86 87 88 90 91 92 93 SW of Bologna. 8 wines, 5 grape varieties. TERRE ROSSE is top estate (***).

Colli Euganei Ven DOC r w dr s/sw (sp) *→*** DYA A DOC SW of Padua for 7 wines. Red is adequate; white and sparkling soft and pleasant. Best producers: Vignalta (***), Cà Lustra.

Colli Orientali del Friuli F-VG DOC r w dr sw **→**** 88 89 90 91 92 93 20 different wines (18 named after their grapes) on hills E of Udine. Whites esp are vg. Top producers: ABBAZIA DI ROSAZZO, BORGO DEL TIGLIO, DORIGO, Livon, RONCO DEL GNEMIZ, Torre Rosazza, VOLPE PASINI.

Colli Piacentini E-R DOC r p w *→** DYA DOC incl traditional GUTTURNIO and Monterosso Val d'Arda among 11 types grown S of Piacenza. Good fizzy MALVASIA. Most wines FRIZZANTE.

Colli del Trasimeno Um DOC r w *→** 90 91 92 93 Often lively wines from Perugia. Best from: La Fiorita, Marella, MARTINI & ROSSI, Morolli.

Collio F-VG DOC r w **→**** 88 89 90 91 92 93 19 wines, 17 named after their grapes, from a small area on the Slovenian border. Vg whites, esp SAUV, PINOT BIANCO and PINOT GRIGIO. Best from: La Castellada, L FELLUGA, GRAVNER, JERMANN, Primosic, Radikon, SCHIOPETTO, VILLA RUSSIZ.

Coltassala Tus r *** 85 86 87 88 90 93 Notable VDT red of SANGIOVESE from the ancient CHIANTI CLASSICO estate of CASTELLO DI VOLPAIA at Radda.

Conterno, Aldo ✶✶✶✶ Legendary grower of BAROLO, etc, at Monforte d'Alba. Good GRIGNOLINO, FREISA, vg CHARD 'Printanier' and 'Bussia d'Oro'. Best BAROLOS are Cicala and Colonello. Barrel-aged NEBBIOLO VDT 'Favot' vg.

Conterno, Giacomo ✶✶✶✶ Top grower of BAROLO etc at Monforte d'Alba. Monfortino Barolo is long-aged, rare, outstanding.

Conterno-Fantino ✶✶✶ Three young families making vg BAROLO etc at Monforte d'Alba.

Contratto PIEDMONT firm known for ASTI, BAROLO, etc.

Contini, Attilio Famous producer of VERNACCIA DI ORISTANO; best is vintage blend 'Antico Gregori'.

Contucci, Conti ✶✶→✶✶✶ Ancient esteemed makers of VINO NOBILE DI MONTEPULCIANO.

Copertino Ap DOC r (p) ✶✶ 87 88 89 90 91 92 93 Savoury age-worthy red wine of NEGROAMARO from the heel of Italy. Look for the RISERVA from the CANTINA SOCIALE.

Coppo Ambitious producers of BARBERA D'ASTI (eg 'Pomorosso').

Cordero di Montezemolo-Monfalletto ✶✶ Tiny maker of good BAROLO.

Cortese di Gavi See Gavi. (Cortese is the grape.)

Corzano & Paterno, Fattoria di ✶✶ Dynamic CHIANTI Colli Fiorentini estate. Vg RISERVA, red VDT Corzano and outstanding VINSANTO.

Costanti, Conti ✶✶✶ Tiny estate for top quality BRUNELLO DI MONTALCINO.

D'Ambra Top producer of ISCHIA wines, esp excellent white BIANCOLELLA ('Piellero' and single-v'yd 'Frassitelli').

D'Angelo Leading producers of admirable DOC AGLIANICO DEL VULTURE. Barrel-aged Aglianico VDT Canneto also vg.

Dal Forno, Romano ✶✶✶ Very high quality VALPOLICELLA and AMARONE from perfectionist grower, bottling only best: 8,000 bottles from 20 acres.

Darmagi Pie r ✶✶✶✶ 82 83 **85 86 87** 88 89 90 91 92 93 CAB S from GAJA in BARBARESCO is one of PIEDMONT's most discussed VDT reds.

Decugnano dei Barbi Top ORVIETO estate with an ABBOCCATO version known as 'Pourriture Noble', and a good red VDT.

Di Majo Norante Lone star of Molise on the Adriatic with vg Biferno DOC MONTEPULCIANO and white Falanghina under the Ramitello label. Also lighter, more aromatic Molf. Fine value. To watch for new ideas.

Dolce Sweet.

Dolceacqua See Rossese di Dolceacqua.

Dolcetto ✶✶→✶✶✶ PIEDMONT's earliest ripening grape, for v attractive everday wines: dry, young-drinking, fruity, fresh, with deep purple colour. Gives its name to several DOCs D d'Acqui, D d'Alba, D di Diano d'Alba (also Diano DOC), D di Dogliani (CHIONETTI and Pecchenino are top growers) and D di Ovada (best from Abbazia di Vallechiara). Dolcetto is made by most BAROLO and BARBARESCO growers.

Donnafugata Si r w ✶✶ Zesty Sicilian whites (best are Vigna di Gabri, Damaskino). Also sound red. Was VDT, now in DOC Contessa Entellina.

Donnaz VdA DOC ✶✶ 85 88 89 90 91 92 93 A mountain NEBBIOLO, fragrant pale and faintly bitter. Aged for a statutory 3 yrs. Now part of the VALLE D'AOSTA regional DOC.

Dorigo, Girolamo ✶✶✶ Top COLLI ORIENTALI DEL FRIULI producer for outstanding white VDT 'Ronc di Juri', CHARD, dessert VERDUZZO and PICOLIT, red Pignolo, REFOSCO, Schioppettino, VDT Montsclapade.

Duca Enrico See Duca di Salaparuta.

Duca di Salaparuta ✶✶→✶✶✶ Popular Sicilian wines. Sound dry reds, pleasant soft whites. Excellent barrique red called Duca Enrico (✶✶✶ 85 86 87 88 89 90 91 92 93) is one of the best reds of Sicily.

Elba Tus r w (sp) ✶ DYA Decent dry red. The island's white is drinkable with fish.

Enfer d'Arvier VdA DOC r ✶✶ 90 91 93 Alpine speciality (see Donnaz); pale pleasantly bitter light red.

Enoteca Wine library. There are many, the impressive original being the Enoteca Italiana of Siena. Also used for wine shops or restaurants.

Erbaluce di Caluso See Caluso Passito.

Est! Est!! Est!!! Lat DOC w dr s/sw ★ DYA Unextraordinary white from Montefiascone, N of Rome. Trades on its odd-ball name.

Etna Si DOC r p w ★→★★ (r) 88 89 90 91 92 93 Wine from volcanic slopes. Red is warm, full, balanced and can age well; white is distinctly grapey.

Falchini ★★ Producer of good DOCG VERNACCIA DI SAN GIMIGNANO and the best reds of the district, eg VDT Campora.

Falerno del Massico Cam DOC r w ★★ 88 **89 90** 91 92 As Falernum, the best-known wine of ancient times. Strong red from AGLIANICO, fruity white from Falanghina. Good producer: VILLA MATILDE.

Fara Pie DOC r ★★ 85 88 **89 90** 91 92 93 Good NEBBIOLO wine from Novara, N PIEDMONT. Fragrant; worth ageing. Small production. Best is Dessilani's Caramino.

Farneta, Tenuta ★★→★★★ Nr Siena but outside CHIANTI CLASSICO, an estate for pure SANGIOVESE VDT: eg Bongoverno (★★★) and Bentivoglio (★★★).

Faro Si DOC r ★★ 88 89 90 91 92 93 Strong Sicilian red from the Straits of Messina. Made only (and rather well) by Bagni.

Favorita Pie w ★→★★ DYA Dry fruity white making friends in BAROLO country. From eg Negro, Sant'Orsola, VOERZIO.

Fazi-Battaglia Well-known producer of VERDICCHIO, etc. White Le Moie VDT is pleasant. Also owns Fassati (VINO NOBILE DI MONTEPULCIANO).

Felluga Brothers Livio and Marco (RUSSIZ SUPERIORE) have separate companies in the COLLIO and COLLI ORIENTALI. Both are highly esteemed.

Felsina-Berardenga ★★★→★★★★ CHIANTI CLASSICO estate with famous RISERVA Vigna Rancia and VDT Fontalloro.

Ferrari Cellars making some of Italy's best dry sparkling wines nr Trento, TRENTINO-ALTO ADIGE. Giulio Ferrari RISERVA is best.

Fiano di Avellino Cam w ★★→★★★ 91 92 93 Considered the best white of Campania. MASTROBERARDINO's Vignadora is best.

Florio The major producer of MARSALA, controlled by CINZANO.

Foianeghe T-AA vdt r (w) ★★ 86 88 89 90 93 TRENTINO CAB-MERLOT red to age 7–10 yrs. White is PINOT BL-CHARD-TRAMINER. Top grower: Conti Bossi Fedrigotti.

Folonari Large run-of-the-mill merchant of Lombardy. See also GIV.

Fontana Candida One of the biggest producers of FRASCATI. Single-v'yd Santa Teresa stands out. See also GIV.

Fontanafredda ★★ Big historic producer of PIEDMONT wines, incl BAROLO from single v'yds and a range of ALBA DOCs. Also very good DOCG ASTI and SPUMANTE Brut.

Fonterutoli High quality (★★★→★★★★) CHIANTI CLASSICO estate at Castellina with noted VDT Concerto and RISERVA Ser Lapo (★★★).

Le Fonti, Fattoria ★★ CHIANTI estate of 30 acres. Panzano still uses ancient 'promisco' mixed cultivation.

Fontodi ★★★★ Top CHIANTI CLASSICO estate at Panzano producing highly regarded RISERVA, red VDT Flaccianello and white vdt 'Meriggio' (a PINOT BIANCO-SAUV-TRAMINER blend).

Franciacorta Pinot Lom DOC w (p sp) ★★→★★★ Pleasant soft white and some vg sparkling wines made of PINOTS BL, N or GR and CHARD. CA'DEL BOSCO is outstanding. BELLAVISTA, CAVALLERI and Monte Rossa also vg.

Franciacorta Rosso Lom DOC r ★★ 90 91 92 93 Lightish red of mixed CAB and BARBERA from Brescia.

Frascati Lat DOC w dr s/sw sw (sp) ★→★★ DYA Best-known wine of Roman hills: should be soft, ripe, golden, tasting of whole grapes. Most is disappointingly neutral today: look for Conte Zandotti, Villa Simone, or Santa Teresa from FONTANA CANDIDA. Sweet is known as Cannellino.

Freisa Pie r dr s/sw sw (sp) ★★ DYA Usually v dry (except nr Turin), often FRIZZANTE red, said to taste of raspberries and roses. With enough acidity can be highly appetizing, esp with salami. Good from: CIGLIUTI, CONTERNO, Cozzo, Gilli, PARUSSO, Pecchenino, Pelissero, Sebaste, Trinchero, VAJRA, VOERZIO.

Frescobaldi Ancient noble family, leading pioneers of CHIANTI at NIPOZZANO, E of Florence. Also white POMINO and PREDICATO SAUV BL (Vergena) and CAB (Mormoreto). See also Montesodi.

Friuli-Venezia Giulia The NE region on the Slovenian border. Many wines; the DOCs COLLIO and COLLI ORIENTALI include most of the best.

Frizzante (fz) Semi-sparkling. Used to describe wines such as LAMBRUSCO.

Gaja ★★★★ Old family firm at BARBARESCO with inspired direction of Angelo G. Top quality – and price – PIEDMONT wines, esp BARBARESCO (single v'yds SORI Tildin, Sorì San Lorenzo, Costa Russi) and BAROLO Sperss (since '88). Now setting trends with excellent CHARD (Gaja & Rey and less expensive Rossj-Bass), CAB (DARMAGI). Vignarey is excellent BARBERA, Vignabajla delicious DOLCETTO.

Galestro Tus w ★ V light grapey white from eponymous shaley soil in CHIANTI country.

Gambellara Ven DOC w dr s/sw (sp) ★ DYA Neighbour of SOAVE. Dry wine similar. Sweet (known as RECIOTO DI GAMBELLARA) agreeably fruity. Also VINSANTO. Outstanding producer, LA BIANCARA (★★★).

Gancia Famous ASTI house also producing vermouth and dry sparkling. New Torrebianco estate in Apulia is making good VDT whites: CHARD, SAUV, PINOT BL, also good single-v'yd BAROLO, 'Cannubi', since '89.

Garganega Principal white grape of SOAVE.

Garofoli, Gioacchino ★★→★★★ Quality leader of the Marches (nr Ancona). Notable style in VERDICCHIO Macrina and Serra Fiorese; also vg sparkling. ROSSO CONERO Piancarda and Grosso Agontano.

Gattinara Pie DOCG r ★★→★★★ 82 85 86 **88** 89 90 93 V tasty BAROLO-type red (from NEBBIOLO, locally known as Spanna). Best are Monsecco and single-v'yd wines from Antoniola. Others incl Nervi, Travaglini.

Gavi (or Cortese di Gavi) Pie w ★★→★★★ DYA At best substantial subtle dry white of Cortese grapes. LA SCOLCA is best known, Castello di Tassarolo top quality, La Giustiniana, Tenuta San Pietro and Villa Sparina are admirable. But high prices are rarely justified.

Ghemme Pie DOC r ★★→★★★ 82 85 86 **88** 89 90 93 Neighbour of GATTINARA, rival in quality but rare. Best is Antichi Vigneti di Cantalupo.

Ghiaie della Furba Tus r ★★★ 85 86 **88** 89 90 93 Bordeaux-style VDT CAB blend from the admirable TENUTA DI CAPEZZANA, CARMIGNANO.

Giacosa, Bruno ★★★ Inspired loner: outstanding BARBARESCO, BAROLO and PIEDMONT wines at Neive. Remarkable ARNEIS white, PINOT N sparkling.

GIV (Gruppo Italiano Vini) Complex of coops and wineries, apparently Europe's largest (60M bottles). Sells 12% of all Italian wine, incl eg BIGI, Conti Serristori, FOLONARI, FONTANA CANDIDA, LAMBERTI, Macchiavelli, MELINI, Negri, Santi...

Goldmuskateller Aromatic ALTO ADIGE grape made into irresistible dry white, esp by TIEFENBRUNNER.

Governo Old Tuscan custom, enjoying mild revival with some producers, in which dried grapes or must are added to young wine to induce secondary fermentation and give a slight prickle – sometimes instead of using must concentrate to increase alcohol.

Gradi Degrees (of alcohol), ie percent by volume.

Grappa Pungent spirit made from grape pomace (skins etc after pressing).

Grasso, Elio ★★★ Hard-working, reliable, quality producer at Monforte d'Alba: outstanding BAROLO (look for Gavarini and Casa Maté), potent barrel-aged BARBERA, VDT Martina, DOLCETTO, etc.

Grattamacco ★★★ Top Tuscan producer on coast outside classic centres (nr SASSICAIA S of Bolgheri). Vg Grattamacco SANGIOVESE-CAB blend.

Grave del Friuli F-VG DOC r w ★★ (r) 88 89 **90** 91 92 93   DOC covering 15 different wines, 14 named after their grapes, from nr the Slovenian border. Good MERLOT and CAB. Best producers: Borgo Magredo, Di Lenardo, Le Fredis, PIGHIN, Teresa Raiz, Vigneti Le Monde.

Gravner, Josko ★★★★   Together with MARIO SCHIOPETTO, spiritual leader of COLLIO: estate with range of excellent whites, led by CHARD and SAUV.

Grechetto White grape with more flavour than the ubiquitous TREBBIANO, increasingly used in Umbria.

Greco di Bianco Cal DOC w sw ★★ 87 88 89 90 91 92 93   An original smooth and fragrant dessert wine from Italy's toe. Best from Ceratti. See also Mantonico.

Greco di Tufo Cam DOC w (sp) ★★→★★★ 91 92 93   One of the best white wines of the south: fruity and slightly 'wild' in flavour. A character. MASTROBERARDINO makes single-v'yd Vignadangelo.

Grignolino d'Asti Pie DOC r ★ DYA   Lively standard light red of PIEDMONT.

Grumello Lom DOC r ★★ 85 86 88 **89** 90 91 92 93   NEBBIOLO wine from VALTELLINA. Can be delicate (or meagre).

Guerrieri-Gonzaga ★★→★★★   Top producer in TRENTINO; esp VDT San Leonardo, a ★★★ CAB-MERLOT blend.

Guerrieri-Rizzardi ★★   Top producer of AMARONE, BARDOLINO, SOAVE and VALPOLICELLA from various family estates.

Gutturnio dei Colli Piacentini E-R DOC r dr (s/sw) ★★ 88 89 90 91 92   BARBERA-BONARDA blend from the hills of Piacenza, often FRIZZANTE.

Haas, Franz Very good ALTO ADIGE MERLOT and PINOT NERO.

Hauner, Carlo ★★→★★★   Island estate for marvellous MALVASIA DELLE LIPARI.

Inferno Lom DOC r ★★ 85 86 88 **89** 90 93   Similar to GRUMELLO and, like it, classified as VALTELLINA SUPERIORE.

Ischia Cam DOC w (r) ★→★★ DYA   Wine of the island off Naples. Slightly sharp white SUPERIORE is best of DOC. But top producer D'AMBRA makes better VDT whites BIANCOLELLA and Forestera and red PER'E PALUMMO.

Isole e Olena ★★★→★★★★   Top CHIANTI CLASSICO estate with fine red VDT Cepparello. Vg VINSANTO, and L'Eremo Syrah.

Isonzo F-VG DOC r w ★★★ (r) 88 89 90 91 92 93   DOC covering 19 wines (17 varietals) in the northeast. Best whites and CAB compare with neighbouring COLLIO wines. Best from Borgo Conventi, Pecorari, Ronco del Gelso, VIE DI ROMANS, Villanova.

Jermann, Silvio ★★★   Family estate in COLLIO: top white VDT, incl singular VINTAGE TUNINA oak-aged white blend and lighter Vinnae. Also fresh Capo Martino (91) and CHARD. 'Where the dreams have no end...'

Kalterersee German name for LAGO DI CALDARO.

Kant, Edi ★★★   Lone star of CARSO with outstanding DOC CHARD, SAUV, MALVASIA and vg red Terrano.

Lacryma (or Lacrima) Christi del Vesuvio Cam r p w dr (sw fz) ★→★★ DYA   Famous but ordinary range of wines in great variety from Vesuvius. (DOC Vesuvio.) MASTROBERARDINO produces the only good example.

Lageder, Alois ★★★   The lion of Bolzano (ALTO A). DOCs: SANTA MADDALENA, etc. Exciting wines, incl oak-aged CHARD and CAB Löwengang. Single-v'yd SAUV is Lehenhof, PINOT BL Haberlehof, PINOT GR Benefizium Porer.

Lago di Caldaro See Caldaro.

Lagrein, Südtiroler, T-AA DOC r p ★★→★★★ 85 86 88 **89** 90 91 93   A Tyrolean grape with a bitter twist. Good fruity wine – at best vg appetizing. The rosé is called Kretzer, the dark Dunkel. Best from Gojer, Gries, Kössler, Maddalena, Niedermayr, Rottensteiner, Schwanburg.

Lamberti Large producers of SOAVE, VALPOLICELLA, BARDOLINO, etc at Lazise on the E shore of Lake Garda. NB LUGANA and VDT Turà. See also GIV.

Lambrusco E-R DOC (or not) r p dr s/sw ★→★★ DYA   Popular fizzy red, best known in industrial s/sw version. Top is SECCO, traditional is with second fermentation in bottle (yeast sediment on bottom). DOCs are L Grasparossa di Castelvetro, L Salamino di Santa Croce and, perhaps best, L di Sorbara. Vg from: Baldini, Barbolini, Bellei, Graziano.

Langhe The hills of central PIEDMONT, home of BAROLO, BARBARESCO, etc. Has become name for recent DOC (r w ★★→★★★) for 6 different wines: ROSSO, BIANCO, FREISA, NEBBIOLO, ARNEIS and FAVORITA. Also for declassified Barolo and Barbaresco (previously only allowed VDT status).

Latisana F-VG DOC r w ★→★★ (r) 90 91 92 93   DOC for 13 varietal wines from 50 miles NE of Venice. Esp good TOCAI FRIULANO.

Leone de Castris ★★   Large producer of Apulian wines with an estate at SALICE SALENTINO, near Lecce.

Lessona Pie DOC r ★★ 85 86 88 89 90 93   Soft dry claret-like wine from the province of Vercelli. NEBBIOLO, Vespolina and BONARDA grapes.

Librandi ★★   Top Calabria producer. Vg red CIRO (RISERVA Duca San Felice is ★★★) and VDT Gravello (v interesting, good value CAB-Gaglioppo blend).

Liquoroso Means strong and usually sweet (whether fortified or not).

Lisini ★★★   Small estate for some of the finest recent vintages of BRUNELLO.

Loazzolo Pie DOC w sw ★★★ 89 90 91 92 93   New DOC for MOSCATO dessert wine from botrytised air-dried grapes: expensive and sweet. Esp from Borgo Maragliano, Borgo Moncalvo, Borgo Sambui, Bricchi Mej, Luja.

Locorotondo Ap DOC w (sp) ★ DYA   Pleasantly fresh southern white.

Lugana Lom and Ven DOC w (sp) ★★ DYA   One of the best whites of S Lake Garda: fragrant, smooth, full of body and flavour. Good from Cà dei Frati, Ottella, Roveglia, Zenato.

Lungarotti ★★→★★★   The leading producer of TORGIANO wine, with cellars, hotel and wine museum nr Perugia. Also some of Italy's best CHARD (Miralduolo and Vigna I Palazzi) and PINOT GR. See Torgiano.

Maculan The top producer of DOC BREGANZE. Also Torcolato, dessert VDT (★★★) and Prato di Canzio (CHARD, PINOT BL and PINOT GR).

Malvasia An important grape of chameleon character: white or red wines, sparkling or still, strong or mild, sweet or dry, aromatic or rather neutral, often as VDT, sometimes as DOC. White, dry to sweet, strong, concentrated: **M di Cagliari** Sar DOC ★★ (eg Meloni); red, fragrant, grapey, sweet, somtimes sparkling: **M di Casorzo d'Asti** Pie DOC ★★ (eg Bricco Mondalino); red, aromatic, sparkling: **M di Castelnuovo Don Bosco** Pie DOC ★★ (eg Gilli); white, rich, strong, long-living: M delle Lipari Si DOC ★★★ (eg Colosi, Hauner); white, dry to semi-sweet, deep bouquet, long-lived: M de Nus VdA DOC ★★★ (eg La Crotta de Vegnerons). See also Torricella.

Manduria (Primitivo di) Ap DOC r s/sw (dr sw fz) ★★ 88 89 **90 91** 92 93   Heady red, naturally strong but often fortified. From nr Taranto. Primitivo grape is related to California's Zinfandel. Esp Vinicola Savese's.

Mantonico Cal w dr sw fz ★★ 86 87 88 89 90 91 92 93   Fruity deep amber dessert wine from Reggio Calabria. Can age remarkably well. Good from Ceratti. See also Greco di Bianco.

Marino Lat DOC w dr s/sw (sp) ★→★★ DYA   A neighbour of FRASCATI with similar wine; often a better buy. Look for COLLE PICCHIONI brand.

Marsala Si DOC br dr s/sw sw fz ★★→★★★ NV   Sherry-type wine invented by the Woodhouse Brothers from Liverpool in 1773; excellent aperitif or for dessert, but mostly used in the kitchen. The dry ('virgin'), sometimes made by the solera system, must be 5 yrs old. Top producers: FLORIO, Pellegrino, Rallo, VECCHIO SAMPERI.

Martini & Rossi Well-known vermouth and sparkling wine house (now controlled by Bacardi group), also famous for its splendid wine museum in Pessione, nr Turin.

Marzemino (Trentino) T-AA DOC r ★→★★ **90 91 92 93**   Pleasant local red. Fruity; slightly bitter. Esp from Bossi Fedrigotti, Casata Monfort, CAVIT, De Tarczal, Gaierhof, Letrari, Simoncelli, Vallarom, Vallis Agri.

Mascarello The name of 2 top producers of BAROLO, etc: Bartolo M and Giuseppe M & Figli. Look for the latter's BAROLO Monprivato.

Masi, Agricola Well-known conscientious and reliable specialist producers of VALPOLICELLA, AMARONE (★★★), RECIOTO, SOAVE, etc, incl fine red Campo Fiorin. Also look for excellent new red VDT Toar.

Mastroberardino **→**** The leading wine producer of Campania (by far). Wines incl FIANO DI AVELLINO, GRECO DI TUFO, LACRYMA CHRISTI and TAURASI (look for Radici).

Melini Long-est'd producers of CHIANTI CLASSICO at Poggibonsi. Good quality-price ratio; look for single-v'yd C Classico Selvanella. See also GIV.

Meranese di Collina T-AA DOC r * DYA Light red of Merano, known in German as Meraner Hügel.

Merlot Adaptable red B'x grape widely grown in N (esp) and central Italy. Merlot DOCs are abundant. Best growers are: HAAS, SCHRECKBICHL and Baron Widman in T-AA, Torre Rosazza (L'Altromerlot) and BORGO DEL TIGLIO in F-VG and the Tuscan Super-VDTS of AMA (L'Apparita), AVIGNONESI and ORNELLAIA (Masseto).

Metodo classico or tradizionale Terms increasingly in use to identify classic method sparkling wines. (See also Classico.)

Moccagatta **→*** Specialist in impressive single-v'yd BARBARESCO: Basarin, Bric Balin (***) and Vigna Cole.

Monferrato Pie DOC r w sw p ** The hills between the river Po and the Apennines give their name to a new DOC that includes ROSSO, BIANCO, CHIARETTO, GRIGNOLINO, FREISA and Casalese CORTESE.

Monica di Sardegna Sar DOC r * DYA Monica is the grape. An ordinary dry light red.

Monsanto Esteemed CHIANTI CLASSICO estate, esp for Il Poggio v'yd.

Montalcino Small town in the province of Siena, Tuscany, famous for its deep red BRUNELLO and younger ROSSO DI MONTALCINO.

Monte Vertine ***→**** Top estate at Radda in CHIANTI. VDT Le Pergole Torte (100% SANGIOVESE) is one of Tuscany's best. Also Sodaccio (Sangioveto plus Canaiolo) and fine VINSANTO.

Montecarlo Tus DOC w r ** DYA (w) Traditional white wine area in N Tuscany: smooth delicate TREBBIANO blended with a range of better grapes. Now applies to a CHIANTI-style red too (eg Rosso di Cercatoia). Good producers: Buonamico, Carmignani, Michi.

Montefalco (Rosso di) Umb DOC r ** 90 91 92 93 Common SANGIOVESE-TREBBIANO-SAGRANTNO blend. ADANTI's Rosso d'Arquata VDT stands out.

Montefalco Sagrantino Umb DOCG r dr sw *** 90 91 92 93 Strong, v interesting SECCO or sweet PASSITO red from Sagrantino grapes only. Good from: ADANTI, Antano, Antonelli, Val di Maggio, Villa Antica.

Montellori, Fattoria di **→*** Tuscan father-son team producing admirable SANGIOVESE-CAB VDT blend 'Castelrapiti Rosso', Viognier VDT 'Bonfiglio', Chardonnay VDT 'Castelrapiti Bianco' and vg SPUMANTE.

Montepulciano An important red grape of central-east Italy as well as the famous Tuscan town (see next entry).

Montepulciano d'Abruzzo (or Molise) Ab (or Mol) DOC r p ** 85 87 88 89 90 91 92 93 Happens rarely, but when it's at its best, one of Italy's tastiest reds, full of flavour and warmth, from the Adriatic coast round Pescara. Good from: Barone Cornacchia, Filomusi-Guelfi, Illuminati, Masciarelli, Nicodemi, Tenuta del Priore, Zaccagnini. See also Cerasuolo and (the best) Valentini.

Montepulciano, Vino Nobile di See Vino Nobile di Montepulciano.

Montesodi Tus r *** 83 85 86 88 90 93 Tip-top CHIANTI RUFINA RISERVA from FRESCOBALDI.

Morellino di Scansano Tus DOC r ** 88 90 93 Local SANGIOVESE of the Maremma, the S Tuscan coast. Cherry-red, lively and tasty. Fattorie Le Pupille, Moris Farms are good.

Moscadello di Montalcino Tus DOC w sw (sp) ** DYA Traditional wine of MONTALCINO, much older than BRUNELLO. Sweet white fizzy, and sweet to high-octane PASSITO MOSCATO. Good producers: BANFI, POGGIONE.

NB This edition introduces a new short-cut vintage category. Vintages in colour are the ones you should choose first for drinking in 1995.

Moscato Fruitily fragrant ubiquitous grape for a diverse range of wines: sparkling or still, light or full-bodied, but always sweet. Most famous is **M d'Asti** Pie DOCG (****→*****): light, aromatic, sparkling and delicious from BERA, Dogliotti, Gatti, RIVETTI, Saracco and Vignaioli di Santo Stefano. Italy's best is from the island of Pantelleria off the Tunisian coast, with top wines from De Bartoli, Murana. And rare but prestigious is **Moscato di Trani** (s'times fortified), best from Nugnes.

Müller-Thurgau Makes wine to be reckoned with in TRENTINO-ALTO ADIGE and FRIULI, esp TIEFENBRUNNER's Feldmarschall.

Nasco di Cagliari Sar DOC w dr sw (fz) ** Sardinian speciality with light bitter taste, high alcohol content. Good from Meloni.

Nebbiolo The best red grape of PIEDMONT and Lombardy.

Nebbiolo d'Alba Pie DOC r dr (s/sw sp) ** 88 89 90 91 93 From ALBA (but not BAROLO, BARBARESCO). Sometimes like lightweight Barolo, but easier to appreciate than the powerful classic wine. Best from Correggia, MASCARELLO, PRUNOTTO, RATTI, Roagna. See also Roero.

Negroamaro Literally 'black bitter'; Apulian red grape with potential for quality. See Copertino.

Nipozzano, Castello di ***→***** FRESCOBALDI estate E of Florence making MONTESODI CHIANTI. The most important outside the CLASSICO zone.

Nosiola (Trentino) T-AA DOC w dr sw ** DYA Light fruity white from dried Nosiola grapes. Also good VINSANTO. Best from Pravis: Le Frate.

Nozzole Famous estate, owned by RUFFINO, in the heart of CHIANTI CLASSICO N of Greve. Also good CAB.

Nuragus di Cagliari Sar DOC w * DYA Lively Sardinian white, not too strong.

Oberto, Andrea *** Hardworking small La Morra producer with top BAROLO and BARBERA D'ALBA.

Oliena Sar r ** Interesting strong fragrant CANNONAU red; a touch bitter.

Oltrepò Pavese Lom DOC r w dr sw sp *→** DOC applicable to 14 wines produced in the province of Pavia, mostly named after their grapes. Top growers incl Cabanon, Doria, Mairano, Tenuta Mazzolino, Monsupello, Montelio.

Ornellaia Tus ***** 85 86 87 88 **89** 90 91 92 93 New 130-acre estate of LODOVICO ANTINORI nr Bolgheri on the Tuscan coast. To watch for CAB-MERLOT and SAUV BL called Poggio delle Gazze. Also Masseto, vg straight Merlot, and blend La Volte (since '91).

Orvieto Umb DOC w dr s/sw **→*** DYA The classical Umbrian golden white: smooth and substantial; formerly rather dull but recently more interesting, esp in sweet versions. Orvieto CLASSICO is better. Only the finest examples (eg BARBERANI, BIGI, DECUGANO DEI BARBI) age well. But see Castello della Sala.

Pagadebit di Romagna E-R DOC w dr s/sw DYA Pleasant traditional 'payer of debts' from around Bertinoro.

Palazzino, Podere Il *** Small estate with admirable CHIANTI CLASSICO and VDT Grosso Sanese.

Panaretta, Castello della ** An estate to follow: v interesting CHIANTI CLASSICO.

Panizzi **→*** Makes top class VERNACCIA DI SAN GIMIGNANO.

Paradiso, Fattoria Century-old family estate near Bertinoro (E-R). Good ALBANA and PAGADEBIT and unique red Barbarossa. Vg SANGIOVESE.

Parrina Tus r w ** 90 91 92 93 Light red and white from S Tuscany.

Parusso *** Tiziana and Marco Parusso are making BAROLO at the highest level (vg single-v'yd Bussia, also Mariondino), also vg BARBERA D'ALBA and DOLCETTO, etc.

Pasolini Dall'Onda Noble family with estates in CHIANTI Colli Fiorentini and Romagna, producing fine traditional-style wines.

Passito (pa) Strong sweet wine from grapes dried on the vine or indoors.

Pelaverga Pie r ** 90 91 92 93 Pale red with spicy perfume, from Verduno. Good producers: Alessandria, Bel Colle, Castello di Verduno.

Peppoli Estate owned by ANTINORI, producing excellent CHIANTI CLASSICO in a full round youthful style – first vintage 85.

Per'e Palummo Cam r ** Appetizing light tannic red from island of ISCHIA.

Piave Ven DOC r w ✳→✳✳ (r) 88 90 93 (w DYA) Flourishing DOC NW of Venice covering 8 wines, 4 red and 4 white, named after their grapes. CAB, MERLOT and RABOSO reds can all age. Good from Molon-Traverso.

Picolit (Colli Orientali del Friuli) F-VG DOC w s/sw sw *** 88 90 93 Delicate well-balanced sweet dessert wine with exaggerated reputation. Like Jurançon. Ages up to 6 yrs, but wildly overpriced. Best from DORIGO, Dri, LIVIO FELLUGA, Livon, Rodaro, RONCO DEL GNEMIZ.

Piedmont (Piemonte) The most important Italian region for top quality wine. Turin is the capital, ASTI and ALBA the wine centres. See Barbaresco, Barbera, Barolo, Dolcetto, Grignolino, Moscato, etc.

Piedmont vintages

1993 Hot summer, good Dolcetto and Barbera, but September rains disrupted Nebbiolo harvest and severe selection was necessary for Barolo and Barbaresco.

1992 An extremely difficult year due to incessant rainfall. Whites good. Nebbiolo wines not so lucky.

1991 Cold April and suddenly v hot in July, harvest then interrupted by rain: some elegant Barolo, Barbaresco and Barbera; Dolcetto and whites fine.

Pieropan *** Outstanding producer of SOAVE and RECIOTO that for once deserves its fame.

Pigato DOC under Riviera Ligure di Ponente. Often outclasses VERMENTINO as Liguria's finest white, with rich texture and structure. Good from: Anfossi, Colle dei Bardellini, Feipu, Lupi, TERRE ROSSE, Vio.

Pighin, Fratelli Solid producers of COLLIO and GRAVE DEL FRIULI.

Pinot Bianco (Pinot Bl) Popular grape in NE for many DOC wines. Best from ALTO ADIGE T-AA ** (top growers: CS St-Michael, LAGEDER, Elena Walch), COLLIO F-VG ** (vg from Keber, Mangilli, Picech, Princic) and COLLI ORIENTALI F-VG **→*** (best from Rodaro and Vigne dal Leon).

Pinot Grigio (Pinot Gr) Tasty low-acid white grape popular in NE. Best from DOCs ALTO ADIGE (LAGEDER, Kloster Muri-Gries, Schwanburg) and COLLIO (Caccese, SCHIOPETTO). AMA in Tuscany makes vg VDT Pinot Gr.

Pinot Nero T-AA DOC r ✳✳ 88 89 90 91 92 93 Pinot Nero (Noir) gives lively light wine in much of NE Italy, incl TRENTINO and esp ALTO ADIGE. Vg results from SCHRECKBICHL, Castelfeder, HAAS, Niedrist. Also fine sparkling. Promising trials elsewhere, eg AMA, FONTODI, Pancrazi and RUFFINO in Tuscany.

Pio Cesare A producer of top-quality red wines of PIEDMONT, incl BAROLO.

Poggio Antico (Montalcino) ***→***** Admirably consistent top level BRUNELLO, ROSSO and red VDT Altero.

Poggione, Tenuta Il * Perhaps the most consistent estate for BRUNELLO and ROSSO DI MONTALCINO.

Pojer & Sandri * Top TRENTINO producers: reds and whites, incl SPUMANTE.

Poliziano * Federico Carletti makes top VINO NOBILE DI MONTEPULCIANO (esp Asinone, Caggiole), VDT Elegia (CAB, SANGIOVESE) and wonderful VINSANTO. V reasonable prices.

Pomino Tus DOC w (r br) *** 85 86 87 88 90 93 Fine white, partly CHARD (Il Benefizio is 100%), and a SANGIOVESE-CAB-MERLOT-PINOT N blend. Also VINSANTO. Esp from FRESCOBALDI.

Predicato Name for 4 kinds of VDT from central Tuscany, illustrating the current headlong rush from tradition. P del Muschio is CHARD and PINOT BL; P del Selvante is SAUV BL; P di Biturica is CAB with SANGIOVESE, P di Cardisco is Sangiovese straight. Esp RUFFINO's Cabreo brand wines.

Primitivo di Apulia See Manduria.

Prosecco di Conegliano-Valdobbiadene Ven DOC w dr s/sw (sp) ** DYA Popular light sparkling wine of the NE. Slight fruity bouquet, the dry pleasantly bitter, the sweet fruity; the best are known as Superiore di Cartizze. CARPENE-MALVOLTI is most renowned producer, now challenged by Adami, Conte da Sacco, Nino Franco, Merotto, Zaredetto.

Prunotto, Alfredo Very serious ALBA company with vg BARBARESCO (esp Montestefano, ★★★★), BAROLO (esp ★★★★ single-v'yd Bussia and Cannubi), NEBBIOLO, etc. Now controlled by ANTINORI.

Querciabella ★★→★★★ Up-coming CHIANTI CLASSICO estate with excellent red VDT Camartina and a dream of a white VDT, Bâtard Pinot (BL and GR).

Quintarelli, Giuseppe ★★★★ True artisan producer of VALPOLICELLA, RECIOTO and AMARONE, at the top in both quality and price.

Raboso del Piave (now DOC) Ven r ★★ 86 88 90 91 92 Powerful sharp interesting country red; needs age. Look for Molon-Traverso.

Ragose, Le ★★★ Family estate, one of VALPOLICELLA's best. AMARONE and RECIOTO top quality; CAB and Valpolicella vg too.

Ramandolo See Verduzzo Colli Orientali del Friuli.

Ramitello See Di Majo Norante.

Rampolla, Castello dei ★★★ Top CHIANTI CLASSICO estate at Panzano; also excellent CAB-based VDT Sammarco.

Ratti, Renato ★★→★★★ Maker of vg BAROLO and other ALBA wines. The late Signor Ratti (d '88) was a highly respected local wine scene leader.

Recioto Wine made of half-dried grapes. Speciality of Veneto since the days of Venetian empire; has roots in famous Roman wine, Raeticus.

Recioto di Gambellara Ven DOC w sw (sp s/sw DYA) ★ Mostly half-sparkling and industrial. Best is strong and sweet. Look for LA BIANCARA (★★★).

Recioto di Soave Ven DOC w s/sw (sp) ★★★ 87 88 90 91 92 93 SOAVE made from selected half-dried grapes: sweet fruity fresh, slightly almondy; high alcohol. Outstanding from ANSELMI and PIEROPAN.

Recioto della Valpolicella Ven DOC r s/sw sp ★★★ 85 86 88 90 93 Strong late-harvest red, s'times sparkling. 'Amabile' is sweet. Vg from ALLEGRINI, Brigaldara, MASI, LE RAGOSE, Le Salette, San Rustico, Speri, TEDESCHI.

Recioto della Valpolicella Amarone See Amarone.

Refosco r ★★ 88 90 91 92 93 Interesting full-bodied dark tannic red, needs ageing. Said to be the same grape as the Mondeuse of Savoie (France). It tastes like it. Best comes from F-VG DOC COLLI ORIENTALI, GRAVE and CARSO (where R is called Terrano). Vg from DORIGO, EDI KANTE, Le Fredis, Livon, Villa Belvedere.

Regaleali ★★★ Owned by the family Conte Tasca D'Almerita, on the way to being the best Sicilian producer; situated between Palermo and Caltanissetta to the SE. Vg VDT red, white and pink 'Regaleali', red 'Rosso del Conte' and CAB.

Ribolla (Colli Orientali del Friuli and Collio) F-VG DOC w ★→★★ DYA Thin NE white. The best come from COLLIO. Top estates: La Castellada, GRAVNER, Krapez, Radikon, Venica & Venica, VILLA RUSSIZ.

Ricasoli Famous Tuscan family, 'inventors' of CHIANTI, whose CHIANTI CLASSICO is named after their Brolio estate and castle.

Riecine Tus r (w) ★★★ First-class CHIANTI CLASSICO estate at Gaiole, created by an Englishman, John Dunkley. Also VDT La Gioia di Riecine.

Riesling Used to mean Italian Ries (Ries Italico or Welschriesling). German (Rhine) Ries, now ascendant, is Ries Renano. Best are DOC ALTO ADIGE ★★ (esp coop Kurtatsch, Ignaz Niedrist, coop La Vis, Elena Walch) and DOC OLTREPO PAVESE Lom ★★ (Brega, Cabanon, Doria, Frecciarossa, coop La Versa), also astonishing from Ronco del Gelso (DOC ISONZO).

Riserva Wine aged for a statutory period, usually in barrels.

Riunite One of the world's largest coop cellars, nr Reggio Emilia, producing huge quantities of LAMBRUSCO and other wines.

Rivera Reliable winemakers at Andria, near Bari, with good red Il Falcone and CASTEL DEL MONTE rosé. Also Vigna al Monte label.

Rivetti, Giorgio (La Spinetta) ★★★ First success with MOSCATO, then with reds. Top Moscato d'Asti, vg BARBERA, v interesting VDT Pin (blend of Barbera and NEBBIOLO).

For key to grape variety abbreviations, see pages 6–9.

Riviera del Garda Bresciano Lom DOC w p r (sp) ★→★★ Simple, sometimes charming cherry-pink CHIARETTO from different grapes, and neutral white from SW Garda. Good producers: Cà dei Frati, Comincioli, Costaripa, Monte Cigogna.

Rocca, Bruno ★★★ Young producer with admirable BARBARESCO (Rabajà).

Rocca di Castagnoli ★★→★★★★ Recent producer of vg CHIANTI CLASSICO (best: Capraia, RISERVA Poggio a'Frati), also vg VDT Stielle and Buriano (blends of CAB and SANGIOVESE).

Rocche dei Manzoni, Podere ★★★ Go-ahead estate at Monforte d'Alba. Excellent BAROLO (best: Vigna Big), BRICCO MANZONI (outstanding NEBBIOLO-BARBERA blend VDT), ALBA wines, CHARD (L'Angelica) and Valentino Brut sparkling.

Roero DOC r ★★ DYA New name for a drink-me-quick NEBBIOLO from ALBA. Can be delicious. Good from: Correggia, Deltetto, Malabaila, Malvirà.

Ronco Term for a hillside v'yd in FRIULI-VENEZIA GIULIA.

Ronco del Gnemiz ★★★ Tiny property with outstanding COLLI ORIENTALI DOCs and VDT CHARD made in barriques.

Rosa del Golfo Ap p ★★ DYA An outstanding VDT rosé of ALEZIO.

Rosato Rosé.

Rosato del Salento Ap p ★★ DYA From nr Brindisi and v like BRINDISI, COPERTINO and SALICE SALENTINO ROSATOS; sometimes strong, but often astonishingly fine and fruity. See Brindisi, Copertino, Salice Salentino for producers.

Rossese di Dolceacqua Lig DOC r ★★ 92 93 Well-known fragrant light red of the Riviera. Good from Cane, Giuncheo, Guglielmi, Lupi, Perrino, Terre Bianche.

Rosso Red.

Rosso Cònero Mar DOC r ★★★ 85 86 88 89 90 91 92 93 Some of the best MONTEPULCIANO (varietal) reds of Italy, eg GAROFOLI'S Grosso Agontano, Moroder's RC RISERVA, UMANI RONCHI'S Cumaro and San Lorenzo.

Rosso di Montalcino Tus DOC r ★★→★★★ 88 89 90 91 92 93 DOC for younger wines from BRUNELLO grapes. Still variable but potentially a winner if the many good producers are not too greedy over prices. For growers see Brunello di M.

Rosso di Montepulciano Tus DOC r ★★ 90 91 92 93 Equivalent of the last for junior VINO NOBILE, recently introduced and yet to establish a style. For growers see Vino Nobile di M.

Rosso Piceno Mar DOC r ★→★★ 90 91 93 Stylish Adriatic red. Can be SUPERIORE from classic zone near Ascoli. Best include Cocci Grifoni, Villamagna.

Rubesco The excellent popular red of LUNGAROTTI; see Torgiano.

Ruchè (also Rouchè or Rouchet) A rare old grape (French origin) giving fruity, fresh, rich bouqueted red wine (s/sw). Ruchè di Castagnole Monferrato is recent DOC, with Piero Bruno best producer. Rouchet Briccorosa is dry and excellent (★★★) from SCARPA.

Ruffino Well known CHIANTI merchants, at Pontassieve. RISERVA Ducale and Santedame are the top wines. NB new PREDICATO wines (red and white Cabreo) and CAB Il Pareto.

Rufina Important subregion of CHIANTI in the hills E of Florence. Best wines from Castello Nipozzano (FRESCOBALDI), SELVAPIANA.

Russiz Superiore (Collio) See Felluga, Marco.

Sagrantino di Montefalco See Montefalco.

Salice Salentino Ap DOC r ★★ 83 85 86 87 88 89 90 91 92 93 Strong red from NEGROAMARO grapes. RISERVA after 2 yrs; smooth when mature. Top makers: Candido, De Castris, Taurino, Vallone.

San Felice ★★ Rising star in CHIANTI with fine CLASSICO Poggio Rosso. Also red VDT Vigorello and PREDICATO di Biturica.

San Giusto a Rentennano One of the best CHIANTI CLASSICO producers (★★★). Delicious but v rare VINSANTO. Excellent VDT red Percarlo.

San Guido, Tenuta ★★★★ See Sassicaia.

Sandrone, Luciano ★★★ Exponent of new-style BAROLO vogue with vg B Cannubi Boschis, DOLCETTO and BARBERA.

Sangiovese or Sangioveto Principal red grape of Italy. High performance only in Tuscany, where its many forms incl CHIANTI, VINO NOBILE, BRUNELLO, MORELLINO, etc. V popular is S di Romagna (E-R DOC r ★→★★), a pleasant standard red. Vg from Cesari, Conti, PARADISO, Trerè, ZERBINA, outstanding ★★★ VDTs Ronco dei Cigliegi and Ronco delle Ginestre from CASTELLUCCIO, and VDT Nespoli (★★★) from Podere dal Nespoli.

Santa Maddalena (or St-Magdalener) T-AA DOC r ⊛ DYA Typical SCHIAVA Tyrolean red, lightish with bitter aftertaste. Best from: CS St-Magdalena, CS Girlan, Gojer, Thurnhof.

Sassella (Valtellina Superiore) Lom DOC r ★★★ 85 86 88 **89** 90 93 Considerable NEBBIOLO wine, tough when young. Known since Roman times; mentioned by Leonardo da Vinci. Neighbour to INFERNO, etc.

Sassicaia Tus r ★★★★ 82' 83' 85' 86 88' 89 90' 91 92 93 Outstanding pioneer CAB, Italy's best, from the Tenuta San Guido of the Incisa family, at Bolgheri nr Livorno.

Sauvignon Sauvignon Blanc is working v well in the northeast, best from DOCs TERLANO, ALTO ADIGE, ISONZO, COLLIO and COLLI ORIENTALI.

Sauvignon (Colli Orientali del Friuli) F-VG DOC w ★★→★★★ 90 91 92 93 Top producers: Torre Rosazza, Vigne dal Leon.

Sauvignon (Collio) F-VG DOC w ★★→★★★ **90 91** 92 93 Top wines from La Castellada, GRAVNER, Primosic, SCHIOPETTO, VILLA RUSSIZ.

Sauvignon (Isonzo) F-VG DOC w ★★→★★★ **90 91** 92 93 V full fruity white, increasingly good quality. Top producers: Pecorari, VIE DI ROMANS.

Savuto Cal DOC r p ★★ **90 91** 92 Fragrant juicy wine from the provinces of Cosenza and Catanzaro. Best producer is Odoardi.

Scarpa Old-fashioned house with full-bodied smooth BARBERA D'ASTI (La Bogliona is ★★★), rare Rouchet (★★★), vg DOLCETTO, BAROLO, BARBARESCO.

Schiava High-yielding red grape of TRENTINO-ALTO ADIGE with characteristic bitter aftertaste, used for LAGO DI CALDARO, SANTA MADDALENA, etc.

Schiopetto, Mario ★★★★ Legendary COLLIO pioneer with brand-new 20,000-case winery; vg DOC SAUV, PINOT GR, TOCAI, VDT blend 'Blanc de Rosis', etc.

Schreckbichl (or Colterenzio CS) No 1 Südtirol CS. Admirable ALTO ADIGE CAB S, Gewürz, PINOT N, (look for Schwarzhaus RISERVA), CHARD, PINOT BL, PINOT GR, SAUV (look for Lafoa), red VDT Cornelius, etc.

Sciacchetrà See Cinqueterre.

Scolca, La Famous estate in GAVI for excellent Gavi and SPUMANTE (look for Extra Brut Soldati La Scolca).

Secco Dry.

Sella & Mosca ★★ Major Sardinian growers and merchants at Alghero. Their port-like Anghelu Ruju (★★★) is excellent. Also pleasant white TORBATO and delicious light fruity VERMENTINO Cala Viola (DYA).

Selvapiana ★★★ CHIANTI RUFINA estate. Top wine is RISERVA Bucerchiale.

Sforzato Lom DOC r ★★★ 82 83 85 86 88 89 90 93 Valtellina equivalent of RECIOTO AMARONE made with partly dried grapes. Velvety, strong, ages remarkably well. Also called Sfursat. See Valtellina.

Sizzano Pie DOC r ★★ 85 86 87 88 **89** 90 93 Full-bodied red from Sizzano, Novara, mostly NEBBIOLO. Ages up to 10 yrs. Esp from: Bianchi, Dessilani.

Soave Ven DOC w ★→★★★ DYA Famous mass-produced Veronese white. Should be fresh with v attractive texture. Standards rising (at last). S CLASSICO is more restricted and better. Esp from ANSELMI, PIEROPAN.

Solaia Tus r ★★★★ 82 83 85 86 88 90 93 V fine Bordeaux-style VDT of CAB S and a little SANGIOVESE from ANTINORI; first made in '78. Extraordinarily influential in shaping VDT (and Italian) philosophy.

Solopaca Cam DOC r w ⊛ 89 90 91 92 93 Up-and-coming from nr Benevento; rather sharp when young, the white soft and fruity. Good from Antica Masseria Venditti.

Sorì Term for a high S, SE or SW oriented v'yd in PIEDMONT.

Spanna See Gattinara.

Spumante Sparkling, as in sweet ASTI or many good dry wines, incl both METODO CLASSICO (best from TRENTINO, A ADIGE, FRANCIACORTA, PIEDMONT, some vg also from Tuscany and Veneto) and tank-made cheapos.

Stravecchio Very old.

Südtirol The local name of German-speaking ALTO ADIGE.

Super-Tuscans Term coined for high-price novelties from Tuscany, usually involving CAB and barriques, and frequently fancy bottles.

Superiore Wine that has undergone more ageing than normal DOC and contains 0.5–1% more alcohol.

Taurasi Cam DOCG r *** 85 86 87 88 89 90 91 92 93 The best Campanian red, from MASTROBERARDINO of Avellino. Harsh when young. RISERVA after 4 yrs. Radici (since '86) is Mastroberardino's top estate bottling.

Tedeschi, Fratelli V reliable and vg producer of VALPOLICELLA, AMARONE (***), RECIOTO and SOAVE. Vg Capitel San Rocco red and white VDT.

Terlano T-AA DOC w **→*** DYA DOC for 8 whites from Bolzano province, named by their grapes, esp SAUV. Terlaner in German. Good growers: Cantina Sociale Terlan, CS Terlan, LAGEDER, Niedrist.

Teroldego Rotaliano T-AA DOC r p **→*** 90 91 92 93 Attractive blackberry-scented red; slight bitter aftertaste; can age v well. Esp Foradori's.

Terre di Ginestra Si w ** Good VDT from Cataratto, SW of Palermo.

Terre Rosse *** Distinguished small estate nr Bologna. Its CAB, CHARD, SAUV BL, PINOT GR, RIES, even Viognier, etc, are the best of the region.

Teruzzi & Puthod (Fattoria Ponte a Rondolino) *** Innovative top producers of San Gimignano with vg VERNACCIA DI SAN G, white VDTs 'Terre di Tufi' and 'Carmen'.

Tiefenbrunner Leading grower of some of the very best ALTO ADIGE white and red wines at Schloss Turmhof, Kurtatsch (Cortaccio).

Tignanello Tus r **** 82 83 85 86 88 90 93 Pioneer and still leader of the new style of Bordeaux-inspired Tuscan reds, made by ANTINORI.

Tocai Mild smooth NE white (no relation of Hungarian or Alsace Tokay). DOC also in Ven and Lom (*→***), but producers are most proud of it in F-VG (esp COLLIO and COLLI ORIENTALI): (**→***). Best producers: BORGO DEL TIGLIO, Castello di Spessa, Keber, Picech, Princic, Raccaro, Ronco del Gelso, RONCO DI GNEMIZ, SCHIOPETTO, Scubla, Specogna, Toros, Venica & Venica, VILLA RUSSIZ, VOLPE PASINI.

Torbato di Alghero Sar w (pa) ** DYA Good N Sardinian table wine. Top maker: SELLA & MOSCA.

Torgiano Umb DOC r w p (sp) **→*** and **Torgiano, Rosso Riserva** Umb DOCG r *** 85 87 88 90 93 (3 yrs ageing) Creation of Lungarotti family. Excellent red from nr Perugia, comparable with top CHIANTI CLASSICO. Rubesco is standard quality. RISERVA Vigna Monticchio is superb; keep 10 yrs. VDT San Giorgio involves CAB to splendid effect. White Torre di Giano, of TREBBIANO and GRECHETTO, also ages well. See also Lungarotti.

Torricella Tus w *** 88 90 93 Remarkable aged, soft, buttery MALVASIA dry white from Brolio. Produced by BARONE RICASOLI.

Toscana Tuscany.

Tuscany vintages

1993 A hot summer was followed by heavy October rains; despite these Chianti Classico generally good, Brunello and Vino Nobile di Montepulciano vg.

1992 Promise of a top quality vintage dispelled for reds by rain. Whites had better luck and are vg.

1991 A difficult vintage: wines to drink quickly, without many positive surprises.

Traminer Aromatico T-AA DOC w **→*** DYA (German: Gewürz) Delicate aromatic soft. Best from: Cantina Sociale Girlan/Cornaiano, CS St-Michael, CS SCHRECKBICHL/ COLTERENZIO, Hofkellerei, Paterbichl, TIEFENBRUNNER.

Trebbiano Principal white grape of Tuscany, found all over Italy. Ugni Blanc in French. Sadly a waste of good v'yd space, with v rare exceptions.

Trebbiano d'Abruzzo Ab, Mol DOC w *→** DYA Gentle neutral slightly tannic. From round Pescara. VALENTINI is much the best producer (also of MONTEPULCIANO D'ABRUZZO).

Trentino T-AA DOC r w dr sw *→★★★   DOC for as many as 20 different wines, mostly named after their grapes. Best are CHARD, PINOT BL, MARZEMINO, TEROLDEGO and esp VINSANTO. The region's capital is Trento.

Umani Ronchi ★★→★★★   A leading producer of quality wines of the Marches; notably VERDICCHIO (Casal di Serra and Villa Bianchi) and ROSSO CONERO (Cumaro and San Lorenzo).

Vajra, Giuseppe Domenico ★★★   Vg consistent BAROLO producer, esp for BARBERA, Barolo, DOLCETTO, etc.

Valcalepio Lom DOC r w *→★★   From nr Bergamo. Pleasant red; lightly scented fresh white. Good from: Bonaldi, Il Calepino, Tenuta Castello.

Valdadige T-AA DOC r w dr s/sw ★   Name for the simple wines of the Adige Valley – in German 'Etschtaler'. Top producer: Armani.

Valentini, Edoardo ★★★   Perhaps the best traditionalist maker of TREBBIANO and MONTEPULCIANO D'ABRUZZO.

Valgella Lom DOC r ★★ 85 86 88 **89** 90 93   One of the VALTELLINA NEBBIOLOS: good dry red. RISERVA at 4 yrs. See Valtellina.

Valle d'Aosta VdA DOC ★★→★★★   Regional DOC for 15 Alpine wines incl DONNAZ. A mixed bag. Vg from monastery-run Institut Agricole Régional, Charrèrre, Crote de Vegnerons, Grosjean.

Valle Isarco (Eisacktal) T-AA DOC w ★★ DYA   A DOC applicable to 5 varietal wines made NE of Bolzano. Good MULLER-T, Silvaner. Top producers are CS Eisacktaler, Kloster Neustift, Kuenhof.

Vallechiara, Abbazia di ★★   New PIEDMONT estate with astonishingly high quality wines, eg DOC Dolcetto di Ovada and DOLCETTO-based VDTS Due Donne and Torre Albarola.

Valpolicella Ven DOC r *→★★ 90 91 92 93   Attractive light red from nr Verona; most attractive when young. Delicate nutty scent, slightly bitter taste. (None of this is true of junk Valpolicella sold in litre and bigger bottles.) CLASSICO more restricted; SUPERIORE has 12% alcohol and 1 yr of age. Good esp from ALLEGRINI, Brigaldara, Brunelli, Corte Sant Alda, Aleardo Ferrari, Fornaser, GUERRIERI-RIZZARDI, LE RAGOSE, MASI, Le Salette, San Rustico, Speri, Vantini, Venturini. DAL FORNO and QUINTARELLI make the best (★★★). Interesting VDTS on the way to a new Valpolicella style are Toar (★★★) from MASI and La Poja (★★★) from ALLEGRINI.

Valtellina Lom DOC r ★★→★★★ 88 89 90 91 92 93   A DOC for tannic wines made mainly from Chiavennasca (NEBBIOLO) grapes in Sondrio province, N Lombardy. V SUPERIORE are GRUMELLO, INFERNO, SASSELLA, VALGELLA. Best from: Conti Sertoli-Salis, Fay, La Castellina, Triacca.

Vecchio Samperi Si ★★★   MARSALA-like VDT from outstanding Sicily estate. The best is barrel-aged 20 years, not unlike amontillado sherry. The owner, Marco De Bartoli, also makes top DOC Marsalas.

Vendemmia Harvest or vintage.

Venegazzù Ven r w sp ★★★ 88 89 90 93   Remarkable rustic Bordeaux-style red produced from CAB grapes nr Treviso. Rich bouquet, soft warm taste. 'Della Casa' and 'Capo di Stato' are best quality. Also sparkling.

Verdicchio dei Castelli di Jesi Mar DOC w (sp) *→★★★ DYA   Ancient famous pleasant fresh pale white from nr Ancona, dating back to the Etruscans. Also CLASSICO. Trad in amphora-shaped bottles. Esp from Brunori, Bucci, GAROFOLI, Monteschiavo, UMANI RONCHI; also FAZI-BATTAGLIA.

Verdicchio di Matelica Mar DOC w (sp) ★★ DYA   Similar to the last, though bigger and less well-known. Esp CS Belisario, Castiglioni, CAVALLERI.

Verduzzo (Colli Orientali del Friuli) F-VG DOC w dr s/sw sw ★★→★★★ 88 89 90 91 92   Full-bodied white from a native grape. The best sweet is called Ramandolo. Top makers: Dario Coos, DORIGO, Giovanni Dri.

Verduzzo (del Piave) Ven DOC w ★ DYA   A dull little white.

Vermentino Lig w DOC ★★ DYA   Best seafood white of Riviera: from Pietra Ligure and San Remo. DOC is Riviera Ligure di Ponente. See Pigato. Esp from: Anfossi, Cascina dei Peri, Colle dei Bardellini, Lambruschi, Lupi.

Vermentino di Gallura Sar DOC w ★★ DYA   Soft dry rather strong white of N Sardinia. Esp from CS di Gallura, CS Giogantinu, CS Del Vermentino.

Vernaccia di Oristano Sar DOC w dr (sw fz) ✶✶✶ 75 78' **81 83 85' 87** 88 91 92 93   Sardinian speciality, like light sherry, a touch bitter, full-bodied and interesting. SUPERIORE with 15.5% alcohol and 3 yrs of age. Top producer Contini also makes ancient solera wine Antico Gregori.

Vernaccia di San Gimignano Tus DOCG w ✶✶ 92 93   Once Michelangelo's favourite, then ordinary tourist wine. Rapid improvement in last few yrs, now newly DOCG with tougher production laws. Best from FALCHINI, Palagetto, PANIZZI, Rampa di Fugnano, San Quirico, TERUZZI & PUTHOD.

Vernatsch German for SCHIAVA.

Vicchiomaggio CHIANTI CLASSICO estate near Greve.

VIDE An association of better-class Italian producers for marketing their estate wines from many parts of Italy.

Vie di Romans ✶✶✶→✶✶✶✶   A young wine genius, Gianfranco Gallo, has built up his father's ISONZO estate to top FRIULI status within a few years. Unforgettable CHARD and SAUV; excellent TOCAI and PINOT GR.

Vietti Excellent small producer of characterful PIEDMONT wines, incl BAROLO and BARBARESCO (both ✶✶✶→✶✶✶✶). At Castiglione Falletto in Barolo region.

Vigna A single vineyard – see Introduction, page 78.

Vignamaggio Historic, beautiful and vg CHIANTI CLASSICO estate nr Greve.

Villa Matilde ✶✶   Top Campania producer. Vg FALERNO and white Falanghina.

Villa Russiz ✶✶   Impressive white DOC COLLIO from Gianni Menotti: eg, SAUV (look for 'de la Tour'), PINOT BL, TOCAI, etc.

Vin Santo Toscano Tus w s/sw ✶✶→✶✶✶   Aromatic rich and smooth. Aged in v small barrels called caratelli. Can be as astonishing as expensive, but a good one is v rare and top producers are always short of it. Best from AVIGNONESI, Cacchiano, CAPEZZANA, CONTUCCI, CORZANO & PATERNO, POLIZIANO, SAN GIUSTO A RENTENNANO, SELVAPIANA.

Vino da arrosto 'Wine for roast meat', ie good robust dry red.

Vino Nobile di Montepulciano Tus DOCG r ✶✶✶ **83 85** 86 87 **88** 90 91 92 93   Impressive SANGIOVESE red with bouquet and style, rapidly making its name and fortune. RISERVA after 3 yrs. Best estates incl AVIGNONESI, Bindella, BOSCARELLI, Canneto, LE CASALTE, Casella, Fattoria del Cerro, CONTUCCI, Dei, Lombardo, Macchione, POLIZIANO, Talosa, Tenuta Trerose, Valdipiatta, Vecchia Cantina (look for the RISERVA). Nobile is so far very reasonably priced.

Vino novello Italy's equivalent of France's primeurs (as in Beaujolais).

Vino da tavola (vdt) 'Table wine': intended to be the humblest class of Italian wine, with no specific geographical or other claim to fame, but recently the category to watch (with reasonable circumspection and a wary eye on the price) for top-class wines not conforming to DOC regulations. New laws introduced in '92 will phase out this situation (see Introduction, page 78).

Vinsanto or Vin(o) Santo Term for certain strong sweet wines esp in Tuscany: usually PASSITO. Can be v fine, esp in Tuscany and TRENTINO.

Vintage Tunina F-VG w ✶✶✶ 88 89 90 91 92 93   A notable blended white from the JERMANN estate.

Voerzio, Roberto ✶✶✶   Young BAROLO pace-setter: Brunate is new-style best.

Volpe Pasini ✶✶✶   Ambitious COLLIO ORIENTALI estate, esp for good SAUV.

VQPRD Often found on the labels of DOC wines to signify Vini di Qualità Prodotti in Regioni Delimitate.

Zanella, Maurizio Owner of CA'DEL BOSCO. His name is on his top CAB-MERLOT blend, one of Italy's best.

Zerbina, Fattoria ✶✶→✶✶✶   New leader in Romagna with best ALBANA DOCG to date (a rich PASSITO), good SANGIOVESE and a barrique-aged Sangiovese-CAB VDT called Marzeno di Marzeno.

Zibibbo Si w sw ✶✶   Fashionable MOSCATO from the island of Pantelleria. Good producer: Murana.

Zonin One of Italy's biggest privately owned estates and wineries, based at GAMBELLARA, with DOC VALPOLICELLA, etc. Others are at ASTI and in CHIANTI, San Gimignano and FRIULI. Also at Barboursville, Virginia, USA.

Germany

The German wine industry is only now beginning to recover from over two decades of drift and demoralization that began with the catastrophic Wine Laws of 1971. They encouraged low standards, over-production and confusing (not to say misleading) labelling. Demoralization, greed and fraud made matters worse. And so did the weather: 20 years with only four really good vintages.

Now quality is reasserting itself. The world is aware once more that Germany's wines reach unassailable levels – when made of the right grapes, above all, of Riesling. Five fine vintages have been matched by new determination among a new generation of winemakers. Germany's best growers (mostly young) have at last resolved to ignore laws that encourage inflation of quantity and dilution of quality, and make the best wine they can. Sugar-watery wines are still made in vast ignoble quantities – largely for the British market. But today a large number are now being made dry or close to dry, with sweetness reserved as the exception, for Spätlesen and Auslesen, and not always for these. Experiments with oak-ageing (though not of Riesling) open up new stylistic possibilities. On the home market, in restaurants, these fine dry wines are all the rage: abroad they have yet to be fully appreciated.

Officially, all German wines are classified according to grape ripeness. Most wines (like most French) need sugar added before fermentation to make up for missing sunshine. But unlike in France, German wine from grapes ripe enough not to need extra sugar is made and sold as a separate product: Qualitätswein mit Prädikat, or QmP. Within this top category, natural sugar content is expressed by traditional terms in ascending order of ripeness: Kabinett, Spätlese, Auslese, Beerenauslese, Trockenbeerenauslese.

Qualitätswein bestimmter Anbaugebiete (QbA), the second level, is for wines that needed additional sugar before fermentation. The third level, Tafelwein, has no pretensions to quality.

Though there is much more detail in the laws, this is the gist of the quality grading. It differs completely from the French system in ignoring geographical difference. There are (at least as yet) no Grands Crus, no Premiers Crus. And in theory all any German vineyard has to do to make the best wine is to grow the ripest grapes – even of inferior grape varieties – which is patent rubbish.

The law distinguishes only between degrees of geographical exactness. In labelling quality wine growers or merchants are given a choice. They can (and generally do) label the relatively small quantities of their best wine with the name of the precise vineyard or Einzellage. Germany has about 2,600 Einzellage names. Obviously only a relative few are famous enough to help sell the wine. Therefore the 1971 law created a second class of vineyard name: the Grosslage. A Grosslage is a group of Einzellagen of supposedly similar character. Because there are fewer Grosslage names, and far more wine from each, they have the advantage of familiarity – a poor substitute for hard-earned fame.

Thirdly, growers or merchants may choose to sell their wine under a regional or Bereich name. To cope with the demand for 'Bernkasteler', 'Niersteiner' or 'Johannisberger' these world-

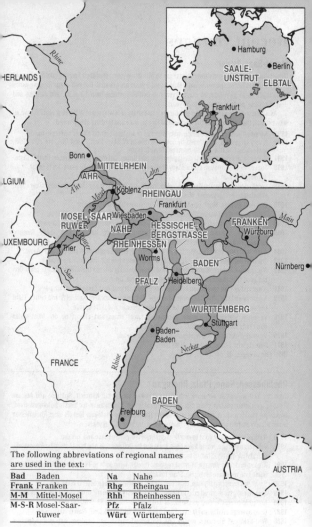

The following abbreviations of regional names are used in the text:

Bad	Baden	**Na**	Nahe
Frank	Franken	**Rhg**	Rheingau
M-M	Mittel-Mosel	**Rhh**	Rheinhessen
M-S-R	Mosel-Saar-	**Pfz**	Pfalz
	Ruwer	**Würt**	Württemberg

famous names were made legal for large districts. 'Bereich Johannisberg' is the whole of Rheingau. Beware the Bereich.

More growers are now simplifying labels to avoid confusion and clutter. Some use the village name only, or indeed sell top wines under a brand name alone as in Italy. But before German wine can fully recover its rightful place, two things are needed: the banning of inferior grapes from top areas, and a thorough classification of which those areas are. A start has at last been made in classifying 'First-class vineyards' – though unofficially, not by the inert government. They are named here and mapped (for the first time) in the 4th edition of The World Atlas of Wine. It is after all (in Germany above all) the vineyard and producer that count.

Recent vintages

Mosel-Saar-Ruwer

Mosels (including Saar and Ruwer wines) are so attractive young that their keeping qualities are not often enough explored and wines older than about 7 years are unusual. But well-made Riesling wines of Kabinett class gain from at least 5 years in bottle, Spätlese from 10 or so, and Auslese and Beerenauslese, anything from 10 to 30 years.

As a rule, in poor years the Saar and Ruwer make sharp thin wines, but in the best years, above all with botrytis, they can surpass the whole world for elegance and thrilling steely 'breed'.

1993 A v small vintage of excellent quality with lots of Auslese/botrytis and nr perfect harmony.
1992 A very large crop, threatened by cold and rain in October. Mostly good QbA, but 30% QmP, some exceptional, esp in Mittelmosel. Start to taste.
1991 A diverse vintage. Bad frost damage in Saar and Ruwer, but many fine Spätlesen. Start to taste.
1990 Superb vintage, though small. Many QmP wines were the finest for 20 years. Try to resist drinking too soon.
1989 Large and outstandingly good, with noble rot giving many Auslesen etc. Saar best; Mittelmosel overproduced. Mostly ready to drink.
1988 Excellent vintage. Much ripe QmP, esp in Mittelmosel. For long keeping.
1987 Rainy summer but warm Sept/Oct. 90% QbA wines, crisp and lively, to drink soon.
1986 Fair Riesling year despite autumn rain: 13% QmP wines, mostly Kabinett. For drinking.
1985 A modest summer but beautiful autumn. 40% of harvest was QmP. Riesling vintage from best v'yds, incl Eiswein. Many still need keeping.
1984 A late and rainy year. Two-thirds QbA, one-third Tafel- or Landwein. Almost no QmP. Avoid.
1983 The best between 76 and 88; 31% Spätlese; Auslesen few but fine. No hurry to drink.
1982 A huge ripe vintage marred by rain which considerably diluted the wines. Most is plain QbA but good sites made Kabinett, Spätlese and Auslese. Drink up.
1981 A wet vintage but some good Mittelmosels up to Spätlese. Also Eiswein. Drinking well.
1979 A patchy vintage after bad winter damage. But several excellent Kabinetts and better. Light but well-balanced wines should be drunk up. Auslesen will still improve.
1976 Vg small vintage, with some superlative sweet wines and almost no dry. Most wines now ready; the best will keep.
1975 Vg; many Spätlesen and Auslesen. Almost all now ready.
1971 Superb, with perfect balance. At its peak.
Older fine vintages: 69, 64, 59, 53, 49, 45.

Rheinhessen, Nahe, Pfalz, Rheingau

Even the best wines can be drunk with pleasure when young, but Kabinett, Spätlese and Auslese Riesling gain enormously in character by keeping for longer. Rheingau wines tend to be longest-lived, improving for 15 years or more, but wines from the Nahe and Pfalz can last as long. Rheinhessen wines usually mature sooner, and dry Franken wines are best at 3–6 years.

1993 A small vintage of v good to excellent quality. Plenty of Spätlese and Auslese.
1992 Very large vintage, would have been great but for October cold and rain. A third QmP wines of rich stylish quality. Start to taste.
1991 A good middling vintage in most regions, though light soils in Pfalz suffered from drought. Some fine wines are emerging. Start to taste.
1990 Small but exceptionally fine. High percentage of QmP will keep beyond 2000.
1989 Summer storms reduced crop in Rheingau. Vg quality elsewhere, up to Auslese level. Try now.
1988 Not quite so outstanding as the Mosel, but comparable with 83. Drinking well.
1987 Good average quality: lively round and fresh. 80% QbA, 15% QmP. Now drinking well.
1986 Well-balanced Rieslings, mostly QbA but some Kabinett and Spätlese, esp in Rheinhessen and Nahe. Good botrytis wines in Pfalz. Now drinking well.
1985 Sadly small crops, but good quality, esp Riesling. Average 65% QmP. Keep the best.
1984 Poor flowering and ripening. Three-quarters QbA. Nothing to wait for.
1983 Vg Rieslings, esp in the Rheingau and central Nahe. Generally about half QbA, but plenty of Spätlesen, now excellent to drink.
1982 A colossal vintage gathered in torrential rain. All 82s should be drunk up.
1981 Rheingau poor, Nahe and Rheinhessen better, Pfalz best. Drink up.
1979 Few great wines but many typical and good, esp in Palatinate. Drink up.
1976 The richest vintage since 21 in places. Very few dry wines. Balance less consistent than 75. Generally mature.
1971 A superlative vintage, now at its peak.
Older fine vintages: 69, 67, 64, 59, 53, 49, 45.

NB On the German vintage notation
Vintage notes after entries in the German section are given in a different form from those elsewhere, to show the style of the vintage as well as its quality. Three styles are indicated:

Bold type (eg **93**) indicates classic, super-ripe vintages with a high proportion of natural (QmP) wines, including Spätlese and Auslese.

Normal type (eg 92) indicates 'normal' successful vintages with plenty of good wine but no great preponderance of sweeter wines.

Italic type (eg *84*) indicates cool vintages with generally poor ripeness but a fair proportion of reasonably successful wines, tending to be over-acid. Few or no QmP wines, but correspondingly more selection in the QbA category. Such wines sometimes mature better than expected.

Where no mention is made the vintage is generally not recommended, or most of its wines have passed maturity.

Achkarren Bad w (r) ✹✹ Village on the KAISERSTUHL, known esp for RULANDER. Best site: Schlossberg. Good wines: DR HEGER and coop.

Adelmann, Graf Grower with 37 acres at Kleinbottwar, WURTTEMBERG. Uses the name 'Brussele'. Reds best.

Ahr Ahr r ✹→✹✹✹ 76 83 85 87 88 89 90 91 92 93 Germany's best-known red wine area, south of Bonn. Very light, pale SPATBURGUNDER, esp from Kloster Marienthal, Meyer-Näkel, STATE DOMAIN.

Amtliche Prüfungsnummer See Prüfungsnummer.

Anheuser, Paul NAHE grower (✹✹) at BAD KREUZNACH.

APNr Abbreviation of AMTLICHE PRUFUNGSNUMMER.

Assmannshausen Rhg r ✹→✹✹✹ 71 75 76 83 85 87 88 **89 90** 91 92 93 RHEINGAU village known for its usually pale, sometimes sweet reds. Top v'yd: Höllenberg. Grosslagen: Steil and Burgweg. Growers incl August Kesseler, Robert König, VON MUMM, and the STATE DOMAIN at ELTVILLE.

Auslese Specially selected wine with high natural sugar; the best affected by 'noble rot' (Edelfäule) and correspondingly unctuous in flavour.

Avelsbach M-S-R (Ruwer) w ✹✹✹ 71 75 76 83 85 87 88 **89 90 91** 92 93 Village nr TRIER. At (rare) best, lovely delicate wines. Esp BISCHOFLICHE WEINGUTER, Staatliche Weinbaudomäne (see Staatsweingut). Grosslage: Römerlay.

Ayl M-S-R (Saar) w ✹✹✹ 71 75 76 83 85 87 88 89 **90** 91 92 93 One of the best villages of the SAAR. First-class v'yd: Kupp. Grosslage: SCHARZBERG. Growers incl BISCHOFLICHE WEINGUTER, Lauer, DR WAGNER.

Bacchus Modern, perfumed, even kitsch, grape. Best for sweet wines.

Bacharach ✹→✹✹✹ District name for southern MITTELRHEIN v'yds downstream from RHEINGAU. Now amalgamated with RHEINBURGENGAU to form the new BEREICH 'Loreley'. Racy RIESLINGS, some v fine. Growers incl Fritz Bastian, TONI JOST, Randolph Kauer, Ratzenberger.

Bad Dürkheim Pfz w (r) ✹✹→✹✹✹ 76 83 85 86 87 88 **89 90** 91 92 93 Main town of MITTELHAARDT, with the world's biggest barrel (converted into a tavern) and a vast ancient September wine festival, the 'Wurstmarkt'. Top v'yds: Michelsberg, Spielberg. Grosslagen: Feuerberg, Hochmess, Schenkenböhl. Growers: Kurt Darting, FITZ-RITTER, Karst, Karl Schäfer.

Bad Kreuznach Nahe w ✹✹→✹✹✹ 75 76 79 83 85 86 87 88 **89 90** 91 92 93 Main NAHE town. Many fine v'yds. First-class: Brückes, Kahlenberg, Krötenpfuhl. Grosslage: Kronenberg. Growers incl ANHEUSER, Finkenauer, PLETTENBERG.

Baden Huge SW area of scattered wine-growing. The style is substantial, generally dry, relatively low in acid, good for mealtimes. Fine Pinots etc and SPATBURGUNDER, less RIES. Best areas: KAISERSTUHL, ORTENAU.

Badische Bergstrasse/Kraichgau (Bereich) Widespread district of N BADEN. WEISSBURGUNDER and RULANDER are best.

Badischer Winzerkeller New name for the ZBW, Germany's (and Europe's) biggest coop, at BREISACH; 25,000 members with 12,000 acres, producing almost half of BADEN's wine at all quality levels.

Badisches Frankenland See Tauberfranken.

Barriques Some German growers are experimenting with fashionable small-barrel new-oak ageing; a quick route to notoriety and higher prices. It can be positive for SPATBURGUNDER, WEISSBURGUNDER or GRAUBURGUNDER, but not RIES.

Bassermann-Jordan 117-acre MITTELHAARDT family estate with many of the best v'yds in DEIDESHEIM, FORST, RUPPERTSBERG, etc. 100% RIES and a formidable track-record.

Becker, J B Dedicated family estate and brokerage house at WALLUF. 30 acres in ELTVILLE, MARTINSTHAL, Walluf. Specialist in dry RIESLINGS.

Beerenauslese Extremely sweet and luscious wine from selected exceptionally ripe individual berries, their sugar and flavour usually concentrated by 'noble rot'. Very rare and expensive.

Bensheim See Hessische Berstrasse.

Bercher KAISERSTUHL estate; 40 acres of white and red Pinots at Burkheim. Good dry wines.

Bereich District within an Anbaugebiet (region). The word on a label should be treated as a warning. As a rule do not buy. See Introduction and under Bereich names, eg Bernkastel (Bereich).

Bergweiler-Prüm-Erben, Weingut Zacharias, See Pauly-Bergweiler, Dr.

Bernkastel M-M w ✶✶→✶✶✶✶ 71 75 76 79 83 *84* 85 86 87 **88** 89 90 91 92 93 Top wine town of the MITTELMOSEL; the epitome of RIES. Great First-class v'yd: Doctor, 8 acres (✶✶✶✶); First-class v'yds: Graben, Lay. Grosslagen: Badstube (✶✶✶) and Kurfürstlay (✶). Top growers incl FRIEDRICH WILHELM GYMNASIUM, HERIBERT KERPEN, LAUERBURG, DR LOOSEN, DR PAULY-BERGWEILER, J J PRUM, Studert-Prüm, THANISCH, WEGELER-DEINHARD.

Bernkastel (Bereich) Wide area of deplorably mixed quality but hopefully flowery character. Mostly MULLER-T. Includes all the MITTELMOSEL.

Biffar, Josef Rising star DEIDESHEIM estate. 40 acres (also WACHENHEIM) of RIES. Intense classic wines.

Bingen Rhh w ✶✶→✶✶✶ 71 75 76 83 85 87 88 89 90 91 92 93 Rhine/NAHE town; fine v'yds: First-class is Scharlachberg. Grosslage: Sankt Rochuskapelle.

Bingen (Bereich) District name for west RHEINHESSEN.

Bischöfliche Weingüter Famous M-S-R estate at TRIER, a union of the cathedral properties with 2 other famous charities, the Bischöfliches Priesterseminar and the Bischöfliches Konvikt. 260 acres of top v'yds, esp in SAAR and RUWER. After recent disappointments there are signs of improvement. Ruwer wines currently best (esp EITELSBACH, KASEL).

Blue Nun The best-selling brand of LIEBFRAUMILCH, from SICHEL.

Bocksbeutel Flask-shaped bottle used for FRANKEN wines.

Bodenheim Rhh w ✶✶ Village nr NIERSTEIN with full earthy wines, esp from First-class v'yds Hoch and Silberberg. Top grower: Kühling-Gillot.

Bodensee (Bereich) Minor district of S BADEN, on Lake Constance.

Brauneberg M-M w ✶✶✶✶ 71 75 76 83 85 86 87 88 89 90 91 92 93 Top M-S-R village nr BERNKASTEL (750 acres), unbroken tradition for excellent full-flavoured RIES. 'Grand Cru' if anything on the Mosel is. Great First-class v'yd: Juffer-Sonnenuhr. First-class v'yd is Juffer. Grosslage: Kurfürstlay. Growers: FRITZ HAAG, WILLI HAAG, Paulinshof, M F RICHTER.

Breisach Bad Frontier town on RHINE nr KAISERSTUHL. Seat of the largest German coop, the BADISCHER WINZERKELLER.

Breisgau (Bereich) Minor BADEN district. Esp v pale pink WEISSHERBST.

Breuer, Weingut G Family estate of 36 acres in RUDESHEIM, with 6 acres of Berg Schlossberg, and 12.5-acre monopole RAUENTHALER Nonnenberg. Fine quality and new ideas, incl sparkling (87) RIES-Pinot Bl-Pinot Gr.

Buhl, Reichsrat von Historic PFALZ family estate, below historic form. 160 acres (DEIDESHEIM, FORST, RUPPERTSBERG...). Now leased by Japanese firm.

Bundesweinprämierung The German State Wine Award, organized by DLG (see next page): gives great (Grosse), silver or bronze medallion labels.

Bürgerspital zum Heiligen Geist Ancient charitable estate at WURZBURG. 333 acres in Würzburg, RANDERSACKER, etc; often magnificent rich dry wines, esp from SILVANER and RIES. 89–92 vintages substandard.

Bürklin-Wolf, Dr Famous PFALZ family estate. 222 acres in FORST, DEIDESHEIM, RUPPERTSBERG and WACHENHEIM. Vg 89s.

Castell'sches, Fürstlich Domänenamt Historic 142-acre princely estate in STEIGERWALD. Noble FRANKEN wines: SILVANER, RIESLANER. Also SEKT.

Chardonnay A small acreage of Chard has been experimentally, and sometimes illegally, planted – it is now legal in PFALZ and BADEN-WURTTEMBERG.

Charta Organization of top RHEINGAU estates making forceful medium-dry RIES to far higher standards than dismally permissive laws require.

Christoffel, J J Tiny domaine in ERDEN, GRAACH, URZIG, WEHLEN. Polished RIES.

Clevner (or Klevner) Synonym in WURTTEMBERG for Blauer Frühburgunder black grape, supposedly a mutation of Pinot N or Italian Chiavenna (early-ripening black Pinot). Also ORTENAU (BADEN) synonym for TRAMINER.

Crusius 30-acre family estate at TRAISEN, NAHE. Vivid RIES from Bastei, Rotenfels and SCHLOSSBÖCKELHEIM. Top wines age v well. Also good SEKT and freshly fruity SPATBURGUNDER dry rosé.

Deidesheim Pfz w (r) ✱✱→✱✱✱✱✱ 71 75 76 83 85 86 87 88 89 90 91 92 93 Biggest top-quality wine village of PFALZ (1,000 acres). Rich high-flavoured lively wines. Also Sekt. First-class v'yds are Grainhübel, Hohenmorgen, Kalkofen, Kieselberg, Langenmorgen, Leinhöhle. Grosslagen: Hofstück (✱✱), Mariengarten (✱✱✱). Esp BASSERMANN-JORDAN, Joseph Biffar, BURKLIN-WOLF, DEINHARD, VON BUHL, Kimmich.

Deinhard Famous old Koblenz merchants and growers of high quality wines in RHEINGAU, MITTELMOSEL, RUWER and PFALZ (see Wegeler-Deinhard), also makers of vg SEKT (eg Lila). Leaders in new ideas. Their Heritage range of single-village (DEIDESHEIM, HOCHHEIM, JOHANNISBERG, etc) TROCKEN wines are well-made but singularly austere.

Deinhard, Dr Fine 62-acre family estate: many of DEIDESHEIM's best v'yds.

Deutsche Weinstrasse Tourist road of S PFALZ, Bockenheim to SCHWEIGEN.

Deutscher Tafelwein Officially the term for v humble German wines. Now confusingly the flag of convenience for some top novelties as well (eg BARRIQUE wines). As in Italy, the law will have to change.

Deutsches Weinsiegel A quality seal (ie neck label) for wines which have passed a statutory tasting test. Seals are: yellow for dry, green for medium-dry, red for medium-sweet.

DLG (Deutsche Landwirtschaftgesellschaft) The German Agricultural Society at Frankfurt. Awards national medals for quality.

Dhron See Neumagen-Dhron.

Diabetiker Wein Wine with minimal residual sugar (less than 4 grams per litre); thus suitable for diabetics – or those who like *very* dry wine.

Diel auf Burg Layen, Schlossgut Fashionable 30-acre NAHE estate; known for ageing RULANDER and WEISSBURGUNDER in French BARRIQUES. Also fine traditional RIES.

Dom German for 'cathedral'. Wines from the famous TRIER cathedral properties have 'Dom' before the v'yd name.

Domäne German for 'domain' or 'estate'. Sometimes used alone to mean the 'State domain' (STAATLICHE WEINBAUDOMANE).

Dönnhoff, Weingut Hermann 23-acre NAHE estate with exceptionally fine RIES from NIEDERHAUSEN, Oberhausen, etc.

Dornfelder New red grape making deep-coloured everyday wines in PFALZ.

Durbach Baden w (r) ✱✱→✱✱✱✱ 76 83 85 87 88 89 90 91 92 93 Village with 775 acres of BADEN's best v'yds. Top growers: A Laible, H Männle, SCHLOSS STAUFENBERG, Wolf-Metternich. Choose their KLINGELBERGERS (RIES) and CLEVNERS (TRAMINER). Grosslage: Fürsteneck.

Edel Means 'noble'. Edelfäule means 'noble rot': the condition which gives the greatest sweet wines (see page 52).

Egon Müller zu Scharzhof Top SAAR estate of 32 acres at WILTINGEN. Its delicate racy SCHARZHOFBERGER RIESLINGS in AUSLESEN vintages are among the world's greatest wines. The best are given gold capsules. 89s and 90s are sublime, honeyed, immortal. Le Gallais is a second estate in WILTINGER Braune Kupp.

Eiswein Wine made from frozen grapes with the ice (ie water content) discarded, thus v concentrated in flavour and sugar – of BEERENAUSLESE ripeness or more. But alcohol content can be as low as 5.5%. High acidity gives them v long life.Rare and v expensive. Sometimes made as late as January or February following the vintage.

Eitelsbach M-S-R (Ruwer) w ✶✶→✶✶✶✶ 71 75 76 83 85 87 88 89 90 91 92 93 RUWER village now part of TRIER, incl superb Great First-class KARTHAUSERHOFBERG estate. Grosslage: Römerlay.

Elbling Traditional grape widely grown on upper MOSEL. Can be sharp and tasteless but capable of great freshness and vitality in the best conditions (eg at Nittel or Schloss Thorn in the OBERMOSEL).

Elbtal Sachsen Former E German region (750 acres) on outskirts of Dresden and Meissen. MULLER-T dominant; also WEISSBURGUNDER, TRAMINER, etc. Schloss Wackerbarth makes good SEKT Graf von Wackerbarth.

Eltville Rhg w ✶✶→✶✶✶✶ 71 75 76 83 85 86 87 88 89 90 91 92 93 Major wine town: cellars of RHEINGAU STATE DOMAIN, FISCHER and VON SIMMERN estates. Excellent wine. First-class v'yd: Sonnenberg. Grosslage: Steinmächer.

Enkirch M-M w ✶✶→✶✶✶✶ 71 76 83 85 87 88 89 90 91 93 Minor MITTELMOSEL village, often overlooked but with lovely light tasty wine. Grosslage: Schwarzlay. Top v'yds: Batterieberg, Zeppwingert.

Erbach Rhg w ✶✶✶→✶✶✶✶ 71 76 83 85 86 87 88 89 90 91 92 93 Top RHEINGAU area: powerful perfumed wines, incl from superb First-class v'yds Hohenrain, MARCOBRUNN, Siegelsberg, Steinmorgen; Schlossberg is another top v'yd. Major estates: SCHLOSS REINHARTS-HAUSEN, SCHLOSS SCHONBORN. Also BECKER, KNYPHAUSEN, VON SIMMERN, etc.

Erben Word meaning 'heirs', often used on old-established estate labels.

Erden M-M w ✶✶→✶✶✶✶✶ 71 75 76 83 *84* 85 86 87 88 89 90 91 92 93 Village between Urzig and Kröv: noble full-flavoured vigorous wine (different in style so without the high repute of neighbouring BERNKASTEL and WEHLEN). Great First-class v'yds: Prälat, Treppchen. Grosslage: Schwarzlay. Growers incl BISCHOFLICHE WEINGUTER, Stefan Ehlen, DR LOOSEN, Meulenhoff, MONCHHOF, Nicolay.

Erstes Gewächs Literally 'first growth'. A new (94) classification for the top vineyards of the RHEINGAU. Applies from '92 vintage.

Erzeugerabfüllung Bottled by producer. Being replaced by 'GUTSABFULLUNG'.

Escherndorf Frank w ✶✶→✶✶✶✶ 76 83 87 88 89 90 91 92 93 Important wine town near WURZBURG. Similar tasty dry wine. Top v'yds: Berg, and First-class Lump. Grosslage: Kirchberg. Growers incl JULIUSSPITAL.

Eser, Weingut August 20-acre RHEINGAU estate at OESTRICH. V'yds also in HALLGARTEN, RAUENTHAL (esp Gehrn, Rothenberg), WINKEL. Model wines.

Eser, Hans Hermann JOHANNISBERG family estate. 45 acres. RIESLINGS that justify the great Johannisberg name.

Filzen M-S-R (Saar) w ✶✶→✶✶✶ 76 83 85 87 88 89 90 91 92 93 Small SAAR village nr WILTINGEN. First-class v'yd: Pulchen. Grower to note: Piedmont.

Fischer, Weingut Dr 60-acre OCKFEN, WAWERN estate: variable quality (83 vg, 90 good).

Fischer Erben, Weingut 18-acre RHEINGAU estate at ELTVILLE with highest traditional standards. Long-lived classic wines.

Fitz-Ritter Reliable BAD DURKHEIM estate. 54 acres, fine RIES.

Forschungsanstalt See Hessische Forschungsanstalt.

Forst Pfz w ✶✶→✶✶✶✶✶ 71 75 76 83 85 86 87 88 89 90 91 92 93 MITTELHAARDT village with 500 acres of Germany's best v'yds. Ripe, richly fragrant, full-bodied but subtle wines. First-class v'yds: Jesuitengarten, Kirchenstück, Pechstein, Ungeheuer. Grosslagen: Mariengarten, Schnepfenflug. Top growers: BASSERMANN-JORDAN, DEINHARD, Georg Mosbacher, Spindler, Werlé.

To decipher codes, please refer to symbols key at front of book, and to 'How to use this book' on page 5.

Franken Franconia. Region of excellent distinctive dry wines, esp SILVANER, always bottled in round-bellied flasks (BOCKSBEUTEL). The centre is WURZBURG. Bereich names: MAINDREIECK, STEIGERWALD. Top producers: BURGERSPITAL, Castell, JULIUSSPITAL, WIRSCHING, etc.

Freiburg Baden w (r) ★→★★ DYA   Wine centre in BREISGAU, N of MARKGRAFLERLAND. Good GUTEDEL.

Freinsheim Pfz w r ✶✶   Well-known village of MITTELHAARDT with high proportion of RIES. Aromatic spicy wines. Top grower: LINGENFELDER.

Friedrich Wilhelm Gymnasium Superb 111-acre charitable estate based in TRIER with v'yds in BERNKASTEL, GRAACH, OCKFEN, TRITTENHEIM, ZELTINGEN, etc, all M-S-R. 90s, 91s, 92s should have been better.

Remember that vintage information for German wines is given in a different form from the ready/not ready distinction applying to other countries. Read the explanation on page 103.

Fuhrmann See Pfeffingen.

Gallais Le See Egon Müller.

Geheimrat 'J' Brand-name of good very dry RIES SPATLESE from WEGELER-DEINHARD, OESTRICH, since '85. Epitomizes new thinking.

Geisenheim Rhg w ★★→★★★ 76 83 85 86 87 88 89 90 91 92 93   Village famous for Germany's best-known wine school and fine aromatic wines. First-class v'yds are Kläuserweg, Rothenberg. Grosslagen: Burgweg, Erntebringer. Many top growers (eg SCHLOSS SCHONBORN) have v'yds here.

Gemeinde A commune or parish.

Gewürztraminer (or Traminer) 'Spicy' grape, speciality of Alsace, used a little in Germany, esp in PFALZ, RHEINHESSEN and BADEN.

Gimmeldingen Pfz w ★→★★ 76 83 85 87 88 89 90 91 92 93   Village just S of MITTELHAARDT. At their best, similar wines. Grosslage: Meerspinne.

Goldener Oktober Brand of RHINE and MOSEL blends from ST-URSULA.

Graach M-M w ★★→★★★ 71 75 76 83 *84* 85 86 87 88 89 90 91 92 93   Small village between BERNKASTEL and WEHLEN. First-class v'yds: Domprobst, Himmelreich, Josephshöfer. Grosslage: Münzlay. Many top growers, eg: KESSELSTATT, DR LOOSEN, J J PRUM, WILLI SCHAEFER, SELBACH-OSTER, WEINS-PRUM.

Grans-Fassian Fine 25-acre MOSEL estate at Leiwen. V'yds there and in PIESPORT, TRITTENHEIM.

Grauburgunder Synonym of RULANDER or Pinot Gris.

Grosser Ring Group of top (VDP) MOSEL-SAAR-RUWER estates.

Grosslage See Introduction, pages 100–101.

Gunderloch Excellent 30-acre NACKENHEIM estate, the best in RHEINHESSEN today. 70% RIES. Best wines from N Rothenberg, but all are vg.

Guntersblum Rhh w ★→★★ 76 83 85 88 89 90 91 92 93   Big wine town S of OPPENHEIM. First-class v'yds: Bornpfad, Himmeltal. Grosslagen: Krötenbrunnen, Vogelsgärten. Top grower: RAPPENHOF.

Guntrum, Louis Fine 164-acre family estate in NIERSTEIN, OPPENHEIM, etc, and reliable merchant house. Fine SILVANERS and GEWURZ as well as RIES.

Gutedel German word for the Chasselas grape, used in S BADEN.

Gutsabfüllung Estate-bottled. A new term limited to qualified estates.

Gutsverwaltung Estate administration.

Haag, Fritz and Willi Two small quality BRAUNEBERG estates. FH is v top league.

Haart, Reinhold Small estate, the best in PIESPORT. Refined aromatic wines, capable of long ageing.

Halbtrocken Medium-dry (literally 'semi-dry'). Containing less than 18 but more than 9 grams per litre unfermented sugar. An increasingly popular category of wine intended for mealtimes, often better balanced than TROCKEN. All CHARTA wines are halbtrocken.

Hallgarten Rhg w ★★→★★★ 71 76 83 85 86 87 88 **89** 90 91 92 93   Small wine town behind HATTENHEIM. Robust full-bodied wines, mysteriously seldom seen. Dominated by coops (unusual for Rhg). Weingut Fred Prinz is emerging as top estate.

Hallgarten, House of Well-known London-based wine merchant.

Hattenheim Rhg w ✶✶→✶✶✶✶ 71 75 76 83 85 87 88 **89 90** 91 92 93
Superlative 500-acre wine town. First-class v'yds are Engelmannsberg, Mannberg, Pfaffenberg, STEINBERG (ORTSTEIL). Vg others incl Nussbrunnen, Wisselbrunnen. Grosslage: Deutelsberg. MARCOBRUNN lies on ERBACH boundary. Many fine estates incl KNYPHAUSEN, RESS, SCHLOSS SCHONBORN, VON SIMMERN, STATE DOMAIN, etc.

Heger, Dr Some of BADEN's best SPATBURGUNDER reds come from old vines on this 28-acre ACHKARREN estate. Also fine GRAUBURGUNDER, WEISSBURGUNDER.

Heilbronn Würt w r ✶→✶✶✶ 76 83 85 87 88 **89 90** 91 92 93 Wine town with many small growers and a big coop. Best wines are RIESLINGS. Seat of DLG competition. Top growers: Amalienhof, Drautz-Able, Heinrich.

Hessen, Prinz von Famous 75-acre estate in JOHANNISBERG, KIEDRICH and WINKEL. Despite gold medals, recent wines raw or sharp, lacking fruit.

Hessische Bergstrasse w ✶✶→✶✶ 76 83 85 87 88 **89 90** 91 92 93 Smallest wine region in former West Germany (1,000 acres), N of Heidelberg. Pleasant RIES from STATE DOMAIN v'yds at Bensheim, Bergstrasser Coop, Heppenheim and Stadt Bensheim.

Hessische Forschungsanstalt für Wein-Obst-& Gartenbau Famous wine school and research establishment at GEISENHEIM, RHEINGAU. Good wines incl reds. The name on the label is Forschungsanstalt.

Heyl zu Herrnsheim Leading 72-acre NIERSTEIN estate, 60% RIES. An excellent record, recently patchy. Now part-owned by VALCKENBERG.

Hochgewächs A superior level of QBA RIES, esp in MOSEL-SAAR-RUWER.

Hochheim Rhg w ✶✶→✶✶✶✶ 71 75 76 79 83 84 85 86 87 88 **89 90** 91 92 93 600-acre wine town 15 miles E of main RHEINGAU area, once thought of as best on Rhine. Similar fine wines with an earthy intensity and fragrance of their own. Top v'yds: Domdechaney, Hölle, Kirchenstück, Königin Viktoria Berg (12-acre monopoly of Hupfeld of OESTRICH, sold only by DEINHARD). Grosslage: Daubhaus. Growers incl ASCHROTT, Hupfeld, FRANZ KUNSTLER, RESS, SCHLOSS SCHONBORN, STAATSWEINGUT, WERNER.

Hock Traditional English term for Rhine wine, derived from HOCHHEIM.

Hoensbroech, Weingut Reichsgraf zu Top KRAICHGAU estate. 37 acres. Excellent dry WEISSBURGUNDER and SILVANER, eg Michelfelder Himmelberg. Some of BADEN's best wines.

Hövel, Weingut von Very fine SAAR estate at OBERMOSEL (Hütte is 12-acre monopoly) and in SCHARZHOFBERG.

Huxelrebe Modern very aromatic grape variety, mainly for dessert wines.

Ihringen Bad r w ✶✶✶✶✶ 83 85 86 87 88 **89 90** 91 92 93 One of the best villages of the KAISERSTUHL, BADEN. Proud of its SPATBURGUNDER red, WEISSHERBST and vg SILVANER. Top growers: Dr Heger, Stigler.

Ilbesheim Pfz w ✶✶✶✶ 83 85 87 88 **89 90** 91 92 93 Base of vast growers' coop of SUDLICHE WEINSTRASSE 'Deutsches Weintor'. See also Schweigen.

Ingelheim Rhh r w ✶ 85 88 **89 90** 91 92 93 Town opposite the RHEINGAU historically known for SPATBURGUNDER. First-class v'yds: Horn, Pares, Sonnenberg, Steinacker.

Iphofen Frank w ✶✶→✶✶✶ 75 76 79 83 85 87 88 **89 90** 91 92 93 Village E of WURZBURG. Superb First-class v'yds: Julius-Echter-Berg, Kalb. Grosslage: Burgweg. Growers: JULIUSSPITAL, Ruck, STAATLICHER HOFKELLER, WIRSCHING.

Jahrgang Year – as in 'vintage'.

Johannisberg Rhg w ✶✶→✶✶✶✶ 71 75 76 83 85 86 87 88 **89 90** 91 92 93 260-acre village with superlative subtle RIES. Top v'yds incl Goldatzel, Klaus. First-class: Hölle, SCHLOSS JOHANNISBERG. Grosslage: Erntebringer. Many good growers. Beware 'Bereich Johannisberg' wines (next entry).

Johannisberg (Bereich) District name for the entire RHEINGAU.

Johner, Karl-Heinz Tiny BADEN estate at Bischoffingen, in the front line for new-look SPATBURGUNDER and oak-aged WEISSBURGUNDER.

Josephshöfer Fine v'yd at GRAACH, the sole property of VON KESSELSTATT.

Jost, Toni Perhaps the top estate of the MITTELRHEIN. 25 acres, mainly RIES, in BACHARACH and also in the RHEINGAU.

Juliusspital Ancient religious charity at WURZBURG with 374 acres of top FRANKEN v'yds and many of the region's best wines. Look for its SILVANERS and RIESLINGS.

Kabinett The term for the lightest category of natural, unsugared (QMP) wines. Low in alcohol (RIES averages 7–9%) but capable of sublime finesse. Do not hurry to drink.

Kaiserstuhl (Bereich) One of the top districts of BADEN, with a notably warm climate and volcanic soil. Villages incl ACHKARREN, IHRINGEN. Grosslage: Vulkanfelsen.

Kallstadt Pfz w (r) ✶✶→✶✶✶✶ 76 83 85 86 87 88 89 90 91 92 93 Village of N MITTELHAARDT. Fine rich wines are frequently underrated. First-class v'yd: Saumagen. Grosslagen: Feuerberg, Kobnert. Growers incl Henninger, KOEHLER-RUPRECHT, Schüster.

Kammerpreismünze See Landespreismünze.

Kanzem M-S-R (Saar) w ✶✶✶ 71 75 76 83 85 87 88 89 90 91 92 93 Small neighbour of WILTINGEN. First-class v'yd: Altenberg. Grosslage: SCHARZBERG. Growers incl Othegraven, Reverchon. Best is J P Reinert.

Karlsmühle Hotelier in MERTESDORF, making top-grade RUWERS in KASEL and his monopole v'yd: Lorenzhof.

Karthäuserhofberg Top RUWER estate of 46 acres at Eitelsbach. Easily recognized by bottles with only a neck-label. Recently back on top form, esp with standard wines.

Kasel M-S-R (Ruwer) w ✶✶→✶✶✶✶ 71 75 76 83 85 86 87 88 89 90 91 92 93 Village with stunning flowery light wines. First-class v'yds: Kehrnagel, Nies'chen. Grosslage: Römerlay. Top growers: KARLSMUHLE, VON KESSELSTATT, WEGELER-DEINHARD.

Keller Wine cellar.

Kellerei Winery.

Kerner Modern grape variety, earlier-ripening than RIES, of fair quality but without the inbuilt harmony of Riesling.

Kerpen, Weingut Heribert Tiny top-class estate in BERNKASTEL, GRAACH, WEHLEN.

Kesselstatt, von The biggest private MOSEL estate, 600 yrs old. Some 150 acres in GRAACH, KASEL, PIESPORT, WILTINGEN, etc, plus substantial rented or managed estates, making aromatic, generously fruity MOSELS. Now belongs to Günther Reh (of Leiwen). Excellent wines since '88.

Kesten M-M w ✶→✶✶✶ 71 75 76 83 85 86 87 88 89 90 91 92 93 Neighbour of BRAUNEBERG. Best wines (from Paulinshofberg v'yd) similar. Grosslage: Kurfürstlay. Top grower: Paulinshof.

Kiedrich Rhg w ✶✶→✶✶✶ 71 76 83 85 86 87 88 89 90 91 92 93 Neighbour of RAUENTHAL; almost as splendid and high-flavoured. First-class v'yds: Gräfenberg, Sandgrub; also good: Wasseros. Grosslage: Heiligenstock. Growers incl FISCHER, KNYPHAUSEN, STATE DOMAIN. R WEIL now top estate.

Klingelberger ORTENAU (BADEN) term for RIESLING, esp in DURBACH.

Kloster Eberbach Glorious 12th-C Cistercian Abbey in the forest at HATTENHEIM, RHEINGAU. Its monks planted the STEINBERG. Now STATE DOMAIN property and HQ of the German Wine Academy.

Klüsserath M-M w ✶✶→✶✶✶ 76 83 85 88 89 90 91 92 93 Minor MOSEL village, good yrs well worth trying. Best v'yd: Bruderschaft. Grosslage: St-Michael. Top growers: FRIEDRICH WILHELM GYMNASIUM, Kirsten.

Knyphausen, Weingut Freiherr zu Noble 50-acre estate on former Cistercian land (see Kloster Eberbach) in ELTVILLE, ERBACH, HATTENHEIM, KIEDRICH and MARCOBRUNN. Top RHEINGAU wines, many dry.

Koehler-Ruprecht Highly-rated little (22-acre) estate; the top grower in KALLSTADT, PFALZ. Ultra-traditional winemaking; v long-lived dry RIESLINGS from K Saumagen are memorable. Now also making outstanding Burgundian Pinot Noirs.

Königin Viktoria Berg See Hochheim.

Kraichgau Small BADEN region S of Heidelberg. Top grower: HOENSBROECH.

Kreuznach District name for the entire northern NAHE, now united with SCHLOSSBOCKELHEIM to form BEREICH 'NAHETAL'. See also Bad Kreuznach.

Kröv M-M w ★→★★★ **88 89 90** 91 92 93   Popular tourist resort famous for its Grosslage name: Nacktarsch, meaning 'bare bottom'. Avoid.

Künstler, Franz Outstanding 12.5-acre HOCHHEIM estate, esp for H Hölle and H Kirchenstück and model CHARTA wines.

Landespreismünze Prizes for quality at state, rather than national, level. Considered by some more discriminating than DLG medals.

Landwein A category of better quality TAFELWEIN (the grapes must be slightly riper) from 20 designated regions. It must be TROCKEN or HALBTROCKEN. Similar in intention to France's vin de pays.

Lauerburg One of the 4 owners of the famous Doctor v'yd, with 10 acres, all in BERNKASTEL. Often excellent racy wines.

Leitz, J Fine little RUDESHEIM family estate for elegant dry RIES. A rising star.

Liebfrauenstift 26-acre v'yd in city of Worms; origin of 'LIEBFRAUMILCH'.

Liebfraumilch Much abused name, accounting for 50% of all German wine exports – to the detriment of Germany's better products. Legally defined as a QBA 'of pleasant character' from RHEINHESSEN, PFALZ, NAHE or RHEINGAU, of a blend with at least 51% RIESLING, SILVANER, KERNER or MULLER-T. Most is mild, semi-sweet wine from Rheinhessen and Pfalz. Rules now say it must have more than 18 grams per litre unfermented sugar. S'times v cheap and of inferior quality, depending on brand or shipper. Its definition makes a mockery of the legal term 'Quality Wine'.

Lieser M-M w ★→★★ **71 76 83 85** 86 87 88 **89 90** 91 92 93   Little-known neighbour of BERNKASTEL. Lighter wines. First-class v'yd: Niederberg-Helden. Grosslage: Kurfürstlay.

Lingenfelder, Weingut Small, innovative Grosskarlbach (PFALZ) estate: some of Germany's top burgundy-style SPATBURGUNDER, full-bodied RIES, etc.

Loosen, Weingut Dr 20-acre St-Johannishof estate in BERNKASTEL, ERDEN, GRAACH, URZIG, WEHLEN. Lovely recent quality: 91 92 were top in M-S-R.

Lorch Rhg w (r) ★→★★ **71 76 83 85** 87 88 **89 90** 91 92 93   At extreme W of RHEINGAU. Some fine light MITTELRHEIN-like RIES. Best grower: von Kanitz.

Loreley (Bereich) New BEREICH name for amalgamated RHEINBURGENGAU and BACHARACH districts.

Löwenstein, Fürst 66-acre FRANKEN estate: classic dry powerful wines. 45-acre HALLGARTEN property is rented by MATUSCHKA-GREIFFENCLAU. V mixed quality in '91 and '92.

Maindreieck (Bereich) District name for central FRANKEN, incl WURZBURG.

Marcobrunn Historic RHEINGAU v'yd; one of Germany's v best. See Erbach.

Markgräflerland (Bereich) District S of FREIBURG, BADEN. Typical GUTEDEL wine can be delicious refreshment when drunk v young, but best wines are the -BURGUNDERS: WEISS-, GRAU- and SPAT-. Also Sekt.

Martinsthal Rhg w ★★→★★★ **71 75 76 83 85** 86 87 88 **89 90** 91 92 93   Little-known neighbour of RAUENTHAL. First-class v'yd: Langenberg; also gd: Wildsau. Grosslage: Steinmächer. Growers incl BECKER, Diefenhardt.

Matuschka-Greiffenclau, Graf Erwein Owner of ancient SCHLOSS VOLLRADS and tenant of WEINGUT FURST LOWENSTEIN at HALLGARTEN. A principal spokesman for German wine, esp dry, and its combination with food.

Maximin Grünhaus M-S-R (Ruwer) w ★★★★ **71 75 76 79 83 85** 86 87 88 89 90 91 92 93   Supreme RUWER estate of 80 acres at MERTESDORF. Wines of firm elegance to mature 20 yrs+.

Mertesdorf See Maximin Grünhaus and Karlsmühle.

Mittelhaardt The north-central and best part of PFALZ, incl DEIDESHEIM, FORST, RUPPERTSBERG, WACHENHEIM, largely planted with RIESLING.

Mittelhaardt-Deutsche Weinstrasse (Bereich) District name for the northern and central parts of PFALZ.

Mittelheim Rhg w ★★ **71 75 76 83 85** 86 87 88 **89 90** 91 92 93   Relatively minor village between WINKEL and OESTRICH.

Mittelmosel The central and best part of the MOSEL, incl BERNKASTEL, PIESPORT, WEHLEN, etc. Its top sites are (or should be) entirely RIESLING.

Mittelrhein Northern Rhine area of domestic importance, incl BACHARACH and Boppard. Some attractive steely RIESLING.

Morio-Muskat Stridently aromatic grape variety now on the decline.

Mosel The TAFELWEIN name of the area. All quality wines from the Mosel must be labelled MOSEL-SAAR-RUWER. (Moselle is the French – and English – spelling for this beautiful river.)

Mosel-Saar-Ruwer (M-S-R) 31,000-acre QUALITATSWEIN region between TRIER and Koblenz. Incl MITTELMOSEL, RUWER, SAAR areas. Natural home of RIES.

Moselland, Winzergenossenschaft Biggest M-S-R coop, based at BERNKASTEL, incl Saar-Winzerverein at WILTINGEN. Its 5,200 members produce 25% of M-S-R wines (incl classic method SEKT), but nothing above average.

Müller zu Scharzhof, Egon See Egon Müller.

Müller-Catoir Outstanding estate of NEUSTADT, PFALZ, with 40 acres and many varieties, incl barrel-aged reds. A name to conjure with.

Müller-Thurgau Fruity early-ripening, usually low-acid grape; commonest in PFALZ, RHEINHESSEN, NAHE, BADEN and FRANKEN; increasingly planted in all areas, incl MOSEL. Should be banned from all top v'yds by law.

Mumm, von 173-acre estate in JOHANNISBERG, RUDESHEIM, etc. Under the same control as SCHLOSS JOHANNISBERG, but v variable quality.

Münster Nahe w ★→★★★★ 71 75 76 83 85 86 87 88 **89 90** 91 92 93 Best village of N NAHE, with fine delicate wines. First-class v'yds: Dautenpflänzer, Felseneck, Kapellenberg, Pittersberg, Schlossberg. Grosslage: Schlosskapelle. Top growers: Kruger-Rumpf, STATE DOMAIN.

Nackenheim Rhh w ★→★★★★ 75 76 83 85 86 87 88 89 90 91 92 93 Neighbour of NIERSTEIN, both have top Rhine terroir. Best wines (esp First-class Rothenberg v'yd) similar. Grosslagen: Spiegelberg (★★), Gutes Domtal (★). Best grower: GUNDERLOCH.

Nahe Tributary of the Rhine and high quality wine region. Balanced fresh clean but full-, even earthy-flavoured wines; RIES best. BEREICH: NAHETAL.

Nahetal (Bereich) BEREICH name for amalgamated KREUZNACH and SCHLOSSBOCKELHEIM districts.

Neckerauer, Weingut Klaus Interesting, out-of-the-way 40-acre estate at Weissenheim-am-Sand, on sandy soil in N PFALZ. Impressive but unpredictable range.

Neef M-S-R w ★→★★ 71 76 83 85 87 88 **89** 90 91 92 93 Village of lower MOSEL with one fine v'yd: Frauenberg.

Neipperg, Graf von 71-acre top WURTTEMBERG estate at Schwaigern, esp known for red wines and TRAMINER.

Neumagen-Dhron M-M w ★★ Neighbour of PIESPORT: fine but sadly neglected.

Neustadt Central town of PFALZ with a famous wine school.

Niederhausen Nahe w ★★→★★★★ 71 75 76 83 85 86 87 88 **89 90** 91 93 Neighbour of SCHLOSS BOCKELHEIM and HQ of the NAHE STATE DOMAIN. Wines of grace and power. First-class v'yds incl Felsensteyer, Hermannsberg, Hermannshöhle. Grosslage: Burgweg. Top growers: CRUSIUS, DONNHOFF, Hehner-Kilz, STATE DOMAIN.

Nierstein Rhh w ★→★★★★ 71 75 76 83 85 86 87 88 **89 90** 91 92 93 Famous but treacherous name. 1,300 acres incl superb First-class v'yds: Bruderberg, Glöck, Heiligenbaum, Hipping, Kranzberg, Oelberg, Orbel, Pettenthal, and their Grosslagen: Auflangen, Rehbach, Spiegelberg. Ripe aromatic wines with great 'elegance'. But beware Grosslage Gutes Domtal: no guarantee of anything. Growers to choose incl H Braun, GUNDERLOCH, GUNTRUM, HEYL ZU HERRNSHEIM, St-Antony, G A Schneider, Seebrich, Strub, Wehrheim.

Nierstein (Bereich) Large E RHEINHESSEN district of v mixed quality.

Nierstein Winzergenossenschaft The leading NIERSTEIN coop, with far above average standards. (Formerly 'Rheinfront'.)

Nobling New white grape: light fresh wine in BADEN, esp MARKGRAFLERLAND.

Norheim Nahe w ★→★★★ 71 76 79 83 85 86 87 88 **89 90** 91 92 93 Neighbour of NIEDERHAUSEN. First-class v'yds: Delchen, Kafels, Kirschheck; Klosterberg comes next. Grosslage: Burgweg. Growers: ANHEUSER, CRUSIUS.

Novum Completely new style of wine from SICHEL, softened by malolactic fermentation. Aromatic, gentle and versatile.

Oberemmel M-S-R (Saar) w **→*** **71 75 76 83 85 86 87 88 89 90 91 92 93** Next village to WILTINGEN. V fine wines from First-class v'yd Hütte, also Karlsberg, etc. Grosslage: SCHARZBERG. Esp VON HOVEL, VON KESSELSTADT.

Obermosel (Bereich) District name for the upper MOSEL above TRIER. Generally uninspiring wines from the ELBLING grape, unless v young.

Ockfen M-S-R (Saar) w **→*** **71 75 76 83 85 86 87 88 89 90 91 92 93** 200-acre village with superb fragrant austere wines. Top v'yd: Bockstein. Grosslage: SCHARZBERG. Growers incl DR FISCHER, FRIEDRICH WILHELM GYMNASIUM, WAGNER, ZILLIKEN.

Oechsle Scale for sugar content of grape juice (see page 212).

Oestrich Rhg w **→*** **71 75 76 83 85 86 87 88 89 90 91 92 93** Big village; variable but capable of splendid RIES AUSLESE. First-class v'yds are Doosberg, Lenchen; Klosterberg is also good. Grosslage: Gottesthal. Major growers: Auerbach, AUGUST ESER, WEGELER-DEINHARD.

Offene weine Wine by the glass: the way to order it in wine villages.

Oppenheim Rhh w *→*** **71 75 76 83 85 86 87 88 89 90 91 92 93** Town S of NIERSTEIN with a spectacular 13th-C church. Best wines (from First-class Herrenberg and Sackträger v'yds) similar. Grosslagen: Guldenmorgen (***), Krötenbrunnen (*). Growers incl GUNTRUM, Carl Koch, Kühling-Gillot. None currently up to full potential.

Ortenau (Bereich) District just S of Baden-Baden. Good KLINGELBERGER (RIES), SPATBURGUNDER and RULANDER. Top village: DURBACH.

Ortsteil Independent part of a community allowed to use its estate v'yd name without the village name, eg SCHLOSS JOHANNISBERG, STEINBERG.

Palatinate English for RHEINPFALZ.

Pauly-Bergweiler, Dr Fine 27-acre estate based at BERNKASTEL. V'yds there and in WEHLEN, etc. 'Peter Nicolay' wines from URZIG and ERDEN are best.

Perlwein Semi-sparkling wine.

Pfalz 56,000-acre v'yd region S of RHEINHESSEN (see Mittelhaardt and Südliche Weinstrasse). Grapes ripen to relatively high degrees. The classics are rich wines, with TROCKEN and HALBTROCKEN increasingly fashionable and well made. Biggest RIES producer after M-S-R. Until recently, known as 'Rheinpfalz'.

Pfeffingen, Weingut Messrs Fuhrmann and Eymael make outstanding RIES and SCHEUREBE on 26 acres of UNGSTEIN.

Piesport M-M w **→**** **71 75 76 83 85 86 87 88 89 90 91 92 93** Tiny village with famous vine amphitheatre, at best glorious gentle fruity RIES. Great First-class v'yd: Goldtröpfchen. Treppchen, on flatter land, far inferior. Grosslage: Michelsberg (mainly MULLER-T; avoid). Esp R HAART, Kurt Hain, KESSELSTADT, Reuscher-Haart, Weller-Lehnert.

Plettenberg, von 100-acre estate at BAD KREUZNACH. Wines recently poor.

Portugieser Second-rate red-wine grape now often used for WEISSHERBST.

Prädikat Special attributes or qualities. See QmP.

Prüfungsnummer The official identifying test-number of a quality wine.

Prüm, J J Superlative and legendary 34-acre MOSEL estate in BERNKASTEL, GRAACH, WEHLEN, ZELTINGEN. Delicate but long-lived wines, esp in WEHLENER SONNENUHR: 81 KABINETT is still young.

Qualitätswein bestimmter Anbaugebiete (QbA) The middle quality of German wine, with sugar added before fermentation (as in French 'chaptalisation'), but controlled as to areas, grapes, etc.

Qualitätswein mit Prädikat (QmP) Top category, incl all wines ripe enough to be unsugared (KABINETT to TROCKENBEERENAUSLESE). See pages 100–101.

Randersacker Frank w **→*** 76 *83* 86 87 88 89 90 91 92 93 Leading village for distinctive dry wine. First-class v'yds: Marsberg, Pfülben. Grosslage: Ewig Leben. Growers incl BURGERSPITAL, Martin Göbel, STAATLICHER HOFKELLER, JULIUSSPITAL, Robert Schmitt, Schmitt's Kinder.

Rappenhof, Weingut 90-acre R'HESSEN estate at Alsheim: wide range incl BARRIQUE-aged CHARD, deep-coloured SPATBURGUNDER. Recent RIES poor.

Rauenthal Rhg w ***→**** 71 75 76 83 85 86 87 88 89 90 91 92 93 Supreme village: spicy complex wine. First-class v'yds: Baiken, Gehrn, Nonnenberg, Rothenberg, Wülfen. Grosslage: Steinmächer. Growers: BREUER, ESER, SCHLOSS REINHARTS HAUSEN, SCHLOSS SCHONBORN, VON SIMMERN, STATE DOMAIN.

Rebholz Top SUDLICHE WEINSTRASSE grower. Many varieties on 25 acres.

Ress, Balthasar R'GAU estate (74 acres of good land), cellars in HATTENHEIM. Also runs SCHLOSS REICHARTSHAUSEN. Variable wines; original artists' labels.

Restsüsse Unfermented grape sugar remaining in (or more often added to) wine to give it sweetness. TROCKEN wines have v little, if any.

Rheinburgengau (Bereich) District name for MITTELRHEIN v'yds around the Rhine gorge. Wines with 'steely' acidity needing time to mature.

Rheinfront, Winzergenossenschaft See Nierstein Winzergenossenschaft.

Rheingau Best v'yd region of Rhine, W of Wiesbaden. 7,000 acres. Classic substantial but subtle RIES. BEREICH name for whole region: JOHANNISBERG.

Rheinhessen Vast region (61,000 acres of v'yds) between Mainz and Worms, bordered by the river NAHE, mostly second-rate, but incl top wines from NACKENHEIM, NIERSTEIN, OPPENHEIM, etc.

Germany's quality levels
The official range of qualities in ascending order are as follows:

(1) Deutscher Tafelwein: sweetish light wine of no special character. (Unofficially, can be very special.)

(2) Landwein: dryish Tafelwein with some regional style.

(3) Qualitätswein: dry or sweetish wine with sugar added before fermentation to increase its strength, but tested for quality and with distinct local and grape character.

(4) Kabinettwein: dry or dryish natural (unsugared) wine of distinct personality and distinguishing lightness. Can be very fine.

(5) Spätlese: stronger, often sweeter than Kabinett. Full-bodied. The trend today is towards drier or even completely dry Spätlese.

(6) Auslese: sweeter, sometimes stronger than Spätlese, often with honey-like flavours, intense and long.

(7) Beerenauslese: v sweet and usually strong, intense; can be superb.

(8) Eiswein: (Beeren- or Trockenbeerenauslese) concentrated, sharpish and very sweet. Extraordinary and everlasting.

(9) Trockenbeerenauslese: intensely sweet and aromatic; alcohol slight.

Rheinhessen Silvaner (RS) New uniform label for dry wines from SILVANER – designed to give a modern quality image to the region.

Rheinpfalz See Pfalz.

Rhodt SUDLICHE WEINSTRASSE village: esa Rietburg coop; agreeable fruity wines.

Richter, Weingut Max Ferd Top 37-acre MITTELMOSEL family estate, based at Mülheim. Fine barrel-aged RIES from: BRAUNEBERG (Juffer-Sonnenuhr), GRAACH, Mülheim (Helenenkloster), WEHLEN (usually models).

Rieslaner Cross between SILVANER and RIES; has made fine AUSLESEN in FRANKEN, where most is grown. Also fine from MULLER-CATOIR.

Riesling The best German grape: fine, fragrant, fruity, long-lived. Only CHARDONNAY can compete as the world's best white grape.

Rosewein Rosé wine made of red grapes fermented without their skins.

Rotwein Red wine.

Rüdesheim Rhg w **→**** 71 75 76 79 81 82 83 84 85 86 87 88 89 90 91 92 93 Rhine resort with excellent v'yds; the 3 best called Rüdesheimer Berg-. Full-bodied wines, fine-flavoured, often remarkable in 'off' years. Grosslage: Burgweg. Most top RHEINGAU estates own some Rüdesheim v'yds. Best growers: G BREUER, J LEITZ, Dr Nägler, SCHLOSS SCHONBORN.

Rüdesheimer Rosengarten RUDESHEIM is also the name of a NAHE village near BAD KREUZNACH. Do not be misled by the ubiquitous blend going by this name. It has nothing to do with RHEINGAU Rüdesheim. Avoid.

Ruländer PINOT GRIS: grape giving soft full-bodied wine, alias (as dry wine) GRAUBURGUNDER. Best in BADEN and southern PFALZ.

113

Ruppertsberg Pfz w ★★→★★★ 75 76 83 85 86 87 88 89 90 91 92 93 Southern village of MITTELHAARDT. First-class v'yds incl Hoheburg, Linsenbusch, Nussbien, Reiterpfad, Spiess. Grosslage: Hofstück. Growers incl BASSERMANN-JORDAN, JOSEPH BIFFAR, VON BUHL, BURKLIN-WOLF, DEINHARD.

Ruwer Tributary of MOSEL nr TRIER. V fine delicate but highly aromatic and well-structured wines. Villages incl EITELSBACH, KASEL, MERTESDORF.

Saale-Unstrut Region in former E Germany, 1,000 acres around confluence of these two rivers at Naumburg, nr Leipzig. Terraced v'yds of WEISS-BURGUNDER, SILVANER, GUTEDEL, etc and red PORTUGIESER and SPATBURGUNDER have Cistercian origins. Quality leader: Landesweingut Kloster Pforta.

Saar Tributary of MOSEL S of RUWER. Brilliant austere 'steely' RIES. Villages incl AYL, OCKFEN, Saarburg, SERRIG, WILTINGEN (SCHARZHOFBERG). Grosslage: SCHARZBERG. Many fine estates.

Saar-Ruwer (Bereich) District covering these 2 regions.

St-Ursula Well-known merchants at BINGEN.

Salm, Prinz zu Owner of SCHLOSS WALLHAUSEN and President of VDP.

Salwey, Weingut Leading BADEN estate at Oberottweil, esp for RIESLING, WEISSBURGUNDER and RULANDER.

Schaefer, Willi The finest grower of GRAACH (but only 5 acres).

Scharzberg Grosslage name of WILTINGEN and neighbours.

Scharzhofberg M-S-R (Saar) w ★★★★ 71 75 76 83 85 86 87 88 89 90 91 92 93 Superlative 67-acre SAAR v'yd: austerely beautiful wines, the perfection of RIESLING. Do not confuse with the previous entry. Top estates: EGON MULLER, VON HOVEL, VON KESSELSTATT.

Schaumwein Sparkling wine.

Scheurebe Fruity grape of high quality (and RIESLING parentage) esp used in PFALZ. Excellent for botrytis wine (BA, TBA).

Schillerwein Light red or rosé QBA, speciality of WURTTEMBERG (only).

Schloss Groenesteyn Formerly top-grade RHEINGAU estate (80 acres) in KIEDRICH and RUDESHEIM. Not on top form.

Schloss Johannisberg Rhg w ★★★ 76 79 83 85 86 87 88 89 90 91 92 93 Famous RHEINGAU estate of 86 acres owned by Prince Metternich and Oetker family. The original Rhine 'first growth'. Wines incl fine SPATLESE, KABINETT TROCKEN; more could be achieved with this truly great v'yd.

Schloss Reichartshausen 10-acre HATTENHEIM v'yd run by RESS.

Schloss Reinhartshausen Fine 175-acre estate in ERBACH, HATTENHEIM, KIEDRICH, etc. Changed hands in '87. The mansion is now a hotel.

Schloss Saarstein SERRIG estate of 25 acres with consistently fine RIESLINGS.

Schloss Salem 188-acre estate of Margrave of BADEN near L Constance in S Germany. MULLER-T and WEISSHERBST.

Schloss Schönborn One of the biggest and best RHEINGAU estates, based at HATTENHEIM. Full-flavoured wines, at best excellent. Also vg SEKT.

Schloss Staufenberg 69-acre DURBACH estate, BADEN. KLINGELBERGER best.

Schloss Thorn Ancient OBERMOSEL estate, remarkable ELBLING, RIES and castle.

Schloss Vollrads Rhg w ★★★ 71 76 83 85 86 87 88 89 90 91 93 Great WINKEL estate since 1300. 116 acres. Dry austere RIES; TROCKEN and HALBTROCKEN are specialities; recently not impressive. See MATUSCHKA-GREIFFENCLAU.

Schloss Wallhausen The 25-acre NAHE estate of the PRINZ ZU SALM, one of Germany's oldest. 65% RIES. Vg TROCKEN.

Schlossböckelheim Nahe w ★★→★★★★★ 71 75 76 79 83 85 86 87 88 89 90 91 92 93 Village with the best v'yds, incl First-class Felsenberg, In den Felsen, Königsfels, Kupfergrube. Firm yet delicate wine. Grosslage: Burgweg. Top growers: CRUSIUS, DONNHOF, STATE DOMAIN.

Schlossböckelheim District name for the whole S NAHE, amalgamated with KREUZNACH to form BEREICH NAHETAL.

Schoppenwein Café (or bar) wine: ie wine by the glass.

Schubert, von Owner of MAXIMIN GRUNHAUS.

For key to grape variety abbreviations, see pages 6–9.

Schwarzer Adler, Weingut Franz Keller and his son make top BADEN GRAU-, WEISS-, also SPATBURGUNDER on 35 acres at Oberbergen.

Schweigen Pfz w ★→★★★ 85 86 87 88 89 90 91 92 93 S PFALZ village. Grosslage: Guttenberg. Best grower is Fritz Becker, esp for SPATBURGUNDER reds.

Sekt German (QBA) sparkling wine, best when label specifies RIES, WEISSBURGUNDER or SPATBURGUNDER. Sekt bA is the same but from specified area.

Selbach-Oster 15-acre ZELTINGEN estate now among MITTELMOSEL leaders.

Serrig M-S-R (Saar) w ★★→★★★★ 71 75 76 83 85 86 87 88 89 90 91 93 Village for 'steely' wine, excellent in sunny yrs. First-class v'yds: Herrenburg, Saarstein, Serriger Schloss, Würzberg. Grosslage: SCHARZBERG. Top grower: VEREINIGTE HOSPITIEN. Others: SCHLOSS SAARSTEIN, BERT SIMON.

Sichel, Söhne H Famous wine merchants of London and Mainz based at Alzey, RHEINHESSEN. Owners of BLUE NUN LIEBFRAUMILCH.

Silvaner The third most-planted German white grape, usually underrated, best in FRANKEN. Worth looking for in RHEINHESSEN and KAISERSTUHL, too.

Simmern, Langwerth von Top 120-acre ELTVILLE family estate. Famous v'yds: Baiken, Mannberg, MARCOBRUNN. Some of v best, most elegant R'GAU RIES.

Simon, Weingut Bert One of largest SAAR estates. 80 acres: KASEL, SERRIG.

Sonnenuhr Sundial. Name of several v'yds, esp one at WEHLEN.

Spätburgunder Pinot Noir: the best red-wine grape in Germany, esp in BADEN and WURTTEMBERG and, increasingly, PFALZ – though its wines are usually found pallid and underflavoured outside their country.

Spätlese Late Harvest. One better (stronger, sweeter) than KABINETT RIESLING. Wines to age at least 5 yrs. Dry Spätlesen can be v fine.

Staatlicher Hofkeller The Bavarian STATE DOMAIN. 287 acres of finest FRANKEN v'yds with spectacular cellars under the great baroque Residenz at WURZBURG. Wines less spectacular.

Staatsweingut (or Staatliche Weinbaudomäne) The State wine estates or domains; esp KLOSTER EBERBACH, SCHLOSS-BOCKELHEIM, TRIER.

State Domain See Staatsweingut.

Steigerwald (Bereich) District name for E part of FRANKEN.

Steinberg Rhg w ★★★ 71 75 76 79 83 85 86 87 88 89 90 91 92 93 Famous 79-acre HATTENHEIM walled v'yd, planted by Cistercians 700 yrs ago. Now owned by STATE DOMAIN, ELTVILLE. Some glorious wines; some feeble.

Steinwein Wine from WURZBURG's best v'yd, Stein. In the past the term was loosely used for all FRANKEN wine.

Stuttgart Chief city of WURTTEMBERG, producer of some pleasant wines (esp RIES), recently beginning to be exported.

Südliche Weinstrasse (Bereich) District name for S PFALZ. Quality improved tremendously in last 25 yrs. See Ilbesheim, Schweigen, Siebeldingen.

Tafelwein Table wine. The vin ordinaire of Germany. Frequently blended with other EC wines. But DEUTSCHER TAFELWEIN must come from Germany alone and may be excellent. (See also Landwein.)

Tauberfranken (Bereich) New name for minor Badisches Frankenland BEREICH of N BADEN: FRANKEN-style wines.

Thanisch, Weingut Wwe Dr H Vg BERNKASTEL estate, incl part of Doctor v'yd.

Traben-Trarbach M-M w ★★ 76 83 85 86 87 88 89 90 91 92 93 Major wine town of 800 acres, 87% of it RIES. Top v'yds: Ungsberg, Würzgarten. Grosslage: Schwarzlay. Top grower: MAX FERD RICHTER.

Traisen Nahe w ★★★ 71 75 76 79 83 85 86 87 88 89 90 91 92 93 Small village incl superlative First-class Bastei and Rotenfels v'yds, making RIES of great concentration and class. Top grower: CRUSIUS.

Traminer See Gewürztraminer.

Trier M-S-R w ★★→★★★★ Top wine city of Roman origin, on MOSEL, nr RUWER, now also incl AVELSBACH and EITELSBACH. Grosslage: Römerlay. Big Mosel charitable estates have cellars here among stunning Roman remains.

Trittenheim M-M w ★★ 71 75 76 83 85 87 88 89 90 91 92 93 Attractive S MITTELMOSEL light wines. Top v'yds were Altärchen, Apotheke, but now incl second-rate flat land: First-class are Felsenkopf, Leiterchen. Grosslage: Michelsberg (avoid). Top growers: GRANS-FASSIAN, Milz.

Trockenbeerenauslese Sweetest, most expensive category of German wine, extremely rare, with concentrated honey flavour. Made from selected shrivelled grapes affected by 'noble rot' (botrytis). TBA for short. See also Edel. Edelbeerenauslese would be a less confusing name.

Trollinger Common (pale) red grape of WÜRTTEMBERG; locally v popular.

Ungstein Pfz w ✱✱→✱✱✱ 71 75 76 83 85 86 87 88 89 90 91 92 93 MITTELHAARDT village with fine harmonious wines. First-class v'yds: Herrenberg, Spielberg, Weilberg. Top growers: Darting, FITZ-RITTER, PFEFFINGEN, Karl Schäfer. Grosslagen: Honigsäckel, Kobnert.

Urzig M-M w ✱✱✱✱ 71 75 76 83 85 86 87 88 89 90 91 93 Village on red sandstone famous for firm, full, spicy wine unlike other MOSELS. First-class v'yd: Würzgarten. Grosslage: Schwarzlay. Growers incl J J Christoffel, DR LOOSEN, MÖNCHHOF, WEINS-PRÜM.

Valckenberg, P J Major merchants and growers at Worms, with Madonna LIEBFRAUMILCH. Also dry Ries. Now part owner of HEYL ZU HERRNSHEIM.

VDP Verband Deutscher Prädikats und Qualitätsweingüter. An important association of premium growers. President: PRINZ ZU SALM.

Vereinigte Hospitien 'United Hospitals'. Ancient charity at TRIER with large holdings in PIESPORT, SERRIG, TRIER, WILTINGEN, etc; but wines recently below their wonderful potential.

Verwaltung Administration (of property/estate etc).

Wachenheim Pfz w ✱✱✱→✱✱✱✱ 71 75 76 79 83 85 86 87 88 89 90 91 92 93 840 acres, incl exceptionally fine RIES. First-class v'yds incl Belz, Gerümpel, Goldbächel, Rechbächel. Top grower: BÜRKLIN-WOLF. Grosslagen: Mariengarten, Schenkenböhl, Schnepfenflug.

Wagner, Dr Saarburg estate. 20 acres of RIES. Fine wines incl TROCKEN.

Waldrach M-S-R (Ruwer) w ✱✱ 76 83 85 88 89 90 91 92 93 Some charming light wines. Grosslage: Römerlay.

Walluf Rhg w ✱✱✱ 75 76 79 83 85 87 88 89 90 91 92 93 Neighbour of ELTVILLE; formerly Nieder- and Ober-Walluf. Underrated wines. First-class v'yd: Walkenberg. Grosslage: Steinmächer. Growers incl BECKER.

Walporzheim Ahrtal (Bereich) District name for the whole AHR VALLEY.

Walthari-Hof Much-discussed estate at Edenkoben, PFALZ, making wine without recourse to the usual sulphur dioxide.

Wawern M-S-R (Saar) w ✱✱→✱✱✱ 71 75 76 83 85 87 88 89 90 91 92 93 Small village, fine RIES. First-class v'yd: Herrenberg. Grosslage: SCHARZBERG.

Wegeler-Deinhard 136-acre RHEINGAU estate. V'yds: GEISENHEIM, MITTELHEIM, OESTRICH, RÜDESHEIM, WINKEL, etc. Consistent quality; dry SPÄTLESE, classic AUSLESE, finest EISWEIN. Also 67 acres in MITTELMOSEL, incl major part of BERNKASTELER Doctor, WEHLENER SONNENUHR, etc, 46 acres in MITTELHAARDT (DEIDESHEIM, FORST, RUPPERTSBERG). Only best sites are named on labels. See also GEHEIMRAT 'J'.

Wehlen M-M w ✱✱✱→✱✱✱✱ 71 75 76 83 85 86 87 88 89 90 91 92 93 Neighbour of BERNKASTEL with equally fine, somewhat richer wine. Great First-class v'yd: SONNENUHR. Top growers: HERIBERT KERPEN, DR LOOSEN, J J PRÜM, WEGELER-DEINHARD, WEINS-PRÜM. Grosslage: Münzlay.

Weil, Robert Fine 84-acre estate at KIEDRICH, now owned by Suntory of Japan. Back on top form from '92.

Weinbaugebiet Viticultural region. For TAFELWEIN (eg MOSEL, RHEIN, SAAR).

Weingut Wine estate.

Weinkellerei Wine cellars or winery. See Keller.

Weins-Prüm, Dr Classic MITTELMOSEL estate; 12 acres at WEHLEN. WEHLENER SONNENUHR is top wine.

Weinstrasse Wine road. Scenic route through v'yds. Germany has several. The most famous is the Deutsche Weinstrasse in PFALZ.

Weintor, Deutsches See Schweigen.

Weissburgunder Pinot Blanc. One of the better grapes for TROCKEN and HALBTROCKEN wines: low acidity, high extract. Also much used for Sekt.

Weissherbst Usually pale pink wine of QBA standard or above, from a single variety, even occasionally BEERENAUSLESE, the speciality of BADEN, PFALZ and WURTTEMBERG. Currently fashionable in Germany.

Werner, Domdechant Fine family estate on best HOCHHEIM slopes. 95% RIES.

Wiltingen M-S-R (Saar) w ★★→★★★★ 71 75 76 83 85 86 87 88 89 90 91 92 93 The centre of the SAAR. 790 acres. Beautiful subtle austere wine. Great First-class v'yd is SCHARZHOFBERG (ORTSTEIL); and First-class are Braune Kupp, Hölle. Grosslage (for the whole SAAR): SCHARZBERG. Top growers: EGON MULLER, LE GALLAIS, VON KESSELSTATT, etc.

Winkel Rhg w ★★★ 71 75 76 83 85 86 87 88 89 90 91 92 93 Village famous for full fragrant wine, incl SCHLOSS VOLLRADS. First-class v'yds incl Hasensprung, Jesuitengarten, Klaus, SCHLOSS VOLLRADS, Schlossberg. Grosslagen: Erntebringer, Honigberg. Growers incl DEINHARD, PRINZ VON HESSEN, VON MUMM, BALTHASAR RESS, SCHLOSS SCHONBORN, etc.

Winningen M-S-R w ★★ Village of lower MOSEL nr Koblenz, producing some fine delicate RIES. Top v'yds: Röttgen, Uhlen. Growers: Franz Dötsch, von Heddesdorf, Heymann-Löwenstein, Richard Richter.

Wintrich M-M w ★★→★★★ 71 75 76 83 85 86 87 88 89 90 91 92 93 Neighbour of PIESPORT; similar wines. Top v'yds: Ohligsberg, Sonnenseite. Grosslage: Kurfürstlay. Good grower: REINHOLD HAART.

Remember that vintage information for German wines is given in a different form from the ready/not ready distinction applying to other countries. Read the explanation on page 103.

Winzergenossenschaft Wine-growers' cooperative, often making sound and reasonably priced wine. Referred to in this text as 'coop'.

Winzerverein The same as the above.

Wirsching, Hans Leading estate in IPHOFEN for some of best FRANKEN wines: firm, elegant and dry. 100 acres in top v'yds: Julius-Echter-Berg, Kalb...

Wonnegau (Bereich) District name for S RHEINHESSEN.

Wolff Metternich Noble DURBACH estate: BADEN's best dry (and sweet) RIES.

Württemberg Vast southern wine area, little known for wine outside Germany. Some good RIES esp from Neckar Valley. Also TROLLINGER.

Würzburg Frank ★★→★★★★ 71 76 79 81 *83* 85 86 87 88 89 90 91 92 93 Great baroque city on the Main, centre of FRANKEN wine: fine, full-bodied, dry. First-class v'yds: Abtsleite, Innere, Leiste, Stein. No Grosslage. See Maindreieck. Growers: BURGERSPITAL, JULIUSSPITAL, STAATLICHER HOFKELLER.

Zell M-S-R w ★→★★ 76 83 88 89 90 91 92 93 The best-known lower MOSEL village, esp for its awful Grosslage: Schwarze Katz ('Black Cat'). RIES on steep slate gives aromatic light wines. Top grower: Albert Kallfelz.

Zell (Bereich) District name for whole lower MOSEL from Zell to Koblenz.

Zeltingen M-M w ★★→★★★★ 71 75 76 79 83 85 86 87 88 89 90 91 92 93 Top MOSEL village nr WEHLEN. Lively crisp RIES. First-class v'yd: SONNENUHR. Grosslage: Münzlay. Many estate-owned v'yds, esp PRUM, SELBACH-OSTER.

Zilliken, Forstmeister Geltz Former estate of the Prussian royal forester at Saarburg and OCKFEN, SAAR. Racy minerally RIESLINGS. Great EISWEIN.

Zwierlein, Freiherr von 55-acre family estate in GEISENHEIM. 100% RIES.

Spain & Portugal

The following abbreviations are used in the text:

Amp	Ampúrdan-Costa Brava
Alen	Alentejo
Bair	Bairrada
B Al	Beira Alta
B Lit	Beira Littoral
Cos del S	Costers del Segre
El B	El Bierzo
Gal	Galicia
La M	La Mancha
Mont-M	Montilla-Moriles
Nav	Navarra
Pen	Penedès
Pri	Priorato
Rib del D	Ribera del Duero
R Alt	Rioja Alta
R Ala	Rioja Alavesa
RB	Rioja Baja
Som	Somontano
Set	Setúbal
U-R	Utiel-Requeña
VV	Vinhos Verdes
g	vino generoso
res	reserva

Spain and Portugal have had nine years, since they joined the European Community, to modernize their venerable wine industries. Much has been done and there is much to do. The continuing state of ferment is highly productive, and some splendid new wines have appeared, both in the few traditional quality areas and in former bulk-wine regions.

Currently in Spain (apart from sherry country), the northeast, Rioja, Navarra, Galicia, Rueda and Ribera del Duero still hold most interest; in Portugal (apart from the port vineyards and Madeira) Bairrada, the Douro, Ribatejo, Alentejo, the central coast and the north. In Portugal especially, newly delimited areas are tending to overshadow such old appellations as eg Dão.

The following listing includes the best and most interesting types and regions of each country, whether legally delimited or not. Geographical references (see map above) are to demarcated regions (DOs and DOCs), autonomies and provinces.

Spain

AGE, Bodegas Unidas R Alt r w (p) dr sw res ★→★★★ 84 85 86 Large BODEGA with a wide range. Red MARQUES DE ROMERAL and Siglo GRAN RESERVA are best. Saco red is reliable if unspectacular; avoid its white counterpart.

Alavesas, Bodegas R Ala r (w) res ★★→★★★ 86 87 91 Pale orange-red Solar de Samaniego is one of the most delicate of these soft, fast-maturing wines. Quality has been seriously variable; some excessively light.

Sherry, port and madeira, still the greatest glories of Spain and Portugal, have a chapter to themselves on pages 133–139.

Albariño Fine aromatic high-quality white grape of GALICIA and its wine. See also Rías Baixas.

Alella Alella r w (p) dr sw ** Small demarcated region just N of Barcelona. Pleasantly fruity wines. (See Marfil, Marqués de Alella, Parxet.)

Alicante Alicante r (w) ★ DO. Wines still tend to be earthy and overstrong.

Almendralejo E Spain r w ★ Wine centre of Extremadura. Much of its wine is distilled to make the spirit for fortifying sherry. See Lar de Barros.

Aloque La M r ★ DYA A light (though not in alcohol) variety of VALDEPEÑAS, made by fermenting red and white grapes together.

Alvear Mont-M g ★★★ The largest producer of excellent sherry-like aperitif and dessert wines in MONTILLA-MORILES.

Ampurdán, Cavas del Amp r w p sp res ★→★★ Producers of big-selling white Pescador, red Cazador table wines and cuve close sparklers.

Ampurdán-Costa Brava Amp r w p dr ★→★★ Demarcated region abutting Pyrenees. Mainly coop-made rosés, reds. See also last entry.

Año Year: 4° Año (or Años) means 4 yrs old when bottled. Common on labels in the past, now largely discontinued in favour of vintages, or terms such as CRIANZA.

Aragonesa, Compañía Vitivinícola Som r w p res ★★→★★★ 89 91 New SOMONTANO estate. Single-varietal wines under Viñas del Vero label: Chard, Ries, Gewürz, Cab S, etc. Vines are still young and oak excessive, but this is an outfit to watch.

Bach, Masia Barcelona r w p dr sw res ✦✦→✦✦✦ 85   Spectacular villa-winery nr SAN SADURNI DE NOYA, owned by CODORNIU. White Extrísimo, formerly sweet and oaky, is now dry. Also good red RESERVAS.

Banda Azul R Alt r   CRIANZA wine from BODEGAS PATERNINA. Once reliable.

Barbier, René Pen r w res ✦✦ 86 87 89   Owned by FREIXENET, known for 'Mediterraneo', fresh white Kraliner, red RB RESERVAS, budget CAVA.

Baron de Ley RB r (w) res ✦✦✦ 85 86   Newish BODEGA linked with EL COTO: good single-estate wines.

Barril, Masia Pri r br res ✦✦ 83 87 91   Tiny family estate in DO PRIORATO: powerful fruity reds – the 83 was 18°! – and superb RANCIO.

Bebidas, Bodegas y Formerly 'Savin'. One of largest Spanish wine companies; wineries all over Spain. Mainly fair quality and value brands. Also controls various prestigious firms, eg CAMPO VIEJO, MARQUES DE PUERTO.

Berberana, Bodegas R Alt r (w) res ✦→✦✦✦ 83 85 86   Fruity full-bodied reds are best: young Carta de Plata, Carta de Oro CRIANZA, velvety RESERVAS.

Berceo, Bodegas R Alt r w p res ✦✦→✦✦✦ 87   Cellar in HARO with vg Gonzalo de Berceo GRAN RESERVA.

Beronia, Bodegas R Alt r w res ✦✦→✦✦✦ 73 78 80 85 87 88   Small modern BODEGA making reds in traditional oaky style and fresh 'modern' whites. Owned by Gonzalez Byass (see page 135).

Bilbainas, Bodegas R Alt r w (p) dr sw res ✦✦ 80 82 85 87 88 89   Large BODEGA in HARO. Wide and usually reliable range incl dark Viña Pomal, lighter Viña Zaco, Vendimia Especial RESERVAS and Royal Carlton CAVA.

Binissalem r w ✦✦   Best-known Mallorca DO. See also Ferrer, José L.

Blanco White.

Bodega Spanish for (i) a wineshop; (ii) a concern occupied in the making, blending and/or shipping of wine; and (iii) a cellar.

Campillo, Bodegas R Ala r (p) res ✦✦✦ 78 82 87   Affiliated with FAUSTINO MARTINEZ, a young BODEGA with wines of consistently high quality.

Campo Viejo, Bodegas R Alt r (w) res ✦→✦✦✦ 70 73 80 82 85 87 88   Makes the popular and tasty young San Asensio and some big fruity red RESERVAS, esp Marqués de Villamagna. See Bodegas y Bebidas.

Can Rafols dels Caus Pen r w ✦✦ 88   Young small PENEDES BODEGA: own-estate fruity Cab, pleasant Chard-Xarel-lo-Chenin. Also gd Cab-Merlot.

Cañamero SW Spain w ✦   Remote village nr Guadalupe whose wines grow FLOR and behave almost like sherry.

Caralt, Cavas Conde de Barcelona r w sp res ✦✦ 85 87   CAVA wines from outpost of FREIXENET, gd pgd vigorous Brut NV; also pleasant still wines.

Cariñena Cariñena r (w p) ✦   Demarcated region and large-scale supplier of strong everyday wine, dominated by coops. Now being invigorated (and its wines lightened) by modern technology.

Casar de Valdaiga El B r w ✦✦   Fruity red from Pérez Carames, N of LEON.

Castellblanch Pen w sp ✦✦ 88 90   PENEDES CAVA firm, owned by FREIXENET. Currently much praised for Brut Zéro and Gran Castell GRAN RESERVAS.

Castillo Ygay 25 34 42 59 62 68   See Marqués de Murrieta.

Cava Official term for any classic method Spanish sparkling wine, and the DO covering the areas up and down Spain where it is made.

Cenalsa See Principe de Viana, Bodegas.

Cenicero Wine township in the RIOJA ALTA with ancient Roman origins.

Cepa Wine or grape variety.

Cervera, Lagar de Gal w ✦✦✦ DYA   Makers of one of best ALBARINOS: flowery and intensely fruity with subdued bubbles and a long finish.

Chacolí nr Nav w (r) ✦ DYA   Alarmingly sharp, often fizzy, wine from the Basque coast, now possessing its own DO, which applies to all 141 acres! It contains only 9–11% alcohol. Best producer: Txomín Etxaníz.

Chaves, Bodegas Gal w ✦✦ DYA   Small firm: good, fragrant, acidic ALBARINO.

Chivite, Bodegas Julián Nav r w (p) dr sw res ✦✦ 85 87 88 89 90   Biggest NAVARRA BODEGA. Full red, flowery well-balanced white. See Gran Feudo.

Cigales Cigales r p ✦→✦✦   Recently demarcated region north of Valladolid, esp for light reds (traditionally known as CLARETES).

Clarete Traditional term, now banned by EC, for light red wine (or dark rosé).

Codorníu Barcelona w sp ✹✹→✹✹✹ One of the two largest firms in SAN SADURNI DE NOYA making good CAVA: v high tech, 10 million bottles ageing in cellars. Non Plus Ultra is matured. Many prefer the fresher Ana de Codorníu (89), the Première Cuvée Brut (86 87) and the Chard (88).

Compañía Vinícola del Norte de España (CVNE) R Alt r w (p) dr sw res ✹✹→✹✹✹ 82 85 86 87 89 Top RIOJA BODEGA. The CRIANZA is among the best young red RIOJAS. Monopole, once one of the best slightly oaky whites, has recently been disappointing. Excellent red Imperial and Viña Real RESERVAS. CVNE is pronounced 'coonay'. See also Contino.

Conca de Barberá Pen w (r p) Demarcated region growing Parellada grapes for making CAVA, shortly to be incorporated in the DO PENEDES. Its best wine is TORRES MILMANDA Chard.

Condado de Huelva DO see Huelva.

Consejo Regulador Official organization for the defence, control and promotion of a DENOMINACION DE ORIGEN.

Contino R Ala r res ✹✹✹ 81 82 84 85 86 87 88 Superb single-v'yd red made by a subsidiary of COMPANIA VINICOLA DEL NORTE DE ESPANA.

Cosecha Crop or vintage.

Cosecheros Alaveses R Ala r ✹✹ 87 88 89 91 92 Up-and-coming RIOJA coop, esp for good young unoaked red Artadi.

Costers del Segre Cos del S r w p sp ✹✹→✹✹✹ Small demarcated area around the city of Lleida (Lérida) and famous for the v'yds of RAIMAT.

Criado y embotellado por... Grown and bottled by...

Crianza Literally 'nursing'; the ageing of wine. New or unaged wine is 'sin crianza' or 'joven' (young). Reds labelled 'crianza' must be at least 2 yrs old (with 1 yr in oak), and must not be released before the third yr.

Cumbrero See Montecillo, Bodegas.

De Muller Tarragona br (r w) ✹✹→✹✹✹ Venerable TARRAGONA firm specializing in altar wine, gd PRIORATO, superb sumptuous v old SOLERA-aged dessert wines. Incl Priorato DULCE, PAXARETE. Also fragrant Moscatel Seco.

Denominación de Origen (DO) Official wine region (see page 118).

Denominación de Origen Calificada (DOCa) Classification for wines of the highest quality; so far only RIOJA benefits (since '91).

Diaz e Hijos, Jesús La M r w p res ✹✹ 86 87 90 91 Unoaked reds from this small BODEGA near Madrid win many prizes.

Domecq R Ala r (w) res ✹✹→✹✹✹ 76 78 81 82 83 85 88 RIOJA outpost of sherry firm. Inexpensive Viña Eguia and excellent Marqués de Arienzo CRIANZAS and RESERVAS, fragrant and medium-bodied.

Don Darias/Don Hugo Alto Ebro r w ✹ Huge selling, modestly priced wines, v like RIOJA, from undemarcated Bodegas Vitorianas. Sound red, white.

Dulce Sweet.

Elaborado y añejado por... Made and aged by...

El Bierzo DO since '90, N of León. See Casar de Valdaiga, Palacio de Arganza.

El Coto, Bodegas R Ala r (w) res ✹✹ 78 82 85 89 BODEGA best known for light, soft, red El Coto and Coto de Imaz.

Espumoso Sparkling (but see Cava).

Evena Nav Gov't research station revolutionizing NAVARRA. Run by J OCHOA.

Fariña, Bodegas Toro r w res ✹✹ 86 87 89 Rising star of new DO TORO: good spicy reds. Gran Colegiata is cask-aged; Colegiata not.

Faustino Martínez R Ala r w (p) res ✹✹→✹✹✹ 82 83 85 86 87 88 Good reds. Light fruity white Faustino V. GRAN RESERVA is Faustino I. Do not be put off by the repellent fake-antique bottles.

Felix Solis Valdepeñas r ✹✹ BODEGA in VALDEPENAS making sturdy oak-aged reds, Viña Albali, RESERVAS (87 88) and fresh white.

Ferrer, José L Mallorca r res ✹✹ 84 85 86 87 The best-known BODEGA of Mallorca, at Binissalem. Second best known is Vinos Oliver, at Felanitx.

Spain entries also cross-refer to Sherry, Port & Madeira, pages 133–139.

Fillaboa, Granxa Gal w ★★★ DYA New small firm: delicately fruity ALBARINO.

Franco-Españolas, Bodegas R Alt r w dr sw res ★→★★ 82 85 87 Reliable LOGRONO wines. Bordón is fruity red. Semi-sweet white Diamante is a Spanish favourite. Also characterful GRAN RESERVA white.

Freixenet Cavas Barcelona w sp ★★→★★★ Huge producer of CAVA, rivalling CODORNIU in size through many acquisitions. Range of good sparklers, notably bargain Cordon Negro in black bottles, Brut Nature (88), Reserva Real and Premium Cuvée DS (87). Also owns Gloria Ferrer in California, Champagne Henri Abelé in Reims and a sparkling wine plant in Mexico. Paul Cheneau is low-price brand.

NB This edition introduces a new short-cut vintage category. Vintages in colour are the ones you should choose first for drinking in 1995.

Galicia Rainy NW Spain: to watch for fresh aromatic whites, esp ALBARINO.

Generoso (g) Aperitif or dessert wine rich in alcohol.

Gonzalez y Dubosc, Cavas Barcelona w sp ★★ A branch of the sherry giant GONZALEZ BYASS. Pleasant sparkling wines exported as 'Jean Perico'.

Gran Feudo Nav w res ★★ 89 Brand name of fragrant white, refreshing rosé, soft plummy red; the best-known wines from CHIVITE.

Gran Reserva See Reserva.

Gran Vas Pressurized tanks (French cuves closes) for making cheap sparkling wines; also used to describe this type of wine.

Guelbenzu, Bodegas Nav r res ★★ 89 90 New 89-acre family estate in Cascante: concentrated full-bodied red from Tempranillo, Cab, Merlot.

Haro Wine centre of the RIOJA ALTA, a small but stylish old town.

Hill, Cavas Pen w r sp res ★★ 87 89 Old PENEDES firm: fresh dry white Blanc Cru, good Gran Civet, Gran Toc reds, delicate RESERVA Oro Brut CAVA.

Huelva Condado de Huelva (DO) r w br ★→★★ W of Cádiz. White table wines and sherry-like GENEROSOS; formerly imp't source of 'Jerez' for blending.

Irache, SL Nav r p (w) res ★ 78 81 82 85 87 91 Well-known BODEGA for cheap everyday reds.

Jean Perico See Gonzalez y Dubosc.

Jerez de la Frontera The capital city of sherry (see page 136).

Joven (vino) Young, unoaked wine.

Jumilla Jumilla r (w p) ★→★★ DO in mountains N of Murcia. Its overstrong (up to 18%) wines are being lightened by earlier picking and better winemaking, esp by French-owned Bodegas VITIVINO (eg Altos de Pío).

Juvé y Camps Barcelona w sp ★★→★★★ Family firm aiming for and achieving top quality CAVA, from free-run juice only, esp Reserva de la Familia (89).

La Rioja Alta, Bodegas R Alt r w (p) dr (sw) res ★★★ 73 75 78 81 82 84 85 86 87 88 Excellent wines, esp red CRIANZA Viña Alberdi, velvety Ardanza Reserva, lighter Araña Reserva, splendid Reserva 904 and marvellous RESERVA 890. Now making only RESERVAS and GRAN RESERVAS.

Laguardia Picturesque walled town at the centre of the RIOJA ALAVESA.

Lagunilla, Bodegas R Alt r ★★ 82 85 86 87 Modern firm owned by British Grand Met. Easy drinking light reds incl Viña Herminia and GRAN RESERVA.

Lan, Bodegas R Alt r (p w) res ★★→★★★ 82 83 85 86 Huge modern BODEGA: aromatic red RIOJAS (good Lanciano and Lander), fresh white Lan Blanco.

Lar de Barros SW r res ★★ 84 87 Meaty RESERVAS from Bodegas Inviosa, the first wines from remote Extremadura to make their mark outside Spain. Also Lar de Larres GRAN RESERVAS.

León León r p w ★→★★ 82 85 86 88 91 Northern region to watch: fruity, dry and refreshing wines, esp from Vinos de León, the former unfortunately named VILE (eg young Coyanza, more mature Palacio de Guzman, full-blooded Don Suero RESERVA). See also El Bierzo.

León, Jean Barcelona r w res ★★★ 78 79 83 85 87 Small firm owned by a Los Angeles restaurateur. Good oaky Chard, deep full-bodied Cab that repays long bottle-ageing, though less so since '80.

Logroño First town of RIOJA region. HARO has more charm (and BODEGAS).

López de Heredia R Alt r w (p) dr sw res ★★→★★★ 64 76 78 80 81 82 83 84 85 86 87 Startlingly old-est'd BODEGA in HARO known for exceptionally long-lasting, v traditional wines, but variable since '85. Viña Tondonia reds and whites are delicate and fine; Viña Bosconia fine and beefy.

López Hermanos Málaga ★★ Large BODEGA for commercial MALAGA wines, incl popular Málaga Virgen and Moscatel Gloria.

Los Llanos La M r (p w) res ★★ 82 83 84 86 87 88 90 One of the growing number of VALDEPEÑAS BODEGAS to age wine in oak. It markets a RESERVA, GRAN RESERVA and premium Pata Negra Gran Reserva of 100% Cencibel (Tempranillo). Also clean fruity white, Armonioso. To watch.

Magaña, Bodegas Nav r res ★★★ 80 81 82 83 85 Tiny young BODEGA: excellent red with Merlot (vines bought from Ch Pétrus), Cab S. Vintages variable.

Málaga Málaga br sw ★★→★★★ Demarcated region around city of Málaga. At their best its dessert wines can resemble tawny port. See Scholtz.

Majorca JOSE FERRER, Miguel Oliver and Jaume Mesquida make the only wines of any interest on the island. On the whole, drink Catalan.

Mancha, La La M r w ★→★★ Large demarcated region N and NE of VALDEPEÑAS. Mainly white wines, the reds lacking the liveliness of the best Valdepeñas but showing signs of improvement. To watch.

Marfil Alella r w (p) ★★ Means 'ivory'. Brand name of Alella Vinícola (Bodegas Cooperativas), oldest-established producer in ALELLA. Now making lively but rather pricey new-style dry white wines.

Marqués de Alella Alella w (sp) ★★ 91 93 (DYA) Light and fragrant white ALELLA wines from PARXET, some from Chard (incl barrel-fermented 'Allier' 91), made by modern methods. Also CAVA.

Marqués de Cáceres, Bodegas R Alt r p w res ★★→★★★ 82 85 86 87 89 Good RIOJAS made by modern French methods from CENICERO (R Alt) grapes; also surprisingly light, fragrant white (DYA) and another, over-oaked.

Marqués de Griñon La M r w ★★★ 87 88 Enterprising nobleman making v fine Cab nr Toledo, S of Madrid, a region not known for wine. Fruity wines to drink fairly young. Also an excellent white Selección Especial 91 made from Verdejo grapes in RUEDA.

Marqués de Monistrol, Bodegas Barcelona w p r sp dr sw res ★★ 85 89 Old BODEGA now owned by Martini & Rossi. Reliable CAVAS.

Marqués de Murrieta R Alt r p w res ★★★→★★★★ 34 42 52 59 62 68 70 78 83 85 Historic, much-respected BODEGA near LOGROÑO, formerly making some of the best of all RIOJAS. Also known for red Etiqueta Blanca, red CASTILLO YGAY, old-style oaky white and a wonderful old-style RESERVA ROSADO. Except for the Rosado, recent quality v disappointing.

Marqués del Puerto R Alt r (p w) res ★★→★★★ 86 87 88 Small firm, was Bodegas López Agos, now owned by BODEGAS Y BEBIDAS. Balanced reliable.

Marqués de Riscal R Ala r (p w) res ★★★ 76 82 87 88 Best-known BODEGA of RIOJA ALAVESA. Its red wines are relatively light and dry. Old vintages are v fine; some more recent ones were poor; current ones are right back on form. Baron de Chirel, 50% Cab S, new in '86, is magnificent. Whites from RUEDA, incl a vg Sauv Bl and oak-aged RESERVA Limousin.

Martínez-Bujanda R Ala r p w res ★★★ 78 81 82 85 86 87 89 91 Refounded ('85) family-run RIOJA BODEGA, remarkably equipped. Excellent wines, incl fruity SIN CRIANZA, irresistible ROSADO, noble Valdemar RESERVAS.

Mascaró, Cavas Barcelona r p w sp ★★→★★★ Maker of some of the best Spanish brandy, good sparkling wine, lemony refreshing dry white Viña Franca, and good (85) Anima Cab S.

Mauro, Bodegas Valladolid r ★★ 84 85 86 87 89 Young BODEGA in Tudela del Duero with vg round fruity Tinto del País (Tempranillo) red. Not DO as it is made by Bodegas Sainz in RUEDA.

Méntrida La M r w ★ DO west of Madrid, source of everyday red wine.

Milmanda ★★★ DYA See Conca de Barberá, Torres.

Monopole See Compañía Vinícola del Norte de España (CVNE).

Montánchez E Spain r g ★ Village near Mérida whose red wines grow FLOR yeast like FINO sherry.

Montecillo, Bodegas R Alt r w (p) res ** RIOJA BODEGA owned by OSBORNE. Wines v appealing young but recent vintages extremely fragile.

Montecristo, Bodegas Mont-M ** Well-known brand of MONTILLA-MORILES.

Monterrey Gal r * Region nr N border of Portugal; strong VERIN-like wines.

Montilla-Moriles Mont-M g **→*** DO nr Córdoba. Its crisp sherry-like FINO and AMONTILLADO contain 14–17.5% natural alcohol and remain unfortified. At best, singularly toothsome aperitifs.

Muga, Bodegas R Alt r (w sp) res *** 82 **85 86 87 88** Small family firm in HARO, known for making some of RIOJA's best reds by strictly traditional methods. Wines are light but highly aromatic, with long complex finish. Best is Prado Enea (82 is outstanding, but 86 87 88 far below par). Whites and CAVA also good.

Navajas, Bodegas R Alt r w res ** 85 89 Small firm with bargain reds, CRIANZAS and RESERVAS, fruity and full-bodied. Also excellent oak-aged white Viura and cherry and vanilla flavoured CRIANZA ROSADO.

Navarra Nav r p (w) ** Demarcated region; mainly rosés and sturdy reds, now well launched on stylish Tempranillo and Cab reds, some RESERVAS up to RIOJA standards. See Chivite, Magaña, Ochoa, Principe de Viana.

Nuestro Padre Jésus del Perdón, Coop de La M r w *→*** 85 86 88 91 DYA Look for bargain fresh white Lazarillo and more-than-drinkable Yuntero; 100% Cencibel (alias Tempranillo) aged in oak.

Ochoa Nav r p w res **→*** 88 89 Small family BODEGA now with an excellent white, but better known for well-made red and rosés, incl outstanding 100% Tempranillo. Cab S and blends are less interesting.

Olarra, Bodegas R Alt r (w p) res ** Vast modern BODEGA nr LOGROÑO, one of the showpieces of RIOJA. Interesting 5–6 yrs ago, esp for silky, well-balanced Cerro Añon reds, but quality now disappointing.

Rioja's characteristic style

To the Spanish palate the taste of luxury in wine is essentially the taste of (American) oak. Oak contains vanillin: hence the characteristic vanilla flavour of all traditional Spanish table wines of high quality – exemplified by the reservas of Rioja (red and white). Fashion swung (perhaps too far) against the oaky flavour of old Rioja whites but the pendulum is swinging back, although to subtler oak flavours than in the old days. The marriage of ripe fruit and oak in red Rioja is still highly appreciated.

Palacio, Bodegas R Ala r p w res ** 81 82 85 86 87 89 **90 91** Seagram-owned, now recovered from dismal standards. Esp Glorioso RESERVA.

Palacio de Arganza El B r p (w) res ** 83 85 Best-known BODEGA in new EL BIERZO DO. Somewhat variable red Almena del Bierzo is worth trying.

Palacio de Fefiñanes Gal w res *** Famous for untypical ALBARINO. No bubbles and oak-aged 3–5 yrs.

Parxet Alella w p sp ** Makers of excellent fresh, fruity, exuberantly fizzy CAVA (only one from ALLELA), and elegant white Allela, 'MARQUES DE ALELLA'.

Paternina, Bodegas R Alt r w (p) dr sw res *→*** 73 A household name, esp for BANDA AZUL. Conde de los Andes label was fine; **64 70 73** were outstanding, but recent vintages, as of other RIOJAS, are disappointing. Most consistent is clean cold-fermented Banda Dorada white (DYA).

Paxarete Traditional intensely sweet dark brown almost chocolatey speciality of TARRAGONA. Not to be missed. See De Muller.

Pazo Gal r p w ** DYA Brand name of the RIBEIRO coop, whose wines are akin to VINHOS VERDES. Rasping red is local favourite. Pleasant slightly fizzy Pazo and Xeito whites are safer; Viña Costeira has quality.

Pazo de Barrantes Gal w *** 91 93 New ALBARINO from RIAS BAIXAS, from an estate owned by the Conde de Creixels of Murrieta. Delicate, exotic and of impeccable quality, but v expensive and hard to come by.

Peñafiel Village on R Duero nr Valladolid. See Bodegas Ribero Duero.

Penedès Pen r w sp *→*** Demarcated region including Vilafranca del Penedès, SAN SADURNI DE NOYA and SITGES. See also Torres.

Perelada Amp w (r p) sp ★★ In the demarcated region of Ampurdán on the Costa Brava. Best known for sparkling, both CAVA and GRAN VAS.

Pérez Pascuas Hermanos Rib del D r (p) res ★★★ 87 88 89 91 Immaculate tiny family BODEGA in RIBERA DEL DUERO. In Spain its fruity and complex red Viña Pedrosa is rated one of the country's best.

Pesquera Rib del D r ★★★ 85 86 87 88 89 90 91 Small quantities of RIBERA DEL DUERO from Alejandro Fernandez. Robert Parker has rated it level with B'x Grands Crus. Janus is special (even more expensive) bottling.

Piqueras La M r ★★ 82 83 85 87 Small family BODEGA. Some of LA MANCHA's best reds: Castillo de Almansa CRIANZA, Marius GRAN RES.

Principe de Viana, Bodegas Nav r w ★★ 89 90 91 Large firm (formerly 'Cenalsa'), blending and maturing coop wines and shipping a range from NAVARRA, incl flowery new-style white and fruity red, Agramont.

Priorato Pri br r ★★★ 83 85 87 88 89 91 DO enclave of TARRAGONA, known for alcoholic RANCIO and splendidly full-bodied, almost black reds, often used for blending, but at brambly best one of Spain's triumphs. Lighter blended is good carafe wine. See Barril, De Muller, Scala Dei.

Protos See Ribero Duero, Bodega.

Raimat Cos del S r w p sp ★★→★★★ (Cab) 83 84 85 86 87 88 89 90 Clean, structured wines from new DO nr Lérida, planted by CODORNIU with Cab, Chard, other foreign vines. Good 100% Chard CAVA. Standards slipping?

Rancio Maderized (brown) white wine.

Raventos i Blanc Barcelona w sp ★★→★★★ 85 86 87 Excellent CAVA aimed at top of market, also fresh El Preludi white (91).

Real Divisa, Bodegas R Alt r res ★★ 85 86 87 90 Picturesque old BODEGA, one of few growing all its own fruit. Esp Marqués de Legarda RESERVAS.

Remélluri La Granja R Ala r res ★★★ 85 87 88 89 Small estate (since '70), making vg traditional red RIOJAS and improving all the time.

Reserva (res) Good quality wine matured for long periods. Red reservas must spend at least 1 yr in cask and 2 in bottle; gran reservas 2 in cask and 3 in bottle. Thereafter many continue to mature for years.

Rías Baixas Gal w ★★→★★★ NW DO embracing subzones Val do Salnés, O Rosal and Condado de Tea, now for some of the best (and priciest) cold-fermented Spanish whites, mainly from ALBARINO grapes.

Ribeiro Gal r w (p) ★→★★ Demarcated region on N border of Portugal: wines similar in style to Portuguese VINHOS VERDES – and others.

Ribera del Duero Rib del D Historic demarcated region E of Valladolid, now revealed as excellent for Tinto Fino (Tempranillo) reds. Vintages are somewhat variable and prices high. See Peñafiel, Pérez Pascuas, Pesquera, Torremilanos, Vega Sicilia. Also Mauro.

Ribera Duero, Bodegas Rib del D r w res ★★→★★★ 76 79 80 82 83 85 86 87 89 Formerly the cooperative of PENAFIEL and the second oldest winery in RIBERA DEL DUERO, recently privatized. Fruity young reds and tasty Protos Reserva. Tasty does not always mean agreeable.

Rioja r p w sp 64 70 73 78 81 82 85 89 90 91 N upland region along River Ebro for many of Spain's best red table wines in some 60 BODEGAS DE EXPORTACION. Mostly from Tempranillo. Other grapes and/or oak added depending on fashion and vintage. Subdivided into 3 areas, each now controlled by a different autonomous government:

Rioja Alavesa N of the R Ebro, produces fine red wines, mostly light in body and colour but particularly aromatic.

Rioja Alta S of the R Ebro and W of LOGRONO, grows most of the finest, best-balanced red and white wines; also some rosé.

Rioja Baja Stretching E from LOGRONO, makes coarser red wines, high in alcohol and often used for blending.

Rioja Santiago R Alt r (p w dr sw) res ★→★★ 81 85 86 87 90 BODEGA at HARO with brands incl the biggest-selling bottled SANGRIA. Its top reds, Condal and Gran Enologica, are respectable.

Riojanas, Bodegas R Alt r (w p) res ✯✯→✯✯✯ 64 70 73 75 78 81 82 83 85 86 88 91 Old BODEGA making good traditional Viña Albina (78 85 86). Its Monte Real RESERVAS (70 82) are big and mellow.

Rosado Rosé.

Rovellats Barcelona w p sp ✯✯→✯✯✯ 91 Small family firm making only gd (and expensive) CAVAS, stocked in some of Spain's best restaurants.

Rovira, Pedro Tar/Pen r p br w dr sw res ✯→✯✯ Large firm with BODEGAS in the DOs TARRAGONA, Terra Alta and PENEDES. A wide range.

Rueda Rueda br w ✯→✯✯ Small historic demarcated area W of Valladolid. Traditional producer of FLOR-growing, sherry-like wines up to 17° alcohol, now for fresh whites, incl those of the MARQUES DE RISCAL and MARQUES DE GRINON. Its secret weapon is the Verdejo grape.

Ruiz, Santiago Gal w ✯✯✯ DYA Most prestigious BODEGA, now owned by Bodegas LAN, in RIAS BAIXAS. Its fresh lemony ALBARINO is one of v best.

Salceda, Bodegas Viña R Ala r res ✯✯ 82 85 88 Makes fruity light but well-balanced red wines.

Sangre de Toro Brand name for a rich-flavoured red from TORRES.

Sangría Cold red wine cup traditionally made with citrus fruit, fizzy lemonade, ice and brandy. But too often repulsive commercial fizz.

Sanlúcar de Barrameda Centre of the Manzanilla district (see Sherry).

San Sadurní de Noya Barcelona w sp ✯✯→✯✯✯ Town S of Barcelona, hollow with cellars where dozens of firms produce CAVA. Standards can be v high, though the flavour (of Parellada and other grapes) is quite different from that of champagne.

San Valero, Bodega Cooperativa Cariñena r p w res ✯→✯✯✯ 85 87 88 Large CARINENA coop with some modern wines. Good red CRIANZA Monte Ducay; fresh Perçebal ROSADO with slight spritz; and good value young unoaked Don Mendo red and white.

Sarría, Bodegas de Nav r (p w) res ✯✯→✯✯✯ 73 74 75 76 78 81 82 84 87 88 89 Model estate BODEGA nr Pamplona: wines up to RIOJA standards.

Scala Dei, Cellers de Pri r w p res ✯✯→✯✯✯ 85 87 88 89 92 One of the few BODEGAS in tiny PRIORATO. Full-bodied reds (esp GRAN RESERVA), some oak-aged, and the region's only white, Scala Dei Blanco; also delicious Tavel-style ROSADO since '92. Less alcohol recently.

Scholtz, Hermanos Málaga br ✯✯→✯✯✯ Makers of the best MALAGA, incl dry 10-yr-old AMONTILLADO, excellent Moscatel and traditional Dulce y Negro. Best of all is the dessert Solera Scholtz 1885.

Seco Dry.

Segura Viudas, Cavas Pen w sp ✯✯→✯✯✯ CAVA of PENEDES (FREIXENET-owned). Buy the Brut Vintage (83), Aria (88) or RESERVA Heredad.

Serra, Jaume Pen r w res ✯✯ 86 88 91 PENEDES firm making refreshing single-variety whites, fruity well-balanced reds and CAVA.

Sin Crianza See Crianza.

Sitges Barcelona w sw ✯✯ Coastal resort S of Barcelona formerly noted for its dessert wine made from Moscatel and Malvasia grapes. Only one maker, Celler Robert, survives.

Somontano Som Pyrenees foothills DO. Best-known BODEGAS: old French-est'd Lalanne (esp Viña San Marcos red: Moristel-Tempranillo-Cab S; white Macabeo, Chard), Coop Somontano de Sobrarbe (esp Montesierra range and oak-aged Señorío de Lazán), new COVISA (Víñas del Vero).

Tarragona Tarragona r w br dr sw ✯→✯✯✯ (i) Table wines from demarcated region (DO); of little note. (ii) Dessert wines from the firm of DE MULLER.

Tinto Red.

Toro Toro r ✯→✯✯ Demarcated region 150 miles NW of Madrid. Formerly made over-powerful (up to 16°) red wines, but now produces some tasty balanced reds. See Bodegas Fariña.

To decipher codes, please refer to symbols key at front of book, and to 'How to use this book' on page 5.

Torremilanos Rib del D r res ★→★★ 85 86 87 88   Label of Bodegas López Peñalba, a fast-expanding family firm near Aranda de Duero (RIBERA DEL DUERO). Their red Tinto Fino (Tempranillo) wines are lighter and more RIOJA-like than most. Also labelled 'Peñalba'.

Torres, Bodegas Pen r w p dr s/sw res ★★→★★★★ 83 85 86 87 88 89 90 91 93   World-famous family firm making most of the best table wines of PENEDES, and a flagship for the whole of Spain. Wines are flowery white Viña Sol, Green Label Fransola Sauv Bl and Parellada, Gran Viña Sol, MILMANDA oak-fermented Chard, semi-dry aromatic Esmeralda, Waltraud Ries, red Tres Torres and Gran Sangre de Toro, superlative Gran Coronas (Cab) RESERVAS, fresh and soft Las Torres Merlot and Santa Digna Pinot N. Mas Borras is a new 100% Pinot N. The family also has v'yds in Chile and California.

Utiel-Requeña U-R r p (w)   Demarcated region W of Valencia. Sturdy reds and chewy vino de doble pasta for blending; also light fragrant rosé.

Valbuena Rib del D r ★★★ 82 83 84 85 86 88   Made with the same grapes as VEGA SICILIA but sold when either 3 or 5 yrs old. Best at about 10 yrs. Some prefer it to its elder brother.

Valdeorras Gal r w ★→★★   Demarcated region E of Orense. Dry and (at best) refreshing wines.

Valdepeñas La M r (w) ★→★★   Demarcated region nr the border of Andalucía. Mainly red wines, high in alcohol but surprisingly soft in flavour. Best wine (eg LOS LLANOS and FELIX SOLIS) now oak-matured.

Valencia Valencia r w ★   Demarcated region exporting vast quantities of clean and drinkable table wine; also refreshing whites, esp Moscatel.

Vallformosa, Masia Pen r w p sp res ★★ 85 87 88   Good PENEDES wine; a fresh dry white Gran Blanc, good Vall Fort red and Vall RESERVAS.

Vega de la Reina Rueda w r res ★★ 70 73 75 78 80 81 82 85   RUEDA BODEGA making complex old-style oaky reds with something of the quality of the famous VEGA SICILIA. Also a characterful white Verdejo.

Vega Sicilia Rib del D r res ★★★★ 41 48 53 59 60 61 62 64 66 67 69 72 73 74 75 76 79 80 82   One of the v best Spanish wines, full-bodied, fruity, piquant, rare and fascinating. Up to 16% alcohol. Reserva Especial is a blend, chiefly of 62 and 79 (!). See also VALBUENA.

Vendimia Vintage.

Verín Gal r ★   Town near N border of Portugal. Its wines are the strongest from GALICIA, without a bubble, and with up to 14% alcohol.

Viña Literally, a vineyard. But wines such as Tondonia (LOPEZ DE HEREDIA) are not necessarily made with grapes from only the v'yd named.

Viña Pedrosa See Pérez Pascuas.

Viña Toña Pen w ★★→★★★ 93 DYA   Clean fresh and fruity white of Xarel-lo and unoaked Chard from the small firm of Celler R Balada. Justifiably high reputation in Spain.

Viñas del Vero Som w p r res ★★→★★★   Worthwhile SOMONTANO wines from COMPANIA VITIVINICOLA ARAGONESA.

Vinícola de Castilla La M r p w ★★ 83 84 87 89 91 92   One of largest LA MANCHA firms. Red and white Castillo de Alhambra: palatable. Top are Cab S, Cencibel (Tempranillo), Señorío de Guadianeja (84) GRAN RESERVAS.

Vinícola Navarra Nav r p w res ★★ 78 82 84 88 90   Old-est'd BODEGA, thoroughly trad NAVARRA. Best: Castillo de Tiebas, Las Campanas (88).

Vinival, Bodegas Valencia r p w ★   Huge Valencian consortium marketing the most widely drunk wine in the region, Torres de Quart (rosé best).

Vino comun/corriente Ordinary wine.

Vino Joven See Joven.

Vitivino, Bodegas Jumilla r w ★★→★★★ 88 89 91   French J-L Gadeau has caused stir with lively or meaty Altos de Pío from local Monastrell grapes.

Yecla Yecla r w ★   DO north of Murcia. Good red from Bodegas Castaño.

Ygay See Marqués de Murrieta.

Yllera Rib del D r ★★ 86 88 89   Good value RIBERO DEL DUERO red from Los Curos (but bottled in RUEDA so not DO).

Portugal

Portugal entries also cross-refer to Sherry, Port & Madeira, pages 133–139.

Abrigada, Quinta de Central Portugal r w res ✹✹ 80 86   Family estate: characterful light whites and cherry-like Castelão Francês (aka0. PERIQUITA). Best are the oak-aged GARRAFEIRAS.

Adega A cellar or winery.

Alenquer r w   Aromatic reds, strong whites from new IPR just N of Lisbon.

Alentejo Alen r (w) *→✹✹✹   Vast tract of S Portugal with only sparse vineyards nr the Spanish border, but rapidly emerging potential for excellent wine. To date the great bulk has been coop-made. Estate wines from ROSADO FERNANDES, Herdade de Mouchão, QUINTA DO CARMO (now Rothschild-owned) and ESPORAO have potency and style. Best coops are at BORBA, REDONDO and REGUENGOS DE MONSARRAZ. Growing excitement here.

Algarve Algarve   r w *   Demoted DO in the holiday area. With few exceptions its wines are nothing to write home about.

Aliança, Caves Bair r w sp res ✹✹→✹✹✹   Large BAIRRADA-based firm making classic method sparkling. Reds and whites incl good Bairrada wines and mature DAOS. Aliança Tinta Velha is the best-selling red in Portugal.

Almeirim Ribatejo r w *   Large new IPR east of ALENQUER. Its coop makes the admirably fruity, extremely inexpensive Lezíria (alias Ramada).

Almodovar, Casa Agricola Alen w r res ✹✹ 84 86 87   The whites of this ADEGA at Vidigueira are better known, but its reds are worth trying.

Amarante Subregion in the VINHO VERDE area. Rather heavier and stronger wines than those from farther north.

Arrábida nr Lisbon r w   New IPR W of SETUBAL. Reds mostly from Castelão Francês (or PERIQUITA) some Cab S allowed.

Arruda, Adega Cooperative de nr Lisbon r res ✹   Vinho Tinto Arruda is a best buy, but avoid the reserva.

Aveleda, Quinta da Douro w ✹✹ DYA   A first-class VINHO VERDE made on the Aveleda estate of the Guedes family of MATEUS fame. Sold dry in Portugal but sweetened for export.

Azeveda, Quinta de VV w ✹✹ DYA   Superior VINHO VERDE from SOGRAPE. 100% Loureiro grapes.

Bacalhoa, Quinta da Set r res ✹✹✹ 81 82 83 84 85 87 88 90   American-owned estate near SETUBAL, famous for harmonious fruity mid-weight Cab S vinified by J P VINHOS.

Bairrada Bair r w sp *→✹✹✹ 78 79 80 81 82 83 84 85 86 87 88 89 90 91 92 93   Demarcated region producing excellent red GARRAFEIRAS. Also good sparkling by the classic method. Now an export hit.

Barca Velha ('Ferreirinha') Douro r res ✹✹✹✹ 78 81 82 83 84 85   Perhaps Portugal's best red, made in v limited quantities in the high DOURO by the port firm of FERREIRA (now owned by SOGRAPE). Powerful resonant wine with deep bouquet, still unchallenged by younger rivals.

Barrocão, Cavas do Bair r w res *→✹✹✹   Based in BAIRRADA; blends good red DAOS and sells first-rate old Bairrada GARRAFEIRAS (60 64).

Basto A subregion of the VINHO VERDE area on the R Tamego, producing more astringent red wine than white.

Borba Alen r *→✹✹   Small IPR area nr Evora, making some of the best wine from ALENTEJO.

Borba, Adega Cooperative de Alen r (w) res *→✹✹✹ 82 84 87 88 89   Leading ALENTEJO coop modernized with stainless steel and oak by EC funding. Big fruity vinho de ano red and vg 82 reserva.

Borges & Irmão Merchants of port and table wines at Vila Nova de Gaia, incl GATAO and (better) Gamba VINHOS VERDES, sparkling Fita Azul.

Braga Subregion of the VINHO VERDE area, good red and white.

Branco White.

Buçaco nr Dão r w (p) res **** (r) 51 53 57 58 60 63 67 70 72 75 77 (w) 56 65 66 70 72 75 78 82   Legendary speciality of the Palace Hotel at Buçaco nr Coimbra, not seen elsewhere. At best incredible quality.

Bucelas w *** 79 84   Tiny demarcated region N of Lisbon. CAVES VELHAS make aromatic whites with 11–12% alcohol. Reliable, not dramatic.

Camarate, Quinta de Lisbon r ** 82 83 84 85 86 87 90   Notable red from FONSECA, S of Lisbon, incl detectable proportion of Cab S.

Campos da Silva Olivera, JC Dão r res ** 84 85   Small ADEGA with v fruity estate DAO, Sete Torres Reserva.

Carcavelos br sw *** normally NV   Minute demarcated region W of Lisbon. Excellent but rare sweet aperitif or dessert wines average 19% alcohol and resemble honeyed MADEIRA. For yrs the only producer was the Quinta do Barão; now J P VINHOS has joined in.

When in Portugal... chose youngest vintages of whites, oldest of red.

Carmo, Quinta do Alen r w res *** 86 87 88 89   Small and beautiful ALENTEJO ADEGA, bought in '92 by the Rothschilds of Lafite. 125 acres, plus cork forests. Ferments its wines in marble 'lagars'. Fresh dry white, but best is the fruity harmonious red.

Cartaxo Ribatejo r w *   A district in the RIBATEJO N of Lisbon, now an IPR area making everyday wines popular in the capital.

Carvalho, Ribeiro & Ferreira N Lisbon r w res **→***   Large merchants blending and bottling SERRADAYRES and excellent RIBATEJO GARRAFEIRAS.

Casa Ferreirinha Douro r res ***   The second wine to BARCA VELHA, made in less than ideal vintages.

Casa da Insua Dão r w **   One of the v few single-estate wines of DAO (but not DO), made with a proportion of Cab S for the proprietors by FONSECA.

Casa de Sezim VV w *** DYA   Top estate-bottled VINHO VERDE from a member of the association of private producers, APEVV.

Casal García Douro w ** DYA   Big-selling VINHO VERDE, made at AVELEDA.

Casal Mendes VV w ** DYA   The VINHO VERDE from CAVES ALIANCA.

Casaleiro Trademark of Caves Dom Teodosio-João T Barbosa, who make a variety of standard wines: DAO, VINHO VERDE, etc.

Castelo Rodrigo NE Portugal r w   Reds resembling DAO.

Cepa Velha VV w (r) ***   Brand name of Vinhos de Monção. Their Alvarinho is one of the best VINHOS VERDES.

Chaves N Portugal r w   New IPR. Sharp pale fizzy reds from granite soils. Rounder ones from schist.

Clarete Relatively light red wine.

Colares Colares r *** TOTB (the older the better)   Small DOC on the sandy coast W of Lisbon. Its antique-style dark red wines, rigid with tannin, are from vines that have never suffered from phylloxera. Drink the oldest available: it needs at least 10 yrs (see Paulo da Silva).

Conde de Santar B Al r (w) res **→*** 78 85 86   Estate-grown DAO, later matured and sold by the port firm of CALEM. Reservas are fruity, full-bodied and exceptionally smooth.

Consumo (vinho) Ordinary wine.

Coruche Coruche r w   Large new IPR of Sorraia river basin NE of Lisbon. Only growth of interest, the botrytis wine made by J P VINHOS.

Corval, Quinta do Pinhão r **   Estate nr Pinhão: good CLARETES.

Côtto, Quinta do Douro r w res *** 82 85 90   Pioneer table wines from port country; red Grande Escolha and Q do Côtto are dense fruity tannic wines that will repay long keeping. Also port.

Cova da Beira r w   Largest of new IPRs on Spanish border. Light reds best.

Dão Dão r w res ** 80 81 82 83 84 85 86 87 88 89 90 91 92 93   Demarcated region round town of Viseu. Produces some of Portugal's best-known, but often dull table wines: solid reds of some subtlety with age; substantial dry whites. Most sold under brand names. But see Duque de Viseu, Casa da Insua, J M da Fonseca, Porta dos Cavalheiros, etc.

DOC (Denominacâo de Origem Controlada) Official wine region. There are 12 in mainland Portugal, incl BAIRRADA, COLARES, DAO, DOURO, SETUBAL, VINHO VERDE.

Doce (vinho) Sweet (wine).

Douro Douro r w **80 81 82 83 84 85 86 87 88 89 90 91** 92 Northern river whose valley produces port and some of Portugal's most exciting new table wines. See Barca Velha, Quinta do Côtto, etc. Watch this space.

Duque de Viseu Dão r **90** High quality branded red DAO from SOGRAPE.

Encostas de Aire Central Portugal r w Fruity high-alcohol wines from large new IPR.

Esporão, Herdade do Alen w r ** **87** 90 Owners Finagra SA spent US $10 million on their space-age winery and planting 900 acres. Their light fresh Roupeiro white and 87 red, with a touch of Cab S, are pleasant but pricey. Wines now made by Australian David Baverstock.

Espumante Sparkling.

Esteva Douro r *→** DYA Very drinkable young DOURO red wine from the port firm FERREIRA.

Evelita Douro r ** Reliable middle-weight red made near VILA REAL by REAL COMPANHIA VINICOLA DO NORTE DE PORTUGAL. Ages well.

Evora Alen r w **86 87 88 89 90 91** Large new IPR south of Lisbon.

Fonseca, JM da Lisbon r w dr sw sp res **→**** Venerable firm in Azeitão nr Lisbon with one of the longest and best ranges in Portugal, incl dry white PASMADOS, PORTALEGRE and QUINTA DE CAMARATE; red PERIQUITA, Pasmados, de Camarate, TERRAS ALTAS DAO; and famous dessert Moscatel de SETUBAL. Fonseca also owns ROSADO FERNANDES and makes the wines for CASA DA INSUA.

Fonseca Internacional, JM da nr Lisbon p sp * Formerly part of the last, now owned by Grand Met. Produces LANCERS rosé and a surprisingly drinkable sparkling Lancers Brut made by a continuous process of Russian invention.

Gaeiras Central Coast r ** Dry full-bodied well-balanced red made nr OBIDOS.

Garrafeira Label term. The 'private reserve' wine of a merchant, aged for a minimum of 2 yrs in cask and 1 in bottle, but often much longer. Usually their best, though traditionally often of indeterminate origin.

Gatão VV w ** DYA Standard VINHO VERDE from BORGES & IRMAO; fragrant but sweetened.

Gazela VV w ** DYA New VINHO VERDE made at Barcelos by SOGRAPE since the AVELEDA estate went to a different branch of the Guedes family.

Generoso Aperitif or dessert wine rich in alcohol.

Grão Vasco Dão r w res ** **82 83 85 87** 88 89 93 One of the best brands of DAO, from a new high-tech ADEGA at Viseu. Fine red RESERVAS; fresh young white (DYA). Owned by SOGRAPE.

Thirty-one new Portuguese wine regions came into play in 1990. These 'IPRs' (Indicacões de Proveniência Regulamentada) are on a six-year probation for DOC status. In EC terminology they are VQPRDs. Those which are really performing are included in this edition.

IPR Indicacões de Proveniência Regulamentada. See above.

J P Vinhos Set r w sp res **→**** One of Portugal's best-equipped and best-run wineries. Wines incl delicious J P Vinhos Branco (Moscato), Catarina (with Chard), dry white and red Santa Marta, red Santo Amaro made by macération carbonique, TINTO DE ANFORA, QUINTA DA BACALHOA, dessert SETUBAL, classic sparkling J P Vinhos Bruto, and now CARCAVELOS.

Lafões r w New IPR between DAO and VINHO VERDE.

Lagosta VV w * DYA VINHO VERDE from the REAL COMPANHIA VINICOLA DO NORTE DE PORTUGAL.

Lancers nr Lisbon p w sp * Sweet carbonated rosé and sparkling white extensively shipped to the US by FONSECA INTERNACIONAL.

Leziria See Almeirim.

Lima Subregion in N of VINHO VERDE area, for mainly astringent red wines.

Madeira br dr sw ★★→★★★★   Source of famous aperitif and dessert wines. See pages 133–139.

Maduro (vinho) A mature table wine – as opposed to a VINHO VERDE.

Mateus Rosé Bair p (w) ★   World's biggest-selling medium-sweet carbonated rosé, made by SOGRAPE at VILA REAL and Anadia in BAIRRADA.

Monção N subregion of the VINHO VERDE area on R Minho: producing the best of them from the Alvarinho grape.

Morgadio de Torre VV w ★★ DYA   A top VINHO VERDE from SOGRAPE. Largely Alvarinho grapes.

Mouchão, Herdade de Alen r res ★★★ 74 82   Perhaps the best ALENTEJO estate, ruined in the '75 revolution; since replanted.

Moura Alen r w 85 86 87 88 89 90 91   New IPR: source of J P VINHOS red and white Santa Marta.

Obidos r w   New IPR nr coast, S of Alcobaça (central coast). Similar wines.

Pacheca, Quinta da Douro r w ★★ 82   Superior DOURO table wines, estate-grown -made and -bottled. Unfortunately not free of faults.

Palacio de Brejoeira VV w (r) ★★★   Outstanding estate-made VINHO VERDE from MONCAO, with astonishing fragrance and full fruity flavour.

Palmela Set r w   New sandy soil IPR NE of SETUBAL. Reds esp long-lived.

Pancas, Quinta de Central Coast r res ★★ 87 90   Red wine to watch from ALENQUER district N of Lisbon.

Pasmados Very tasty FONSECA red from the SETUBAL peninsula.

Paulo da Silva, Antonio Bernardino Colares r (w) res ★★→★★★ 68 70 74 77 79 80 83 84 85   His COLARES Chita is one of the very few of those classics still made (by the ADEGA Regional).

Pedralvites, Quinta de Bair w ★→★★★ 93   Pleasant BAIRRADA white with apple and apricot flavours from the Maria Gomes grape, by SOGRAPE.

Penafiel Subregion in the S of the VINHO VERDE area.

Periquita Lisbon r ★★ 85 86 87 88   One of Portugal's most enjoyable robust reds, made by FONSECA S of Lisbon. Periquita is an alias of Castelão Francês, a grape much grown in the ALENTEJO.

Pinhel B Al w (r) sp ★   IPR region E of DAO: similar white, mostly sparkling.

Pires, Vinhos João See J P Vinhos.

Planalto Douro w ★★ 90   Good white wine from SOGRAPE.

Planalto Mirandês r w   Large new IPR NE of DOURO. Port grapes in reds. Verdelho in whites.

Ponte de Lima, Cooperativa de VV r ★★   Maker of one of the best bone-dry red VINHOS VERDES, and first-rate dry and fruity white.

Porta dos Cavalheiros Dão ★★ 80 83 85   One of the best red DAOs, matured by CAVES SAO JOAO in BAIRRADA.

Portalegre Alen r w 85 86 87 88 89 90   Important new IPR on Spanish border. Strong fragrant reds with potential to age. Alcoholic whites.

Quinta Estate.

Raposeira Douro w sp ★★   Well-known fizz made by the classic method at Lamego. Ask for the Bruto. An outpost of Seagram.

Real Companhia Vinícola do Norte de Portugal Giant of the port trade (see page 138); also produces EVELITA, LAGOSTA, etc.

Redondo Alen r w   Nr Spanish border. One of Portugal's best-kept secrets. Newly granted IPR status.

Reguengos de Monsarraz, Cooperativa de Alen r (w) res ★★ 80 81 82 83 84 85 86 87 88 89 90   Important coop making steadily better wines; the best of them red, esp Terras d'el Rei Reserva 86.

Ribatejo r w 80 81 82 83 84 85 86 87 88 89 90 91   Region on R Tagus north of Lisbon. Several good GARRAFEIRAS etc.

Ribeirinho, Quinta de Bair r sp ★★ 80 85   Luis Pato makes some of the best estate-grown BAIRRADA: fruity red and fresh classic method sparkling.

For key to grape variety abbreviations, see pages 6–9.

Rosa, Quinta de la Douro r ★★ Firm oak-aged red from v'yds formerly used for port. Also young peppery Quinta das Lamelas. Both made by Australian David Baverstock.

Rosado Rosé.

Rosado Fernandes, José de Sousa Alen r res ★★ 75 79 83 86 Small firm recently acquired by FONSECA, making the most sophisticated of the full-bodied wines from the ALENTEJO, fermenting them in earthenware amphoras and ageing them in oak.

Santarém r w New central Portugal IPR. Reds and whites fruity and strong; reds will age.

São Claudio, Quinta de VV w ★★★ DYA Estate at Esposende: perhaps the best VINHO VERDE outside MONCAO.

São João, Caves Bair r w sp res ★★→★★★ 78 80 82 83 One of the best firms in BAIRRADA, known for fruity and full-bodied reds and PORTA DOS CAVALHEIROS DAOS. Also fizz.

Seco Dry.

Serradayres r (w) res ★ Blended RIBATEJO table wines from CARVALHO, Ribeiro & Ferreira. Usually sound and v drinkable; recently too tart.

Setúbal Set br (r w) sw (dr) ★★★ Small demarcated region S of the River Tagus, where FONSECA make a highly aromatic dessert Muscat (80 81 82 83 84 85 86 87 88 89 90 91 92 93).

Sogrape Sociedad Comercial dos Vinhos de Mesa de Portugal. Largest wine concern in the country, making VINHOS VERDES, DAO, BAIRRADA, MATEUS ROSE, VILA REAL red, etc, and now owners of FERREIRA port.

Solar das Boucas VINHO VERDE estate. Its dry aromatic wine is a model.

Terra Franca Bair r res ★★ 85 87 88 90 Good red BAIRRADA from SOGRAPE, available also as a GARRAFEIRA.

Terras Altas Dão r w res ★★ 82 83 84 85 86 87 88 89 Good DAO from FONSECA.

Tinto Red.

Tinto da Anfora Set r ★★ 84 85 86 87 Deservedly popular juicy and fruity red from J P VINHOS. Repays at least 5 yrs in bottle.

Tomar r w New central Portugal IPR for acidic whites, smooth reds.

Torres Vedras r w ★ Area N of Lisbon famous for Wellington's 'lines'. Major supplier of bulk wine; one of biggest coops in Portugal.

Valpaços r New IPR N of DOURO. Wines like CHAVES' (esp from schist soils).

Velhas, Caves Bucelas r w res ★★→★★★ Until very recently the only maker of BUCELAS; also good DAO and (80) Romeira GARRAFEIRAS.

Vidigueira Alen w r Famous for traditionally-made unmatured whites from volcanic soils. Newly awarded IPR status.

Vila Real Douro r ★→★★ Town in the DOURO. Some good reds.

Verde Green (see Vinhos Verdes).

Vinhos Verdes VV and Douro w ★→★★★ r ★ Demarcated region between R Douro and N frontier with Spain, producing 'green wines': wine made from barely ripe grapes and (originally) undergoing a special secondary fermentation to leave it with a slight sparkle. Today the fizz is usually just added CO_2. Ready for drinking in spring after harvest, it may be white or red. 'Green wine' is not an official term.

Dull technical stuff

The alcohol content of wine varies from as little as 7% by volume to as much as 16%, depending on the sugar content of the grapes (and the possible addition of sugar or 'chaptalisation', before fermentation).

Low strength does not mean low quality; nor vice versa. Finest Mosel Rieslings can balance alcoholic lightness with brilliant fruit-acid intensity. On the other hand a basic over-produced red at 10 or 11% will taste feeble.

Most top-quality wines, red or white, in the French style contain between 11.5 and 13%. Above this figure the risk is an over-'heady' smell, unless it is balanced by great intensity of flavour (sweetness). Fortified wines vary from 17 to 18% (fino sherry) to about 20% (vintage port).

Sherry,
Port & Madeira

The original authentic sherries of Spain, ports of Portugal and madeiras of Madeira are listed below. No other wines that use these names have a moral right to them; nor do any compare in quality and value for money with good examples of the originals.

The map on page 119 locates the port and sherry districts. Madeira is an island 400 miles out in the Atlantic from the coast of Morocco, a port of call for west-bound sailing ships: hence its historical market in North America.

In this section most of the entries are shippers' names followed by a brief account of their wines. The names of wine types are also included in the alphabetical listing.

Abad, Tomas Small sherry bodega owned by LUSTAU. Vg light FINO.

Almacenista Individual matured but unblended sherry; high quality, usually dark dry wines for connoisseurs. Often superb quality and value. See Lustau.

Amontillado A FINO which has been aged in cask beyond its normal span to become darker, more powerful and pungent. The best are natural dry wines. In general use means medium sherry.

Amoroso Type of sweet sherry, v similar to a sweet OLOROSO.

Barbadillo, Antonio Much the largest SANLUCAR firm, with a range of 50-odd MANZANILLAS and sherries mostly excellent of their type, incl Sanlúcar FINO, superb SOLERA manzanilla PASADA, Fino de Balbaina, austere Principe dry AMONTILLADO. Also young Castillo de San Diego table wines.

Barbeito Shippers of good-quality madeira, one of the last independent family firms, now Japanese controlled. Wines incl aperitif Island Dry, superior Crown range and rare vintage wines, eg MALMSEY 1901 and the latest, BUAL 1960.

Barros Almeida Large family-owned port house with several brands (including Feuerheerd, KOPKE): excellent 20-yr-old TAWNY and many COLHEITAS.

Bertola Sherry shippers, best known for their Bertola CREAM SHERRY.

Blandy Historic family firm of madeira shippers and one of two top names used by MADEIRA WINE CO. Duke of Clarence MALMSEY is their most famous wine. 10-year-old reservas (VERDELHO, BUAL, MALMSEY) are vg. Many glorious old vintages.

Blázquez Sherry bodega at JEREZ owned by DOMECQ. Outstanding FINO, Carta Blanca, v old SOLERA OLOROSO Extra, and Carta Oro AMONTILLADO al natural (unsweetened).

Bobadilla Large JEREZ bodega, best known for v dry Victoria FINO and Bobadilla 103 brandy, esp among Spanish connoisseurs. Also excellent sherry vinegar.

Brown sherry British term for a style of budget dark sweet sherry.

Bual One of the best grapes of madeira, making a soft smoky sweet wine, not usually as rich and sweet as MALMSEY.

Burdon English-founded sherry bodega owned by CABALLERO. Light FINO, Don Luis AMONTILLADO and raisiny Heavenly Cream are top lines.

Borges, H M Independent MADEIRA shipper of old repute.

Burmester Old, small, family-owned port house with fine soft sweet 20-yr-old TAWNY; also vg range of COLHEITAS. Vintages: **48 55 58 60 63 70 77 80 84 85 89 91**.

Caballero Important sherry shippers at PUERTO DE SANTA MARIA, best known for Pavon FINO, Mayoral Cream OLOROSO, excellent BURDON sherries and PONCHE orange liqueur.

Cálem Old family-run Portuguese house with fine reputation, esp for vintage wines. Owns excellent Quinta da Foz (**82** 84 86 87 88 89 90 92). Vintages: 50 55' 58 60 63' 66 70 75 77' 80 83 85 91. Good light TAWNY; exceptional range COLHEITAS: **48** 50 52 57 60 62 65 78 84 85 86.

Churchill The only recently founded port shipper, already highly respected for excellent vintages 82 and 85, also 91. Also a vg CRUSTED. Quinta da Agua Alta is Churchill's single-QUINTA port: 83 87 90 92.

'All wine would be port if it could.'
– old English saying

Cockburn British-owned (Allied-Hiram Walker) port shippers with a range of good wines incl the v popular fruity Special Reserve. Fine vintage port from high v'yds can look deceptively light when young, but has great lasting power. Vintages: 55 60 63' 67 70' 75 83 85 91.

Colheita Vintage-dated port of a single yr, but aged at least 7 winters in wood: in effect a vintage TAWNY. The bottling date is also shown on the label. Good examples come from KOPKE, CALEM and Krohn.

Cossart Gordon Leading firm of madeira shippers founded 1745, with BLANDY, now one of the two top-quality labels of the MADEIRA WINE CO. Wines slightly less rich than Blandy's. Best known for Good Company range but also producing 5-yr-old Reservas, old vintages (latest, 52) and SOLERAS (esp superb SERCIAL Duo Centenary).

Côtto, Quinta do Single-v'yd port from Miguel Champalimaud, best-known of a new wave of grower-bottlers up the DOURO. Vg vintage 82. See also in Portugal section.

Cream Sherry A style of amber sweet sherry made by sweetening a blend of well-aged OLOROSOS. It originated in Bristol, England.

Croft One of the oldest firms shipping vintage port: since 1678. Now owned by Grand Met Co. Well-balanced wine tend to mature early (since 66). Vintages: 55 60 63' 66 67 70' 75 77' 82 85' 91; and lighter vintage wines under the name of their Quinta da Roeda in several other years (78 80 83 87). Distinction is their most popular blend. MORGAN is a small separate company (see also Delaforce). Also now in the sherry business with Croft Original (PALE CREAM). Particular (medium), Delicado (FINO, also medium), and good PALO CORTADO.

Crusted Term for a vintage-style port, but usually blended from several vintages not one. Bottled young, then bottle-aged, so it forms a 'crust'. Needs decanting.

Delaforce Port shippers owned by CROFT, best known in Germany. His Eminence's Choice is a v pleasant TAWNY; VINTAGE CHARACTER is also good. Vintage wines are v fine, among the lighter kind: 55 58 60 63' 66' 70 74 75 77' 82 83 85'; Quinta da Côrte in 78 80 84 87 91.

Delgado Zuleta Old-established SANLUCAR firm best known for marvellous La Goya MANZANILLA PASADA.

Diez-Merito SA Fast-growing JEREZ firm owned by Bodegas INTERNACIONALES specializing in 'own-brand' sherries. Owns Zoilo Ruiz-Mateos, formerly part of the ill-fated Rumasa empire. Its own FINO Imperial and OLOROSO Victoria Regina are excellent. DON ZOILO wines are superb.

Domecq Giant family-run sherry bodegas at JEREZ; bought by Hiram Walker in '94, famous also for Fundador brandy. Double Century Original OLOROSO is their biggest brand, La Ina their excellent FINO. Other famous wines incl Celebration CREAM, Botaina (old AMONTILLADO) and the magnificent Rio Viejo (v dry amontillado) and Sibarita (PALO CORTADO). Recently: a range of wonderful old SOLERA sherries (Sibarita, Amontillado 51-1A and Venerable Oloroso). Also in RIOJA and Mexico.

Sherry, Port & Madeira entries also cross-refer to Spain and Portugal sections, respectively pages 118–127 and 128–132.

Don Zoilo Luxury sherries, including velvety FINO, sold by DIEZ-MERITO.

Dow Old port name, well-known for relatively dry but splendid vintage wines, said to have a faint 'cedarwood' character. Also very good VINTAGE CHARACTER and Boardroom, a 15-year-old TAWNY. Quinta do Bomfim is their single-QUINTA port **(78 79 82 84 86 87 88 89 90 92)**. Vintages: **55 60 63' 66' 70' 72 75 77' 80 83 85' 91**. Dow, GOULD CAMPBELL, GRAHAM, QUARLES HARRIS, SMITH WOODHOUSE and WARRE all belong to the Symington family.

Dry Fly A household name in the UK. A crisp nutty AMONTILLADO made in JEREZ for its British proprietors, Findlater Mackie Todd & Co.

Dry Sack See Williams & Humbert.

Duff Gordon Sherry shippers best known for El Cid AMONTILLADO. Also good FINO Feria and Nina Dry OLOROSO. Owned by OSBORNE.

Duke of Wellington A luxury range of sherries from BODEGAS INTERNACIONALES. Fine quality.

Eira Velha, Quinta da Small port estate with old-style vintage wines shipped by MARTINEZ. Vintages: 78 82 87 92.

Ferreira One of the biggest Portuguese-owned port growers and shippers (since 1751), recently bought by SOGRAPE (see Portugal). Largest selling brand in Portugal. Well-known for old TAWNIES and juicily sweet, relatively light vintages: **60 63' 66 70' 75 77' 78 80 82 85' 87 91**. Also Dona Antónia Personal Reserve, splendidly rich tawny Duque de Bragança and single-QUINTA wines Quinta do Seixo (83) and Quinta do Leda (90).

Fino Term for the lightest and finest of sherries, completely dry, v pale and with great delicacy. Fino should always be drunk cool and fresh: it deteriorates rapidly once opened. TIO PEPE is the classic example. Use half bottles where possible.

Flor A floating yeast peculiar to FINO sherry and certain other wines that oxidize slowly and tastily under its influence.

Fonseca Guimaraens British-owned port shipper of stellar reputation, connected with TAYLOR'S. Robust deeply coloured vintage wine, among the v best. Vintages: Fonseca **60 63' 66' 70' 75 77' 80 83 85' 92**; Fonseca Guimaraens **76 78 82 84 86 87 88 91**. Quinta do Panascal 78 is a new single-QUINTA wine. Also delicious VINTAGE CHARACTER Bin 27.

Forrester Port shippers and owners of the famous Quinta da Boa Vista, now owned by Martini & Rossi. Their vintage wines tend to be round, 'fat' and sweet, good for relatively early drinking. Baron de Forrester is vg TAWNY. Vintages: (Offley Forrester) **55 60 62' 63' 66 67 70' 72 75 77' 80 82 83 85' 87 89**.

Garvey Famous old sherry shippers at JEREZ. Their finest wines are deep-flavoured FINO San Patricio, Tio Guillermo Dry AMONTILLADO and Ochavico Dry OLOROSO. San Angelo Medium amontillado is the most popular. Also Bicentenary PALE CREAM.

Gonzalez Byass Enormous family-run firm shipping the world's most famous and one of the very best FINO sherries: TIO PEPE. Brands include La Concha Medium AMONTILLADO, Elegante Dry fino and new El Rocío Manzanilla Fina, San Domingo PALE CREAM, Nectar CREAM and Alfonso Dry OLOROSO. Amontillado del Duque is on a higher plane, as are Matusalem and Apostoles: respectively sweet and dry old OLOROSO sherries of rare quality. The company is now linked with Grand Metropolitan.

Gould Campbell See Smith Woodhouse.

Graham Port shippers famous for some of the richest, sweetest and best of VINTAGE PORTS, largely from their own Quinta dos Malvedos (52 57 58 61 65 68 76 78 79 82 84 86 87 88 90 92). Also excellent brands, incl Six Grapes RUBY, LBV, and 10- and 20-yr-old TAWNIES. Vintages: **55' 60 63' 66' 70' 75 77' 80 83 85' 91**.

Guita, La Famous old SANLUCAR bodega (owned by Perez Marin) and its v fine MANZANILLA PASADA. Also vg vinegar.

Harvey's The largest sherry firm: owner of PALOMINO and DE TERRY and linked to BOBADILLA and GARVEY; itself owned by Allied-Hiram Walker. World-famous Bristol shippers of Bristol Cream and Bristol Milk (sweet), Club AMONTILLADO and Bristol Dry (medium), Luncheon Dry and Bristol FINO (not v dry), and Tico, an odd sweet fino. More to the point is their very good '1796' range of high quality sherries and Adorno OLOROSO. Harvey's also control COCKBURN.

Henriques & Henriques Now the largest independent madeira shippers of Funchal: wide range of rich and toothsome wines. Also a good dry aperitif, Monte Seco; and v fine old reservas.

Hidalgo, Vinícola Old SANLUCAR family firm best known for high quality sherries: pale MANZANILLA La Gitana, fine OLOROSO Seco and Jerez CORTADO.

Internacionales, Bodegas Once the pride of the now-defunct Rumasa company, incorporating such famous houses as BERTOLA, VARELA and DIEZ-MERITO. Now the cornerstone of a new empire embracing PATERNINA and FRANCO-ESPANOLAS in RIOJA. Their best sherries are the DUKE OF WELLINGTON range.

Jerez de la Frontera Centre of the sherry industry, between Cádiz and Seville in S Spain. The word 'sherry' is a corruption of the name, pronounced in Spanish 'hereth'. In French, Xérès.

Kopke The oldest port house, founded by a German in 1638. Fair quality vintage wines (55 58 60 63 65 66 67 70 74 75 77 78 79 80 82 83 85 87 89 91) and excellent COLHEITAS.

Late-bottled vintage (LBV) Port of a single vintage kept in wood for twice as long as VINTAGE PORT (about 5 yrs), therefore lighter when bottled and ageing quicker. A real LBV will 'throw a crust' like vintage port. Few (eg WARRE, SMITH WOODHOUSE) qualify.

Leacock One of the oldest madeira shippers, now a label of the MADEIRA WINE CO. Basic St John range is v fair; 10-yr-old Special Reserve MALMSEY and 13-yr-old BUAL are excellent.

Urgent notice: sherry, port, madeira and food
By a quirk of fashion the wines of sherry, madeira and to some extent port are currently being left on the sidelines by a world increasingly hypnotized by a limited range of 'varietal' wines. Yet all three include wines with every quality of 'greatness', and far more gastronomic possibilities than are commonly realized. It is notorious that for the price of eg a bottle of top-class white burgundy you can buy three of the very finest fino sherry, which with many dishes (see Wine & Food) will make an equally exciting accompaniment. Mature madeiras give the most lingering farewell of any wine to a splendid dinner. Tawny port is a wine of many uses, especially wonderful at sea. Perhaps it is because the New World cannot rival these Old World classics that they are left out of the headlines.

Lustau One of the largest family-run sherry bodegas in JEREZ (now controlled by CABALLERO), making many wines for other shippers, but with a vg Dry Lustau range (esp FINO and OLOROSO) and Jerez Lustau PALO CORTADO. Pioneer shippers of excellent ALMACENISTA and 'landed age' wines; AMONTILLADOS and olorosos aged in elegant bottles before shipping. See also Abad.

Macharnudo One of the best parts of the sherry v'yds, N of JEREZ, famous for wines of the highest quality, both FINO and OLOROSO.

Madeira Wine Company In 1913 all the British madeira firms (26 in total) amalgamated to survive hard times. Remarkably, three generations later the wines, though cellared together, preserve their house styles. BLANDY and COSSART GORDON are top labels. New investment by Symingtons (see Dow) promises a bright future.

Malmsey The sweetest form of madeira; dark amber, rich and honeyed yet with madeira's unique sharp tang.

Manzanilla Sherry, normally FINO, which has acquired a peculiar bracing salty character from being kept in bodegas at SANLUCAR DE BARRAMEDA, on the Guadalquivir estuary nr JEREZ.

Manzanilla Pasada A mature MANZANILLA half-way to an AMONTILLADO-style wine. At its best (eg LA GUITA) one of the most appetizing of all sherries.

Passing the Port

Vintage port is almost as much a ritual as a drink. It always needs to be decanted with great care (since the method of making it leaves a heavy deposit in the bottle). The surest way of doing this is by filtering it through clean muslin or a coffee filter-paper into either a decanter or a well-rinsed bottle. All except very old ports can safely be decanted the day before drinking. A week may not be too long. At table the decanter is traditionally passed from guest to guest clockwise. Vintage port can be immensely long-lived. Particularly good vintages older than those mentioned in the text include 04 08 11 20 27 34 35 45 50.

Marqués del Real Tesoro Old sherry firm, famous for MANZANILLA and AMONTILLADO, bought by the enterprising José Estevez. Shrugging off the current slump in sales he has built a spanking new bodega – the first in years. Tio Mateo is a vg FINO.

Martinez Gassiot Port firm, subsidiary of COCKBURN, known esp for excellent rich and pungent Directors 20-yr-old TAWNY, CRUSTED and LBV. Vintages: **55 60 63 67 70 75** 82 85 87 91.

Medina A SANLUCAR family bodega doing well; linking with small companies to become a major exporter.

Miles Formerly Rutherford & Miles, MADEIRA shippers famous for Old Trinity House BUAL etc. Now a label of the MADEIRA WINE CO.

Morgan A subsidiary of CROFT port, best known in France.

Niepoort Small (Dutch) family-run port house with long record of fine vintages (**42 45 55 60 63 66 70 75 77 78 80 82 83 85 87 91** 92) and exceptional COLHEITAS.

Noval, Quinta do Historic port house now French (AXA) -owned. Intensely fruity, structured and elegant vintage port; a few ungrafted vines still at the QUINTA make a small quantity of Nacional – extraordinarily dark, full, velvety and slow-maturing wine. Also vg 20-yr-old TAWNY. Vintages: **55' 58 60 63 66' 67 70' 75 78** 82 85' 87 91.

Offley Forrester See Forrester.

Oloroso Style of sherry, heavier and less brilliant than FINO when young, but maturing to greater richness and pungency. Naturally dry, but generally sweetened, for sale as CREAM.

Osborne Enormous Spanish firm with well-known brandy but also good sherries incl FINO QUINTA, Coquinero dry AMONTILLADO, 10 RF (or Reserva Familiale) OLOROSO. See also Duff Gordon.

Pale Cream Popular style of pale sherry made by sweetening FINO, pioneered by CROFT's Original.

Palo Cortado A style of sherry close to OLOROSO but with some of the character of an AMONTILLADO. Dry but rich and soft. Not often seen.

Palomino & Vergara Historic sherry shippers of JEREZ bought in '86 by HARVEY'S, best known for Palomino CREAM, Medium and Dry.

Pasada Style of FINO or MANZANILLA which is close to AMONTILLADO: a stronger drier wine without FLOR character.

Poças Junior Family port firm specializing in TAWNIES and COLHEITAS.

Ponche An aromatic digestif made with old sherry and brandy, flavoured with herbs and orange, presented in eye-catching silvered bottles. See Caballero and de Soto.

Puerto de Santa María Second city and port of the sherry area, with important bodegas.

PX Short for Pedro Ximénez, the grape part-dried in the sun used in JEREZ for sweetening blends.

Quarles Harris One of the oldest port houses, since 1680, now owned by the Symingtons (see Dow). Small quantities of LBV, mellow and well-balanced. Vintages: **60 63' 66' 70' 75 77' 80 83 85' 91**.

Quinta Portuguese for 'estate'. Also used to denote vintage ports which are usually, but not invariably, from the estate's v'yds, made in good but not exceptional vintages.

Rainwater A fairly light, not very sweet blend of madeira – traditionally popular in N America.

Ramos-Pinto Dynamic small port house specializing in single-QUINTA TAWNIES of style and elegance.

Real Companhia Vinícola do Norte de Portugal Aka Royal Oporto Wine Co and Real Companhia Velha; the largest port house, with a long political history. Many brands and several QUINTAS, incl Quinta dos Carvalhos which makes TAWNIES and COLHEITAS. Vintage wines generally dismal.

Rebello Valente Name used for the VINTAGE PORT of ROBERTSON. Light but elegant and well-balanced, maturing rather early. Vintages: **55' 60 63' 66' 67 70' 72 75 77' 80 83 85'**.

La Riva Distinguished firm of sherry shippers, now controlled by DOMECQ, making one of the best FINOS, Tres Palmas, among many good wines.

Rivero, JM The famous CZ brand of the oldest sherry house now belongs to Antonio Núñez, who makes Rivero sherries as well as his own.

Robertson Subsidiary of SANDEMAN, shipping REBELLO VALENTE VINTAGE, LBV, Robertson's Privateer Reserve, Game Bird TAWNY, 10-yr-old Pyramid and 20-yr-old Imperial. Vintages: **63' 66' 67 70' 72 75 77' 80 83 85'**.

Rosa, Quinta de la Fine single-QUINTA port of the Bergqvist family at Pinhão. Recent return to traditional methods and stone lagars. Esp **85 88 90**.

Rozes Port shippers controlled by Moët Hennessy. RUBY V popular in France; also TAWNY. Vintages: **63 67 77' 78 83 85 87 91**.

Ruby Youngest (and cheapest) port style: simple, sweet and red. The best are vigorous, full of flavour; others can be merely strong, rather thin.

Sanchez Romate Family firm in JEREZ since 1781. Best known in Spanish-speaking world, esp for brandy Cardinal Mendoza. Good sherry: FINO Cristal, OLOROSO Don Antonio, AMONTILLADO NPU ('Non Plus Ultra').

Sandeman A giant of the port trade and a major figure in the sherry one, owned by Seagram. Founder's Reserve is their well-known VINTAGE CHARACTER; TAWNIES are much better. Partners' Ruby is new (94). Vintage wines are at least adequate – some of the old vintages were superlative (55' 57 58 60' 62' 63' 65 66 67 68 70' 72 75 77 78 80 82 85 88). Of the sherries, Medium Dry AMONTILLADO is best-seller, Don FINO is vg, and a range of wonderful luxury old sherries incl Royal Ambrosante, Imperial Corregidor, Royal Esmerelda is not to be missed.

Sanlúcar de Barrameda Seaside sherry town (see Manzanilla).

Sercial Madeira grape for driest of the island's wines – a supreme aperitif.

Shortridge Lawton MADEIRA shipper (part of MADEIRA WINE CO) with v dry Reserva SERCIAL and v tangy 10-yr-old Special Reservas.

Smith Woodhouse Port firm founded in 1784, now owned by the Symington family (see Dow). Gould Campbell is a subsidiary. Relatively light and easy wines incl Old Lodge TAWNY, Lodge Reserve VINTAGE CHARACTER (widely sold in USA). Vintages (v fine): **60 63' 66' 70' 75 77'' 80 83 85' 91 92**. GC Vintages: **60 63 66 70 75 77 80 83 85 91**.

Solera System used in making both sherry and (in modified form) madeira, also some port. It consists of topping up progressively more mature barrels with slightly younger wine of the same sort, the object being to attain continuity in the final wine. Most sherries when sold are blends of several solera wines.

Soto, José de Best known for inventing PONCHE, this family firm also makes a range of good sherries, esp Dry OLOROSO.

Tawny Style of port aged for many yrs in wood (VINTAGE PORT is aged in bottle) until tawny in colour. Many of the best are 20-yrs-old. Low-price tawnies are blends of red and white ports. Taste the difference.

138

Taylor, Fladgate & Yeatman (Taylor's) Perhaps the best port shippers, esp for full rich long-lived VINTAGE wine and TAWNIES of stated age (40-yr-old, 20-yr-old, etc). Their VARGELLAS estate is said to give Taylor's its distinctive scent of violets. Vintages: **55' 60' 63' 66' 70' 75** 77' 80 83' 85' 92'. Quinta de Vargellas is shipped unblended in certain (lesser) years (**67 72 74** 76 78 82 84 86 87 88 91). Also now Terra Feita single-QUINTA wine (82 86 87 88 91). Their LBV is also better than most.

Since January '93, madeiras labelled Sercial, Verdelho, Bual or Malmsey must be at least 85% from that grape variety. The majority, made using the chameleon Tinta Negra Mole grape, which vinified similarly easily imitates each of these grape styles, may only be called seco (dry), meio seco (medium dry), meio doce (medium sweet) or doce (sweet) respectively. Meanwhile replanting is building up supplies of the (rare) classic varieties.

Terry, Fernando A de Magnificent bodega at PUERTO DE SANTA MARIA with an undistinguished range of sherries (but famous brandies), bought in '86 by HARVEY'S.

Tio Pepe The most famous of FINO sherries (see Gonzalez Byass).

Valdespino Famous family-owned bodega at JEREZ, owner of the Inocente v'yd and making the excellent aged FINO of that name. Tio Diego is their dry AMONTILLADO, Solera 1842 an OLOROSO, Del Carrascal their best amontillado. Matador is the name of their popular range.

Varela Sherry shippers best known for their Medium and CREAM.

Vargellas, Quinta de Hub of the Taylor's empire since 1893, giving its very finest ports. The label for in-between vintages. See Taylor Fladgate & Yeatman.

Verdelho Madeira grape for fairly dry but soft wine without the piquancy of SERCIAL. A pleasant aperitif. Some glorious old vintage wines.

Vesuvio, Quinta de Enormous 19th C FERREIRA estate in the high DOURO. Bought '89 by Symington family. 130 acres planted. Esp 88 89 90 91 92.

Vintage Character Somewhat misleading term used for a good quality, full and meaty port like a first-class RUBY, made by a version of the SOLERA system. Lacks the splendid 'nose' of VINTAGE PORT.

Vintage Port The best port of exceptional vintages is bottled after only 2 yrs in wood and matures very slowly for up to 20 or more in bottle. Always leaves a heavy deposit and therefore needs decanting.

Warre The oldest of all British port shippers (since 1670), owned by the Symington family (see Dow) since the 1950s. Fine elegant long-maturing vintage wines, a good TAWNY (Nimrod), VINTAGE CHARACTER (Warrior), and excellent LBV. Their single-v'yd Quinta da Cavadinha is a new departure (78 79 82 84 86 87 88 89 90 92). Vintages: **55' 58 60 63' 66' 70 75** 77' 80 83 85' 91.

White Port Port made of white grapes, golden in colour. Formerly made sweet, now more often dry: a fair aperitif but a heavy one.

Williams & Humbert Famous first-class sherry bodega, now owned by ANTONIO BARBADILLO. Dry Sack (medium AMONTILLADO) is its best-seller; Pando an excellent FINO; Canasta CREAM and Walnut BROWN are good in their class; Dos Cortados is its famous dry old OLOROSO.

Wisdom & Warter Not a magic formula for free wine, but an old bodega with good sherries, especially AMONTILLADO Tizon and v rare Solera. Also FINO Olivar.

Switzerland

Switzerland has no truly great wines, but almost all (especially whites) are enjoyable and satisfying – and very expensive. Switzerland has some of the world's most efficient and productive vineyards; costs are high and nothing less is viable. All the most important are in French-speaking areas, along the south-facing slopes of the upper Rhône Valley and Lake Geneva, respectively the Valais and the Vaud. Wines from German- and Italian-speaking zones are mostly drunk locally. Wines are known by place names, grape names and legally controlled type names and are usually drunk young. 1993 saw the establishment of a Swiss cantonal and federal appellation system, but controlled indication of orgin is still under discussion.

Aargau Wine-growing canton in E Switzerland. Best for light RIES-SILVANER, rich BLAUBURGUNDER and pleasant country wines.

Aigle Vaud r w **→*** Well-known for balanced whites and supple reds.

Aligoté Old White Burgundy variety doing well in the VALAIS and GENEVA.

Amigne Traditional white grape of the VALAIS, esp around VETROZ. Full-bodied tasty wine, often made sweet.

Arvine Old VALAIS white grape (also 'Petite Arvine'): dry and sweet, elegant long-lasting wines with characteristic salty finish. Best in SIERRE, SION.

Beerliwein Original name for wine of destemmed E Swiss BLAUBURGUNDER (now general practice). Today used for wine fermented on skins traditionally rather than in pressure tanks.

Bern Swiss capital and canton of same name. V'yds in W (BIELERSEE) and E (Thunersee, Laufental: BLAUBURGUNDER, RIES-SILVANER); 610 acres.

Béroche, La Neuchâtel r p w *→** Wine-growing region on Lake Neuchâtel incl communes of Gorgier, Fresens, St-Aubin, Vaumarcus.

Bex Vaud r w ** CHABLAIS appellation, esp for red wines.

Bielersee r p w *→** Wine region on N shore of the Bielersee (dry light CHASSELAS, PINOT N, SPEZIALITATEN) and at the foot of Jolimont.

Blauburgunder German-Swiss name for PINOT N. (Aka Clevner.)

Bonvillars Vaud r p w ** Characterful red from N shore of Lake Neuchâtel.

Bündner Herrschaft Grisons r p w **→*** Best E Swiss wine region incl top villages: Fläsch, Jenins, Maienfeld, Malans. Serious BLAUBUR-GUNDER ripens unusually well, cask-aged is vg. Also matured CHARD.

Calamin Vaud w **→*** Village next to DEZALEY: lush fragrant whites.

140

Chablais Vaud w (r **→*** Robust full-bodied reds and whites from VAUD subsection. Best villages: AIGLE, BEX, Ollon, VILLENEUVE, YVORNE.

Chamoson Valais r w **→*** Largest VALAIS commune, esp for SILVANER.

Chardonnay Long-established in W, now also in more favourable parts.

Chasselas (Gutedel) Top white grape of W, neutral in flavour so takes on local character: lean (GENEVA), refined (VAUD), potent (VALAIS), pleasantly sparkling (BIELERSEE, L Neuchâtel, Murtensee). Not usually on label.

Completer Native white grape, only in GRISONS. Aromatic generous wines which keep well. Also Beerenauslese types from BUNDNER HERRSCHAFT.

Cornalin Local red grape making VALAIS speciality; dark spicy v strong wine. Best from SALGESCH, SIERRE.

Cortaillod Neuchâtel r (p w) ** Small village S of NEUCHATEL making good CHASSELAS and OEIL DE PERDRIX, but esp famous for PINOT N.

Côte, La Vaud r p w *→*** Largest VAUD wine area, on N shore of Lake Geneva. Whites with finesse; harmonious reds.

Côtes de l'Orbe Vaud r p w ** Light fruity reds from N VAUD appellation between NEUCHATEL and Lake Geneva.

Dézaley Vaud w (r) *** Famous LAVAUX v'yd on slopes above L Geneva, once tended by Cistercian monks. Unusually powerful CHASSELAS, needs ageing. Red Dézaley is a GAMAY-PINOT N-MERLOT-SYRAH rarity.

Dôle Valais r **→*** Appellation for blend of (at least 51%) PINOT N with GAMAY: full-bodied, supple. Dôle Blanche is a v lightly pressed rosé. Eg from MARTIGNY, SIERRE, SION, VETROZ.

Epesses Vaud w (r) **→*** LAVAUX appellation: supple full-bodied whites.

Ermitage The Marsanne grape; a VALAIS SPEZIALITAT. Concentrated full-bodied dry white, often with residual sugar. Esp from FULLY, SION.

Federweisser E Swiss name for white wine from BLAUBURGUNDER.

Fendant Valais w *→** VALAIS appellation for CHASSELAS. Wide range of wines. Better ones now use village names only (FULLY, SION, etc).

Flétri/Mi-flétri Late-harvested grapes from which sweet and slightly sweet wine (respectively) is made; SPEZIALITAT in VALAIS.

Fribourg Small W Swiss region (260 acres, nr VULLY and Lake Neuchâtel). Esp for BLAUBURGUNDER, CHASSELAS, GAMAY, SPEZIALITATEN.

Fully Village nr MARTIGNY making excellent ERMITAGE and GAMAY.

Gamay The red Beaujolais grape abounds in the west. Fairly thin wine.

Geneva Capital of, and west Swiss wine canton; the third largest (3,700 acres). Key areas: Mandement, Entre Arve et Rhône, Entre Arve et Lac. Mostly CHASSELAS, GAMAY. Also RIES-SILVANER, PINOT N, good ALIGOTE.

Gewürztraminer Grown in Switzerland as a SPEZIALITAT variety.

Glacier, Vin du (Gletscherwein) Fabled oxidized white (from rare Rèze grape) of Val d'Anniviers; offered by thimbleful to visiting dignitaries.

Goron DOLE that fails to make the grade (83° Oechsle).

Grand Cru Quality designation for top wines. Implication differs by canton: in VALAIS and GENEVA used where set requirements fulfilled, in VAUD, for any top-of-the-range wine.

Grisons (Graubünden) Mountain canton, partly in E (BUNDNER HERRSCHAFT, Churer Rheintal; esp BLAUBURGUNDER) and partly in TICINO (Misox, esp MERLOT); 910 acres. Tiny quantities of Puschlav wine (Italian grapes). RIESLING-SILVANER is commonest white.

Heida (Païen) Old VALAIS white grape for country wine of upper V (originally from v'yds at 1,000 m+), so successful that now in lower V too.

Humagne Strong native white grape (a SPEZIALITAT). Humagne Rouge (unrelated, from VALAIS) also sold. Mostly from CHAMOSON and Leytron.

Lagewein (Origin-describing names.) In Switzerland 'Clos', 'Domaine', 'Château' or 'Abbaye' may only be used when the exclusive origin.

Landwein (Vin de pays) Traditional light easy white and esp red from E.

Lausanne Capital of VAUD. No longer with v'yds in town area, but longtime owner of classics: Abbaye de Mont, Château Rochefort (LA COTE); Clos des Moines, Clos des Abbayes, Dom de Burignon (LAVAUX). Pricey.

Lavaux Vaud r w *→*** Scenic wine region on N shore of Lake Geneva. Delicate refined whites, good reds. Best from CALAMIN, Chardonne, DEZALEY, EPESSES, Lutry, St-Saphorin, Vevey-Montreux, Villette.

Légèrement doux Any Swiss wine not completely esp dry must say this.

Martigny Valais w r ** Lower VALAIS commune esp for HUMAGNE rouge.

Merlot Grown in Italian Switzerland (TICINO) since 1907 (after phylloxera destroyed local varieties): aromatic, soft. Also used with Cab. See Viti.

Mont d'Or, Domaine du Valais w s/sw **→*** Well-sited property nr SION: rich concentrated demi-sec wine, notable SILVANER. Controlled by SCHENK.

Morges Vaud r p w *→** LA COTE/VAUD appellation: fruity balanced reds.

Muscat Grown in VAUD as a SPEZIALITAT variety.

Neuchâtel City and canton on N shore of lake (W Switz). V'yds from L Neuchâtel to BIELERSEE. Mainly CHASSELAS: fragrant lively (sur lie, sp). PINOT N also gd (esp OEIL DE PERDRIX). PINOT GR, CHARD increasing.

Nostrano Word meaning 'ours', applied to lesser red wine of TICINO, made from native and Italian grapes (Bondola, Freisa, Barbera, etc).

Oeil de Perdrix Pale PINOT N rosé. Esp from NEUCHATEL and the VAUD.

Perlan Name for usually thin CHASSELAS grown in the GENEVA area.

Pinot Gris Widely planted white grape for dry and residually sweet wines. Makes v fine Spätlese in VAUD (called Malvoisie).

Pinot Noir Top Swiss black grape. Best: BUNDNER HERRSCHAFT, NEUCHATEL, VAUD.

Rauschling Old white ZURICH grape; esp for quality fruit and elegant acidity.

Riesling (Petit Rhin) Mainly in the VAUD. Excellent botrytis wines.

Riesling-Silvaner Swiss for Müller-THURGAU (E's top white; SPEZIALITAT in W).

St-Gallen E Swiss wine canton nr L Constance. Esp for BLAUBURGUNDER, RIES-SILVANER, SPEZIALITATEN. Incl Altstätten, Berneck, Rhine Valley, Thal.

Salquenen Valais r w *→** Village nr SIERRE. First to use 'GRAND CRU'.

Salvagnin Vaud r *→** GAMAY and/or PINOT N appellation. (See also Dôle.)

Schaffhausen E Swiss canton and town on R Rhine. Esp BLAUBURGUNDER; also some RIESLING-SILVANER and SPEZIALITATEN (eg Perle von Alzey).

Schafis Bern r p w *→** Top wine commune of BIELERSEE and the name for all wines from its N shore. Twann is similar.

Schenk Europe-wide wine giant, founded and based in Rolle (VAUD). Owns firms in Burgundy, Bordeaux, Germany, Italy, Spain.

Sierre Valais r w **→*** Sunny resort and famous wine town. Known for Fendant, PINOT N, ERMITAGE, Malvoisie. Vg DOLE.

Sion Valais r w *→*** Capital/wine centre of VALAIS. Esp FENDANT de Sion.

Silvaner (Johannisberg, Gros Rhin) SPEZIALITAT in VAUD. Heady and spicy: some with residual sweetness, some Spätlese. Also rich and potent from hot VALAIS v'yds.

Spezialitäten (Spécialités) Wines of unusual grapes: vanishing local Gwass, Elbling, Bondola, etc, or modish Chenin Bl, Sauv, Cab (first grown experimentally). Eg VAUD: 38 of its 42 varieties are considered 'spezialitäten'.

Süssdruck Dry bright red wine retaining some residual sweetness.

Thurgau E Swiss canton beside Bodensee (625 acres). Top wines from Warth, Seebachtal, Rhine Valley, south shore of the Untersee (esp BLAUBURGUNDER). Good RIES-SILVANER (ie Müller-T, born in the region).

Ticino Italian-speaking S Switzerland (with Misox), growing mainly MERLOT (good from mountainous Sopraceneri region). Trying out Cab S (cask-matured Bordeaux style), Sauv Bl, Sém, Merlot rosé.

Valais The Rhône Valley from the Grimselpass round to St Gingolph on L Geneva: the largest, sunniest wine canton in W Switzerland. Nr perfect climatic conditions; 42 grape varieties: FENDANT, SILVANER, GAMAY, PINOT N, plus many SPEZIALITES. Esp white. See also Fendent.

Vaud Region of L Geneva and the Rhône. W Switzerland's second largest wine canton incl CHABLAIS, LA COTE, LAVAUX and appellations Bonvillars, Côtes de l'Orbe, VULLY. CHASSELAS stronghold. Also GAMAY, PINOT N etc.

Vétroz Valais w r ★★→★★★ Top village nr SION, esp famous for AMIGNE.

Vevey-Montreux Vaud r w ★★ Up-and-coming appellation of LAVAUX. Famous wine festival held about every 30 years; next in 1999.

Villeneuve Vaud w (r) ★★→★★★ Nr L Geneva: powerful yet refined whites.

Viti Quality designation for the traditional MERLOT wine of TICINO.

Vully Vaud w (r) ★→★★ Good refreshing sparkling from Rhine catchment.

Winzerwy Quality label (E Swiss) for cantons AARGAU, Appenzell, Basel, BERN, GRAUBUNDEN, ST-GALLEN, SCHAFFHAUSEN, THURGAU and ZURICH.

Yvorne Vaud w (r) ★★★ Top CHABLAIS appellation: strong fragrant whites.

Zürich Capital of largest E wine canton (same name). Mostly BLAUBURG-UNDER; also PINOT GR and GEWURZ, and esp RIES-SILVANER and RAUSCHLING.

Austria

Austria has recently emerged as a vigorous and well-regulated producer of hearty white wines, including aromatic ones in the modern German style (but more potent), liquorous ones closer to Sauternes, and increasingly fine 'international' sorts. Her red wines (20% of vineyards) have yet to make an international reputation but this will come. New laws, passed in 1985 and revised for the 1993 vintage, include curbs on yields (Germany please copy) and impose higher levels of ripeness for each category than their German counterparts. Many regional names, introduced under the 1985 law, are still unfamiliar outside Austria. This is a country to explore.

Recent vintages

1993	Frost damage caused a smaller than average yield which produced excellent wines.
1992	Extremely hot summer may have led to acidity problems in some areas. Very good wines from the Wachau, Kamptal-Donauland and Styria. Good red wine year (esp Burgenland).
1991	Good to average quality along with a few vg wines from Burgenland.
1990	One of the best vintages of the last 50 yrs.
1989	Some weather problems reduced crop. Quality fair to good, best in Burgenland and Styria.
1988	Good quantity, some excellent wines.
1987	A third small harvest, but quality is reasonable.
1986	An outstanding vintage in most cases, though small.
1985	A small but excellent quality harvest.

Ausbruch PRADIKAT wine (v sweet) between Beerenauslese and Trockenbeerenauslese in quality. Traditionally produced in RUST.

Ausg'steckt ('hung up') HEURIGEN are not open all year. To show potential visitors wine is being served a green bush is hung up above the door.

Banderol Quantity control label carrying the red-white-red of the national flag: obligatory for all Austrian wines since '86.

Bergwein Legal classification for wines made from grapes grown on slopes with an incline of over 26%.

Blauburger Austrian red grape variety. A cross between BLAUER PORTUGIESER and BLAUFRANKISCH. Dark-coloured wine with little body.

Blauer Burgunder (Pinot N) A rarity in Austria. Vintages fluctuate. Best in BURGENLAND, KAMPTAL, THERMENREGION. Esp BRUNDLMAYER, STIEGELMAR.

Blauer Portugieser Produces light, fruity wines which may be drunk slightly chilled when young. Mostly made for local consumption.

Blauer Wildbacher Grape used to make SCHILCHER wines.

Blauer Zweigelt Austrian cross between BLAUFRANKISCH and ST-LAURENT: high yields, rich colour. Quality-conscious producers (Heinrich, Pfaffl, Pöckl) have gained it general recognition.

Blaufränkisch (Lemberger in Germany, Kékfrankos in Hungary) Austria's most widely planted black grape, esp in MITTELBURGENLAND for peppery acidity, fruity taste of cherries. Often blended with Cab. Best: GESELLMANN, Iby, IGLER, Krutzler, Nittnaus, E Triebaumer, WENINGER.

Bouvier Indigenous grape, producing light wines with low alcohol but plenty of nose, esp good for Beeren- and Trockenbeerenauslese.

Bründlmayer, Willi **→**** Leading LANGENLOIS-KAMPTAL estate. Vg wines: both local (RIES, GRUNER V) and international (CHARD, red) styles.

Burgenland Province and wine area (50,000 acres) in E next to Hungarian border. Warm climate. Ideal conditions, esp for botrytis wines nr NEUSIEDLER SEE, also reds. Four wine regions: MITTELBURGENLAND, NEUSIEDLERSEE, NEUSIEDLERSEE-HUGELLAND and SUDBURGENLAND.

Buschenschank Country cousin of Viennese HEURIGE.

Cabernet Sauvignon Increasingly cultivated in Austria; used esp in blends.

Carnuntum Recognised wine region since '94, E of Vienna, bordered by the Danube to the north. Best producers: Glatzer, Pitnauer.

Chardonnay Increasingly grown, mainly barrique-aged. Also traditional in STYRIA as 'MORILLON' (unoaked) with strong fruit taste and lively acidity. Esp from BRUNDLMAYER, SATTLER, STIEGELMAR, WENINGER.

Deutschkreutz r (w) Red wine area in MITTELBURGENLAND, esp for BLAUFRÄNKISCH. Best producers: IGLER, GESELLMANN.

Donauland (Danube) w (r) Recognised wine region since '94, situated W of Vienna. Incl KLOSTERNEUBURG and Wagram regions S of Danube. Mainly whites, esp GRUNER VELTLINER. Best producers: Chorherren Klosterneuburg, Leth, Neumayer, Wimmer-Cerny, Zimmermann.

Dürnstein w Wine centre of the WACHAU with famous ruined castle. Mainly GRUNER V and RIES. Esp from FREIE WEINGARTNER WACHAU, Schmidl.

Eisenstadt r w d sw Capital of BURGENLAND and historic seat of Esterházy family. Top producers: Barmherzigen Brüder, Esterházy, Erwin Tinhof.

Falkenstein w dr Wine centre in eastern Weinviertel nr Czech border. Good GRUNER VELTLINER. Best producers: Jauk, Luckner, SALOMON.

Federspiel Medium quality level of the VINEA WACHAU categories, roughly corresponding to Kabinett. Fruity, elegant wines.

Fels am Wagram r w Large wine region with loess terraces in DONAULAND. Best producers: Leth, Wimmer-Cerny.

Freie Weingärtner Wachau *→*** Large important winegrowers' cooperative in DURNSTEIN. Excellent GRUNER VELTLINER and RIES.

Gamlitz w Largest oldest region of S STYRIA: Lackner-Tinnacher, SATTLER.

Gemischter Satz A blend of grapes (mostly white) grown, harvested and vinified together. Traditional wine, still served in HEURIGEN today.

Gesellmann, Engelbert **→*** Wine estate in DEUTSCHKREUTZ. Vg red and white: both traditional and international styles.

Gols r w d sw Largest BURGENLAND wine region (N shore of NEUSIEDLER SEE). Best producers: Beck, Heinrich, Leitner, Nittnaus, Renner, STIEGELMAR.

To decipher codes, please refer to symbols key at front of book, and to 'How to use this book' on page 5.

Grinzing w   District of Vienna, famous for its HEURIGEN.

Grüner Veltliner 'National' white grape. Fruity, racy, lively wines. Distinguished age-worthy Spätlesen. Best producers: Aigner, BRUNDLMAYER, FREIE WEINGARTNER WACHAU, HIRTZBERGER, KNOLL, Leithner, MANTLER, PICHLER, PFAFFL, PRAGER, Walzer.

G'spritzter Popular refreshing summer drink, usually white wine-based; made sparkling by adding soda or mineral water. Esp in HEURIGEN.

Gumpoldskirchen w (r) dr sw   Popular village S of Vienna, for HEURIGEN. Centre of THERMENREGION. Distinctive wines from ZIERFANDLER and ROTGIPFLER grapes. Best producers: Biegler, Schellmann.

Heurige The wine of the most recent harvest, called 'new wine' for one year, then classified as 'old'. Heurigen are the wine houses where growers-cum-patrons serve their wine by the glass or bottle, together with simple local food – an institution, esp in VIENNA. (The first Heurige licence was granted by Emperor Josef II in 1784.)

Hirtzberger, Franz ***→*****   Leading producer with 22 acres at Spitz an der Donau, WACHAU; RIESLING, GRUNER VELTLINER, Neuburger.

Horitschon MITTELBURGENLAND region for reds. Best: Anton Iby, WENINGER.

Igler, Hans **→***   Leading DEUTSCHKREUTZ estate; pioneer of A's reds.

Illmitz w (r) dr sw   SEEWINKEL region famous for Beeren- and Trockenbeerenauslese. Best from KRACHER, Alois und Helmut Lang, Opitz.

Jamek, Josef **→***   Outstanding, well-known estate and restaurant at Joching in the WACHAU. Pioneer of dry whites since the '50s.

Jurtschitsch/Sonnhof *→***   Domaine run by three brothers: outstanding whites (RIES, GRUNER VELTLINER, CHARD).

Kamptal r w   Wine region since '94, along R Kamp. Top v'yds: LANGENLOIS, STRASS, Wichtigste Orte, Zöbing. Best growers: BRUNDLMAYER, Dolle, Ehn, Hiedler, Hirsch, JURTSCHITSCH, Leithner, Loimer, METTERNICH-SANDOR.

Kattus *→**   Producer of traditional Sekt in VIENNA.

Kellergassen Picturesque alleyways lined with wine presses and cellars, devoted exclusively to production, storage and consumption of wine, situated outside the town, typical of the WEINVIERTEL region.

Klöch W STYRIA wine town famous for Traminer. Best from Stürgkh.

Klosterneuburg r w   Wine district rich in tradition, N of Vienna, with a famous Benedictine monastery and a wine college dating back to 1860. Best producers: Chorherren Klosterneuburg, Zimmermann.

Kloster Und Wine tasting centre in a restored Capuchin monastery near KREMS, run by ERICH SALOMON.

KMW Abbreviation for 'Klosterneuburger Mostwaage' (must level), the unit used in Austria to measure the sugar content in grape juice.

Knoll, Emmerich **→*****   V traditional estate in Loiben, WACHAU producing showpiece wines from GRUNER VELTLINER and RIESLING.

Kollwentz-Römerhof **→***   Innovative wine producer in Grosshöflein nr EISENSTADT: Sauv Bl, Eiswein and reds.

Kracher, Alois **→*****   First class small producer in ILLMITZ; speciality: PRADIKAT wines, some aged in barriques and others not.

Krems w (r) dr (sw)   Ancient wine town on the Danube, W of VIENNA. Capital of KREMSTAL. Good for GRUNER VELTLINER and RIES. Best from Aigner, Ditz, SALOMON, Walzer, Weingut Stadt Krems, WINZER KREMS.

Kremstal w (r)   Wine region since '94 (3,700 acres). Esp Ditz, Geyerhof, MALAT-BRUNDLMAYER, MANTLER, Nigl, SALOMON, Weingut Stadt Krems.

Langenlois r w   Major wine town in KAMPTAL with 50,000 acres of vines. Best producers: BRUNDLMAYER, Ehn, Hiedler, JURTSCHITSCH.

Lenz Moser *→**   Major producer nr KREMS, now in 5th generation. Lenz Moser III invented a high vine system. Also incl wines from Schlossweingut Malteser Ritterorden (wine estate of the Knights of Malta) in Mailberg-Weinviertel and Klosterkeller Siegendorf in BURGENLAND.

Loiben w   Wine region in lower, wider part of Danube Valley (WACHAU) where conditions are ideal for RIES and GRUNER VELTLINER. Best from Alzinger, Dinstlgut Loiben, KNOLL, Mittelbach, FRANZ X PICHLER.

Malat-Bründlmayer ★→★★★ Modern Danube producer: vg traditional and 'international' wines. Interesting bottle-fermented sparkling.

Mantler, Josef ★★→★★★ Leading traditional estate in Gedersdorf nr KREMS. Vg RIES, GRUNER VELTLINER, CHARD, and rare red Veltliner.

Mayer, Franz ★→★★★ With 90 acres, the largest producer in VIENNA. Traditional jug wines (HEURIGE: Beethovenhaus), as well as wines more than a year old including excellent RIESLING.

Metternich-Sándor, Schlossweingüter ★→★★ Large wine estate in Strass; 173 acres of v'yd jointly run with Adelsgütern Starhemberg, Abensberg-Traun and Khevenhüller-Metsch estates.

Mittelburgenland r (w) dr (sw) Wine region on Hungarian border protected by three hill ranges. Large quantities of red (esp BLAUFRANKISCH). Best producers: GESELLMANN, Iby, IGLER, WENINGER.

Mörbisch r w dr sw Region on W shore of NEUSIEDLER SEE. Schindler is good.

Morillon Name given in STYRIA to CHARDONNAY.

Müller-Thurgau See Riesling-Sylvaner.

Muskateller Rare aromatic grape, recently popular again as aperitif. Best in STYRIA. Top growers: Gross, Lackner-Tinnacher, Polz, SATTLER.

Muskat-Ottonel Fragrant, often dry, whites; also interesting PRADIKATS.

Neuburger Indigenous white grape: nutty flavour; mainly in the WACHAU (delicate flowery), in the THERMENREGION (mellow, well-developed) and in N BURGENLAND. Best from Alphart, Heinrich, HIRTZBERGER, Pöckl.

Neusiedler See V shallow BURGENLAND lake on Hungarian border. Warm temperatures, autumn mists encourage botrytis. Gives name to wine regions of NEUSIEDLERSEE-HUGELLAND and NEUSIEDLERSEE.

Neusiedlersee r w dr sw Region N and E of NEUSIEDLER SEE. Best growrs: Beck, Heinrich, KRACHER, Nittnaus, Pöckl, STIEGELMAR, UMATHUM.

Neusiedlersee-Hügelland r w dr sw Wine region W of NEUSIEDLER SEE based around OGGAU, RUST and MORBISCH on the lake shores, and EISENSTADT in the foothills of the Leitha Mts. Best producers: Feiler-Artinger, KOLLWENTZ, Mad, Prieler, Schröck, Ernst Triebaumer.

Niederösterreich (Lower Austria) With 58% of Austria's v'yds: CARNUNTUM, DONAULAND, KAMPTAL, Kremstal, THERMENREGION, WACHAU, WEINVIERTEL.

Nikolaihof ★→★★ Estate in Mautern-Wachau for top RIES and GRUNER V.

Nussdorf VIENNA district famous for HEURIGEN and vg Ried Nussberg.

Oggau Wine region on the W shore of NEUSIEDLER SEE. Best producers: Mad-Haus Marienberg, Thometitsch.

Pichler, Franz X ★★★→★★★★ Leading RIES, GRUNER V in Oberloiben-Wachau.

Prädikatswein Quality graded wines from Spätlese upwards (Spätlese, Auslese, Eiswein, Strohwein, Beerenauslese, AUSBRUCH and Trockenbeerenauslese). See Germany, page 100.

Prager, Franz ★★→★★★ Together with Josef Jamek, pioneer of WACHAU dry white. His son-in-law Anton Bodenstein carries on the tradition developing new varieties and great PRADIKAT wines.

Retz r w Important region in W WEINVIERTEL. Esp Weinbauschule Retz.

Ried Single v'yd: when named on the label it is usually a good one.

Riesling On its own always means German RIESLING. WELSCHRIESLING (unrelated) is labelled as such. Top growers: BRUNDLMAYER, FREIE WEINGARTNER WACHAU, HIRTZBERGER, KNOLL, MANTLER, F X PICHLER, PRAGER.

Riesling-Sylvaner Name used for Müller-T, which accounts for about 10% of Austria's grapes grown. Best producer: HIRTZBERGER.

Rotgipfler Fragrant, indigenous grape of THERMENREGION. With ZIERFANDLER makes lively, interesting wine. Esp Biegler, Schellmann, Stadelmann.

Rust (r) w; dr sw BURGENLAND region, famous since 17th C for AUSBRUCH. Now also for red and dry white. Esp from Feiler-Artinger, Schandl, Heidi Schröck, Ernst Triebaumer, Paul Triebaumer, Wenzel.

St-Laurent Traditional red wine grape with cherry aroma, believed to be related to Pinot N. Esp from Fischer, Heinrich, Mad, Pöckl, UMATHUM.

Salomon-Undhof ★→★★ Vg producer of RIES, WEISSBURGUNDER, Traminer in KREMS. Erich Salomon also owns/runs KLOSTER UND wine tasting centre.

Salon Österreichischer Wein Austrian wine fair: excellent new annual exhibition of 200 of Austria's best wines.

Sattler, Willi ★★→★★★ Top S STYRIA (Gamlitz) grower. Esp Sauv Bl, MORILLON.

Schilcher Rosé wine from indigenous BLAUER WILDBACHER grapes (high acidity). Speciality of W STYRIA. Vg: Klug, Lukas, Reiterer, Strohmeier.

Schlumberger ★→★★ Largest sparkling wine maker in Austria (VIENNA); bottle-fermented according to their own 'Méthode Schlumberger'.

Seewinkel ('Lake corner'.) Name given to the S part of NEUSIEDLERSEE incl Apetlon, ILLMITZ and Podersdorf. Ideal conditions for botrytis.

Smaragd Highest quality category of VINEA WACHAU, similar to Spätlese.

Spätrot See Zierfandler.

Spätrot-Rotgipfler Typical THERMENREGION (SPATROT and ROTGIPFLER) wine.

Spitz an der Donau w W WACHAU region: vg individual microclimate (wide day-night temp variations): fine wines. Esp HIRTZBERGER, Högl, Lagler.

Steinfeder VINEA WACHAU quality category for light, fragrant wines.

Stiegelmar, Georg ★→★★★ Gols grower: consistently vg, unusual specialities.

Strass w (r) Wine centre in the KAMPTAL region for good Qualität white wines. Best producers: Dolle, METTERNICH-SANDOR, Sturm, Topf.

Styria (Steiermark) The southernmost wine region of Austria. Recently good Qualitätswein. Incl SUDSTEIERMARK, SUD-OSTSTEIERMARK and WESTSTEIERMARK (S, SW and W Styria).

Südburgenland r w Small S BURGENLAND wine region: good red wines. Best producers: Krutzler, Körper-Faulhammer, Wachter, Wiesler.

Südsteiermark (S Styria) w Best wine region of STYRIA: v popular whites (MORILLON, MUSKATELLER, WELSCHRIESLING and Sauv Bl). Top producers: Gross, Lackner-Tinnacher, Muster, Polz, SATTLER, Tement, Wohlmuth.

Süd-Oststeiermark (SW Styria) w (r) STYRIAN wine region with 'islands' of v'yds. Best producers: Neumeister, Stürgkh, Winkler-Hermaden.

Thermenregion r w dr sw Wine region of lower Austria, S of VIENNA, for indigenous speciality grapes (eg ZIERFANDLER, ROTGIPFLER) and good reds. Main centres: Baden, GUMPOLDSKIRCHEN. Top producers: Alphart, Biegler, Fischer, Reinisch, Schafler, Schellmann, Stadelmann.

Uhudler Rare wine produced in SUDBURGENLAND from non-grafted American vines and only allowed again officially since '93.

Umathum, Josef ★★→★★★ Distinguished producer in Frauenkirchen (NEUSIEDLERSEE) for vg reds, and white wines from Burgunder grapes.

Vienna w (r) The Austrian capital is a wine region in its own right (1,800 v'yd acres in suburbs). Simple lively wines served in HEURIGEN and increasingly for quality: Breyer, MAYER, Schilling, WENINGER.

Vinea Wachau WACHAU appellation started by winemakers in '83 with three categories of wine: STEINFEDER, FEDERSPIEL and SMARAGD.

Wachau w Wine region on the bank of the Danube, W of KREMS: some of Austria's best wines, incl RIES and GRUNER V. Top producers: Alzinger, HIRTZBERGER, Högl, JAMEK, KNOLL, Lagler, Nikolaihof, F X PICHLER, Rudolf Pichler, PRAGER, Schmelz, Schmidl.

Weinviertel (Wine Quarter) w (r) Largest Austrian wine region (44,500 acres), between the Danube and Czech border. Mostly light refreshing whites. Best producers: Hardegg, Jauk, Luckner, Lust, Malteser Ritterorden, Minkowitsch, Pfaffl, Taubenschuss, Zull.

Weissburgunder (Pinot Bl) Grown in all Austria, good dry wines and PRADIKATS. Esp Beck, Heinrich, HIRTZBERGER, Fischer, Gross, Neumayer.

Weststeiermark (West Styria) p Smallest Austrian wine region which specialises in SCHILCHER. Esp from Klug, Lukas, Reiterer, Strohmeier.

Welschriesling White grape, not related to RIESLING, grown in all wine regions: light, fragrant, young-drinking dry wines and good PRADIKATS.

Wieninger, Fritz ★→★★★ Vg VIENNA-Stammersdorf grower: CHARD and red.

Winzer Krems ★→★★ Wine growers' co-operative in KREMS: good whites.

Zierfandler (Spätrot) White grape grown almost exclusively in the THERMENREGION, with the ROTGIPFLER produces v robust, lively wines which age well. Best producers: Biegler, Schellmann, Stadelmann.

Central &
Southeast Europe

Prague ◆

CZECH
REPUBLIC

GERMANY

AUSTRIA

Bratislava

Budapest

SLOVENIA

Ljubljana

Drava

CROATIA

Zagreb

Sava

BOSNIA–
HERZEGOVINA

Split

Sarajevo

ITALY

Dubrovnik

Adriatic
Sea

POLA

SLOVA
REPUB

Danube

To say that parts of the region covered by this map are somewhat provisional these days is an understatement. But new regional autonomies and new statehoods are frequently being followed by higher aspirations in winemaking and new international interest and/or investment. So far Hungary and Czechoslovakia, and perhaps Moldova, as well as Bulgaria, have taken the lead in what has become an area to follow with fascination. The potential of other ex-communist states is still on hold.

In this section references are arranged country by country, each shown on the map on this page. Labelling in all the countries involved, except Greece and Cyprus, is broadly based on the international pattern of place name and grape variety. Main grape varieties are therefore included alongside place areas and other terms in the alphabetical listings.

Heavily shaded areas are
the wine-growing regions

UKRAINE

MOLDOVA

Kishinev

Prut

NGARY

Tirnave

ROMANIA

Olt

lgrade

Danube

Bucharest

Danube

RBIA

Varna

BULGARIA

Black
Sea

Sofia

Plovdiv

Euros

MACEDONIA

Skopje

Istanbul

BANIA

Thessaloniki

Aegean
Sea

GREECE

TURKEY

Patras

Athens

Hungary

Hungary is the unquestioned regional leader in terms of tradition, although neighbouring Austria is now ahead in quality. Magyar taste is for fiery, hearty, full-blooded wines, which their traditional grapes (mainly white) perfectly provide, but which are being superseded in many cases by 'safer' international varieties. Since the end of Communism several French, German and other concerns have bought land or entered into joint ventures, especially in Hungary's most famous region, Tokay. Expect to hear much more of this. Meanwhile visitors to the country will find plenty of original wines in the old style.

Alföld Hungary's Great Plain, producer of much everyday wine and some much better, esp at HAJOS, HELVECIA, KECSKEMET, KISKUNHALAS, Szeged.

Aszú Rotten: applied to v sweet wines esp TOKAY (Tokaji), where the aszú is late-picked and 'nobly rotten' as in Sauternes (see page 52.) Used to designate both the sweet wine and the rotten berries.

Aszú Eszencia Tokaji br sw **** 57 63   Second highest TOKAY quality seen commercially: superb amber, like Sauternes with a hint of fino sherry.

Badacsony Balaton w dr sw **→**** Famous 426-m hill on the N shore of LAKE BALATON whose basalt soil can give rich high-flavoured white wines, among Hungary's best.

Balaton Balaton r w dr sw *→**** Hungary's inland sea and Europe's largest freshwater lake. Many good wines take its name. The ending 'i' (eg Balatoni, Egri) is the equivalent of -er in Londoner.

Balatonboglár Balaton r w p *→** Progressive cellars with sound modern-style wines, esp whites. Also cuve close sparkling.

Balatonfüred Balaton w (r) dr sw ** Town on the N shore of LAKE BALATON, centre of the Balatonfüred-CSOPAK district. Softer, less fiery wines.

Bársonyos-Csàszàr Northern area for traditional dry whites.

Bikavér Balaton r * 'Bulls Blood', the historic name of the best-selling red wine of EGER: at best full-bodied and well-balanced, but dismally variable in its export version today. A three-variety blend (minimum), mostly KEKFRANKOS and Cab. Now also made in SZEKSZARD.

Csárfás Royal v'yd, still state-owned, at Tarcal; perhaps the finest in TOKAJI.

Csopák Village next to BALATONFURED, with similar wines but drier whites, incl good Chard, Sauv Bl, SZURKEBARAT, etc.

Debrö Mátraalja w sw ** Town famous for mellow aromatic HARSLEVELU.

Disznókö Important French insurance (AXA) investment in first-rate TOKAY land at Szombor. 100+ acres.

Edes Sweet (but not as luscious as ASZU wine).

Eger Eger district r w dr sw *→** Best-known red wine centre of N Hungary; a baroque city of cellars full of BIKAVER. Also fresh white LEANYKA (perhaps its best product today), OLASZRIZLING, Chard and Cab.

Eszencia The fabulous quintessence of TOKAY (Tokaji): intensely sweet wine from grapes wizened by botrytis. Formerly grape juice of v low, if any, alcoholic strength, reputed to have miraculous properties: this is now called NEKTAR. Today's Eszencia must attain 6% alcohol, which makes it, in reality, a super ASZU Eszencia.

Etyek Nr Budapest. Source of modern standard wines, esp Chard, Sauv Bl.

Ezerjó The grape grown at MOR to make one of Hungary's best dry white wines; potentially distinguished, fragrant and fine.

Felsöbabad Regional cellar S of Budapest with authentic (but in Hungary unauthorised) fragrant Pinot N.

Francois President French founded (1882) sparkling wine producer at Budafok, nr Budapest. Vintage wine: President.

Furmint The classic grape of TOKAY (Tokaji), with great flavour and fire, also grown for table wine at LAKE BALATON and in SOMLO.

Gyöngyös Mátraalja w (r) ✹✹ City with real promise in dry white SZURKEBARAT, Chard, MUSKOTALY, Sauv, etc. Recent French and Australian investment.

Hajós Alföld r ✹ Village in S Hungary known for good lively Cab S reds of medium body and ageing potential. Also gd (if unauthorised) Pinot N.

Hárslevelü The 'lime-leaved' grape used at DEBRO and as the second main grape of TOKAY. Gentle mellow wine.

Helvécia (Kecskemét) Historic ALFOLD cellars. V'yds ungrafted: phylloxera cannot negotiate sandy soil. Whites and rosés modernist; reds trad.

Hétszölö Noble first-growth 116-acre estate at TOKAJ bought by Grands Millésimes de France and Suntory. Second label: Dessewffy.

Hungarovin Traders/producers with huge cellars at Budafok nr Budapest: mainly 'western varietals', also cuve close, transfer, classic sparkling.

Izsák Major sparkling wine producer; the majority by cuve close.

Kadarka Hungary's commonest red grape. Vast quantities for light everyday wine in the south, but capable of ample flavour and interesting maturity (eg at SZEKSZARD and VILLANY). Gamza in Bulgaria.

Kecskemét Major town of the ALFOLD. Much everyday wine, some better.

Kékfrankos Hungarian Blaufränkisch; reputedly related to Gamay. Good light or full-bodied reds, esp at SOPRON. Used in BIKAVER at EGER.

Kéknyelü High-flavoured white grape making the best and 'stiffest' wine of MT BADACSONY. It should be fiery and spicy stuff.

Kiskunhalas Huge-scale plains winery, good esp for KADARKA.

Különleges Minöség Special quality: highest official quality grading.

Lang and Lauder New partnership of famous international Hungarians to make TOKAY at Mád.

Leányka or Király Old Hungarian white grape also grown in Transylvania. Makes admirable aromatic faintly Muscat dry wine in many areas. Kiraly ('Royal') Leányka is supposedly superior.

Mátraalja Wine district in the foothills of the Mátra range in N Hungary, incl DEBRO, GYONGYOS and NAGYREDE.

Mecsekalja District in S Hungary, known for the good whites of PECS.

Médoc Noir The Merlot grape.

Minöségi Bor Quality wine. Hungary's appellation contrôlée.

Mór N Hungary w ✹✹→✹✹✹ Town esp for fresh dry EZERJO. Now Ries, Sauv.

Muskotály Makes light, though long-lived, Muscat wine in TOKAY (Tokaji) and EGER. Very occasionally makes ASZU in Tokaji.

Nagyburgundi Literally 'great burgundy' – an indigenous grape and not Pinot N as sometimes thought. Makes sound solid wine in S Hungary, esp around VILLANY and SZEKSZARD.

Nagyréde Mátraalja Foothill winery. Competent and modern.

Nektár New legal term for the unfermented juice formerly called ESZENCIA.

OBI Official laboratory based in Budapest, responsible for labelling, quality control and export licence. Old notions being modernized.

Olaszrizling Hungarian name for the Italian Riesling or Welschriesling.

Oporto Red grape increasingly used for soft jammy wines to drink young.

Oremus Ancient TOKAJI v'yd of founding Rakóczi family at Sárospatak, being reconstituted by owners of Vega Sicilia.

Pécs Mecsek w (r) ✹→✹✹ Major S wine city. Esp OLASZRIZLING, Pinot Bl, etc.

Pezsgö Sparkling wine, mostly transfer method, can often be v palatable.

Pinot Noir Normally means NAGYBURGUNDI. But see Felsöbabad.

Puttonyos The measure of sweetness in TOKAY (Tokaji). A 7-gal container from which ASZU is added to SZAMORODNI. One 'putt' makes it sweetish; 6 v sweet indeed. Each putt is a 20–25 kilo hod of ASZU grapes added to 136 litres of base wine. The minimum now made is 3 putts, the maximum 6. Tokay of 4 putts is often best-balanced.

Royal Tokay Wine Co Early Anglo-Danish-Hungarian joint venture at Mád (TOKAJI). 150 acres, largely first or second growth. First wine a revelation.

Siklós Southern district known for its white wines.

Somló N Hungary w ✹✹ Isolated small v'yd district N of BALATON: white wines (formerly of high repute) from FURMINT and ancient Juhfark grapes.

Sopron W Hungary r ✷✷   Little enclave S of the Neusiedler See (see Austria). Light KEKFRANKOS reds and some Austrian-style sweet wines.

Szamorodni Word meaning 'as it comes'; used to describe TOKAY without the addition of ASZU grapes. Can be dry or (fairly) sweet, depending upon proportion of aszú grapes naturally present. Sold as an aperitif.

Száraz Dry, esp of TOKAJI SZAMORODNI.

Szekszárd r ✷✷   District in south-central Hungary. KADARKA red wine which needs age (say 3–4 yrs). Also good organic wines and (now) BIKAVER.

Szürkebarát Literally means 'grey friar': Pinot Gr, which makes rich (not necessarily sweet) wine in the BADACSONY v'yds and elsewhere.

Tokay (Tokaji) Tokaji w dr sw ✷✷→✷✷✷✷✷   The ASZU is Hungary's famous liquorous sweet wine, comparable to a highly aromatic and delicate Sauternes, from hills in the NE close to the Russian border. The appellation covers 13,500 acres. See Aszú, Eszencia, Furmint, Puttonyos, Szamorodni. Also dry table wine of character.

Villány Siklós r p (w) ✷✷   Southernmost town of Hungary and well-known centre of red wine production. Villányi Burgundi is largely KEKFRANKOS and can be good. Cabs S and F are v promising. See also Nagyburgundi.

Villány-Siklós Wine region named after the two towns.

Zweigelt Indigenous (S) red grape: deep-coloured spicy flavoursome wine.

Bulgaria

In little more than a decade Bulgaria has come from nowhere to be the world's second-largest exporter of bottled wines after France, trading 90% of its production. Enormous new vineyards and industrial-sized wineries have overwhelmed an old, if embattled, wine tradition. The formerly state-run and state-subsidized wineries learnt almost everything from the New World and offer Cabernet, Chardonnay and other varieties at bargain prices (ousting many native varieties). Controlled appellation ('Controliran') wines, introduced in 1985, have been joined by wood-aged 'Reserve' bottlings, simpler wines of Declared Geographical origin and Country Wines. Bulgaria is divided into five main wine regions: the Danube, the eastern Black Sea region, Stara Planina, Haskovo and Harsovo.

The recent drop in sales to Russia has led to new emphasis on quality, somewhat higher prices and a ban on planting outside the 27 Controliran regions.

In 1990 the organizing monopoly, Vinprom, was disbanded to give wineries autonomy (30 at first; the number continues to increase, as does privatization). A brisk air of competition is now provoking even greater efforts towards quality.

Asenovgrad Main MAVRUD-producing cellar on the outskirts of PLOVDIV – new stainless steel being introduced. Mavrud and CAB can last well.

Boyar, Domaine Bulgaria's first independent wine merchants for almost 50 yrs: based in Sofia, set up '91, now marketing in the UK.

Burgas Black Sea resort and source of easy whites, incl a MUSCAT blend.

Cabernet Sauvignon The Bordeaux grape is highly successful in Bulgaria (with 4 times as much acreage as California). Dark vigorous fruity and well-balanced wine, v drinkable young, but top qualities age with good.

Chardonnay Rather less successful. V dry but full-flavoured wine, improves with a yr in bottle. Some recent oak-aged examples are promising.

Controliran Top quality wines (single grape variety) of AC-style status.

Country Wines Regional wines, often a blend of 2 varieties for original taste.

HUNGARY / BULGARIA

Damianitza MELNIK winery with gd Strambolovo MERLOT and Melnik CAB.

Danube Cool northern region, mostly for reds: incl SUHINDOL and SVISHTOV.

Dimiat The common native white grape, grown in the E towards the coast. Agreeable dry white without memorable character.

Euxinograd (Château) Ageing cellar on the coast, part of the ex-King's palace. Wines reserved for State functions and top restaurants.

Gamza Good red grape, the Kadarka of Hungary. Aged wines, esp from LOVICO SUHINDOL, can be delicious.

Han Krum The most modern makers of white wine, esp oak-aged CHARD, nr VARNA in the east. Also lighter CHARD and SAUV BL.

Harsovo Southwest region, esp for MELNIK.

Haskovo Southern region, principal source of MERLOT for export. Incl ASENOVGRAD, ORIACHOVITSA, PLOVDIV, STAMBOLOVO, SLIVEN, and areas.

Iskra Sparkling wine, normally sweet but fair quality. Red, white or rosé.

Karlovo Town famous for its 'Valley of Roses' and pleasant white MISKET.

Korten Subregion of SLIVEN. Korten CAB is more structured than most.

Lovico Suhindol Neighbour of PAVLIKENI, site of Bulgaria's first coop (1909). Good for GAMZA (CONTROLIRAN), CAB, MERLOT, PAMID and blends. First to declare independence after state monopoly's collapse in '90. Privatized in '92. Now Bulgaria's most important winery.

Mavrud Grape variety and darkly plummy red from S Bulgaria, esp ASENOVGRAD. Can mature 20 yrs. Considered the country's best.

Melnik City of the extreme southwest and its highly prized grape. Dense red wine that locals say can be carried in a handkerchief. Needs at least 5 yrs and lasts for 15. Also CAB, ripe and age-worthy.

Merlot Soft red grape variety grown mainly in HASKOVO in the south.

Misket Indigenous Bulgarian grape: mildly aromatic wines, often used to fatten up white blends.

Muscat Ottonel Normal Muscat grape, grown in E for med-sweet fruity white.

Novi Pazar Controlled appellation CHARD winery nr VARNA with finer wines.

Novo Selo Controliran red GAMZA from the north.

Oriachovitsa Major S area for Controliran CAB-MERLOT. Rich savoury red best at 4–5 yrs. Recent RESERVE Cab releases have been good, esp 84 86.

Pamid The light soft everyday red of the southwest and northwest.

Pavlikeni Northern wine town with a prestigious estate specializing in GAMZA and CAB of high quality. Also light COUNTRY WINE MERLOT and Gamza blend.

Petrich Warm SW area for soft fragrant MELNIK, also blended with CAB.

Pleven N cellar for PAMID, GAMZA, CAB. Also Bulgaria's wine research station.

Plovdiv Southern HASKOVO wine town and region, source of good CAB and MAVRUD. Winemaking mostly at ASENOVGRAD.

Preslav Bulgaria's largest white wine cellar, in NE region. Esp for SAUV BL and RESERVE CHARD. Also makes rather good brandy.

Provadya Another centre for good white wines, esp dry CHARD.

Reserve Used on labels of selected and oak-aged wines. Usually with 3–4 yrs in oak vats (often American), may or may not be CONROLIRAN.

Riesling (In Bulgaria) normally refers to Italian Riesling (Welschriesling). Some Rhine Riesling is grown: now made into Germanic-style white.

Rkatziteli One of Russia's favourite white grapes for strong sweet wine. Produces bulk dry or medium whites in NE Bulgaria.

Russe NE wine town on the Danube. Some fresh high-tech whites: Welsch-riesling-MISKET blends, straight medium-dry Welschries, CHARD, MUSCAT and gd Aligoté. Now also reds, esp CONTROLIRAN YANTRA VALLEY CAB S.

Sakar SE wine area for CONTROLIRAN MERLOT, some of Bulgaria's best.

Sauvignon Blanc Grown in E Bulgaria, recently released for export.

Schumen Eastern region, especially for whites.

Silvaner Some pleasant dry Silvaner is exported as 'Klosterkeller'.

Sliven S region, esp for CAB S. Also MERLOT and Pinot N (Merlot is blended with Pinot N in a COUNTRY WINE). Also Silvaner, MISKET and CHARDONNAY.

Sonnenkuste Brand of medium-sweet white sold in Germany.

Stambolovo Wine area esp for CONTROLIRAN MERLOT from HASKOVO.

153

Stara Planina Balkan mountain region of central Bulgaria, incl KARLOVO.

Stara Zagora S region producing CAB and MERLOT to RESERVE quality.

Suhindol See Lovico Suhindol.

Sungarlare E town giving its name to a dry CONTROLIRAN MISKET; also CHARD.

Svishtov CONTROLIRAN CAB-producing winery by the Danube in the north. A front-runner in Bulgaria's controlled appellation wines.

Tamianka Sweet white wine based on aromatic grape also of this name; the same as Romania's Tamaioasa.

Targovichte Independent wine cellar nr SCHUMEN. Esp med and sweet whites.

Tirnovo Strong sweet dessert red wine.

Varna Major coastal appellation for CHARD (buttery and unoaked), SAUV BL. Also Aligoté, Ugni Bl.

Yantra Valley DANUBE region, CONTROLIRAN for CABERNET SAUVIGNON.

The Former Yugoslav States

Before its disintegration in 1991 Yugoslavia was well-established as a supplier of wines of international calibre, if not generally of exciting quality. Now there are barely enough for export. Current political disarray makes commercial contacts difficult except in Slovenia, whose 'Riesling' was the pioneer export, since followed by Cabernet, Pinot Blanc, Traminer and others. All regions except the central Bosnian highlands make wine, almost entirely in giant cooperatives. The Dalmatian (Croatian) coast and Macedonia have good indigenous wines whose roots go deep into the ancient world.

In this edition the wines of Serbia, Bosnia-Herzegovina and Macedonia are omitted.

Slovenia

Bela Krajina SAVA district with speciality 'Ledeno Laski Ries' – from late-collected frozen grapes (in best yrs).

Beli Pinot The Pinot Bl, a popular grape variety.

Belo vino White wine.

Bizeljsko-Sremic SAVA district. Full-flavoured local variety reds and LASKI R.

Crno vino Red (literally 'black') wine.

Cvicek Traditional pale red or dark rosé of the SAVA VALLEY.

Dolenjska SAVA region: CVICEK, LASKI RIZLING and Modra Frankinja (dry red).

Drava Valley (Podravski) Largest Slovene wine region. Mainly whites from aromatic (Welschies, Muscat Ottonel) to flamboyant (Ries and Sauv).

Grasevina Slovenian for Italian RIES. The normal 'Riesling' of the region.

Jerusalem Slovenia's most famous v'yd, at LJUTOMER. Its best wines are late-picked RAJNSKI RIZLING, LASKI RIZLING.

Kakovostno Vino Quality wine (one step down from VRHUNSKO).

Kontrolirano poreklo Appellation. Wine must be 80% from that region.

Koper Hottest area of LITTORAL between Trieste and Piran. Full rich MERLOTS.

Kraski Means grown on the coastal limestone or Karst. A region famous for REFOSCO wines eg Kraski Teran and oak-aged Teranton.

Laski Rizling Yet another name for Italian RIES. Best-known Slovene wine, not best-quality. Top export brand: 'Cloburg' from Podravski (DRAVA) region.

Littoral Coastal region bordering Italy and the Mediterranean.

Ljutomer (or Lutomer) -Ormoz Slovenia's best-known, probably best white wine district, in NE (DRAVA); esp LASKI RIZLING: at its best rich and satisfying. Ormoz winery also has sparkling and late-harvest.

Malvasia Ancient white grape giving luscious wine.

Maribor Important centre in the northeast (DRAVA). White wines, mainly from VINAG, incl LASKI RIZLING, RIES, Sauv Bl, Pinot Bl, Traminer. Slovenska Bistica and S Konjice wineries also good for Laski R.

Merlot Reasonable in Slovenia. Comparable with neighbouring NE Italian.

Namizno Vino Table wine.

Radgona-Kapela DRAVA district next to Austrian border, esp late-harvest wines, eg RADGONSKA RANINA, also classic method sparkling.

Radgonska Ranina Ranina is Austria's Bouvier grape. Radgona is nr MARIBOR. The wine is sweet. Trade name is Tigrovo Mljeko (Tiger's Milk).

Rajnski (or Renski) Rizling The Rhine RIESLING: rare in these regions, but grown a little in LJUTOMER-ORMOZ.

Refosco Vg Italian red grape grown in east and in ISTRIA (Croatia) as TERAN.

Riesling Used without qualification formerly meant Italian Riesling. Now legally limited to real Rhine Riesling.

Sava Valley Central Slovenia: light dry reds, eg CVICEK. Northern bank is for whites, eg LASKI RIZLING, Silvaner and recent Chard and Sauv Bl.

Sipon Name for Furmint of Hungary.

Slamnak A late-harvest LJUTOMER estate RIES.

Tigrovo Mljeko See Radgonska Ranina.

Tocai The Pinot Gr, making rather heavy white wine.

Vinag Huge production cellars at MARIBOR. Top wine: Cloburg LASKI RIZLING.

Vipava Lowland LITTORAL region with tradition of export to Austria and Germany: good Cab S, MERLOT, Barbera.

Vrhunsko Vino Top quality wine.

Croatia

Babic Standard red of DALMATIA, ages better than ordinary PLAVAC.

Banat Partly in Romania: up-to-date wineries making adequate RIES.

Baranjske Planote SLAVONIA area for Ries and BIJELI BURGUNDAC.

Bogdanusa Local white grape of the DALMATIAN islands, esp Hvar and Brac. Pleasant, refreshing faintly fragrant wine.

Burgundac Bijeli Chard, grown in SLAVONIA.

Dalmacijavino Important coop based at Split and selling a full range of DALMATIAN coastal and island wines.

Dalmatia The coast of Croatia, from Rijeka to Dubrovnik. Has a remarkable variety of characterful wines, most of them potent.

Dingac Heavy sweetish PLAVAC red, speciality of mid-DALMATIAN coast.

Faros Substantial age-worthy PLAVAC red from the island of Hvar.

Grasevina Local name for ubiquitous LASKI RIZLING.

Grk White grape, speciality of the island of Korcula, giving strong, even sherry-like wine, and also a lighter pale one.

Istria Peninsula in the N Adriatic, Porec its centre: a variety of pleasant wines, MERLOT as good as any. V dry TERAN is perfect with local truffles.

Marastina Strong dry DALMATIAN white, best from Cara Smokvica on Hvar.

Opol Pleasant light pale PLAVAC red from Split and Sibenik in DALMATIA.

Plavac Mali Native red grape of DALMATIA; wine of body, strength, ageability. See Dingac, Opol, Postup, etc. There is also a white, Plavac Beli.

Portugizac Austria's Blauer Portugieser: plain red wine.

Posip Pleasant white of the DALMATIAN islands, notably Korcula.

Postup Sweet and heavy DALMATIAN red from the Peljesac peninsula nr Korcula. Highly esteemed locally.

Prosek Dessert wine from DALMATIAN: 15–16˚ (can be almost port-like).

Slavonia N Croatia, on the Hungarian border between Slovenia and Serbia (incl parts of SAVA and DRAVA valleys). A big producer of standard wines, mainly white, incl most of the former 'Yugoslav Riesling'.

Teran Stout dark red of ISTRIA. See Refosco (Slovenia).

Vugava Rare white variety of Vis in DALMATIA. Linked (at least in legend) with the Viognier of the Rhône Valley.

Former Czechoslovakia

Re-established January '93 as the Czech (Moravia and Bohemia) and Slovak republics. While there is little or no tradition of exporting wines from this mainly white wine region, there are good wines to be had. Labels will say whether they are blended or single varietal but origin and grapes are not always indicated. All are worth trying for value.

Moravia Favourite wines in Prague: variety and value. V'yds situated along Danube tributaries. Many wines from Austrian border: similar grapes, Grüner Veltliner, Müller-T, Sauv Bl, Traminer, St-Laurent, Pinot N, Blauer Portugieser, Frankovka, etc; and similar wines, eg from Mikulov (white, red, dry and sweet classic-method sparkling; esp Valtice Cellars, est'd 1430, and Vino Mikulov), Satov (modern, mostly white, grapes from local farms and coops) and Znojmo (long-established, ideal limestone soil; local white Palova grape). Other regions: Jaroslavice (wood-matured reds), Prímetice (full aromatic whites), Blatnice, Hustopece, Saldorf (all with vg wineries) and Velké Pavlovice (some good sparkling).

Bohemia Winemaking since 9th C. Same latitude and similar wines to eastern Germany. Best: N of Prague, in Elbe Valley, and (best known) nr Melník (King Karel IV bought in Burgundian vines in 15th C; today Ries, Rulander and Traminer predominate). 'Bohemia Sekt' is growing, eg from Stary Plzenec: tank-fermented (mostly), some oak used, with grapes from SLOVAKIA and MORAVIA too; French advice. Top wineries: Lobkowicz (at Melnik), Roudnice, Litomerice, Karlstein.

Slovakia Warmest climatic conditions and most of former Czechoslovakia's wine. Best in E, neighbouring Hungarian Tokay v'yds. Slovenia uses Hungarian varieties and makes good Tokay too. Key districts: Malokarpatská Oblast (largest region, in foothills of Little Carpathians, incl Rulander, Ries, Traminer, Limberger, etc), Malá Trna, Nové Mesto, Skalice (small, mainly reds), and (in Tatra foothills) Bratislava, Pezinok, Modra. Best recent vintages: 71, 79, 81, 83, 89, 92.

Romania

Romania has a long winemaking tradition and good potential for quality, wasted during decades of supplying the Soviet Union with cheap sweet wine. The present political situation sadly allows little progress. Quantity is still the goal (domestic wine consumption is large). But with cleaner winemaking, earlier bottling and carbonic maceration, there is certainly the potential to rival the success of Bulgaria.

Alba Iulia Town in warm TARNAVE area of TRANSYLVANIA, known for off-dry white (Italian RIES, FETEASCA, MUSKAT-OTTONEL), bottle-fermented sparkling.

Aligoté The junior white burgundy grape makes pleasantly fresh white.

Babeasca Traditional red grape of the FOCSANI area: agreeably sharp wine tasting slightly of cloves. (Means 'grandmother grape'.)

Banat Plain on border with Serbia. Workaday Italian RIES, SAUV BL, MUSKAT-OTTONEL; light red CADARCA, CABERNET and Merlot.

Cabernet Sauvignon Increasingly grown, esp at DEALUL MARE, to make dark intense wines, though sometimes too sweet for Western palates.

Cadarca Romanian spelling of the Hungarian Kadarka.

156

Chardonnay Used at MURFATLAR for sweet dessert wine. Dry and oak-aged too.

Cotesti Part of the FOCSANI area making reds of PINOT N, Merlot, etc, and dry whites claimed to resemble Alsace wines.

Cotnari Region at N limit of v'yds in Moldavia. Romania's most famous (but rarely seen) historical wine: a light dessert white from local varieties (GRASA, FETEASCA ALBA, TAMAIOASA). Rather like v delicate Tokay.

Dealul Mare Important up-to-date v'yd area in the SE Carpathian foothills. Red wines from CAB, Merlot, PINOT N, etc. Whites from TAMAIOASA, etc.

Dobrudja Sunny dry Black Sea region. Incl MURFATLAR. Quality is good.

Dragasani Region on the R Olt south of the Carpathian Mts. Both traditional and 'modern' grapes. Good MUSKAT-OTTONEL and reds.

Feteasca Romanian white grape with spicy, faintly Muscat aroma. Two types: F Alba (same as Hungary's Leányka, considered more ordinary, but base for sparkling wine and sweet COTNARI) and F Regala (F Alba x Furmint cross, good acidity and good for sparkling).

Feteasca Neagra Red Feteasca. Light wines, made coarse by clumsiness, good when aged (blackcurranty and deep red).

Focsani Important MOLDAVIA region incl COTESTI, NICORESTI and ODOBESTI.

Grasa A form of the Hungarian Furmint grape grown in Romania and used in, among other wines, COTNARI. Prone to botrytis.

Iasi Region for fresh acidic whites (F ALBA, Welschriesling, ALIGOTE, MUSKAT OTTONEL): eg 'Bucium', 'Copu', 'Tomesti'.

Istria-Babadag Newish wine region N of MURFATLAR (CAB S, Merlot, F ALBA etc).

Jidvei Winery in the cool Carpathians (TIRNAVE) among Romania's N-most v'yds. Good whites: FETEASCA, Furmint, RIES, SAUV BL.

Lechinta Transylvanian wine area. Wines noted for bouquet (local grapes).

Moldavia NE province. Largest Romanian wine region with 12 subregions incl IASI, FOCSANI. Temperate, with good v'yd potential.

Murfatlar Big modern v'yds nr the Black Sea, specializing in sweet wines incl CHARD (good botrytis conditions). Now also full dry reds and whites.

Muskat Ottonel The E European Muscat, a speciality of Romania, esp cool climate TRANSYLVANIA.

Nicoresti Eastern area of FOCSANI, best known for its red BABEASCA.

Odobesti The central part of FOCSANI: white wines of FETEASCA, RIES, etc.

Oltenia Wine regions including DRAGASANI. Sometimes also a brand name.

Perla The speciality of TARNAVE: a pleasant blended semi-sweet white of Italian RIES, FETEASCA and MUSKAT-OTTONEL.

Pinot Noir Grown in the south: can surprise with taste and character. Becoming popular in supermarkets as cheap alternative to burgundy.

Pitesti Principal town of the Arges region south of the Carpathian Mts. Traditionally whites from FETEASCA, TAMAIOASA, RIES.

Premiat Reliable range of higher quality wines for export.

Riesling Actually Italian Riesling. V widely planted. No exceptional wines.

Sadova Town in the SEGARCEA area exporting a sweetish rosé.

Sauvignon Blanc Romania's tastiest white, esp blended with FETEASCA.

Segarcea Southern wine area near the Danube. Rather sweet CAB.

Tamaioasa Traditional white grape known as 'frankincense' for its exotic scent and flavour. Pungent sweet wines often have botrytis.

Tarnave Important Transylvanian wine region (Romania's coolest), known for its PERLA. Well-situated for dry and aromatic wines, eg JIDVEI's. Also bottle-fermented sparkling.

Trakia Export brand. Better judged for Western palates than most.

Transylvania See Alba Iulia, Lechinta, Tarnave.

Valea Calugareasca 'The Valley of the Monks', part of DEALUL MARE with a well-known, go-ahead research station – currently proposing new AC-style rules. CAB (esp Special Reserve 85), Merlot and PINOT N are admirable, as are Italian RIES, Pinot Gr.

For key to grape variety abbreviations, see pages 6–9.

Greece

Since Greece's entry into the EC its antique wine industry has started moving into higher gear. Some is still fairly primitive, but a new system of appellations is in place and the past five years have seen substantial investment in equipment and expertise. Modern, well-made, still authentic Greek wines are worth tasting.

Achaia-Clauss Well-known wine merchant with cellars at PATRAS, N PELOPONNESE. Makers of DEMESTICA, etc.

Agiorgitiko Widely planted red-wine grape in the NEMEA region.

Agioritikos Country wine appellation of good medium dry white and rosé from Agios Oros or Mount Athos, the monastic peninsula in Halkidiki. Source of Cab and other grapes for TSANTALI.

Amintaion Light red or rosé, often pétillant, from MACEDONIA.

Ankiralos Fresh white from the Aegean-facing v'yds of Thessaly.

Attica Region round Athens, the chief source of RETSINA.

Autocratorikos New sparkling medium-dry white from TSANTALI.

Botrys Old-established Athenian wine and spirits company.

Boutari Merchants and makers with high standards in MACEDONIAN and other wines, esp NAOUSSA and SANTORINI. Grand Réserve is best (84).

Cair Label of the RHODES coop. Makes Greece's only classic sparkling wine.

Calliga Modern winery with 800 acres on CEPHALONIA. ROBOLA white and Monte Nero reds from indigenous grapes are adequately made.

Cambas, Andrew Important wine-growers and merchants in ATTICA.

Carras, John Estate at Sithonia, Halkidiki, N Greece. Interesting reds and whites under appellation COTES DE MELITON. Ch Carras is a Bordeaux-style barrel-aged red (75 79 81 83 84 85 87 90) worth 10–20 yrs in bottle. Dom Carras is second label. Also non-appellation wines, eg Sauv.

Cava Legal term for blended aged red and white. Eg, Cava Boutari (NAOUSSA-NEMEA blend) and Cava Tstantalis (NAOUSSA-Cab).

Cephalonia (Kephalonia) Ionian (western) island with good white ROBOLA and red Thymiatiko. See Calliga.

Corfu Adriatic island with wines scarcely worthy of it. Ropa is trad red.

Côtes de Meliton Appellation (since '81) of CARRAS estate: red (esp Cab and Limnio) and white (again, Greek and French grapes), incl Ch Carras.

Crete Island with name for some of Greece's good red wine. Appellations are: Archanes, Daphnes and Peza (dry or sweetish reds) and Sitia (strong aromatic red). Cretan white can also be suprisingly good.

Danielis One of the best brands of dry red wine, from ACHAIA-CLAUSS.

Demestica A reliable brand of dry red and white from ACHAIA-CLAUSS.

Emery Maker of good CAVA Emery red and vg Villare white on RHODES.

Epirus Central Greek region with high-altitude vines (at 1,200 metres): 'Katoyi' Cab is celebrated expensive red.

Gamalafka Speciality of Mykonos. Alarmingly like sherry vinegar.

Gentilini New ('84) up-market white from CEPHALONIA; a ROBOLA blend, soft and appealing. Now a v promising oak-aged version. To watch.

Goumenissa (Appellation) Good quality oak-aged mid-weight red from western MACEDONIA. Look for BOUTARI.

Hatzimichali Small Atalanti estate and its wines. The whites are Greek-grape-based; the reds incl Cab S and Merlot.

Ilios Very drinkable standard RHODES wine from CAIR.

Kokkineli The rosé version of RETSINA: like the white. Drink cold.

Kouros Highly rated white from Kourtakis of ATTICA; also red from NEMEA.

Kourtakis, D Athenian merchant with mild RETSINA and good dark NEMEA.

Kretikos White wine made by BOUTARI from CRETAN varieties.

Lac des Roches Sound blended white from BOUTARI.

Lemnos (Appellation) Aegean island: sweet golden Muscat RETSINA, KOKKINELI.

Lindos Higher quality RHODES wine (from Lindos or not). Acceptable, no more.

Macedonia Quality wine region in the north, for XYNOMAVRO, esp NAOUSSA.

Malvasia Famous grape said to be from Monemvasia (south PELOPONNESE).

Mantinia (Appellation) A fresh white from the PELOPONNESE, now widely made.

Mavro Black – the word for dark (often sweet) red wine.

Mavrodaphne (Appellation) 'Black laurel'. Dark, sweet, port/recioto-like conc red; fortified to 15°. Speciality of PATRAS, N PELOPONNESE. Should be aged.

Mavroudi Red wine of Delphi and N shore of Gulf of Corinth: dark, plummy.

Metsovo Town in Epirus (north) producing Cab blend called Katoi.

Minos Popular CRETAN brand; the Castello red is best.

Moscophilero Lightly spicy grape that makes MANTINIA.

Dull technical stuff

The fashion of flavouring wine with oak began in California in the 1960s. Formerly, oak barrels were used for their virtues as strong movable containers with enough porosity to allow very gradual oxidation of their contents. New barrels were needed for transport, but were used for storage only for the very finest, most concentrated wines, whose expected life was decades – by which time any oak flavour would be lost.

The slower oak grows, the better its physical properties and the less pungent its aroma/flavour. American oak is very pungent; Baltic oak the opposite. Of the famous French oak forests, western ('Limousin') is relatively pungent and coarse, usable only for red wines; the central ('Allier', 'Nevers'; 'Tronçais' is top grade) are most delicate, best for white or red wines; eastern ('Bourgogne', 'Champagne', 'Vosges') is intermediate.

Barrels are put together over a fire which helps bend the staves. How much this burns (or 'toasts') the oak affects the wine as much as its origin.

Naoussa (Appellation) Above average strong dry XYNOMAVRO red from MACEDONIA in the north, esp from BOUTARI, the coop and TSANTALI.

Nemea (Appellation) Town in the E PELOPONNESE famous for its lion (a victim of Hercules), its fittingly forceful MAVRO and its AGIORGITIKO grape for unique spicy red (coop's is best, esp Cava Nemea, also Grand Palais).

Patras (Appellation) White wine (eg plentiful dry Rhoditis and rarer Muscats) and wine town on the Gulf of Corinth. Home of MAVRODAPHNE.

Pegasus, Château NAOUSSA estate for superior red (esp 81 86 88).

Peloponnese Southern landmass of mainland Greece, with half of the country's v'yds, incl NEMEA and PATRAS; vines mostly used for currants.

Rapsani Young-drinking rasping red from Thessaly's Mt Ossa.

Retsina White wine with Aleppo pine resin added, tasting of turpentine and oddly appropriate with Greek food. ATTICA speciality. Much modern retsina is disappointingly mild. (So is commercial Taramasalata.)

Rhodes Easternmost Greek island. Chevalier de Rhodes is a pleasant red from CAIR. Makes Greece's best sparkling. See also Cair, Emery, Ilios.

Robola (Appellation) The dry white of CEPHALONIA, island off the Gulf of Corinth. Can be a pleasant soft wine of some character.

Samos (Appellation) Island off the Turkish coast with an ancient reputation for its sweet pale golden Muscat and Malvasia. Best are (fortified) Anthemis and (natural) Nectar.

Santorini Dramatic volcanic island N of CRETE: sweet Vinsanto (sun-dried grapes), v dry white Thira, dry red Santino, Atlantis. Has potential.

Semeli, Château Estate nr Athens making good white and red, incl Cab S.

Strofilia Brand name for the wines of a small 'boutique' winery estate at Anavissos. Good whites, and reds incl Cab S.

Tsantali Producers at Agios Pavlos with a wide range of country and appellation wines, incl MACEDONIAN and wine from the monks of Mt Athos, NEMEA, NAOUSSA and Muscat from SAMOS and LIMNOS. CAVA is a blend.

Vaeni Promising red from NAOUSSA producers' coop.

Xynomavro The tastiest of many indigenous Greek red grapes – though its name means sour. Basis for NAOUSSA and other northern wines.

Zitsa (Appellation) Region of 6 villages in mountainous N Epirus. Delicate Debina (grape) white, still or fizzy.

Cyprus

Cyprus exports 75% of its production, mostly strong wines of reasonable quality, especially low-price Cyprus 'sherry', though old Commandaria, a treacly dessert wine, is the island's finest product. As with Bulgaria, the fall of the old USSR as a major wine market has been a serious blow. Until recently only two local grapes were grown. Now a dozen other native varieties are on trial, and the international standards are inevitably being planted. The island has never had phylloxera.

Afames Village at the foot of Mt Olympus, giving its name to dry tangy red (MAVRO) wine from SODAP.

Alkion A new smooth light dry KEO white (XYNISTERI grapes from Limassol).

Aphrodite Consistent medium-dry XYNISTERI white from KEO, named after the Greek goddess of love.

Arsinöe Dry white wine from SODAP, named after an unfortunate female whom Aphrodite turned to stone.

Bellapais Fizzy medium-sweet white from KEO, named after the famous abbey nr Kyrenia. Essential refreshment for holidaymakers.

Commandaria Good quality brown dessert wine since ancient times in hills N of LIMASSOL, from 15 specified villages; named after a crusading order of knights. Made by solera maturation of sun-dried XYNISTERI and MAVRON grapes. Best (as old as 100 yrs) is superb, of incredible sweetness, fragrance, concentration. Most is just standard Communion wine.

Domaine d'Ahera Modern-style lighter estate red from KEO. (From Grenache – recent on the island – and local Lefkas grapes.)

Emva Brand name of well-made fine, medium and cream SHERRIES.

Etko See Haggipavlu.

Haggipavlu Well-known wine merchant at LIMASSOL. Trades as Etko.

Keo The biggest and most go-ahead firm at LIMASSOL. Standard Keo Dry White and Dry Red are vg value. See also Othello and Aphrodite.

Khalokhorio Principal COMMANDARIA village, growing only XYNISTÉRI.

Kokkineli Rosé: the name is related to 'cochineal'.

Kolossi Crusaders' castle nr Limassol; gives name to table wines from SODAP.

Laona The largest of the small independent regional wineries at Arsos. Good range of wines incl a 'nouveau' and an oak-aged red.

Limassol 'The Bordeaux of Cyprus'. Southern wine port and its region.

Loel Major producer, with Amathus and Kykko brands, Command Cyprus SHERRY and good Negro red.

Mavron The black grape of Cyprus (and Greece) and its dark wine.

Monte Roya Modern regional winery at Chryssoroyiatissa Monastery.

Mosaic KEO's brand of Cyprus SHERRIES. Includes a fine dry wine.

Muscat All major firms produce pleasant low-price 15° Muscats.

Opthalmo Black grape (red/rosé): lighter, sharper than MAVRON. Not native.

Othello A good standard dry red (MAVRO and OPTHALMO grapes from PITSILIA). Solid satisfying wine from KEO. Best at 3–4 yrs.

Palomino Soft dry white made of this (sherry) grape by LOEL. V drinkable ice-cold. Makes Cyprus SHERRY too.

Pitsilia Region S of Mt Olympus for the best white and COMMANDARIA wines.

Rosella Light dry fragrant rosé from KEO. OPTHALMO from PITSILIA.

St Panteleimon Brand of medium-sweet white from KEO.

Semeli Good traditional red from HAGGIPAVLU. Best at 3–4 years old.

Sherry Cyprus makes a full range of sherry-style wines, the best (particularly the dry) of fair quality.

SODAP Major wine coop at LIMASSOL.

Thisbe Fruity medium-dry light KEO wine, (XYNISTERI grapes from LIMASSOL).

Xynisteri The native white grape of Cyprus.

Yerasa Principal COMMANDARIA village on lower slopes of Troodos Mts.

Zoopiyi Principal COMMANDARIA village, growing MAVRO grapes.

Asia & North Africa

Algeria   As a combined result of Islam and the EC, the once massive vineyards of Algeria have dwindled in the last decade from 860,000 acres to under 200,000; many vines are 40+ yrs old and won't be replaced. Red, white and esp rosé wines of some quality are still made in the coastal hills of Tlemcen (powerful), Mascara (good red and white), Haut-Dahra (strong red, rosé), Zaccar, Tessala, Médéa and Ain-Bessem (Bouira esp good). Sidi Brahim is a drinkable red brand. All had VDQS status in French colonial days. Local finds are often the best.

China   Germans and Russians started making wine on the Shantung (now called Shandong) peninsula in the early 1900s. Since 1980 a modern industry, initiated by Rémy Martin, has produced the adequate white Dynasty and Tsingtao wines (Tsingtao is on same latitude as southern France), and new more sophisticated plantings of better varieties in Shandong and Tianjin (further north) promise more interest in the future. Basic table wines are made of the local Dragon Eye and Muscat Hamburg grapes (especially in Tianjin). In Qingdao (with China's only maritime climate) the Huadong winery has made very palatable Welschriesling and Chardonnay and is experimenting with Cabernet Sauvignon, Syrah and Gewürztraminer. Dragon Seal Wines (nr Peking, since '87) have Dragon Eye grapes, recent Chardonnay (with oak), and more planned. As of 1992 Rémy Martin are making 'Imperial Court', China's first classic method sparkling wine, near Shanghai.

India   In 1985 a Franco-Indian firm launched a Chardonnay-based sparkling wine, Omar Khayyam, made at Narayangoan, near Poona, SE of Bombay. It sets an astonishing standard. Plans are to export up to 2 million bottles and to add still wines of Chardonnay and Cabernet. Pompadour follows, also slightly drier Princess Jaulke, made with advice from Charbaut of Champagne. Now near Bangalore there is Cabernet Sauvignon, from Grover Vineyards in the Dodballapur Hills.

Japan   Japan has a small wine industry in Yamanashi Prefecture, west of Tokyo. Most of production here is blended with imports from South America, Eastern Europe, etc. But Premium wines of Sémillon, Chardonnay, Cabernet Sauvignon and the local white grape, Koshu, are the new surprise. Top producers are Mann's, Mercian and Suntory. Château Mercian and Suntory lead the way with high quality Chardonnay, Cabernet, etc. The most interesting (and expensive) are Suntory's Sauternes-like Château Lion, and (since '85) Mercian's Kikyogahara Merlot and especially Jyonohira Cabernet of extraordinary denseness and quality. Mann's not only have Chardonnay and Cabernet (French oak aged) but emphasize local varieties (Kôshû and Zenkôji, the latter the same as China's Dragon Eye) and local-Euro crosses (adapted to Japan's rainy climate) too. Regrettably, Japanese labelling laws have been so lax that misrepresentation of imported wines as 'Japanese' has in the past been the rule rather than exception. A new law stipulates that if the percentage of imported bulk wine in the bottle is above 50% it must be indicated on the label (the larger percentage should be written before the smaller).

For key to grape variety abbreviations, see pages 6–9.

Lebanon The small Lebanese wine industry, based on Ksara in the Bekaa Valley northeast of Beirut, continues against all odds to make red wine of real vigour and quality. There are 3 wineries of note. Château Musar (***) produces splendid matured reds claret-like, largely of Cabernet Sauvignon; a full-blooded white, surprisingly capable of ageing 10–15 yrs; and recently a lighter red wine, 'Tradition', which is 75% Cinsaut, 25% Cabernet Sauvignon. Ksara is the largest and oldest (Jesuit-founded) winery. Kefraya more dynamic: 'Rouge de K' is a Cinsaut-Carignan blend, 'Château Kefraya' is fragrant and from best yrs only; there is rosé and white too; all early-drinking.

Morocco Morocco today makes North Africa's best wine (85% of it red, from Cinsaut, Grenache, Carignan grapes), from vineyards along the Atlantic coast (Rabat to Casablanca, light fruity with speciality white – 'Gris' – from red grapes) and around Meknés and Fez (solid full-bodied), also further east around Berkane (tangy earthy) and in the Gharb and Doukkalas regions. In 10 years they have declined in area from 190,000 to 35,000 acres. The main producers are Domaine de Sahari (near Meknés, with French investment, a new winery in '93, and Cab S, Merlot, along with local grapes), Chaudsoleil, Meknés Vins and Sincomar. Chantebled, Tarik and Toulal are three drinkable reds. Vin Gris (esp de Boulaoune) is the best bet for hot-day refreshment.

Tunisia Tunisia now has 22,000 acres of vines (compared with 120,000 10 years ago). Her speciality is sweet Muscat, but reasonable reds and rosés come from Cap Bon, Carthage, Mornag, Tébourba and Tunis. Trying to improve quality; state and coop wines best.

Turkey Most of Turkey's 1.5 million acres of vineyards produce table grapes. But her wines, from Thrace, Anatolia and the Aegean, are very drinkable. Indigenous varieties such as Emir, Narince (for white) and Bogazkere, Oküzgözü (for red) are used along with Riesling, Sémillon, Pinot Noir and Gamay. Trakya (Thrace) white (light Sém) and Buzbag (E Anatolian) red are the well-known standards of Tekel, the State producer (with 21 state wineries). Doluca, Karmen, Kavaklidere and Taskobirlik are private firms of good quality. Doluca's Villa Neva red from Thrace is well made, as is Villa Doluca. Kavaklidere makes good light Primeurs (white 'Cankaya' and red 'Yakut') from local varieties. But Buzbag remains Turkey's most original and striking wine.

The Former Soviet Union

Over 3 million acres of v'yds make the republics of the former USSR collectively the world's fourth-biggest wine producer. Ukraine (incl Crimea) is the largest, followed by Moldova, the Russian Republic and Georgia. The Soviet consumer has a sweet tooth, for both table and dessert wines.

Crimea and Ukraine Crimea produces first-class dessert wines. Sotheby's auction house disclosed as much in '90, with sales of old wines from the Tsar's Crimean cellars at Massandra (Muscats and port- and madeira-like wines of v high quality); classic method sparkling from Novi Svet and Grand Duchess (the latter from Odessa Winery founded by Louis Roederer in 1896) are also adequate. Reds have good potential (eg Alushta from Massandra). All are still produced under state monopoly. Ukraine is good for Aligoté and Artemosk sparkling; mostly Romanian varieties.

Moldova   With the most temperate climate (same latitude as N France) and now the most modern outlook, Moldova has high potential: esp whites from centre, reds from south, and red and fortified nr the Black Sea (west). Grapes incl Cab, Pinot N, Merlot, Saperavi (fruity), Ries, Pinot Gr, Aligoté, Rkatsiteli. Former Moscow bottling was disastrous. But the 63 Negru de Purkar released in '92 gave a startling glimpse of Moldova's potential, reinforced by following vintages (with 4 yrs oak, and v best from Cab S-Saperavi-Rara Negre blends (like 63)). Purkar may be the best winery. Krikova is also good: esp Kodru 'Claret' blend, Krasny Reserve Pinot N-Merlot-Malbec. Romanesti winery (since '82) has wines from French varieties and Yaloveni, fino and oloroso-style 'flor sherries'. Abrodsov is classic method sparkling. Investment from Germany, Italy, UK and from Australia (Penfolds) at Hincesti, enables local clean bottling and better winemaking. Progress is not smooth, but well worth watching. (NB Moldavia is neighbouring Romanian region.)

The Russian Republic   Makes fair Ries (Anapa, Arbau, Beshtau) and sweet sparkling Tsimlanskoye 'Champanski'. Also Chard, Sauv Bl, Welschriesling (heavy, often oxidized).

Georgia   Uses antique methods to make extremely tannic wines for local drinking, slightly newer techniques for export blends (Mukuzani, Tsinandali); Georgians are disinclined to modernize. Kakhetià, E Georgia, is famed for v tannic red and white. Imeretia (west) makes milder, highly original wines. Sparkling is v cheap, drinkable. When equipment (incl bottles and stoppers) and techniques improve Georgia will be an export hit.

Israel

Israeli wine, since the industry was re-established by Baron Edmond de Rothschild in the 1880s, has been primarily of kosher interest until recently, when Cabernet Sauvignon, Chardonnay, Merlot, Riesling, Sauvignon Blanc, Sémillon, Petite Sirah and Grenache of fair quality have been introduced. Wines from the new cooler northern Golan Heights region are v well-made. Three-quarters of Israel's annual 15-million-bottle production is white.

Ashkelon Family-owned firm making red and white wines. Labels are Segal's and Ben-Ami.

Baron Small family grower. Vg whites, esp dry Muscat and Sauv Bl. Also some Cab S.

Carmel Coop, est 1882, with Israel's two largest wineries (at Zichron-Yaacov and Richon-le-Zion). Top wines are Rothschild series, esp Cab S and Emerald Ries. Also good 'Carmel Selected' Sauv Bl, Chard and Dry Muscat (second series), and Galil (third series).

Eliaz Medium-sized winery producing light-style red and white wines.

Galilee Region incl Golan Heights (Israel's top v'yd area).

Gamla, Golan Soft fruity Cab S and Chard and grassy Sauv Bl, produced by YARDEN.

Samson Central coastal plain v'yds (SE Tel Aviv to W Jerusalem).

Shomron V'yd area around Zichron-Yaacov, nr Haifa.

Yarden Young ('83) modern winery in the Golan Heights, involving Californian oenologists and setting highest standards for Israel. Over 20 wines: top is full-bodied oaky Galil Cab S (85 89); good Merlot, crisp Sauv Bl and barrel-fermented Chard; recently some classic method sparkling.

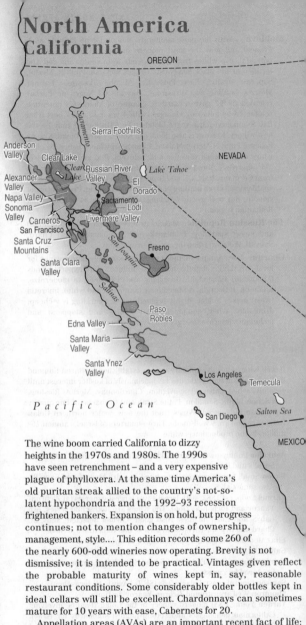

North America
California

OREGON

Sacramento

Sierra Foothills

NEVADA

Anderson
Valley

Clear Lake

*Clear
Lake*

Russian River
Valley

Lake Tahoe

Alexander
Valley

El
Dorado

Napa Valley

Sacramento

Sonoma
Valley

Lodi

Carneros

Livermore Valley

San Francisco

San Joaquin

Santa Cruz
Mountains

Fresno

Santa Clara
Valley

Salinas

Paso
Robles

Edna Valley

Santa Maria
Valley

Santa Ynez
Valley

Los Angeles

Temecula

Pacific Ocean

Salton Sea

San Diego

MEXICO

The wine boom carried California to dizzy
heights in the 1970s and 1980s. The 1990s
have seen retrenchment – and a very expensive
plague of phylloxera. At the same time America's
old puritan streak allied to the country's not-so-
latent hypochondria and the 1992–93 recession
frightened bankers. Expansion is on hold, but progress
continues; not to mention changes of ownership,
management, style.... This edition records some 260 of
the nearly 600-odd wineries now operating. Brevity is not
dismissive; it is intended to be practical. Vintages given reflect
the probable maturity of wines kept in, say, reasonable
restaurant conditions. Some considerably older bottles kept in
ideal cellars will still be excellent. Chardonnays can sometimes
mature for 10 years with ease, Cabernets for 20.

Appellation areas (AVAs) are an important recent fact of life:
they are being registered thick and fast; the current total is over
50, with nine in Napa alone. But it is too soon to use them as a guide
to style. Listed below are the regions usually referred to. Grapes
and brand names, though, remain the key to California wine.

Principal vineyard areas

Central Coast

A long sweep of coast with scattered though increasing wine activity, from San Francisco Bay south to Santa Barbara.

Hecker Pass Pass through the SANTA CRUZ MTS S of San Francisco Bay with a cluster of small old-style wineries.

Livermore Valley E of San Francisco Bay long famous for white wines but now largely built-over.

Monterey See Salinas Valley.

Salinas Valley/Monterey The Salinas Valley runs inland SE from Monterey. After frenzied expansion in the '70s, many vines were removed. What are left make wines of singular character. Currently refining its internal divisions: Arroyo Seco AVA (esp Chard and Ries), Santa Lucia Highlands AVA (Chard, has hopes for Pinot N), San Lucas AVA (steady commercial wines), and coastal Carmel Valley (tiny, sometimes impressive Cab and Chard).

San Luis Obispo Edna Valley just S of San Luis Obispo (1,000 acres, esp Chard) and scattered v'yds nr Paso Robles (6,000 acres, esp Zin).

Santa Barbara Santa Maria Valley is dominant, esp for vg Chardonnay and distinctive Pinot N. The smaller Santa Ynez Valley also has cool foggy conditions: good for Burgundian varieties at seaward end, Bordeaux varieties in warmer inland areas.

Santa Cruz Mts Wineries (though few v'yds) are scattered round the Santa Cruz Mts S of San Francisco Bay, from Saratoga down to HECKER PASS.

Temecula (Rancho California) Small area in S California, 25 miles inland, halfway between San Diego and Riverside. Mainly white/sparkling.

North Coast

Encompasses Lake, Menodocino, Napa and Somoma counties, all north of San Francisco.

Alexander Valley/Russian River (Sonoma) Top quality area from Alexander Valley (N of Napa Valley) towards the sea (Russian River). Incl Dry Creek Valley. Most varieties thrive.

Carneros, Los Important cool region N of San Francisco Bay, shared between NAPA and SONOMA counties. Esp for Chard and Pinot N.

Lake Clear Lake AVA: warm climate, most impressive for Sauv Bl, good for Cab S. Small Guenoc Valley AVA similar.

Mendocino Northernmost coastal wine country; a varied climate coolest in Anderson Valley nr the coast, warm around Ukiah inland.

Napa The Napa Valley, N of San Francisco Bay. The oldest and most-honoured of California wine valleys busily fragmenting itself: Stag's Leap AVA (Cab), CARNEROS AVA (shared with SONOMA, good Chard, Pinot N and sparkling), Mt Veeder (Cab), Howell Mountain AVA (Cab, Zinfandel, Chard), Atlas Peak AVA (Sangiovese) and new AVAs on the valley floor, Rutherford and Oakville.

Russian River See Alexander Valley.

Sonoma County N of San Francisco Bay, between rival NAPA and the sea. California's most divided wine area. Includes historic Sonoma Valley AVA ('Valley of the Moon', versatile, partly in CARNEROS, see Napa); far west, Russian River Valley AVA (increasinlgy devoted to Chard, Pinot N, sparkling, encompassing Chalk Hill and Sonoma-Green Valley AVAs); warmer inland, Alexander, Dry Creek and Knights Valley AVAs (Cab S, Zin, increasingly Rhône types).

The Interior

Amador County in the SIERRA FOOTHILLS E of Sacramento. Grows vg Zinfandel, esp in Shenandoah Valley AVA.

Lodi Town and district at the N end of the SAN JOAQUIN VALLEY, its hot climate modified by a westerly air-stream.

San Joaquin Valley The great central valley of California, fertile and hot, the source of most of the jug and dessert wines in the state. (Incl LODI AVA and the Clarksburg AVA on the Sacramento River delta.)

Sierra Foothills Encompasses AMADOR (Shenandoah Valley, Fiddletown AVAs), El Dorado (AVA of the same name), Calaveras counties, among others. Zin is universal grape; Rhône and Italian varieties seen more and more.

Recent vintages

The Californian climate is far from being as consistent as its reputation. Although, on the whole, grapes ripen regularly, they are subject to spring frosts in many areas, sometimes a wet harvest-time and too often drought.

Wines from the San Joaquin Valley tend to be most consistent year by year. The vintage date on these, where there is one, is more important for telling the age of the wine than its character.

Vineyards in the Central Coast region are widely scattered; there is little pattern. The Napa and Sonoma valleys are the areas where comment can usefully be made on the last dozen or more vintages of the top varietal wines: Cabernet Sauvignon and Chardonnay.

Chardonnay

NB These ageing assessments are based on well-balanced wines with fruit flavours dominant. Very rich and oaky examples tend to be v short-lived: 2 yrs at most. Marker wines for good ageing qualities incl eg Chappellet, Clos du Bois-Calcaire, Dehlinger, Freemark Abbey, Matanzas Creek, Shafer, Silverado, Simi, Sonoma-Cutrer, Trefethen.

1993 Big crop; stop-and-go harvest led to some unevenness; at the very least sound short-termers.
1992 Comfortable growing year; agreeable wines with full flavours, good but not long-keeping balance.
1991 Abundant but delayed harvest. Showing more resolve than earlier; many just starting to open up.
1990 Healthy and trouble-free. Coming along as an irreproachable vintage but not a grand one.
1989 Ups and downs after rainy harvest, but the ups reach some of the decade's highest peaks. Some of the best wines still special.
1988 Big soft quick-developers. Many lack focus. Drink up soonish.
1987 Ideal weather; vg wines to drink now.
1986 Many solid and worthy. Nothing to wait for.
1985 Big crop, good acidity, excellent and maturing well. Mostly ready.
1983 Good once, but only the very best carry on.
1982 Cool harvest; the best wines were lean and tart and have aged well.

Cabernet Sauvignon

NB As with Chardonnays, over-rich and over-oaky wines usually collapse quickly. The markers for the assessments below are not Reserves, but fine standard Cabernets from eg Beaulieu, Beringer (Knights Valley), Caymus, Chappellet, Clos du Val, Fetzer (Barrel Select), Freemark Abbey, Hafner, Jordan, Laurel Glen, Louis Martini (Monte Rosso), Parducci, Raymond, Shafer, Silverado.

1993 Winemakers predicting wines of early approachability.
1992 Charming fruit flavours at v least. Many show good balance for medium-term. Much like 90.
1991 Long cool summer, ideal autumn. Uncommon depth, yet at the same time a subtlety and finesse of texture that promise rewarding evolution if kept.
1990 Wonderfully fleshy, flavourful wines in the vein of '78 when fruit flavours were irresistible early but wines still held on well. No hurry.
1989 Many beautifully dark, flavoury wines with solid structure for ageing; some got caught in rains.
1988 If not charming, pretty close to empty.
1987 Evolving as perhaps the best of the decade overall.
1986 Quickly approachable vintage. Baby fat is now fleshy.
1985 Lean, firm to hard, deep-flavoured. Slow-maturing but impressive.
1984 Showy early: ripe and fragrant. Possibly best now and 3 more years.
1983 Several awkward hard wines. The best have depth but still need time to reveal it.
1982 Epitome of a charming vintage, good now and (for the best) a while longer.
1981 Promptly picked examples have substance and depth. Probably at peak.
1980 High reputation but merely good and solid. Over-tannic. Ready to drink.
1979 Apparently lightish, but the best keep going sturdily.
1978 Excellent. Generally ready, and many fading.
1977 Attractive wines now mainly crumbling.
1976 Drought made v concentrated wines. Good ones are v ripe and potent now.
1975 Delicate, charming; mature.
1970 One of the best ever. Mature.

California wineries

Acacia Napa *** (Chard) 81 83 87 89 90 91 (Pinot N) 79 80 85 87 88 90 91 92
  Specialist in single-v'yd CARNEROS Chard (Marina) and Pinot (Lund, St-
  Clair, Madonna): depth, durability. Owned by CHALONE. 25,000 cases.

Adelaida Cellars San Luis Obispo ** Soft Paso Robles Chard and supple Cab.

Alderbrook Sonoma ** (Chard) 86 87 88 89 90 91 Indelibly flavoured,
  age-worthy Dry Creek Sém, crisp Chard, Sauv. Recent new owners.

Alexander Valley Vineyards Sonoma ** Long-lived rich Cab leads list. Also
  dark sturdy Pinot, mild Ries. Technical problems recently. 40,000 cases.

Almaden San Joaquin * Famous pioneer name, now a HEUBLEIN-owned
  everyday brand, operated from Madera. 1 million+ cases.

S Anderson Vineyard Napa **→*** (Chard) 87 88 89 90 91 92 Robust Chard;
  robuster classic sparkling. Début Cab from neighbour v'yd stunning.

Arrowood Sonoma **→*** (Chard) 86 88 89 90 91 92 (Cab S) 87 88 89 90
  Long-time CHATEAU ST JEAN winemaker Dick A makes leaner wines on
  his own behalf. 15,000 cases.

Atlas Peak Napa Huge international (incl Antinori) investment in E hills.
  Sangiovese and Sangiovese-Cab 'Consenso' extremely promising.

Au Bon Climat Sta Barbara ** (Chard) 87 88 90 (Pinot N) 87 88 89 90
  Ultra-toasty Chard; well-wooded Pinot N. Dynamic experimental little
  winery also for QUPE and VITA NOVA (Santa Maria V) wines. 5,000 cases.

Beaucanon Napa ** Owners of Bordeaux Ch Lebegue turning out
  consistently supple stylish Cab S, Merlot, Chard from own 250 acres.
  Aim is for pleasant drinking.

Beaulieu Vineyard Napa *** (Cab S) 36 45 49 58 65 70 80 83 85 89 90 Long-
  time growers and makers of justly famous age-worthy Georges Delatour
  Private Reserve Cab (87 88 89 not so special). Also vg Rutherford Cab,
  approachable Beautour Cab and crackerjack dry oak-free Sauv Bl.

Bel Arbors Oddly spelt second label of FETZER.

Belvedere Sonoma ** Bold Chard, Cab S and Zin from individual v'yds are
  top of line; Grove Street series is value. 250,000 cases.

Benziger All SONOMA wines. Family sold off GLEN ELLEN Private Reserve and
  M G Vallejo labels to HEUBLEIN. Fruit flavours foremost from Cab, Merlot,
  Chard, Sauv, Sém. Also red and white 'A Tribute' Meritage blends.

Beringer Napa **→*** (Chard) 79 82 83 87 89 90 91 92 (Cab S) 78 79 81
  82 84 85 87 88 89 90 Century-old winery restored to front rank.
  Reserve Chard and esp Reserve Cab are wines to bank on. Solid Fumé,
  Zin, Knights Valley Cab. 1.4 million cases. Everyday label: Napa Ridge.

Black Mountain Sonoma ** Chard, Sauv Bl, Zin. Second label: J W Morris.

Boeger El Dorado ** Steady SIERRA FOOTHILLS Cab S, Merlot, Zin, Sauv Bl.

Bonny Doon Sta Cruz Mts *** (Chard) Rabid francophile led charge
  towards Rhône varieties: esp red Cigare Volant (Grenache-Mourvèdre),
  white Cuvée des Philosophes (Marsanne-Roussanne), Le Sophiste and
  Viognier. Now trying Italian. All worth tasting. Never a dull moment.

Bouchaine Napa ** (Chard) 89 90 91 Specialist in well-wooded CARNEROS
  Chard, Pinot N and so far vg bone-dry Gewürz (88 89).

Brander Vineyard Sta Barbara ** Impressive intense Sauv (90) from Sta
  Ynez V. Good Cab F-S Bouchet (84 85 86 87), 87 Merlot. 8,000 cases.

Bronco Wine Company High-capacity winery. Owns LAURIER, Grand Cru,
  Hacienda, Napa Creek and part of Montpellier labels; also Forest Glen
  (good value LODI Chard and Cab). C C Vineyard and J F J Cellars are
  labels for generic and varietal wines.

Bruce, David Sta Cruz Mts ** (Chard) 91 (Pinot N) 85 89 91 Long-time
  source of heavyweight (now moderated) Chard. Pinot Noir is forte
  (superior 87 89 91, vg 88 90). 32,000 cases.

---

*NB This edition introduces a new short-cut vintage category. Vintages in
colour are the ones you should choose first for drinking in 1995.*

Buehler Napa ** (Cab S) 87 89 90 Impressive 20,000-case E hills estate has turned sharp corner: recent Cabs, Zins to watch. Vg Pinot Bl.

Buena Vista Sonoma ** (Chard) 86 87 88 89 90 91 92 (Cab S) 81 83 85 86 88 89 90 Historic name now German-owned. An utterly reliable source of taste-the-grapes Chard, Sauv Bl, Cab S, Merlot, Gewürz, Ries, mainly from own 1,100-acre v'yd in CARNEROS. 110,000 cases.

Burgess Cellars Napa ** (Chard) 87 88 89 90 91 92 (Cab S) 80 81 82 83 84 85 86 87 88 90 (Zin) 82 83 85 86 87 Emphasis on dark weighty well-oaked reds. 30,000 cases.

BV Abbreviation of BEAULIEU VINEYARD used on its labels.

Davis Bynum Sonoma ** (Chard) 87 89 90 91 (Pinot N) 84 87 90 91 Reliable, sometimes stylish wines go beyond special selection Chard, Cab S to include correct Pinot N, enticing dry Gewürz. 28,000 cases.

Byron Vineyards Sta Barbara *** (Chard) 91 (Pinot N) 84 85 86 87 88 90 ROBERT MONDAVI-owned source of tasty polished Pinot N and vg Chard from estate v'yds. Also some Cab S and Sauv Bl from nearby.

Cain Cellars Napa ** (Cain Five) 85 86 87 88 90' Focal point is Cain Five, blended from Cab varieties grown in estate v'yd on Spring Mt. Cain Cuvée is declassified C Five; the white is Sauv Musqué from MONTEREY.

Cakebread Napa *** (Chard) 90 91 (Cab S) 80 81 82 85 87 88 89 90 Bold style rules in memorable Sauv, excellent Chard and Cab. 40,000 cases.

Calera San Benito *** (Chard) 87 88 89 90 91 (Pinot N) 82 84 85 87 89 90 91 Heady, dark, often tannic estate Pinot Ns are much in fashion; each named after a section of the hilly chalky v'yd (Jensen, Selleck, Reed). Also smoky well-knit Chard; now Viognier. 10,000 cases.

Callaway S California ** (Chard) 88 89 90 91 Mild easy whites incl lees-aged Chard, oak-aged Fumé. 150,000 cases. Reds coming.

Cambria Sta Barbara Affiliate of KENDALL-JACKSON produces extra-smoky rather sweet Chard (but getting drier) and well-oaked Pinot N from own grapes. 18,000 cases and growing fast.

Carey Cellars Sta Barbara ** (Chard) 87 88 89 90 91 Impressive since acquisition by FIRESTONE (mainly estate wines): vg Chard, Merlot, Sauv.

Carmenet Sonoma **→*** (Cab S blend) 88 89 90 CHALONE-owned mountain v'yd and winery above SONOMA town: classy plummy Cab-based blend. Also Edna Valley white based on Sauv Bl. 27,000 cases.

Carneros Creek Napa *** (Chard) 89 90 91 92 (Pinot N) 78 80 85 87 90 91 92 Resolute explorer of climates and clones in CARNEROS focuses on Pinot N. Well-oaked Reserve, lightheartedly fruity Fleur and reliable estate bottlings. Also deftly oaked Chard. 25,000 cases.

Caymus Napa ***→**** (Cab S) 73 74 75 78 79 80 81 85 86 87 88 89 90 Dark firm herbaceous estate Cab Special Selection is the celebrated core; slightly lighter Napa Valley covers the flanks. Also dark Zin, ultra-ripe Pinot. Good value second label: Liberty School. 35,000 cases.

Chalk Hill Sonoma ** In hills nr Windsor, revitalized winemaking leading to oakier Chard, Sauv Bl, Cab S from large estate v'yd. 65,000 cases.

Chalone Monterey ***→**** (Chard) 89 90 91 92 (Pinot) 82 Unique hilltop estate high in Gavilan Mts; source of smoky, woody, flinty, slow-ageing Chard and (latterly) dark tannic Pinot N, both meant to imitate burgundies. Also Pinot Bl and Chenin styled after Chard. 25,000 cases. Also owns ACACIA, CARMENET, EDNA V, Gavilan. Links with (Lafite) Rothschilds.

Chappellet Napa *** (Chard) 82 86 87 91 (Cab S) 75 76 78 82 84 86 87 88 89 90 Beautiful amphitheatrical hill v'yd: lean racy Cab, understated Chard and California's best dry Chenin Bl – all long-lived. 30,000 cases.

Chateau De Baun Sonoma ** Young winery doing well by Chard and Pinot N from RUSSIAN RIVER estate v'yd.

Chateau Montelena Napa *** (Chard) 79 82 85 88 90 91 Understated firm age-worthy Chard and epically tannic, potent Cab to age forever.

Château Potelle Napa **→**** French-owned new producer of balanced quietly impressive NAPA Chard (with fruity and toasty Reserve versions), also Cab S and Mt Veeder Zin. 22,000 cases.

Chateau St Jean Sonoma *** (Chard) 88 90 91 Intensely flavoured, richly textured, individual-v'yd Chards (Robert Young, Belle Terre, McCrea), Fumé Bls (Petite Etoile), and sweet botrytised Ries and Traminers (Robert Young, Belle Terre). Now reds (Cab, Pinot) again. Idiosyncratic classic sparkling (separate winery). Owned by Suntory. 150,000 cases.

Château Souverain Sonoma ** (Chard) 86 88 91 (Cab S) 85 87 89 90 Reliable accessible wines. Price-worthy Reserve Chard, Cab S and Dry Creek Zin, all distinctive, not overdone. 150,000 cases.

Château Woltner Napa *** (Chard) 90 91 92 Ex-owners of Ch La Mission Haut Brion now encamped on NAPA hillside making 4,000 cases of wine a year. Pricey Chards from 3 separate blocks of their v'yd.

Chimney Rock Napa ** (Cab S) 86 87 88 89 90 91 Chard and recently impressive Cab S from Stag's Leap District. 12,000 cases.

Christian Brothers Madera (San Joaquin Valley) ** Since '89 acquisition by HEUBLEIN, settling in at low end of price scale. Sound. Volume in flux.

Cline Cellars Carneros (Sonoma) Rhône Ranger Mourvèdre etc. 5,000 cases.

Clos du Bois Sonoma **→*** (Chard) 85 88 90 91 (Cab S) 81 85 87 89 90 Sizeable Allied-Hiram Walker firm at Healdsburg has consistent Cab, Chard, Gewürz. Single-v'yd Chard (Calcaire, Flintwood), Cab S (Briarcrest), Cab S blend (Marlstone), from ALEXANDER and Dry Creek valleys, can be memorable. 320,000 cases.

Clos Pegase Napa **→*** (Chard) 87 88 90 91 92 (Cab S) 86 87 89 90 91 92 Post-modernist winery-cum-museum (or vice versa) with ever-improving, deftly understated wines. 40,000 cases.

Clos du Val Napa *** (Chard) 87 88 89 90 91 (Cab) 72 74 75 77 78 79 80 81 82 83 85 86 87 88 89 90 91 French-run. Supple polished Cab, Merlot, bold Zin from Stag's Leap District; improving Chard, Pinot from CARNEROS. Joli Val is non-estate wine (Chard, Cab, Sém). 55,000 cases.

Codorníu Napa *** CARNEROS arm of great Catalan cava co is competing well with local Champenois.

Concannon Livermore ** WENTE BROS now own this historically famous source of Sauv Bl. Also Chard, Cab S. 85,000 cases.

Conn Creek Napa **→*** (Chard) 88 89 90 91 (Cab S) 83 85 87 88 89 90 Best known for supple, almost juicy Cab. Chard gaining reputation. Owned by Château Ste Michelle (Washington). 30,000 cases.

Cooks 'Cooks Champagne', see Guild.

Corbett Canyon San Luis Obispo ** (Chard) 89 90 91 (Pinot N Res) 85 86 87 89 90 91 Recently memorable Reserve Pinot N is best. Reserve lots small, good value. Coastal Classics line abundant. 300,000 cases.

Corison Napa Valley *** Long-time CHAPPELLET winemaker on her own making supple flavoury Cab S promising to age well.

Crichton Hall Napa Yountville vines: deep distinct NAPA Chard. 4,000 cases.

Culbertson Temecula ** Sparkling wine specialist blends local and STA BARBARA grapes with medal-winning results. Recently table wines too.

Cuvaison Napa *** (Chard) 83 86 89 90 91 (Cab S) 84 85 87 88 89 90 Lean crisp CARNEROS Chard is steadily top rank. Dark ripe Merlot, up-valley Cab following suit. Pinot is new (début 91 pretty good). 65,000 cases.

Dehlinger Sonoma **→*** (Chard) 85 88 90 91 (Pinot N) 84 85 86 87 89 90' 91 92 Firm fruit-filled Chard (less now but improving), and dark full complex focal point Pinot N (regular and Reserve) from RUSSIAN RIVER estate. Both long-lived. 9,000 cases.

DeLoach Vineyards Sonoma *** (Chard) 87 88 90 91 92 (Zin) 81 87 88 90 92 Unctuous super-fruity Chard and dark slow-ageing Pinot N are best known. Bold, often heady Zin (and uncommonly fine white Zin) should be. Also solid Gewürz, Sauv Bl. 70,000 cases.

deLorimier Sonoma ** Still settling into style, but estate ALEXANDER VALLEY Chard, Sauv-Sém and Cab family blends show promise. 5,000 cases.

Diamond Creek Napa *** (Cab S) 76 78 79 80 81 82 83 84 85 86 87 89 90 Austere long-ageing Cabs from hilly v'yd nr Calistoga go by names of v'yd blocks, eg Gravelly Meadow, Volcanic Hill. 3,000 cases.

Domaine Carneros Napa (★★★)   Showy US outpost of Taittinger in CARNEROS echoes austere style of its parent in Champagne. 25,000+ cases.

Domaine Chandon Napa ★★→★★★   Californian outpost of Moët & Chandon is most broadly known for reliable Brut and Blanc de Noirs; most praised for Reserve, locally available Club Cuvée and luxury cuvée Etoile. Shadow Creek is second (non-Napa) label. 500,000 cases.

Domaine Napa Napa ★★→★★★ (Chard) 87 89 90 91 (Cab) 83 85 86 87 89 90   French owner/grower of consistently supple balanced Chard, Cab, Sauv.

Dominus Napa (★★★★) 83 84 85 86 87 88 89 90 91 92   Partnership of Christian Moueix of Pomerol and inheritors of INGLENOOK makes increasingly intense, massively tannic Cab-based blend. Little of it is even nearly mature. 89 looks magnificent.

Dry Creek Vineyard Sonoma ★★   Unimpeachable source of dry tasty whites, esp Chard and Fumé Bl, but also Chenin Bl. Cab S and Zin rather underrated. David Stare is label for somewhat weighty reserve Cab blend, Sauv blend, and Chard. 80,000 cases.

Duckhorn Vineyards Napa (Cab) 81 82 83 84 85 86 87 88 90'   Known for dark, tannic, almost plummy-ripe reds, eg single-v'yd Merlot (Three Palms, Vine Hill). Also Sauv. 18,000 cases.

Dunn Vineyards Napa (★★★) (Cab S) 80 81 82 83 84 85 86 87 88 89 90 91 92   EX-CAYMUS winemaker Randall Dunn makes dark tannic austere Cab from Howell Mt, slightly milder from valley floor. 4,000 cases.

Durney Vineyard Monterey ★★ (Cab S) 83   Estate in Carmel Valley. Dark robust Cab. Chard joining list. 15,000 cases.

Eberle Winery San Luis Obispo ★★   Oaky fat supple Paso Robles Chard, Cab.

Edna Valley Vineyard San Luis Obispo ★★→★★★ (Chard) 86 87 90 91   Characterful Chard from a joint venture of local grower and CHALONE. Pinot N starts well but fades quickly in most vintages. 48,000 cases.

Estancia See Franciscan.

Etude Napa ★★→★★★   Winemaker-owned cellar of Tony Soter (long-time CHAPPELLET, now respected consultant). Front-rank CARNEROS Pinot N (87 89 90 91), excellent Cab: both burnished and supple. 4,000 cases.

Far Niente Napa ★★★ (Chard) 91 (Cab) 83 87 89 90   V oaky Chard, more restrained Cab at high prices. 36,000 cases.

Ferrari-Carano Sonoma ★★★ (Chard) 88 90 91 (Cab S) 87 88 89   Stylish Chard (Reserve seriously over-oaky), Fumé Bl and, more recently, Merlot and Cab S from 1,000 still-developing acres in ALEXANDER, Dry Creek and Knights valleys. 50,000 cases.

Fetzer Mendocino ★★→★★★ (Chard) 89 90 91 (Cab S) 85 88 89 90   Rapidly expanding with reliable (Sun Dial Chard, Valley Oaks Fumé), s'times memorable (Barrel Select Chard, Cab and Reserve Zin) range. Bel Arbors is value second label. 1.5 M cases. Sold to Brown-Forman Distillers.

Ficklin San Joaquin ★★★   First in California to use Douro grapes. Still California's best 'port', Tinta. Sometimes vintages. 10,000 cases.

Field Stone Sonoma ★★   Sturdy, increasingly steady: Petite Sirah. Also Cab.

Firestone Sta Barbara ★★★ (Chard) 86 89 90 91 (Merlot) 86 89 90 91   Fine Chard overshadows but does not outshine delicious Ries. Merlot good; Cab one of region's best; Sauv, Gewürz also vg. Also owns nearby CAREY.

Fisher Sonoma ★★   Mountain estate for often fine Chard; NAPA grapes dominate steady Cab. 10,000 cases.

Flora Springs Wine Co Napa ★★★ (Chard) 87 90 91 (Cab S) 80 81 85 87 88 89 90   Old stone cellar. Fine Sauv Bl Soliloquy parallels oak-fermented Chard, flavoury Reserve Cab and luxury Cab blend Trilogy: all are top-line Flora Springs. Regular bottlings are 'Floréal'. 18,000 cases.

Fogarty, Thomas Sta Cruz Mts ★★   Fine Gewürz from VENTANA sets the pace; whole line is well made.

To decipher codes, please refer to symbols key at front of book, and to 'How to use this book' on page 5.

Folie à Deux Napa ★★ Impeccable Chards; unexpectedly fine Chenin Bl. Cab a recent addition. 8,000 cases. Current financial troubles.

Foppiano Sonoma ★★ Long-est'd wine family annually turns out fine reds, esp transcendent Petite Sirah. Reserve label for Chard, Cab (fine 85 87) is Fox Mountain; good value second label is Riverside Farms.

Forman Napa ★★★ The winemaker who brought STERLING its first fame in the '60s now makes excellent Cab, Chard on his own. 15,000 cases.

Foxen Sta Barbara ★★★ Memorable Pinot, Cab, Chard etc; Sta Maria grapes.

Franciscan Vineyard Napa ★★ (Chard) 84 89 90 91 (Cab) 79 80 85 86 87 88 89 90 Substantial v'yd at Oakville: increasingly stylish Chard, Cab and Cab blend MERITAGE. Sister label Estancia goes on value Sauv Bl and MONTEREY Chard. Third label, Pinnacles, is for MONTEREY grapes.

Franzia San Joaquin ★ Penny-saver wines (eg Franzia label); varietals under William Bates brand. All say 'Made and bottled in Ripon'. 5M cases.

Freemark Abbey Napa ★★★→★★★★ (Chard) 81 84 85 87 89 90 91 (Cab S) 67 70 73 74 75 77 78 79 80 81 85 87 88 90 91 Inexhaustible stylish Cabs (esp single-v'yd Bosché, Sycamore) of great depth. Almost-bold Chard, incl s-v'yd Carpy. Late harvest Ries Edelwein always among finest.

Fritz, J Sonoma ★★ Splendid Dry Creek Zin, fine RUSSIAN RIVER Chard from 12,000-case winery deserving greater fame.

Frog's Leap Napa ★★→★★★ Small winery, charming as its name (and T-shirts). Rich-flavoured Zin (81 85 86 87 88 89 90), solid Cab (82 84 85 87 88 89 90 91). Chard and Sauv worth second looks too. 16,000 cases.

Gainey Vineyard, The Sta Barbara ★★ Chard, Cab and recent Sauv Bl and Merlot. Pinot N from Benedict v'yd. Also good Ries. 12,000 cases.

Gallo, E & J San Joaquin ★→★★★ (Cab S) 80 81 82 (Zin) 81 84 The world's biggest winery: pioneer in quantity and quality. Family-owned. Hearty 'Burgundy' and 'Chablis Blanc' set national standards. Wide acclaim won for vintage Cab. Varietals from huge SONOMA v'yds aimed up-mkt. Also André fizz etc. 40 million+ cases. 'Super-premium' wines coming.

Gan Eden Sonoma (★★) Kosher producer of serious Chard and Cab won wide critical acclaim for early vintages. 25,000 cases.

Gary Farrell Sonoma (★★★→★★★) Winemaker's label for brilliant well-oaked full-flavoured Pinot Ns (Howard Allen Ranch, RUSSIAN RIVER V). Also vg Chards and Sauv Bl and increasingly good Russian River Zin.

Geyser Peak Sonoma ★→★★ Since brief marriage with Penfolds of Australia, extensive v'yds of Henry Trione in ALEXANDER and RUSSIAN RIVER valleys (lovely grapes) make oaky Aussie-style wine. Canyon Road is second label for grapey good-value varietals. 500,000 cases.

Giumarra San Joaquin ★ Penny-saver everyday wines. 500,000+ cases.

Glen Ellen Sonoma ★★→★★★ Fast-growing brand built by BENZIGER, now HEUBLEIN-owned. Was value-for-money but misnames Proprietor's Reserve line of easy quaffers. Also M G Vallejo, priced one step up.

Gloria Ferrer Sonoma ★★ Substantial classic sparkling winery of Spain's Freixenet has scored well, esp for Cuvée Royale and Cuvée Carneros.

Green and Red Napa ★★ Tiny winery. Vigorous Italianate Zin. 2,000 cases.

Greenwood Ridge Mendocino ★★ (Pinot N) 89 90 91 92 Est'd specialist in Anderson V Ries now offers attention-getting Cab (83 84 90), Sauv (88 92), Zin (92). 3,000 cases. Vg MENDOCINO Chard and Pinot N too.

Grgich Hills Cellars Napa ★★★ (Chard) 82 89 90 91 (Cab S) 80 83 84 87 88 Winemaker Grgich and grower Hills join forces on a stern Chard, impressively rich Cab, Sauv Bl, and – too little noticed – Spätlese-sweet Ries. Also plummy thick SONOMA Zin. 40,000 cases.

Groth Vineyards Napa ★★★ (Chard) 87 90 91 92 (Cab S) 82 83 84 85 87 88 89 90 Estate at Oakville challenges leaders with polished refined Cab (and weightier woodier Reserve). Also vg Chard. 30,000 cases.

Guenoc Vineyards Lake County ★★ Ambitious winery/v'yd venture just N of NAPA county line. NB for Zin (81 84 85 88), Petite Sirah, other reds. Chard coming nicely. Property once belonged to Lillie Langtry, hence Reserve Langtry label for MERITAGES (red and white). 75,000 cases.

Guild San Joaquin ★ Ex-coop owned by Canandaigua of New York. B Cribari is top table wine, Cooks American Champagne a runaway success among tank-fermented sparklers. Also owns Dunnewood V'yds (ex-Cresta Blanca) in MENDOCINO. 3 million cases?

Gundlach-Bundschu Sonoma ★★→★★★ (Chard) 85 87 90 91 92 (Cab S) 82 86 87 89 90 Pioneer name solidly revived by newest generation. Rhine-farm V'yd signals worthy-to-fine Gewürz, Cab, Chard. 50,000 cases.

Hagafen Napa ★★ First and perhaps still finest of the serious kosher producers. Cab, Chard, Johannisberg Ries. 6,000 cases.

Handley Cellars Mendocino ★★ (Chard) 87 89 90 91 92 Winemaker-owned small producer of refined Chard and Gewürz (90 92), classic sparkling and refreshing Brightlighter (Gewürz-based). 12,000 cases.

Hanna Winery Sonoma 600 acres of RUSSIAN RIVER and ALEXANDER valleys coming on stream with v promising Chard, Cab, Sauv Bl.

Hanzell Sonoma ★★★ (Chard) 87 88 89 90 91 (Pinot N) 86 87 88 89 90 91 92 The late founder revolutionized California Chards, Pinot Ns in late '60s. Two owners later Hanzell remains a throwback source of its original ripe full-flavoured style. 2,000 cases.

Haywood Vineyard Sonoma ★★ Source of intense Zin and conventional Chard under German (Racke) ownership. 34,000 cases before sale. Vintner Select is bought-in wine.

Heitz Napa ★★★★ (Cab S) 68 69 70 73 74 75 78 79 81 84 85 88 89 90 An individualist winemaker has set lofty standards for his peers with his dark deep emphatic Cabs, esp Martha's Vineyard but also Bella Oaks and Napa Valley. Other wines eccentric or worse. 40,000 cases.

Hess Collection, The Napa ★★→★★★★ (Chard) 90 91 (Cab S) 85 87 89 90 A Swiss art collector's winery-cum-museum in former Mont La Salle winery of CHRISTIAN BROTHERS. Steadily improving Cab, Chard. Hess Selection label is v gd value. 75,000 cases, aiming for 50,000.

Heublein Vast drinks firm with ambivalent interest in wine (see Almaden, Beaulieu, Christian Bros, Glen Ellen, Inglenook, Niebaum Collection).

Hidden Cellars Mendocino-Lake ★★ Ukiah producer of oaky, steady Zin ('Pacini' best) and Chard. 20,000 cases.

Hill Winery, William Napa ★★★ (Chard) 92 (Cab S) 81 83 85 87 88 89 90 V'yds high in Mayacamas Mts yield steady Chard; ever more stylish Cabs. 12,000 cases. Same owners as CALLAWAY, CLOS DU BOIS.

Hop Kiln Sonoma ★★ Good source of bold-as-brass Petite Sirah and Zin. Even Gewürz is full-flavoured and large-scale. 10,000 cases.

Husch Vineyards Mendocino ★★ Reliable Chard, Sauv Bl, Cab; sometimes outstanding Pinot N and Gewürz from Anderson Valley. 15,000 cases.

Inglenook Napa ★★→★★★ (Chard) 86 90 91 (Cab) 55 56 62 68 78 81 87 88 89 Great old NAPA winery, has three separate lines from penny-savers to underrated and recently improved Napa, esp supple Cab, heartier Cask (Reserve) Cab and thoroughly tannic Reunion Cab. Also Merlot, Gravion (Sauv Bl-Sém) and Reserve Chard. 60,000 cases of Napa.

Iron Horse Vineyards Sonoma ★★★ (Chard) 90 91 (Cab) 88 89 90 Substantial RUSSIAN RIVER property concentrates increasingly on v successful classic sparkling with real finesse, but continues with Chard and Pinot from same estate v'yd. Cab, Sauv Bl from affiliated ALEXANDER V v'yd can be memorable. Laurent-Perrier joint venture on the way. 40,000 cases.

Jekel Vineyards Monterey ★★ (Chard) 88 90 91 Jekel's ripe juicy Ries is most successful wine from SALINAS v'yds. Also good Chard, intensely regional (fruit-flavoured) Cab. 60,000 cases.

Jepson Vineyards Mendocino ★★ Chard, Sauv Bl, classic sparkling, and pot-still brandy from estate in Ukiah area. 30,000 cases.

Jordan Sonoma ★★★ (Chard) 90 91 (Cab S) 80 81 82 83 85 86 88 89 90 Extravagant ALEXANDER VALLEY estate models its Cab on supplest Bordeaux. But it lasts. (Chard is less successful.) Separate classic sparkling called simply 'J' is deft, soft, luxurious. 75,000 cases.

Karly Amador ★★ Among more ambitious sources of SIERRA FOOTHILLS Zin.

Keenan Winery, Robert Napa ** (Chard) 89 90 91 (Cab S) 82 85 86 87 88 89 90   Winery on Spring Mountain has veered away from overweight heavily oaked to more restrained Cab, Merlot, Chard. 12,000 cases.

Kendall-Jackson Lake County ** (Chard) 89 90 91 92 93 (Cab S) 86 87 90   Dynamic maker of popular slightly sweet Chards and Sauv Bls; v oaky Cab. Owns Vinwood Winery (SONOMA), CAMBRIA, Durrell (memorable single-v'yd Sonoma Syrah), Edmeades, LA CREMA (label only), J Stonestreet and an ex-WM HILL v'yd (for Cardinale and s-v'yd Cab). 1 M+ cases.

Kenwood Vineyards Sonoma **→*** (Chard) 88 90 91 92 (Cab S) 87 88 89 90   Substantial producer of vg winning Sauv Bl and Zin, solid Chard (incl single-v'yd Beltane) and Cab S (single-v'yd Jack London can challenge the best). 150,000 cases.

Kistler Vineyards Sonoma *** (Chard) 88 89 90 91   Chards much in the smoky buttery style. Pinot N and Cab more recent. 9,000 cases.

Konocti Cellars Lake County **   Excellent value Sauv Bl, Chard, Cab from small coop. Recent MERITAGES (red, white) show promise. 40,000 cases.

Korbel Sonoma **   Long-established classic sparkling specialists place extra emphasis on fruit flavours, lots of fizz. Natural, Brut and Blanc de Blancs are best. 1.5 million cases.

Krug, Charles Napa ** (Chard) 90 91 92 (Cab S) 64 73 74 78 79 81 84 85 88 89 90 91   Historically important winery with generally sound wines. Cabs at head of list. CK-Mondavi is jug brand. 200,000 cases.

Kunde Estate Sonoma **   Long-time growers turned winemakers ('88). Good (Chard) to brilliant (Sauv) early results. Cab, Cab Reserve, Merlot and Zin: similar promise.

La Crema Sonoma (Chard) 88 89 90 91 (Pinot N) 86 88 89 90 91   Deftly oaked Chard and often deep-flavoured Pinot. Now KENDALL-JACKSON-owned.

Lakespring Napa **   Merlot, Cab, Chard, Sauv. 18,000 cases.

Landmark Sonoma **→*** (Chard) 83 85 87 89 90 91 92   Ever steadier Chard-only producer offers 3 (SONOMA COUNTY, basic; Sonoma Valley Two Williams; ALEXANDER VALLEY Damaris), moving from crisp fresh to me-too toasty-buttery. 15,000 cases.

Laurel Glen Sonoma *** (Cab S) 81 82 85 86 89 90 91   Fine, distinctly regional Cab from steep v'yd in Sonoma Mountain AVA. 5,000 cases.

Laurier Sonoma *** (Chard) 90 91' 92'   Crown-jewel label of the FRANZIAS' BRONCO WINE CO. Formerly lovely wines. Currently aiming high with Chard. No Cab S for years; Pinot N begins with 93.

Lazy Creek Mendocino **   'Retirement hobby' of a long-time restaurant waiter yields serious Anderson Valley Gewürz and Chard. Also Pinot N.

Leeward Winery Ventura (Chard) 89 90 91   Ultra-toasty Central Coast Chards are the mainstay. 18,000 cases.

Lohr, J Central Coast **   Wide range of steady varietals from wineries at San José and Paso Robles (SAN LUIS OBISPO), v'yds in PR and Clarksburg.

Long Vineyards Napa *** (Chard) 89 90 91 92 93 (Cab) 79 80 81 82 83 84 85 86 87 90   Tiny neighbour of CHAPPELLET: lush Chard, flavoury Cab.

Lyeth Vineyard Sonoma **   Former winery, now a brand owned by J C Boisset (Burgundy). Christophe is more modest label for bought wines.

Lytton Springs Sonoma **   Now RIDGE-owned: ink-dark hard heady Zins.

MacRostie Sonoma **   Veteran winemaker producing silky CARNEROS Chards, increasingly buttery-toasty. Good Pinot N and Merlot too.

Madrona El Dorado **   Loftiest v'yds in SIERRA FOOTHILLS good for steady Chard (among others). 10,000 cases.

Maison Deutz San Luis Obispo ***   Californian arm of Champagne Wm Deutz shows a firm sense of style: grapes from nr STA BARBARA.

Marimar Torres Sonoma (***)   Sister of Catalan hero makes ultra-buttery Chard; estate in W RUSSIAN RIVER VALLEY promises lovely Pinot N.

Mark West Vineyards Sonoma **   V satisfactory Gewürz from v'yd in coolest part of RUSSIAN RIVER. Also rustic Chard, Pinot N and, at times, classic Blanc de Noirs sparkling. 22,000 cases. Now owned by Marion Wine Group, with Marion label for less expensive wines.

Markham Napa **→*** (Chard) 87 89 90 91 92 (Cab S) 88 89 90 Japanese-owned. Recently good to excellent, esp Merlot and Bx-style blend 'Laurent'. 20,000 cases.

Martin Bros San Luis Obispo ** (Chard) 87 88 89 90 Fine dry Chenin Bl, good oaked Chard. Family winery aims to establish Paso Robles as California's Piedmont with Nebbiolo, and is developing Italian theme with Aleatico, 'Vin Santo', Cab-Sangiovese etc.

Martini, Louis M Napa **→*** (Chard) 89 90 91 92 (Cab S) 52 55 59 64 68 70 74 76 78 79 80 83 85 87 88 89 90 Family-owned winery with high standards, esp single v'yd Cab (Monte Rosso), Merlot (Los Vinedos del Rio). NAPA Chard is lovely, light, crisp. Second label Glen Oaks.

Masson Vineyards Monterey *→** Chard, Ries, Cab, Pinot N on a big scale.

Matanzas Creek Sonoma *** (Chard) 87 89 90 91 (Merlot) 88 89 Fine ripe fruity (increasingly toasty-oaky) Chard, Sauv, and renowned Merlot.

Maurice Car'rie Temecula ** Setting standards for its region with reliable, approachable Chard, Sauv Bl and others.

Mayacamas Napa *** (Chard) 76 79 85 87 90 (Cab S) 69 73 78 81 85 87 88 89 90 Vg small v'yd with rich Chard and firm (but no longer steel-hard) Cab. Some Sauv Bl, Zin. 5,000 cases.

McDowell Valley Vineyards Mendocino ** Obligatory Chard, Cab, but owners' hearts are with Rhône varieties, esp ancient-vine Syrah and Grenache (Les Vieux Cépages). 40,000 cases. Currently cash-strapped.

Meridian San Luis Obispo **→*** Nestlé-owned latecomer property. Impressive single-v'yd Edna Valley Chard (87 89 90 91); Pinot N (88) and Paso Robles Syrah (88), Cab also good. 300,000 cases.

Meritage Trademarked name for reds or whites using Bordeaux grape varieties. Aiming for 'varietal' status and gaining ground.

Merry Vintners Sonoma (**) Winemaker-owned producer of well-oaked regular and Reserve Chards, also Pinot N. Current financial problems.

Merryvale Vintners Napa ** St-Helena partnership with solid Chard and better Cab. Sauv-Sém White Meritage is best wine. 12,000 cases. Second label: Sunny St-Helena.

Mill Creek Sonoma ** Cab, Merlot, Chard, Sauv Bl. 15,000 cases.

Mirassou Central Coast ** Fifth-generation grower in Sta Clara, pioneer in Monterey (SALINAS VALLEY). Value Cab, Chard, Sauv Bl, Gewürz, Pinot N and v pleasant classic sparkling. 350,000 cases.

Mondavi, Robert Napa **→***** (Chard) 79 81 82 85 90 91 (Cab) 71 73 75 77 79 81 84 85 87 88 89 90 Winery with brilliant quarter-century record of innovation in styles, equipment, technique. Famous successes: Sauv ('Fumé Bl'), Cab, Chard, even Pinot N. 'Reserves' are marvels, regularly among NAPA's best. 500,000 cases. Less pricey California appellation varietals: Mondavi-Woodbridge. See also Opus One.

Mont St John Napa ** Old NAPA wine family makes good value Pinot N, Chard from own CARNEROS v'yd; buys in for solid Cab. 20,000 cases.

Monterey Peninsula Monterey ** Small winery in MONTEREY town: chunky long-living reds, esp Zin, Cab, from SALINAS grapes and others.

Monterey Vineyard, The Monterey ** Seagram-owned label for Chard, Pinot N, Cab: Classic and more costly Limited Release. 550,000 cases.

Monteviña Amador ** Major force in revitalizing hearty-style SIERRA FOOTHILL Zins. Now, under ownership of SUTTER HOME, also turning to a major exploration of Italian varieties. 50,000 cases.

Monticello Cellars Napa **→*** (Cab S) 83 85 86 87 88 89 90 Ultra-modern winery nr Napa City. Outstanding Gewürz (now v limited) first caught the eye. Refined Jefferson Ranch, darkly tannic Corley Reserve Cabs, sternly oaky Chard now the major effort. 25,000 cases.

Morgan Monterey **→*** (Chard) 89 90 91 92 Winemaker-owner: steady local Chard, fine ALEXANDER V Sauv. Also vg Pinot. 20,000 cases.

Mount Eden Vineyards Sta Cruz Mts ** (Chard) 87 88 89 90 91 92 Expensive big-scale Chard from old Martin Ray v'yds and gentler one from MONTEREY. Also Pinot N, Cab. 4,000 cases.

Mount Veeder Napa ★★ (Chard) 89 90 91 (Cab S) 74 81 87 89 90   Once oaky Chards and austere Cabs are gentler and better balanced since acquired by FRANCISCAN. Now MERITAGE (88 89 90). About 8,000 cases.

Mumm Napa Valley ★★★   G H Mumm-Seagram joint venture out of the box fast with fine vintages (85 86) and NV Brut. Also distinctive single-v'yd Winery Lake 'cuvée'. 125,000 cases.

Murphy-Goode Sonoma ★★   Substantial ALEXANDER VALLEY estate. Pinot Bl interesting, Sauv Bl important. 40,000 cases.

Nalle Sonoma ★★→★★★ (Zin) 85 86 88 89 90 91   Winemaker-owned Dry Creek cellar gets to the very heart of Zin. Wonderfully berryish young; that and more with age. Now also a trickle of Cab. 2,500 cases.

Navarro Vineyards Mendocino ★★→★★★ (Chard) 83 85 86 88 89 90 91   Firm fine Chard, outstanding dry Gewürz and Ries from cool Anderson Valley. Pinot N begins to find a footing. 12,000 cases.

Newton Vineyards Napa ★★★ (Chard) 91 (Cab S) 83 85 86 88 89 90   Luxurious estate growing more so; formerly ponderous style now reined back to the merely opulent for Chard, Cab, Merlot.

Niebaum Collection Napa ★★→★★★   HEUBLEIN-owned label: small lots from some of highest quality v'yds they acquired with BEAULIEU and INGLENOOK. V superior Chards (Reference, Laird, Bayview), Sém (Chevrier), good Cabs from winemaker Judy Matulich-Weitz. 20,000 cases.

Niebaum-Coppola Estate   ★★★ Francis Ford Coppola's luxurious hobby. Rubicon is a Cab blend from old INGLENOOK v'yds, now technically much improved (by Tony Soter – see Etude).

Opus One Napa ★★★★ (Cab S) 80 81 83 85 86 87 88 89 90   Joint venture of R MONDAVI and Baronne Philippine de Rothschild. Spectacular new winery opened '92. Wines are showpieces too. 10,000 cases.

Parducci Mendocino ★★ (Cab S) 80 85 87 89 90   Long-est'd v'yds and winery: ever reliable Cab, Cab-Merlot, Zin, Barbera. No-oak Chard, off-dry Sauv.

Pecota, Robert Napa ★★   Cab, Sauv Bl, Chard, Gamay. 18,000 cases.

Pedroncelli Sonoma ★★ (Chard) 89 90 91 (Cab S) 83 85 88 89 90 91   Old family firm with above-average sturdy vinous Cab, Zin (esp Reserves). Chard, Sauv Bl growing stylish. 125,000 cases.

Pepi, Robert Napa ★★→★★★ (Chard) 87 89 90 91 (Cab S) 84 85 87 89 90   Originally Sauv Bl specialist; now thoughtfully restrained Chard, Cab, winning Sangiovese Grosso (Colline di Sassi 89).

Phelps, Joseph Napa ★★★ (Chard) 87 88 90 91 92 (Cab S) 75 81 85 87 88 89 90 91   Deluxe winery and beautiful v'yd: impeccable standards. Vg Chard, Cabs (esp Backus Vineyard, vg 90), Rhône varieties (under Vin du Mistral label) and splendid late-harvest Ries, Gewürz. Reserve red Insignia Cab has tamed tannin and is now consistently impressive.

Philippine Baronne P de Rothschild's new brand. (See also Opus One.)

Philips, R H Yolo ★★   Large producer worth seeking out esp for some of California's most stylish tributes to the Rhône.

Pine Ridge Napa ★★→★★★ (Chard) 90 91 92 (Cab S) 80 81 82 84 85 86 87 88 89 90 91   Winery nr Stag's Leap makes consistently well-oaked Chard, Cab (several) and Merlot. 50,000 cases.

Piper Sonoma Sonoma ★★★   Venture of Piper-Heidsieck: mostly RUSSIAN RIVER grapes. Vg classic sparklers esp gd with bottle-age. 125,000 cases.

Preston Sonoma ★★★ (Cab S) 86 87 89 90   Small winery with excellent Dry Creek Valley v'yd esp for Zin, Cab, Syrah and other Rhône reds and whites. Also Sauv Bl 'Cuvée du Fumé. 25,000 cases.

Quady Winery San Joaquin ★★   Imaginative dessert wines from Madera incl chocolate orangey 'Muscat Essencia', dark Muscat Elysium and, latest, Moscato d'Asti-like Electra. Port-like Starboard is from Amador.

Quail Ridge Napa ★★ (Chard) 90 91   Specialist in barrel-fermented Chard. Also Cab. Recently added vg Sauv Bl and Merlot. Owned by HEUBLEIN.

For key to grape variety abbreviations, see pages 6–9.

Quivira Sonoma ★★ Fine melony Sauv Bl and intensely berryish Zin lead list. Cab Cuvée is a MERITAGE-like blend. Recently more oaky.

Qupé Sta Barbara ★★→★★★ Never-a-dull-moment cellar-mate of AU BON CLIMAT. Marsanne, Pinot Bl, Syrah are well worth trying.

Rafanelli, A Sonoma ★★ (Cab S) 84 88 89 90 (Zin) 82 86 87 89 90 Hearty, somewhat rustic Dry Creek Zin; Cab of striking intensity. 6,000 cases.

Rancho Sisquoc Sta Barbara ★★ Highly personal little winery shows vivid quality of Sta Maria Valley grapes, incl Ries, Chard, even Silvaner.

Ravenswood Sonoma ★★ Best known for dark, sturdy Zins. 15,000 cases.

Raymond Vineyards and Cellar Napa ★★★ (Chard) 85 86 89 90 91 (Cab S) 75 77 80 82 83 84 87 88 89 90 Old NAPA wine family now with Japanese partners. Emphatically fruity Chard and Sauv Bl; dark sturdy keeper Cabs, esp Reserve. 110,000 cases.

Ridge Sta Cruz Mts ★★★★ (Cab S) 83 85 86 87 88 89 90 Winery of highest repute among connoisseurs draws from NAPA, SONOMA, SAN LUIS OBISPO and its own mountain v'yd for concentrated v tannic Cabs and Zins, needing long maturing in bottle. Most notable efforts from single v'yds, esp Monte Bello, York Creek (Spring Mt) Cabs, Geyserville, Dusi Zins. Now also extremely smoky Chard. 40,000 cases.

Rochioli, J Sonoma ★★ Owners of v'yd famed for Pinot N now making vg example of their own. Also fine Sauv Bl.

Roederer Estate Mendocino ★★★ Anderson V branch of Champagne house (est '88). Resonant Roederer style apparent. Potentially 90,000 cases.

Rombauer Vineyards Napa ★★ Well-oaked Chard, dark Cab (esp Reserve-style 'Meilleur du Chai'). 15,000 cases.

Roudon-Smith Sta Cruz Mts ★★ Chard, Cab. 10,000 cases.

Round Hill Napa ★★ Formerly diverse range now narrowed to Cab, Chard, Merlot, Sauv Bl, but in 3 price ranges: bargain California, regular Round Hill, separate top-of-the-line Rutherford Ranch. 350,000 cases.

Rutherford Hill Napa ★★→★★★ (Chard) 88 89 90 91 (Cab S) 82 85 87 88 89 90 Larger stable-mate of FREEMARK ABBEY. Good with several flavoury Chards (Jaeger, XVS), sturdy Cabs (XVS) and Merlots. Merlot to be future main line: 80% of production. 100,000 cases.

Rutherford Ranch See Round Hill.

Rutherford Vintners Napa ★★ (Chard) 87 (Cab S) 77 79 81 Subtle but eminently age-worthy Cabs are the main event; Château Rutherford is Reserve lot. 12,000 cases.

St Andrews Napa ★★ (Chard) 85 90 91 92 (Cab S) 83 84 85 86 87 88 90 Excellent Chard estate on Silverado Trail nr Napa City. Cab abandoned. Recently acquired by CLOS DU VAL, now up for sale again.

St Clement Napa ★★→★★★ (Chard) 89 90 91 (Cab) 77 79 86 87 89 90 Austere Chard, sturdy Cab, Merlot. Distinctive ageable Sauv. Japanese-owned.

St Francis Sonoma ★★ (Chard) 89 90 91 92 (Cab S) 86 88 89 90 Gaining speed after slow start. Firm v tasty Sonoma Valley estate Chard (esp 90). Steady Merlot. Also Cab. Abandoning the Gewürz. 34,000 cases.

St Supery Napa ★★ French-owned, supplied by 500-acre estate v'yd in Pope Valley. Good Sauv Bl, accessible Cab. Also Chard – and now Merlot. 25,000 cases, able to expand tenfold.

Saintsbury Napa ★★★ (Chard) 81 85 89 90 91 (Pinot N) 85 86 87 89 90 91 92 CARNEROS' finest (and slowest-ageing) Pinot N. Lighter Pinot N Garnet and less-oaky-than-formerly Chard also vg. 35,000 cases.

Sanford Sta Barbara ★★★ (Chard) 88 89 90 91 (Pinot N) 81 84 85 86 87 89 90 91 Specialist in clean-fruity intense age-worthy Pinot N (esp Barrel Select). Exceptionally bold Chard; firmly regional Sauv Bl and a little Pinot N 'Gris'. 30,000 cases.

Santa Barbara Winery Sta Barbara ★★ (Chard) 86 87 89 90 91 (Pinot) 87 89 90 91 Former jug-wine producer, now among regional leaders, esp for Reserve Chard. Also Pinot N, Zin, Cab. 28,000 cases.

Santa Cruz Mountain V'yd Sta Cruz Mts ★★ Huge, tannic, heady Pinot N and Cab dominate. 2,500 cases.

Santa Ynez Valley Winery Sta Barbara ** Sauv Bl, Chard and Merlot. 20,000 cases.

Santino Amador ** Stylish SIERRA FOOTHILLS Zins (Fiddletown, Grand Père); also crackerjack white Zin. Italian varieties too. Money problems.

Scharffenberger Mendocino *** First to try MENDOCINO for serious classic sparkling. Now Clicquot-owned and doing well. 25,000 cases.

Schramsberg Napa **** Dedicated specialist: California's best sparkling. Historic caves. Reserve splendid. Bl de Noir outstanding, deserves 2–10 yrs. Luxury cuvée J Schram from '92 is America's Krug.

Schug Cellars Sonoma (Chard) 89 90 91 German-born and trained owner-winemaker developing refined Chard and Pinot N from CARNEROS. Relocated from NAPA to Carneros in '91. 10,000 cases.

Sebastiani Sonoma ** Substantial old family firm works on several different market levels: SONOMA appellations at top (esp Reserve), North Coast varietals in middle, August Sebastiani Country wines in jugs. Also Vendange penny-saver label. 4 million cases.

Seghesio Sonoma ** (Chard) 87 89 90 91 92 (Zin) 85 86 88 90 91 Long-time jug-wine producer recently turned to bottling its own wines with striking results. Vg Chard, Pinot N; often exceptional Zins (esp Dry Creek, ALEXANDER VALLEY Reserves). 85,000 cases.

Sequoia Grove Napa **→*** (Chard) 82 87 88 89 90 Vg Chards age well. NAPA Cabs (2 labels): dark and firm.

Shadow Creek See Domaine Chandon.

Shafer Vineyards Napa **→*** (Chard) 89 90 91 92 (Cab S) 78 80 84 85 86 87 88 89 90 Polished Chard (new 80 acres in CARNEROS), stylish Cab (esp Hillside Select) and Stag's Leap District Merlot.

Sierra Vista El Dorado ** Steady Chard, Cab S, Zin, Syrah from SIERRA FOOTHILLS grapes. 6,000 cases.

Silver Oak Napa **→*** Cabs, excessively American-oaked, incl pricey Bonny's V'yd. 24,000 cases.

Silverado Vineyards Napa *** (Chard) 83 85 87 90 91 (Cab S) 82 85 86 87 88 89 90 91 Showy hilltop Stag's Leap District winery. Cab, Chard, Sauv Bl all consistently refined; Cabs from '81 on ageing well.

Simi Alexander Valley *** (Chard) 80 84 85 88 90 91 (Cab S) 74 81 85 87 90 91 Restored historic winery has flowered under expert direction of Zelma Long. Wonderfully long-lived Chard, Sauv Bl. Fruity Chenin Bl and seductive Cab rosé for summer fests. Vg Cab recently austere. New Sauv Bl-Sém Sendal. 130,000 cases.

Smith & Hook Monterey ** (Cab S) 83 86 88 90 Specialist in dark intensely regional Cabs – so herbaceous you can taste dill. Also Merlots. Lone Oak is second label for Cab, Chard. 10,000 cases.

Smith-Madrone Napa ** Soft, round, durable Spring Mt Ries; Cab, Chard.

Sonoma-Cutrer Vineyards Sonoma ***→**** (Chard) 81 84 87 88 90 91 Ultimate specialist in Chard. Advanced techniques display characters of individual v'yds, as in Burgundy. Les Pierres is No 1 ager; Russian River Ranches is quickly accessible. 75,000 cases.

Spottswoode Napa ***→**** (Cab S) 83 85 86 87 89 90 Seductive resonant luxury Cab from tiny estate v'yd right in St Helena town. Also supple polished Sauv Bl. 3,500 cases.

Stag's Leap Wine Cellars Napa ***→**** (Chard) 85 88 90 91 (Cab S) 75 77 78 82 83 84 86 88 89 90 91 Celebrated v'yd and cellar for Cabs (NAPA, Stag's Leap V'yd, and recently controversial top-of-line Cask 23). Also vg Chard, Ries, improving Sauv Bl. 40,000 cases.

Stags' Leap Winery Napa ** Neighbour to above with more tannic, austere Cab and muscular Petite Syrah. 25,000 cases.

Sterling Napa *** (Chard) 84 85 88 90 91 (Cab S) 78 80 81 85 87 88 89 90 Proficient (also scenic) winery owned by Seagram. Strong tart Sauv Bl and Chards. Burly Cab, Reserve (Cab-based) and v'yd designated Three Palms Merlot. Winery Lake V'yd Pinot N still promises more than it performs. Vg Merlot. 150,000 cases.

Stony Hill Napa ✱✱✱ (Chard) 73 75 76 81 85 88 90 91 Hilly v'yd and winery for many of California's v best whites over past 30 yrs. Founder Fred McCrea died in '77, widow Eleanor in '91; son Peter carries on powerful tradition. Chard less steely, more fleshy than before. Oak-tinged Ries and Gewürz understated but age-worthy. 4,000 cases.

Stratford Napa ✱✱ Merchant label for reliable Cab, Merlot and Chard.

Strong Vineyard, Rodney Sonoma ✱✱ (Chard) 86 87 89 90 91 (Cab S) 87 88 90 Formerly Sonoma V'yds, draws mostly on RUSSIAN RIVER VALLEY for steady Chards (esp Chalk Hill V'yd) and Pinot N; ALEXANDER VALLEY for Cabs (esp single-v'yd Alexander's Crown) and Sauv Bl. 375,000 cases.

Sutter Home Napa ✱✱ (Zin) 68 73 77 83 85 89 90 91 Best known for sweet white Zin; most admired for sometimes heady Amador Zin. Also bargain-priced Cab, Chard. 3 million cases.

Swan, Joseph Sonoma ✱✱ (Zin) 77 78 79 80 81 82 83 84 85 86 Ultra-bold Zins and Pinots of late Joe Swan, now under direction of his son-in-law.

Swanson Napa ✱✱→✱✱✱ Estimable age-worthy Chards lead list; Cab and Merlot worth note. Also pursuing Italian (esp Sangiovese) and Rhône reds.

Taft Street Sonoma ✱✱ After muddling along, has hit an impressive stride with good value RUSSIAN RIVER Chards, good Sauv Bl. 18,000 cases.

Talbott, R Monterey Wealthy owner doing well with Chards from Santa Lucia Highlands AVA, Carmel Valley.

Trefethen Napa ✱✱→✱✱✱ (Chard) 79 81 82 83 85 86 87 90 91 (Cab) 75 78 79 80 82 84 85 87 88 89 90 Respected family winery. Vg dry Ries, tense Chard for ageing (late-released Library wines show how well). Cab shows increasing depths. Value in low-priced blends: Eshcol Red, White.

Tudal Napa ✱✱ (Cab S) 80 82 84 86 88 89 Tiny estate winery N of St Helena; steady source of dark firm ageable Cabs.

Tulocay Napa ✱✱ (Pinot N) 82 85 89 90 Tiny winery at Napa City. Chard and esp Pinot can be v accomplished. Cab is also worth attention.

Turnbull Wine Cellars Napa ✱✱ (Cab) 81 82 83 84 85 86 87 88 89 90 Rich full minty Cab from estate facing ROBERT MONDAVI winery; SONOMA Chard.

Ventana Monterey ✱✱ (Chard) 87 89 90 '78 winery on large v'yd keeps shuffling its range, but Chards (fresh fruity Gold Stripe, oakier Barrel Fermented) remain top, with Sauv (Sauv-Musqué) increasingly notable.

Viader Napa Argentine Delia Viader fled to California to do her own thing: fine Cab-based blend from estate in hills above St Helena.

Viansa Sonoma ✱✱ Reliable source of NAPA-SONOMA Chard, Sauv Bl and Cab, now concentrating on everything Italian: Nebbiolo, Sangiovese, Sangio-Cab ('Thalia'), etc. No 91 wine made.

Vichon Winery Napa ✱✱→✱✱✱ (Chard) 85 90 91 (Cab S) 82 85 88 89 90 91 MONDAVI-owned. Subtle agreeable Chevrignon (Sauv Bl-Sém) equally worthy Cab. Stern oaky Chard. 50,000 cases.

Villa Mt Eden Napa ✱✱ (Chard) 88 89 90 91 (Cab S) 75 85 86 88 89 90 Rich, nearly plummy Cab made the name of this small Oakville estate. Bought by Château Ste Michelle group (see Washington) and improving strongly. Two lines: Grand Reserve (Cab S, Chard, Pinot N) and Cellar Select. 24,000 cases and expanding.

Vine Cliff Napa New well-heeled family winery in E hills above Oakville. Likeable early Chard, tannic portentous Cab.

Vita Nova Sta Barbara Label from stable of AU BON CLIMAT. To watch.

Weibel Alameda and Mendocino ✱→✱✱ Mainly tank-made sparklers; also range of accessible table wines. 200,000 cases. Serious money problems.

Wente Bros Livermore and Monterey ✱→✱✱ Historic specialists in whites, esp LIVERMORE Sauv, Sém. MONTEREY sweet Ries can be exceptional. Of growing importance for classic sparkling. 300,000 cases.

White Oak Sonoma ✱✱ (Chard) 85 88 89 90 91 92 (Zin) 87 88 90 91 Source of underrated, vibrantly fruity ALEXANDER VALLEY Chards and Sauv Bls.

Whitehall Lane Napa ✱✱ Recently bought from Japanese owners by San Francisco family. Obligatory Chard, Cab, weighty Knights Valley Merlot. Formerly fresh lively Pinot N. 20,000 cases.

Wild Horse Winery San Luis Obispo ✦✦→✦✦✦ (Pinot) **84 86 87** 89 90 Reaches into STA BARBARA for impressive Pinot. Good Merlot. Also Chard, Cab.

William Wheeler Sonoma ✦✦ French owners (J-C Boisset). Historic emphasis on dark, tannic Cab and lively Sauv from Dry Creek. Also affable Rhône-type RS Reserve. 19,000 cases. Now a label only, winery up for sale.

Williams & Selyem Sonoma ✦✦✦→✦✦✦✦ (Pinot N) **85** 87 **88 89 90 91** Intense smoky pricey Pinot of emphatic character, esp Rochioli and Allen v'yds.

Zaca Mesa Sta Barbara ✦✦ (Chard) **87 89** 90 91 (Pinot N) 88 90 Deliberately down-sized from 80,- to 35,000 cases and refocussed on buttery Chard, well-wooded Pinot N. Increased emphasis on Syrah.

ZD Napa ✦✦→✦✦✦ (Pinot N) **86** 89 90 91 Lusty Chard scarred by American oak is the ZD signature wine. Pinot N is often finer. 18,000 cases.

The Pacific Northwest

America's main quality challenge to California lies in Oregon and Washington, on the same latitudes on the Pacific Coast as France is on the Atlantic. As in California, the modern wine industry dates back to the 1960s. Each of the northwestern states (Oregon, Washington, Idaho) has developed a distinct identity. The small production of British Columbia fits in here, too.

Oregon's vines (about 6,000 acres) lie mainly in the cool temperate Willamette and warmer Umpqua valleys between the Coast and Cascade Ranges, in sea-tempered climates not unlike those of France, leading to delicate flavours.

Washington's vineyards (about 15,000 acres) are mostly east of the Cascades in a dry, severe climate scarcely tempered by the Yakima and Columbia rivers. Idaho's are east of Oregon along the Snake River. Both regions have hot days and cold nights which preserve acidity and intensify flavours.

Most of Oregon's 85 wineries are small and highly individual. Vintages are as uneven as in Burgundy, whose Pinot Noir is the state's most celebrated (also controversial) grape. A rare succession of good vintages for Pinot Noir, '88, '89 and '90, also yielded notable Chardonnay and Pinot Gris.

The Washington industry, with about 100 wineries, is remarkably consistent over a wide range. Cabernet and Merlot grow excellently, as well as all the classic white varieties. A run of fine vintages, '88, '89, '90, '91, has coincided with maturing winemaking talent. Despite small harvests in 1990 and 1991, most wines remain excellent bargains.

Oregon

Adelsheim Vineyard Willamette (Chard) 90 (Merlot) 88 92 (Pinot) 88 **90** 91 92 Nicely oaked Pinot, Chard best early. Pinots Gr, Bl: clean, bracing.

Alpine Vineyards Willamette Small estate winery: good Pinot N, Ries.

Amity Willamette (w) **90 91 92**   Distinctive Pinot N, several styles; excellent dry Gewürz and dry Ries.

Argyle (Dundee Wine Co) Willamette (w) **90** (sp) **87 88** Since '87, Australia's NW outpost, led by Brian Croser. Dry Ries, Chard; vg classic sparkling.

Beaux Freres Willamette Big, extracted, oaky, somewhat controversial Pinot N (91 92). (V'yd partly owned by wine critic Robert Parker.)

Bethel Heights Willamette (Pinot N) **88** 90 91 92 Deftly made, rising-star Pinot N ('early release', vintage and selected) from estate nr Salem; top quality. Also adequate Chard.

Bridgeview Vineyards Rogue Valley (w) 91 (Pinot N) 91 92   Starting to command attention, esp whites: good Gewürz, also Chard and Pinot.

Cameron Willamette (Pinot) 85 91   Nr KNUDSEN-ERATH. Eclectic producer of Pinot N, Chard: some great, others conversation pieces. Vg Pinot Bl.

Château Benoit Willamette   Most consistent successes have been Müller-T and Ries. Pioneer sparkling wines. Currently solid, unexciting.

Chehalem N Willamette (Pinot N) 90 91 92   Small premium estate winery, since '90. Big Pinot N. Also Chard, Pinot Gr and 'Cerise' (Passetout-grains-style Gamay-Pinot N).

Cristom N Willamette (r) 92   First vintage '90. Vg Pinot Noir and Chard.

Domaine Drouhin Willamette   Bold enterprise of one of Beaune's great names (since '88); superb quality. Fine Pinot N (88 89 90 91 92), tiny production of estate Chard.

Elk Cove Vineyards Willamette   Pinot N has been somewhat erratic, steadier now and can rival best (esp estate 'La Boheme': 88 89 90 91 92). Also fresh Ries (and late-harvest 86 92), well-oaked Chard and Pinot Gr.

Eola Hills Nr Salem (Willamette)   Consistently good Chardonnay (4 acre v'yd-designated) and Pinot Noir.

Evesham Wood Willamette   Tiny family winery nr Salem. Esp Pinot Gr; Pinot N (91) often vg too.

Eyrie Vineyards, The Willamette   Pioneer ('65) winery with Burgundian convictions. Oregon's most famous consistent Pinot and v oaky Chard (91). Also Pinots Gr (irreplaceable with salmon), Meunier, dry Muscat.

Foris Vineyards S Oregon   Value Pinot N, Chard and Gewürztraminer from warmer Rogue Valley.

Henry Estate Umpqua Valley   Distinctive Pinot N (American oak), gd Gewürz.

Hinman Vineyards S Willamette   Eugene winery focussing on quality: Pinot Gr, Gewürz, Ries all vg. Sliven Ridge is the premium label.

King Estate N Willamette   Huge (nr Eugene). First wines: 92 Pinot Gr, Chard.

Knudsen-Erath Willamette (Pinot N) 86 91   Oregon's second-largest winery (est '72). Big turnaround in last 3 yrs: value Pinot N improving, dry Ries and Gewürz v fine. Chard still inconsistent. Pinot Gr since '91.

Lange Winery Yamhill County (Willamette)   Small family winery, occasionally brilliant Pinot N and Pinot Gr.

Laurel Ridge Winery Willamette   Washington County winery with v'yds in Yamhill. Reliable classic method sparkling and Sauv Bl.

Montinore Vineyards Willamette   Ambitious winery with, for Oregon, huge 465-acre v'yd nr Forest Grove. New French winemaker since '92. Chard and Pinot N improving.

Oak Knoll Willamette   Started with fruit wines but has turned into one of Oregon's larger Pinot N producers. Recently inconsistent.

Panther Creek Willamette (Pinot N) 89 90 91 92   Tiny McMinnville winery: excellent beefy Pinot N, luscious Melon de Bourgogne.

Ponzi Willamette Valley (Pinot N) 88 89 90 91 92   Small winery almost in Portland, well-known for Ries. Also Pinot Gr, Chard and delicate full, (French) oaky, cellarable Pinot N.

Rex Hill Willamette (Pinot N) 83 88 90 91 92   Well-financed assault on top Pinots and Chards: consistent success, esp single v'yds. Also Ries.

St-Innocent Willamette   Up-and-coming Eola Hills winery: Chard, Pinot N.

Shafer Vineyard Cellars Willamette   Small producer of frequently good Pinot N, delicate Chard. Currently rather inconsistent.

Sokol Blosser Willamette (Pinot N) 90 91 92   One of the larger Oregon wineries; aim is popular taste with easy, accessible Chard, Pinot (vg 91 92). Also Ries, Sauv, Merlot (seldom grown in Oregon): recently rough.

Tempest Vineyards Willamette (Pinot N) 89 (Chard) 90   Family winery nr Amity: excellent Pinot Gr, Chard; sometimes fine Pinot N.

Tualatin Vineyards Willamette (Pinot) 92 (Chard) 91 92   Substantial estate winery: v consistent Chard, Gewürz, Ries. Pinot N currently weak.

Tyee Willamette   Recent arrival: family-owned and run, now well-established. Early vintages of Gewürz, Chard, Pinot N are well made.

Valley View Vineyards S Oregon   Rogue Valley estate since '90. Focus is top Cab (90 91 92), Merlot, Chard (90), Sauv (91): continually improving.

Van Duzer Eola and Amity Hills (N Willamette)   William Hill-owned (see California). Exciting Ries, vg Pinot N, Chard since '90.

Veritas Vineyard N Willamette   Erratic, but recent Pinot and Chard look gd.

Willamette Valley Vineyards Willamette   New, large, nr Salem. Moderate to high quality Chard, Ries, Pinot N. Founders' Reserve wines best.

Yamhill Valley Vineyards Willamette   Young estate near college town of McMinnville focuses on Pinot Gr, Chard and Pinot N (avoid 91 92).

Washington and Idaho

Arbor Crest Spokane (Washington)   Expanding winery has had ups and downs. Ups are Chard (88), Sauv Bl and late-harvest Ries (86).

Barnard Griffin Prosser (Washington)   Small producer of well-made Merlot (89), Chard (esp barrel-fermented, 92) and Sauv Bl.

Caterina NE Washington   New Spokane grower (Cab, Merlot, Chard, Sauv).

Château Ste Michelle (ubiquitous in Washington)   Regional giant growing ever larger. Owners had Château Ste M and COLUMBIA CREST at 750,000 cases before '91 acquisition of SNOQUALMIE, then the state's second-largest producer. Major v'yd holdings, first-rate equipment and skilful winemakers keep Chard (91 92), Sém, Sauv Bl, Ries, Cab (83 85 87 89) and Merlot in the front ranks. First serious efforts at sparkling are attractive. Newest reds and Chards v exciting.

Chinook Wines Yakima Valley (Washington)   Owner-winemakers Kay Simon and Clay Mackey buying in Yakima Valley grapes for sturdy Chard, Sauv Bl and Merlot. Excellent Sém too (90).

Columbia Crest Columbia Valley (Washington)   Separately run CHATEAU STE MICHELLE label for delicious well-made accessible wines priced one cut lower, most of them from big River Run v'yd. Reserve line is for best Cab, Merlot (88) and Chard. Reds are esp good value.

Columbia Winery Woodinville (Washington) (Cab) 79 85 88 87   Pioneer ('62, as Associated Vintners): still a leader. Balanced stylish understated single-v'yd wines, esp Merlot (Milestone), Cabs (Otis, Red Willow), Syrah (Red Willow). Oak-fermented Woodburne Chard, elegant Pinot, vg fruity long-lived Sém. Reds consistently among the country's finest.

Covey Run Yakima Valley (Washington) (Chard) 90 91 92   Mostly estate. Intriguing Aligoté and Caille de Fumé; intense heady Merlot, Cab.

De Stefano See Whittlesey-Mark.

Gordon Brothers Columbia Valley (Washington)   Tiny cellar for consistent Chard (Reserve 91), Merlot and Cab (89).

Hedges Cellars Puget Sound (Washington)   Esp for Washington's first (vg) Cab-Merlot blend. Began as négociant label, now with own v'yd.

Hogue Cellars Yakima Valley (Washington) (Cab) 85 87 88 89 90 91 92   Leader in region, best known for off-dry whites (esp Ries, Chenin, Sauv), but recently for stylish balanced Chard, Merlot, Cab. Value.

Kiona Vineyards Yakima Valley (Washington) (Cab) 83 85 86   Good v'yd for substantial Cabs and (Austrian) Lembergers; fruity Chard and Ries. Also v fine late harvest Ries (88) and Gewürz.

Latah Creek Spokane (Washington)   Small cellar, mainly for off-dry Chenin Bl, Ries. Erratic, esp with drier oak-aged types and reds.

Leonetti Walla Walla (Washington) (r) 83 85 86 87 88   Harmonious individualistic Cab and fine big-scale Merlot: bold, delicious, ageworthy.

McCrea Seattle (Washington)   Small winery for delicious Chard and Grenache. Experiments with Rhône blends are in progress.

Neuharth W Washington   Olympic Peninsula winery uses Yakima Valley grapes for supple balanced Cab (Chard fair, though not equal to reds).

Preston Wine Cellars Columbia Valley (Washington)   Early winery with wide range of wines. Some eccentric, some conventional/sound. Occasionally wonderful Cab or Merlot.

Quilceda Creek Vintners Puget Sound (Washington) (Cab) 83 85 **86** 87 88 89 90 91 92   Leading ripe well-oaked Cab S from Columbia Valley grapes is the speciality.

Ste Chapelle Caldwell (Idaho, nr Boise)   Top-drawer winemaking keeps intensely flavoured, impeccably balanced Chard, Ries from Washington and local v'yds nr forefront in NW. Reds on the rise. Attractive, good value sparkling wines.

Salishan Vancouver (Washington)   Promising Pinot N and occasionally brilliant dry Ries from nr Willamette Valley.

Silver Lake nr Seattle (Washington)   Fine regular and reserve Chard and Sauv Bl; also fine Cab, Merlot.

Snoqualmie Consistent quality. Whites best.

Staton Hills Yakima Valley (Washington)   Recently inconsistent, but s'times excellent Cab; gd off-dry white (Ries, Chenin, Gewürz). Also sparkling.

Stewart Vineyards Yakima Valley (Washington)   Estate v'yds well-suited to whites, esp Chard and Ries. Latterly some promising Cabs.

Thomas, Paul Bellevue (Washington)   Started as (still is in part) a fruit winery; now: full-flavoured Chard, Sauv, Chenin Bl. Reds show promise.

Thurston Wolfe Tiny eclectic Yakima-based winery: excellent Lemberger (red), late harvest Sauv Bl and Black Muscat.

Washington Hills Cellars Yakima Valley (Washington)   Newly est'd. Winemaker Brian Carter making solid attractive Sém, Fumé and Cab. Value. Apex label is premium line for Sauv, Cab, late harvest white.

Waterbrook Walla Walla (Washington) (r) 85 **87** 89 90 91 92   Young winery has now hit its stride: consistently big and oaky Cab, Merlot, Sauv Bl. Wines with style and personality.

Whittlesey-Mark Seattle (Washington)   Small winery for classic method sparkling. Changing label to De Stefano in late '94.

Will, Andrew Seattle   Exciting Cab and Merlot from E Washington grapes.

Woodward Canyon Walla Walla (Washington) (r) 81 82 83 84 85 86 87 88 89 90 91 92   Small top-notch cellar with well-oaked ultra-bold Cab and buttery Chard. Also Charbonneau blends (Merlot-Cab and Sauv-Sém) and late harvest Ries.

British Columbia

A small but locally significant wine industry has developed since the '70s in the Okanagan Valley, 150 miles east of Vancouver, in climatic conditions not very different from eastern Washington.

Gehringer Bros Okanagan Valley, BC. Good Ries, Ehrenfelser, Müller-T.

Gray Monk USA's N'most v'yd (Okanagan Valley, BC). Good Kerner, Pinot Bl.

Summerhill Entered British Columbia with a bang. Heavy investment; charming results in sparkling Riesling and ice wine.

The Eastern States & Ontario

Producers in New York (there are now 97) and other eastern states, as well as Ohio and Ontario, traditionally made wine from hardy native grapes, varieties of Vitis labrusca whose wine has strong 'foxy' flavour, off-putting to non-initiates. To escape the labrusca flavour, growers then turned to more nuanced French-American hybrids. Today fashion has largely bypassed these, although Seyval Blanc and Vidal keep their fans. European varieties, esp Chardonnay and Riesling are the current trend. Success is mixed (the winter of 1993/94 took its toll), but progress, from Virginia to Ontario, is accelerating.

Allegro Established Pennsylvania (LANCASTER VALLEY AVA) producer of noteworthy Chard, Cab, late harvest Seyval Blanc.

Aurora (Aurore) One of the best white French-American hybrids; the most widely planted in New York. Good for sparkling.

Baco Noir One of the better red French-American hybrids: high acidity but clean dark wine which usually needs ageing.

Banfi V'yd at Old Brookville, LONG ISLAND, with good Chards.

Bedell LONG ISLAND winery known for first-class Merlot.

Brights-Cartier Canada's biggest producer (Ontario). Wine from Canadian and foreign grapes. Sawmill Creek label incl worthy Chard (first Chards in the '50s were failures), Fumé Bl, BACO NOIR, Merlot-Baco Noir blend. Also in British Columbia.

Canandaigua Wine Co FINGER LAKES winery. Major producer (second largest in the US, behind Gallo) of labrusca, table and sparkling wines. Owns Manischewitz, the best-selling kosher wine. Bought WIDMER'S in '86.

Catawba Old native American grape, perhaps the second most widely grown. Pale red and 'foxy' flavoured. Appears in crowd-pleasing, dry, off-dry and sweet styles.

Cave Spring Ontario boutique: sophisticated Chard and Ries.

Cayuga White hybrid created at Cornell Uni. Delicate fruity off-dry wine.

Chaddsford Pennsylvania (LANCASTER VALLEY AVA) producer since '82; esp for burgundy-style Chard.

Chamard Connecticut's best winery, owned by Tiffany's chairman. Top Chard.

Chambourcin Red grape of French origin; under-appreciated Bordeaux-like reds and agreeable rosé.

Château des Charmes Mid-sized Ontario winery. Good Chard, Aligoté, Cab.

Chautauqua Ohio wine area with encouraging initial plantings of vinifera varieties. Lake islands nr Sandusky have best potential.

Chelois Popular red hybrid. Dry medium-bodied burgundy-style wine.

Clinton Vineyards Hudson River winery known for clean dry Seyval Bl and spirited Seyval sparkling.

Concord Labrusca variety, by far the most widely planted grape in New York. Heavy 'foxy' sweet red wines, but mostly grape juice and jelly. Long a staple of kosher wines.

Debonné Vineyards Popular Ohio estate: hybrids, eg CHAMBOURCIN and VIDAL; and vinifera, eg Chard, Ries.

De Chaunac French-American hybrid found in New York and Canada. Too often the usually full dark wine can be disagreeable.

Erie-Chautauqua The biggest of 6 NY state AVAs (this one partly in Ohio). WOODBURY is top v'yd.

Finger Lakes Beautiful historic upstate NY cool-climate region, source of most of the state's best wines (48 producers), and the seat of its 'vinifera revolution'. CANANDAIGUA is most important winery.

Firelands Ohio estate on Isle St George in LAKE ERIE, growing Chard and Cab. Owned by Meier's Wine Cellars, Ohio's biggest producer.

Frank, Dr Konstantin (Vinifera Wine Cellars) Small but influential winery. The late Dr F was a pioneer in growing European vines in the FINGER LAKES. Wines good, if uneven. Vg new Chateau Frank sparkling.

Glenora Wine Cellars Established FINGER LAKES producer of outstanding sparkling wine and good Chard.

Gristina Promising young winery on LONG ISLAND'S NORTH FORK AVA.

Hamptons (Aka South Fork.) LONG ISLAND AVA. Top wineries are Le Rêve and Sag Pond.

Hargrave Vineyard Pioneering, well-established winery on NORTH FORK of LONG ISLAND. Good Cab and Chard.

Hillebrand Estates Aggressive Ontario producer attracting attention with Chard, VIDAL ICE WINE and Ries.

Hudson River Region America's oldest winegrowing district (21 producers). Straddles the river, two hours' drive N of Manhattan.

Ice wine Wine made from frozen grapes. See Eiswein, page 106.

Inniskillin Top Ontario winery at Niagara-on-the-Lake. Skilful burgundy-style Chard, Pinot N; Ries, stunning VIDAL ICE WINE ('91 is award-winning). Good MARECHAL FOCH.

Knapp Versatile FINGER LAKES winery. Tasty Cab, Ries, Bl de Bls sparkling.

Lake Erie The biggest grape-growing district in the east; 25,000 acres along the shore of Lake Erie, incl portions of New York, Pennsylvania and Ohio. 90% is CONCORD, most heavily in CHAUTAUQUA County.

Lamoreaux Landing New FINGER LAKES house: promising Chard and Ries.

Lancaster Valley Pennsylvania AVA nr Maryland border (for vinifera and hybrid vines). Incl ALLEGRO, CHADDSFORD, Naylor, Twin Brook wineries.

Lenz Classy winery of NORTH FORK AVA. Good Chard, Gewürz, Merlot.

Long Island The most talked about new wine region E of the Rockies. Still defining itself: currently 1,300 acres all vinifera (47% Chard) and 2 AVAs (NORTH FORK and HAMPTONS). Most of its 17 wineries are on the North Fork. Best varieties: Chard, Cab, Merlot. A long growing season.

Maréchal Foch Workmanlike red French hybrid. Depending on vinification, yields boldly flavoured or nouveau-style wines.

Michigan Good Chard, Ries, Merlot and Gamay. Disparate wineries: from Tabor Hill (nr Indiana border) to Chateau Grand Travers (nr lake M).

Millbrook The No 1 HUDSON RIVER REGION winery. Money-no-object viticulture has lifted Millbrook into New York's firmament. Chards are splendid, Cab F can be delicious.

Niagara Quintessential labrusca greenish-white grape, sometimes called 'white Concord'. Makes lovely aromatic sweet wine and wants to be gobbled right off the vine.

North Fork LONG ISLAND AVA (of 2). Top wineries: BEDELL, Bidwell, GRISTINA, LENZ, PALMER, PINDAR.

Ontario Ries, Chard, Gewürz, Auxerrois, Gamay, Pinot N, Cab from eg BRIGHTS, Chateau Gai, INNISKILLIN. Ice wine is the state's best success.

Palmer Superior LONG ISLAND (NORTH FORK) producer becoming a byword in the rough-and-tumble metropolitan market. Good Chard and Cab.

Pindar Vineyards Huge 250-acre mini-Gallo winery of NORTH FORK, LONG ISLAND. Wide range of popular varietals, incl Chard, Merlot, and an esp good Bordeaux-type red blend, Mythology.

Ravat (Vignoles) French-American white hybrid of intense flavour and high acidity, often made in yummy 'late harvest' style.

Rivendell Hudson River producer now a hot property winning countless awards for Chard, Seyval Bl and proprietary blends.

Sakonnet Largest New England winery, based in Little Compton, Rhode Island. Its regional reputation, resting on Chard, VIDAL and dry Gewürz, has blossomed since '85.

Stonington Casual Connecticut estate. Peppy wines.

Swedish Hill Creditable Ries from FINGER LAKES. Also Chancellor and late-harvest Vignoles.

Tomasello Progressive New Jersey winery. Good Bl de Noirs sparkling and CHAMBOURCIN.

Treleaven Promising FINGER LAKES winery. Good Ries and Chard.

Vidal Mainstay French-American hybrid: full-bodied personable dry whites.

Vineland Estates Good Ontario producer whose VIDAL ICE WINE, dry and semi-dry Ries and Ries Ice Wine are admired.

Vinifera Wine Cellars Top FINGER LAKES winery, with an off-shoot for sparkling, 'Chateau Frank'.

Wagner Vineyards Jewel of a winery in the FINGER LAKES – arguably New York's best – for succulent barrel-fermented Chard, dry and sweet Ries, RAVAT ICE WINE and NIAGARA. Still has non-vinifera wines, too.

Widmer's Big FINGER LAKES winery specializing in native American wines, esp a fine sparkling NIAGARA.

Wiemer, Hermann J Creative, German-born FINGER LAKES winemaker. Interesting Ries incl vg sparkling and 'late harvest' versions.

Woodbury Top LAKE ERIE-CHAUTAUQUA winery. Good Chard, Ries, sparkling.

Other eastern states

Virginia Virginia's significant modern wine-growing (since '72) is making its name. Whites, especially Chardonnay, lead the way. With 43 wineries producing good Cabernets Sauvignon and Franc, Riesling, Sauvignon Blanc and Merlot from 1,341 acres of grapes, Virginia is one of the more versatile new wine states. There are now 5 AVAs. Monticello has most important producers: Prince Michel Vineyards (the largest, with esp good 'Le Ducq' Cabernet), Barboursville (excellent Malvaxia Reserve), Montdomaine Cellars, Piedmont Vineyards and Rapidan River. Others are Ingleside Plantation, Linden, Naked Mountain, Meredyth, Oasis (for its 'champagne'), Tarara and the Williamsburg Winery.

Missouri A blossoming industry with 30 producers. Best wines: Seyval, Vidal and sweet Vignoles. Best estate is Stone Hill, in Hermann (founded 1847) with a rich red from an American grape known as Norton (or Cynthiana). Hermannhof in the same town (founded 1852), is drawing notice for the same varieties. Mount Pleasant, in Augusta, makes a rich 'port' and a nice sparkler. To watch: Augusta Winery, Blumenhof, Les Bourgeois, Montelle, Röbller Vineyard, St James.

Maryland The state has 9 wineries. Basignani makes good Merlot, Chard and Ries. Catoctin, a boutique winery with mountain v'yds, is building a reputation for solid, modestly priced tannic Cab S, Chard and Ries. Elk Run's Chard is respectable. The state's best-known producer, Boordy Vineyards, gets good marks for Seyval, Vidal and Cab. Woodhall scores with Seyval. Catoctin Valley AVA is main Cab and Chard area.

The Southwest

Texas

In the past fifteen years a brand-new Texan wine industry has sprung noisily to life. It is already past the experimental stage, with 450 growers and 25 wineries now active (10 in Hill Country, with 3 new AVAs). The wines have begun to show some form, the best comparable with those of northern California.

Bell Mountain Hill Country AVA with just one winery:
Bell Mountain Vineyards TEXAS HILL COUNTRY winery at FREDERICKSBURG. 52 acres. Erratic but known for Cab S.
Cap Rock 120 acres nr Lubbock since '90. Chard, Chenin Bl, Sauv Bl and sparkling all promising.
Cordier Estates (Ste-Genevieve V'yds) Largest producer by far: 1,000 acres for Sauv Bl and range of varietals. Links with Bordeaux's Cordier.
Fall Creek Vineyards TEXAS HILL COUNTRY estate with 65 acres, making fine Sauv Bl and Chard. Also Cab S.
Fredericksburg Hill Country AVA.
Leftwich Tiny amount of good Chard from v'yds at Lubbock; winery nr Austin.
Llano Estacado The pioneer; nr Lubbock with 220 acres (210 leased). Known for Chard and Cab S.
Pheasant Ridge Lubbock estate founded '78. Now 36 acres. Esp for reds.
Texas Hill Country One of 3 Hill Country AVAs (S of Lubbock, W of Austin).

New Mexico etc

At present **New Mexico** is known for one wine, the remarkable Gruet sparkling, but other sparklers (Mont Jallon and Domaine Cheurlin) and Anderson Valley winery varietals, have proved the potential of the Rio Grande Valley. **Colorado** and **Arizona** will no doubt feature in our 1996 edition.

South America
Argentina

Argentina has the world's fifth-largest wine production, most of
it uncritically consumed within South America. But things are
stirring. The country's crop of gold medals at Vinexpo Bordeaux
from '87 onwards surprised everyone. Quality vineyards (all
irrigated) are concentrated in Mendoza province in the Andean
foothills at about 2,000 feet. San Juan, to the north, is the second
largest vineyard area. San Rafael, 140 miles south of Mendoza
city, is slightly cooler. Salta to the north and Rio Negro, south,
also produce interesting wines. Denomination of Origin
regulations for each are on the way. Malbec is the most planted
grape; Cabernet, Pinot and other French varieties are on the
increase – reds generally being better than the whites.
Modernization is now rapid; exports have increased by four times
over the last decade, while the domestic market is beginning to
demand higher standards.

Bianchi, Bodegas Well-known premium wine producer at San Rafael
owned by Seagram. Don Valentin Cab, Bianchi Borgoña and Malbec-
Barbera blend are best-sellers. 'Particular' is their top Cabernet. Also
Sauv Bl.

Bosca, Bodegas Luigi Small Mendoza (Maipu) winery with excellent
Malbec, Cab and Syrah; also interesting Chard, Sauv, Pinot and Ries.

Canale, Bodegas The Premier Rio Negro winery: Cab and Sém both won
Bordeaux gold medals, Merlot good too. Whites do well here, esp
Torrontes.

Catena Modern California-influenced Mendoza winery, one of A's best.

Crillon, Bodegas Owned by Seagram, only for tank-method sparkling.

Esmeralda Producers of a good Cab and Chard, St Felician, at Mendoza.

Etchart Salta winery. Typical aromatic but dry Torrontes white (gold
medal at Bordeaux, '87); sound range of reds (mainly Cab S) in Salta
and Mendoza.

Finca Flichman Old Mendoza firm now owned by a bank (investing heavily
in wine). Top Caballero de la Cepa Cab and Chard, plus Syrah, Merlot
and other single-varietals.

Goyenechea, Bodegas Basque family firm in San Rafael making old-style
wines (esp Cab, Syrah, Malbec, Merlot and Aberdeen Angus red), but
now modernizing.

Lopez, Bodegas Family firm best known for their Château Montchenot red
and white and Château Vieux Cab.

M Chandon Producers of Baron B and M Chandon sparkling wine under
Moët & Chandon supervision. Also still reds and whites including vg
Castel Chandon, less exciting Kleinburg (whites), smooth Comte de
Valmont, Beltour and Clos du Moulin reds. Soon to introduce single-
varietals.

Martins Recent notable Merlot and Malbec from Mendoza.

Nacari, Bodegas Small La Rioja cooperative. Its Torrontes white won a
gold medal and Oscar at Vinexpo, Bordeaux '87.

Navarro Correas 3 wineries: Vg Malbec, sparkling and Spätlese-style Ries.

Norton, Bodegas Old firm, originally English, now Austrian-owned, being
thoroughly updated. Reds (esp Malbec) are best. Perdriel is premium
brand. Also good sparkling.

Orfila, José Long-established bodega at St Martín, Mendoza. Top wines:
Cautivo Cab and white Extra Dry (Pinot Bl). Now making sparkling
wine in France for local sale.

Peñaflor Argentina's biggest wine co, reputedly the world's third largest. Bulk wines, but also some of Argentina's finest: TRAPICHE (esp Medalla), Andean V'yds, Fond de Cave (Chard, Cab). Aiming to export competitively. Also 'Sherry': Tío Quinto.

Perez Cuesta Small new winery with outstanding reds, esp Syrah (Gold Medal at Vinexpo '91) and Malbec.

H Piper Sparkling wine made under licence from Piper-Heidsieck.

Rural, Bodegas La ('San Filipe') Family-run winery at Coquimbito (Mendoza) making some of Argentina's best Ries and Gewürz whites and some good reds. Also a charming wine museum.

San Telmo Modern winery with a Californian air and outstanding fresh full-flavoured Chard, Chenin Bl, Merlot and esp Malbec and Cab 'Cruz de Piedra-Maipu'. 230 hectares.

Santa Ana, Bodegas Said to be S America's biggest. Old-established family firm at Guaymallen, Mendoza. Wide range incl good Syrah, Merlot-Malbec, Pinot Gr 'blush' and sparkling (Chard-Chenin Bl) 'Villeneuve'.

Suter, Bodegas Swiss-founded firm owned by Seagram making best-selling Etiquetta Marron white and good classic 'JS' red.

Toso, Pascual Old Mendoza winery at San José, making one of Argentina's best reds, Cabernet Toso. Also Ries and sparkling wines (incl one classic method).

Trapiche Premium label of PENAFLOR and a spearhead of technical advance. Single-grape wine range incls Merlot, Malbec, Cab S, Pinot N, Chard and Torrontes. Also 'Oak Cask' selection, rosé Cab and native grapes.

Weinert, Bodegas Small winery. Tough old-fashioned reds led by good Cab-Merlot-Malbec Cavas de Weinert and promising Sauv Bl.

Chile

Conditions are ideal for wine-growing in central Chile, the Maipo Valley near Santiago, and for 150 miles south. But the country's potential has only started to emerge in the past seven years. So far wines are good – not yet fine. Irrigation is universal. Chilean Cabernets have led the way with original flavours, rapidly gaining in quality. Other varieties, especially Sauvignon Blanc and Chardonnay, now show equal promise. Stainless steel and new oak have bought international standards. A new region (Casablanca), between Santiago and Valparaíso on the coast, is proving especially good for Chardonnay. Top wineries, including most of those following, are members of the Asociación de Exportadores y Embotelladores de Vinos AG. Many long-time growers are no longer supplying large bodegas but branching out, even exporting, alone.

Agrícola Aquitania Joint venture of Bordeaux's Paul Pontallier and Bruno Prats with Felipe de Solminihac near COUSINO MACUL. Red wines only, from '94. 'Paul Bruno' is to be their label.

Bisquertt Colchagua winery (1,056 acres) for generations owned by family of same name. Began exporting in '91.

Caliterra Former venture of ERRAZURIZ and Franciscan of California. Now solely owned by Errázuriz. Good value Chard, Cab.

Cánepa, José Chile's most modern big bodega, of Italian origin, handling wine from several areas. Vg frank and fruity Cab from Lontué, Curicó, and 100 miles south; recently particularly good Chard (some oak-aged), RIES and Sauv Bl. Top wines from Domaine Caperana.

Carmen, Viña Previously a second bodega of SANTA RITA. Now with its own new winery and v'yds.

Carta Vieja 770 acres in Maule. Del Pedregal family-owned for 6 generations.

Casablanca Second bodega of VINA SANTA CAROLINA. For premium wines.

Chateau Los Boldos French-owned winery at the foot of the Andes in Requinoa. 618 acres. Cab S, Sauv Bl and some Chard under Los Boldos de Santa Amalia label.

Concha y Toro Biggest, most outward-looking wine firm, with several bodegas and v'yds all over Chile, mainly at Maipo and Rapel, totalling 5,880 acres. Remarkable dark deep Cab, Merlot, Petit Verdot. Brands are Marqués de Casa Concha, Casillero del Diablo. Chard and Sauv Bl now well established. New top wine: Don Melchor Cab. Banfi (USA) are minority shareholders.

Cousiño Macul Distinguished and beautiful old estate nr Santiago. V dry Sém and Chard. Don Luis light red, Don Matias dark and tannic, are good Cabs. Antiguas Reservas is top export Cab.

Domaine Oriental French-owned modern winery in Maule Valley, Talca.

Domaine Rabat Since 1927 in Maipo and Colchagua; offers Cab, Chard, Sauv Bl. Different labels from each estate incl Dom Rabat, Santa Adela. Joined forces with Grand Marnier in '94.

Echeverría Grower from Curicó now producing good Sauv Bl.

Errázuriz Historic firm in Aconcagua Valley, North of Santiago, modernized and making very rich full-bodied wines, esp Cabernet Don Maximiano.

Exposición Label of Talca Coop. Growers cover 1,625 v'yd acres.

Lomas de Cauquenes Cooperative formed by Cauquenes growers after 1939 earthquake. Grapes from 650 acres.

Montes 250-acre estate at Curicó emerging as a quality leader with good fresh Sauv Bl; Chard and Fumé Bl aged in American oak; light Merlot, good Montes Cab S and excellent Montes Alpha (89) from French oak. Nogales and Villa Montes are unoaked, less expensive wines.

Porta Viña, Newly created winery in Rancagua. Cabs look promising.

Portal del Alto Viña, Small bodega with excellent Cab-Merlot blend. 120 acres, half in Maipo, half in San Fernando.

Robles, Los Label of coop of Curicó. Wines incl Cab and Merlot. 'Flying winemaker' Peter Bright is consultant.

Saint Morillon Lontué bodega with Sauv Bl, Chard, Cab, Cab Reserva. Now favouring Valdivieso label incl popular sparkling wine.

San Pedro Long established at Lontué, Curicó. One of the biggest exporters: range is good to vg. Gato Negro and Gato Blanco are top sellers. Castillo de Molina is top (2,600 acres in Molina). Santa Helena is assoc. Jacques Lurton of Bordeaux is consultant.

Santa Carolina Viña, Architecturally splendid old Santiago bodega with old-style 'Reserva de Familia'. Recent extensive modernization, now concentrating on Casablanca Valley and quality. Other labels: CASABLANCA, Ochagavía.

Santa Ema 550-acre Maipo estate in family since 1955. Esp Cab, Merlot, Sauv Bl and Chard. Reserva Cab 88 (French oak) is their pride.

Santa Emiliana Co-owned with CONCHA Y TORO. Second label popular in Canada and USA, Walnut Crest.

Santa Inés Successful small family winery in Isla de Maipo. Labels: De Martino, Santa Inés.

Santa Mónica Rancagua winery; the best label is Tierra del Sol. Producing quality wine.

Santa Rita, Viña, Long-established bodega in the Maipo Valley S of Santiago. Medalla Real Cab and '120' are best-sellers abroad. New top wine is excellent Casa Real Cab.

Segu Ollé Linares estate owned by two Catalan families. Labels: Caliboro and Doña Consuelo.

Tarapacá Ex-Zavala Producer rated in Chile for red wines. New plantations and conversion to imported oak underway.

For key to grape variety abbreviations, see pages 6–9.

Torreón de Paredes Recent family-owned bodega (253 acres). Modern; no expense spared. Good Reserva Cab.

Torres, Miguel Enterprise of Catalan family firm (see Spain) at Lontué sets a modern pace. Good Sauv Bl (Bellaterra is oak-aged) and Chard, vg Ries. Cab is made more 'elegantly' than other Chileans.

Undurraga Famous family business; one of first to export to the USA. Old and modern style wines: good clean Sauv Bl, oaky yellow Viejo Roble.

Vascos, Los Family estate in Colchagua Province. 400 acres. Some of Chile's best Cab (Bordeaux- and California-influenced). Also stylish Sauv-Sém. Made headlines in '88 by link with Lafite-Rothschild (50% owners). Wines from '87 on have been excellent.

Villard Recent venture of Frenchman Thierry Villard.

Vinícola Montealegre CANEPA'S 2nd bodega. Labels: Rowan Brook, Peteroa.

Brazil

European grape variety plantings are transforming Brazilian wines. International investments, esp in Rio Grande do Sul and Santana do Liuramento, esp from France (eg Moët & Chandon), are significant. Exports are beginning. Large home market too. Equatorial v'yds (eg nr Recife) can have two grape crops a year.

Mexico

The oldest American wine industry is reviving. Best in Baja California (85% of total) and at Aguascalientes. Some of the better Baja C producers are L A Cetto (in Valle de Guadaloupe, the largest, esp for Cabernet Sauvignon, Nebbiolo and Syrah), Bodegas Santo Tomas (since 1888, Mexico's oldest), Monte Xanic (with Napa-award winning Cabernet), Bodegas San Antonio, and Cavas de Valmar.

Peru

Viña Tacama near Ica exports some promising wines, especially the Gran Vino Blanco white; also Cabernet Sauvignon and classic method sparkling. But serious phylloxera.

Uruguay

Winemaking since 1700s, influenced along the way by France, Spain, Germany and Italy. Great efforts are currently being made, with French advice and grape varieties, to improve wine from the 30,000 acres of warm, humid vineyards (eg along Rio de la Plata and the Brazilian border, esp Bella Unión). 50% is planted with hybrids. At present the wine is of local and tourist interest only.

Australia

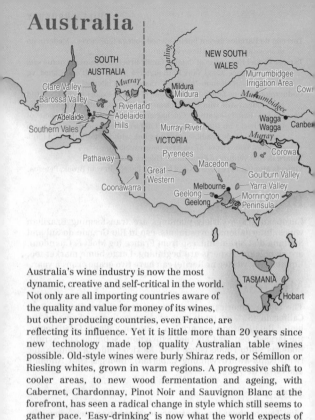

Australia's wine industry is now the most
dynamic, creative and self-critical in the world.
Not only are all importing countries aware of
the quality and value for money of its wines,
but other producing countries, even France, are
reflecting its influence. Yet it is little more than 20 years since
new technology made top quality Australian table wines
possible. Old-style wines were burly Shiraz reds, or Sémillon or
Riesling whites, grown in warm regions. A progressive shift to
cooler areas, to new wood fermentation and ageing, with
Cabernet, Chardonnay, Pinot Noir and Sauvignon Blanc at the
forefront, has seen a radical change in style which still seems to
gather pace. 'Easy-drinking' is now what the world expects of
Australia. But the best wines have greater character than ever.
And they can age splendidly.

The export story has been astonishing: climbing in eight years
from 8 to 125 million litres – with Britain much the biggest export
market. But it is a job to keep tabs on individual wines. There are
now about 700 wineries. Labels are becoming less garrulous (but
less informative) as Australian consumers become more sophisticated. Such information as they give can be relied on, and prizes
in shows (which are highly competitive) mean a great deal. In a
country lacking any formal grades of quality the buyer needs all
the help he or she can get. Value for money is generally high.

Wine areas

Adelaide Hills (SA) Spearheaded by PETALUMA: 22 wineries at v cool, 450-
metre sites in the Mt Lofty ranges.

Adelaide Plains (SA) Small area immed N of Adelaide, formerly known as
Angle Vale. Top wineries include Lauriston, Minton Grove, PRIMO ESTATE.

Barossa (SA) Australia's most imp't winery (though not v'yd) area;
grapes from diverse sources (local, to MURRAY VALLEY; high quality cool
regions: from adjacent hills, to COONAWARRA far S) make diverse wines.

Bendigo/Ballarat (Vic) Widespread small v'yds, some of vg quality, re-creating glories of the last century. 19 wineries incl BALGOWNIE, CH LE AMON, HEATHCOTE.

Canberra District (ACT) 18 wineries now sell 'cellar door' to local and tourist trade. Quality is variable, as is style.

Clare Watervale (SA) Small, high quality area 90 miles north of Adelaide, best for Riesling; also Shiraz and Cabernet. 23 wineries spill over into new subdistrict, Polish Hill River.

Coonawarra (SA) Southernmost and finest v'yd of state: most of Australia's best Cab, successful Chard and Shiraz. New arrivals incl Balnaves, PARKER ESTATE, PENLEY ESTATE.

Geelong (Vic) Once famous area destroyed by phylloxera, re-established mid-'60s. Very cool dry climate: firm table wines from good quality grapes. Names incl BANNOCKBURN, IDYLL, SCOTCHMAN'S HILL.

Goulburn Valley (Vic) Mixture of v old (eg CHATEAU TAHBILK) and relatively new (eg MITCHELTON) wineries in a temperate region; full table wines.

Granite Belt (Qld) Rapidly developing, high altitude, (relatively) cool region just N of NSW border; 15 wineries. Esp spicy Shiraz and rich Sem-Chard.

Great Western (Vic) Temperate region in central W of state. High quality table and sparkling wines. Now 9 wineries, 7 of recent origin.

Hunter Valley (NSW) Great name in NSW. Broad, soft, earthy Shiraz and Sem that live for 30 yrs. Cab not important; Chard increasingly so.

Margaret River (WA) Temperate coastal area with superbly elegant wines 174 miles S of Perth. 30 operating wineries; others planned.

Mornington Peninsula (Vic) Exciting wines in new cool coastal area 25 miles S of Melbourne. 400 acres. 28 commercial wineries on dolls-house scale incl DROMANA, ELGEE PARK, Merricks.

Mount Barker/Frankland River (WA) New, far-flung, cool area in S of state; GOUNDREY and PLANTAGENET are two biggest/best wineries.

Mudgee (NSW) Small isolated area 168 miles NW of Sydney. Big reds of colour and flavour, full Chards; from 23 wineries.

Murray Valley (SA, Vic & NSW) Vintages not normally important   Key irrigated v'yds nr Mildara, Swan Hill (Vic and NSW), Berri, Loxton, Morgan, Renmark and Waikerie (S Aus). Principally 'cask' table wines. 40% of total Australian wine production.

NE Victoria Historic area incl Corowa, Rutherglen, Wangaratta. Generally heavy reds and magnificent sweet dessert wines. 25 wineries.

Padthaway (SA) Large v'yd area (no wineries) developed as an over-spill of COONAWARRA. Cool climate; some good Pinot N and excellent Chard (esp LINDEMANS and HARDY'S), also Chard-Pinot sparkling wines.

Perth Hills (WA) Fledgling area 19 miles E of Perth with 11 wineries and a larger number of growers on mild hillside sites.

Pyrenees (Vic) Central Vic region with 8 wineries: rich minty reds and some interesting whites, esp Fumé Bl.

Riverina (NSW) NV Large-volume producer centred around Griffith; good quality 'cask' wines (esp white), great sweet botrytised Sem.

Southern Vales (SA) Covers energetic McLaren Vale and Reynella on S outskirts of Adelaide. Big reds now rapidly improving; also vg Chard.

Swan Valley (WA) The birthplace of wine in the west, on the N outskirts of Perth. Hot climate makes strong low-acid table wines, but good dessert wines. Declining in importance viticulturally.

Tasmania 38 v'yds now offer wine for commercial sale: over 700,000 litres. Great potential for Chard, Pinot N and Ries in cool climate.

Upper Hunter (NSW) Est'd in early '60s; irrigated wines (mainly whites), lighter and quicker-developing than Lower Hunter's. Often value.

Yarra Valley ('Lilydale') Superb historic area nr Melbourne: 33 small wineries. Growing emphasis on v successful Pinot. Noble varieties only.

For key to grape variety abbreviations, see pages 6–9.

Wineries

Alkoomi Mount Barker ✷✷→✷✷✷ (Ries) 80' 82' 84' 86' 87' 88' 90' 92' 93' (Cab S) 77' 80' 83' 84' 86' 87' 90' 25-year veteran producing 15,000 cases of fine steely Ries and potent long-lived reds incl rare Malbec.

All Saints NE Vic ✷→✷✷ Once famous old family winery bought in '92 by BROWN BROTHERS.

Allandale Hunter Valley ✷→✷✷ Small winery without v'yds, buying selected local grapes. Quality variable; can be good, esp Chard.

Allanmere Hunter Valley ✷✷→✷✷✷ (Chard) 85' 86' 88' 90' 91' 93' Small winery run by expat English doctor: excellent Sem, Chard; smooth reds.

Angove's Riverland (SA) ✷→✷✷ Long-est MURRAY VALLEY family business in Adelaide and Renmark. Value Cab and whites, esp Chard.

Arrowfield Upper Hunter ✷✷ Large irrigated v'yd. Light Cab, succulent Reserve Chard; also wooded Sem. Majority owned by Japanese firm.

Bailey's NE Vic ✷✷→✷✷✷✷ Rich old-fashioned reds of great character, esp Bundarra Hermitage, and magnificent dessert Muscat and 'Tokay'. Now part of ROTHBURY group.

Balgownie Bendigo/Ballarat ✷✷✷ (Cab S) 73' 74' 75' 76' 78' 80' 85' 86' 88' 90' 91' Fine reds, particularly straight Cab. Also occasional exceptional Chard. Now owned by MILDARA.

Bannockburn Geelong ✷✷✷ (Chard) 80' 85' 86' 87' 89' 90' 91' 92' (Pinot N) 81' 86' 87' 89' 90' 91' 92' Intense complex Chard and Pinot N made using Burgundian techniques. 6,000 cases.

Basedow Barossa Valley ✷✷→✷✷✷ Smallish winery buying grapes for reliably good range of red and white; Sem 'White Burgundy' esp good.

Berri-Renmano Coop Riverland (SA) ✷→✷✷ See Renmano.

Best's Great Western ✷✷→✷✷✷ (Shiraz) 62' 64' 70' 77' 78' 84' 85' 87' 88' 90' 91' 92' Conservative old family winery in GREAT WESTERN with good mid-weight reds, and Chard not half bad.

Blass, Wolf (Bilyara) Barossa ✷✷✷ (Cab blend) 75 78 80 82 83 84 86 87 88 90 The ebullient German winemaker merged his business with MILDARA late '91. Dazzling labels, extraordinary wine-show successes, mastery of blending varieties and areas, and lashings of new oak all continue, though signs are that less extreme sensations are on the way.

Botobolar Mudgee ✷✷ Marvellously eccentric little organic winery which exports successfully to the UK.

Bowen Estate Coonawarra ✷✷✷ (Shiraz) 78 81 82 84 87 90 91 (Cab) 79 80 82 84 86 90 91 Small winery; intense not heavy Cab and spicy Shiraz.

Brand Coonawarra ✷✷→✷✷✷ (Shiraz) 77' 78' 82 84 85 87 90 91 (Cab S) 70 71 74 79 81 82 84 87 90 91 Family estate now half owned by McWILLIAMS. Fine bold and stylish Chard, Cab and Shiraz under Laira label. A few quality blemishes in late '70s/early '80s now rectified.

Bridgewater Mill Adelaide Hills ✷✷✷ Second label of PETALUMA; suave wines, Sauv Bl and Shiraz best.

Brokenwood Hunter Valley ✷✷✷ (Shiraz) 75 79 80 82 83 86 87 89 91 (Cab S) 75 77 80 81 83 86 87 89 91 Exciting quality of Cab and Shiraz since '73 – Graveyard Shiraz is outstanding. New winery in '83 added high quality Chard and Sem.

Brown Brothers Milawa (Vic) ✷→✷✷✷ (Chard) 80 82 84 86 88 90 91 (Noble Ries) 70 72 74 76 78 82 84 85 Old family firm with new ideas: wide range of delicate single-grape wines, many from cool mountain districts. Chard, Ries. Dry white Muscat outstanding. See also All Saints.

Buring, Leo Barossa ✷✷→✷✷✷ (Ries) 70 71 73 75 79 82 84 86 87 88 90 91 'Chateau Leonay', old white-wine specialists, now owned by LINDEMANS. Steady Reserve Bin Ries is great with age.

Campbells of Rutherglen NE Vic ✷✷ Smooth ripe reds and good dessert wines, the latter in youthful fruity style.

Cape Clairault Margaret River ✷✷ Progressive producer of Sem, Sauv Bl and Cab, in reasonable quantities, with good progress in quality.

NB This edition introduces a new short-cut vintage category. Vintages in colour are the ones you should choose first for drinking in 1995.

Cape Mentelle Margaret River **→**** (Zin) 81 83 84 87 88 **90** 91 (Cab S) 78 81 82 83 86 88 **90** 91 Idiosyncratic robust Cab can be magnificent; also Zinfandel and v popular Sem. David Hohnen also founded Cloudy Bay, NZ. Both were bought in '90 by Veuve Clicquot.

Capel Vale SW (WA) *** (Ries) 84 86 88 89 **90** 91 93 (Chard) 85 86 87 89 **90** 91 93 Outstanding range of whites, incl Ries, Gewürz. Also vg Cab.

Cassegrain Hastings Valley (NSW) **→*** New winery on NSW coast, taking grapes both from local plantings and from HUNTER VALLEY.

Chambers' Rosewood NE Vic **→*** Good cheap table and great dessert wines, esp 'Tokay'.

Chapel Hill McLaren Vale (SA) **→**** (Shiraz, Cab) **90** 91 Once tiny, now booming: extra-rich fruity-oaky Chard, Shiraz, Cab; big show successes.

Chateau Le Amon Bendigo ** Stylish minty Cab, peppery Shiraz. V quiet.

Chateau Francois Hunter Valley ** Idiosyncratic operation of former Fisheries director: clean reds, soft whites and great olives.

Chateau Hornsby Alice Springs (N Territory) * A charming aberration and magnet for tourists to Ayer's Rock.

Chateau Rémy Great Western/Avoca ** (Cab S) 82 84 86 88 **90** 91 Owned by Rémy Martin. Sparkling based on Chard and Pinot N is much improved. Also good Blue Pyrenees Cab S.

Chateau Reynella S Vales *→**** ('Vintage Port') 67 70 71 72 75 77 79 81 82 87 88 Historic winery serving as HQ for BRL Hardy group. Pleasant table wines, superb vintage 'Port'.

Chateau Tahbilk Goulburn Valley **→*** (Marsanne) 70 72 74 75 80 82 86 88 89 **90** 92 (Shiraz) 68 71 76 79 80 81 84 86 88 91 92 (Cab) 62 64 65 66 71 76 79 81 83 86 88 **90** Beautiful historic family estate: long-lived Cab, Shiraz, Ries, Marsanne. Private Bins outstanding; value for money ditto. Sadly, Eric Purbrick died in '91. His grandson presses on.

Chateau Yaldara Barossa *→** A plethora of brands incl Acacia Hill, Ch Yaldara, Lakewood, Robert Thumm: oaky, slightly sweet, cheap.

Coldstream Hills Yarra Valley ***→**** (Chard) 86 88 **90** 91 92 (Pinot N) 87 88 **90** 91 92 (Cab S) 85 86 88 **90** 91 92 Well-known winery, est'd '85 by wine critic James Halliday. International acclaim for prize-winning Pinot, vg Chard (esp Reserve wines), delicate Cab and Merlot.

Conti, Paul Swan Valley ** Elegant Hermitage; fine Chard and other whites.

Coriole S Vales **→*** (Shiraz) 70 74 75 77 80 84 88 89 **90** 91 Shiraz (esp Lloyd Reserve) from old vines; nicely balanced by oak best, others solid.

Craigmoor Mudgee ** Oldest district winery, now part of ORLANDO group. Good Chard and Sem (the two are also blended), and Cab-Shiraz.

Croser Adelaide Hills ***→**** 87 88 **90** 92 93 Now Australia's top sparkling Chard-Pinot N blend. Offshoot of PETALUMA with Bollinger as partner. Lean, fine, with splendid backbone from Pinot N.

Cullens Willyabrup Margaret River *** (Chard) 81 82 85 86 87 88 **90** 92 93 (Cab S-Merlot) 80 81 82 84 86 87 89 **90** 91 Mother-daughter team pioneered the region with butch but kindly Cab-Merlot, substantial but subtle Sauv Bl and bold Chard: all real characters.

Dalwhinnie Pyrenees **→**** (Chard) 80 82 84 86 88 **90** 91 92 (Cab S) 80 82 85 86 88 **90** 91 3,500-case producer of concentrated rich Chard, Shiraz and Cab S, arguably the best in PYRENEES.

d'Arenberg S Vales *→*** Old-style family firm: big rustic red and Ries.

De Bortoli Griffith (NSW) *→*** (Noble Sem) 82 84 85 87 88 **90** 91 Irrigation-area winery. Standard reds and whites but magnificent sweet botrytised Sauternes-style Sem. See also next entry.

De Bortoli Yarra Valley **→*** (Chard) 88 **90** 91 92 (Cab S) 88 **90** 91 92 Formerly Ch Yarrinya: bought by De Bortoli and now YARRA's largest producer. Main label good to adequate; second, Windy Peak, vg value.

Delatite Central Vic ✱✱✱ (Ries) **82 83 86** 87 90 92 93 Rosalind Ritchie makes appropriately willowy and feminine Ries, Gewürz, Pinot N and Cab from this v cool mountainside v'yd.

Diamond Valley Yarra Valley ✱✱→✱✱✱ (Pinot N) 81 82 85 86 87 88 90 91 92 Producer of outstanding Pinot N in significant quantities; other wines good rather than great.

Domaine Chandon Yarra Valley ✱✱✱ The showpiece of the YARRA VALLEY. Sparkling wine from grapes grown in all the cooler parts of Australia, with strong direction from owner Moët & Chandon. Immediate success in UK under Green Point label.

Drayton's Bellevue Hunter Valley ✱✱ (Hermitage) 73 75 79 81 85 86 87 91 Traditional Hermitage and Sem, occasionally good Chard; recent quality improvements after a lapse.

Dromana Estate Mornington Peninsula ✱✱✱ (Chard) **86 88 90 91 92** (Cab-Merlot) **85 86** 88 90 92 Largest and best producer in district. Great skill in light fragrant Cabs, Pinots, Chards. Second label: Schinus Molle.

Dull technical stuff
Experiments to make palatable low-alcohol wine have made progress recently – notably in Australia, where Penfolds and Orlando have both used a technique known as the 'spinning cone' to remove alcohol: a method related to distillation. Wine enters a column of spinning cones at the top, nitrogen at the bottom. As the wine falls in a thin film, its alcohol (and some flavour) is driven off and collected by the nitrogen.

The winemaker then blends the two resulting fractions, one with alcohol and one without, into a palatable drink at the strength he wants – which for best results is about half-strength, or 6%. How good it tastes depends of course on the grapes; Chardonnay works well. Move over Diet Coke.

Eaglehawk Clare ✱→✱✱ Formerly Quelltaler. Once known for Granfiesta 'Sherry'. Recently good Ries and Sem. Owned by MILDARA BLASS.

Elgee Park Mornington Pensinsula ✱✱ Region's longest-established v'yd, producing good Cab-Merlot, Chard, Ries and a hatful of Viognier.

Evans Family Hunter Valley ✱✱✱ (Chard) **82 84 86 87** 88 91 93 Excellent Chard from small v'yd owned by family of Len Evans and made at ROTHBURY ESTATE. Fermented in new oak. Repays cellaring.

Evans and Tate Swan Valley ✱✱→✱✱✱ (Sem) **82 83 84** 88 89 91 92 93 (Cab) 81 82 84 86 88 90 91 Fine elegant Sem, Chard, Cab, Merlot from MARGARET RIVER, Redbrook. SWAN VALLEY Gnangara v'yds give useful Cab-Shiraz.

Forest Hills Mount Barker ✱✱→✱✱✱ Pioneer v'yd in region, now in common ownership with VASSE FELIX. Ries and Chard can be and usually are excellent.

Freycinet Tasmania ✱✱→✱✱✱ (Pinot N) **90 91 92** 93 East coast winery producing voluptuous rich Pinot N, good Chard and Cab.

Geoff Merrill S Vales ✱→✱✱✱ (Sem-Chard) 82 84 86 87 88 89 90 91 (Cab) 80 82 84 85 86 88 90 91 Ebullient maker of Geoff Merrill, Mt Hurtle and Cockatoo Ridge wines, sometimes elegant, sometimes a little thin.

Giaconda Central Vic ✱✱✱ (Chard) **86 88 90 91 92** (Pinot N) 88 89 91 92 Very small but ultra-fashionable winery nr Beechworth, producing eagerly sought Chard and Pinot N.

Goundrey Wines Great Southern (WA) ✱✱✱ (Ries) **82 85** 88 90 91 93 (Cab S) 77 81 83 85 87 88 89 90 Recent expansion and quality upgrade. Now in first rank: esp good Cabernet and wooded whites.

Grange See Penfolds.

Grant Burge Wines Barossa ✱✱→✱✱✱ Rapidly expanding output of silky-smooth reds and whites (vg Chard 93) from the best grapes of Burge's v'yd holdings. Burge was founder of KRONDORF. 70,000 cases.

Green Point See Domaine Chandon.

Hanging Rock Macedon (Vic) ✱→✱✱✱ (Shiraz) 87 88 90 91 Eclectic range: budget Picnic White/Red; huge Heathcote Shiraz; complex sparkling.

Hardy's S Vales, Barossa, Keppoch, etc *→**** (Eileen Chard) 85 86 89 90 91 ('Vintage Port') 56 65 69 71 75 76 80 81 82 87 88 Historic company using and blending wines from several areas. Best are Eileen Hardy and Thomas Hardy series and (Australia's greatest) 'Vintage Ports'. Hardy's bought HOUGHTON and CH REYNELLA and, more recently, STANLEY. Ch Reynella's beautifully restored buildings are now group headquarters. '92 merger with BERRI-RENMANO and public ownership (BRL Hardy) makes this Australia's second largest wine company.

Heathcote Bendigo ** Stylish producer of eclectic range showing abundant flavour and technical skill, but tends to syrupy Chard.

Heemskerk Tasmania *** (Ries) 84 86 88 90 91 92 93 (Chard) 82 84 86 87 88 90 91 92 A major commercial operation: herby Cab, promising Chard, also Pinot N and Ries. Recent partnership with Louis Roederer produced Jansz sparkling wine.

Heggies Adelaide Hills ** (Ries) 79 80 82 84 86 88 90 91 (Chard) 85 87 88 90 91 (Botrytis Ries) 84 86 88 90 91 92 V'yd at 500 metres in eastern Barossa Ranges owned by S SMITH & SONS; separately marketed: excellent Ries and Botrytis Ries.

Henschke Barossa ***→***** (Shiraz) 52 56 59 61 62 66 67 72 78 80 82 84 86 88 90 91 (Cab S) 78 80 81 84 85 86 88 90 91 125-year-old family business, perhaps Australia's best, known for delectable Shiraz (esp Hill of Grace), vg Cab and red blends. New high-country v'yds on ADELAIDE HILLS add excitement.

Hill-Smith Estate Adelaide Hills ** Another separate brand of S SMITH & SONS; Sauv Bl and Cab-Shiraz can be outstanding value.

Hollick Coonawarra *** (Chard) 84 86 87 90 91 (Cab S-Merlot) 84 85 86 89 90 91 Hollick family plus former TOLLANA winemaker: good Chard, Ries; much-followed reds, Whilga and Ravensworth.

Houghton Swan Valley *→*** (Supreme) 81 82 84 86 87 89 91 93 The most famous old winery of WA. Soft ripe Supreme Chard is their top wine; a national classic. Also excellent Cab, Verdelho, etc. See Hardy's.

Huntington Estate Mudgee **→*** (Cab S) 75 77 79 81 83 84 86 89 91 Small winery; the best in MUDGEE. Fine Cabs, clean Sem and Chard. Invariably under-priced.

Idyll Geelong ** Small winery making Gewürz and Cab in v individual style. Also 'Blush' rosé. A pioneer exporter.

Jim Barry Wines Clare **→*** (Armagh) 85 87 88 89 90 Hard-working family firm now doing esp well with Ries; The Armagh is a spectacular (and expensive) pretender to the throne of GRANGE Hermitage.

Kaiser Stuhl Barossa *→** Now part of PENFOLDS; a huge winery taking fruit from diverse sources. Diminishing importance as a brand.

Katnook Estate Coonawarra *** (Chard) 80 82 84 86 90 (Cab S) 80 81 82 85 86 90 91 Excellent pricey Cab and Chard; also Sauv, Pinot N, Ries.

Krondorf Wines Barossa **→*** Part of MILDARA BLASS group with niche market brands: Show Reserve wines are best.

Lake's Folly Hunter Valley **** (Chard) 81 82 85 86 87 89 91 92 93 (Cab S) 69 72 75 77 78 81 83 85 87 89 91 The work of an inspired surgeon from Sydney. Cab is v fine, complex. Chard exciting and age-worthy.

Lark Hill Canberra District **→*** Best and most consistent CANBERRA producer, making esp attractive Ries.

Leasingham Clare *→*** Important medium-sized quality winery purchased by HARDY's in '87. Good Ries, Sem, Chard and Cab-Malbec blends under Domaine label.

Leconfield Coonawarra **→*** (Ries) 84 86 88 90 91 (Cab S) 80 82 84 88 90 91 COONAWARRA Cab of great style. Ries and Chard improving under former TYRRELL winemaker.

Leeuwin Estate Margaret River **→**** (Chard) 80 82 83 85 86 87 89 (Cab S) 79 81 82 84 85 87 88 89 Leading W Australia estate, lavishly equipped, producing superb (and v expensive) Chard; developing fine Pinot N, vg Ries, Sauv Bl and Cab.

Lehmann Wines, Peter Barossa ★★→★★★ Defender of BAROSSA faith, Peter Lehmann makes vast quantities of wine (some sold in bulk), with v fine 'special cuvées' under own label; now public listed and flourishing.

Lindemans originally Hunter Valley, now everywhere ★→★★★ (Hunter Sem) 66 67 70 72 75 79 80 86 87 91 92 (Hunter Shiraz) 59 65 66 70 73 75 79 82 83 86 87 (Padthaway Chard) 83 85 86 87 88 90 91 92 (Coonawarra Red) 76 78 80 82 85 86 88 90 91 One of the oldest firms, now a giant owned by PENFOLDS. Owns BURING in BAROSSA, ROUGE HOMME in COONAWARRA, and imp't v'yds at PADTHAWAY. Outstanding Chard and Coonawarra reds. Pioneer of new styles, yet still makes fat, old-style 'Hunters'. Bin-number Classics can be vg. Dominant performer at wine shows.

Little's Hunter Valley ★★ Popular little winery with wide range of wines; energetic exporters.

Marsh Estate Hunter Valley ★★→★★★ Substantial producer of good Sem, Shiraz and Cab of growing quality.

McWilliams Hunter Valley & Riverina ★→★★★ (Elizabeth Sem) 74 79 80 81 82 84 86 87 88 89 91 Famous family of HUNTER VALLEY winemakers at Mount Pleasant: Hermitage and Semillon – 'Elizabeth' is the only bottle-aged Sem (6 yrs) sold and is very good value. Also pioneers in RIVERINA with noble varieties, incl Cabernet Sauvignon and sweet white Lexia. Quality is showing marked improvement.

Mildara Coonawarra & Murray Valley ★→★★★★ (Coonawarra Cab) 63 64 68 70 71 78 79 80 82 85 86 88 90 'Sherry' and brandy specialists at Mildara on the Murray River, also make fine Cab S and Riesling at COONAWARRA. Now own BALGOWNIE, BLASS, KRONDORF and YELLOWGLEN too.

Miramar Mudgee ★★→★★★ Some of MUDGEE's best whites, esp Chard.

Mitchells Clare ★★★ (Ries) 82 85 86 87 90 91 93 (Cab S) 76 77 80 82 85 87 90 91 92 Small family winery making excellent Riesling and Cab S.

Mitchelton Goulburn Valley ★★→★★★ Big, modern winery. A wide range incl a vg wood-matured Marsanne, Shiraz, Cab from COONAWARRA; classic Ries from GOULBURN VALLEY is one of Australia's v best. Second label, Thomas Mitchell, is esp good value.

Montrose Mudgee ★★→★★★ Reliable underrated producer of vg Chard and Cab blends. Now part of the ORLANDO group.

Moondah Brook Estate Gingin (WA) ★★ HOUGHTON v'yd 80 km NW of Perth: v smooth flavourful Chard, Chenin Bl, Verdelho and Cab.

Moorilla Estate Tasmania ★★★ (Ries) 81 82 83 88 89 90 91 93 Senior winery on outskirts of Hobart on Derwent River: vg Ries, Traminer and Chard; Pinot N disappointing.

Morris NE Vic ★★→★★★★★ Old winery at Rutherglen for Australia's greatest dessert Muscats and 'Tokays'; also recently v good low-price table wine.

Moss Wood Margaret River ★★★★ (Sem) 80 81 82 83 85 86 87 88 91 92 93 (Chard) 80 85 89 90 92 93 (Cab) 74 77 80 81 83 86 87 90 91 92 To many the best MARGARET RIVER winery (only 29 v'yd acres). Sem, Cab, Pinot, Chard, all with rich fruit flavours, not unlike top California wines.

Mount Avoca Pyrenees ★→★★★ Solid alcoholic and at times distinctly rustic wines with considerable impact; the best age well.

Mount Helen Strathbogie Ranges (Vic) ★→★★★ The high-altitude v'yd owned by TISDALL with its own brand; complex high-flavoured wines which only occasionally reach their full potential.

Mount Langi Ghiran Great Western ★★→★★★ (Shiraz) 82 84 85 86 88 89 90 91 92 Producer of superb rich peppery Rhône-like Shiraz, vg Cab and less exhilarating Ries.

Mount Mary Yarra Valley ★★★★ (Pinot N) 78 79 82 83 85 86 87 89 90 91 (CabS-CabF-Merlot) 76 78 79 80 82 84 85 86 88 90 91 Dr John Middleton is a perfectionist making tiny amounts of suave Chard, vivid Pinot N, and (best of all) Cab S-Cab F-Merlot. All age well.

Mountadam Barossa ★★★ (Chard) 82 84 87 89 90 91 92 High Eden winery of David and Adam Wynn. Chardonnay is rich, voluptuous and long. Other labels include David Wynn, Eden Ridge.

Murray Robson Wines Hunter Valley ★★ The reincarnation of Murray Robson in a winery nr ROTHBURY.

Orlando (Gramp's) Barossa ★★→★★★ (St Hugo Cab S) 80 82 84 85 86 88 90 91 Great pioneering company, bought by management in '88 but now owned by Pernod Ricard of France. Full range from best-selling Jacob's Creek 'Claret' to excellent Jacaranda Ridge Cab from COONAWARRA. See also Wyndham Estate.

Parker Estate Coonawarra ★★★ New estate making exceptional Cab, esp Terra Rossa First Growth.

Penfolds orig Adelaide, now everywhere ★→★★★★ (Grange) 55 62 63 66 67 71 75 76 80 83 85 86 88 90 (Bin 707) 64 65 66 78 80 83 84 86 88 90 91 (Bin 389) 66 70 71 82 83 86 87 88 90 91 Ubiquitous excellent company in BAROSSA, CLARE, COONAWARRA, RIVERINA, etc. Bought LINDEMANS in '90. Its Grange Hermitage (78 80 82') is deservedly ★★★★. Bin 707 Cab not far behind. Other bin-numbered wines (eg Cab-Shiraz 389) can be outstanding. Grandfather 'Port' often excellent. Consistently Australia's best red-wine co. The Penfolds/Lindemans group was taken over by South Australian Brewing Co, already owner of SEPPELT, in '90.

Penley Estate Coonawarra ★★→★★★ High profile, no-expense-spared newcomer: rich, textured, fruit-and-oak Cab; also Shiraz-Cab and Chard.

Petaluma Adelaide Hills ★★★★ (Ries) 79 80 82 84 86 87 90 91 93 (Chard) 77 78 82 85 86 87 88 90 91 92 (Cab S) 79 82 85 86 88 90 91 A rocket-like '80s success with COONAWARRA Cab S, ADELAIDE HILLS Chard, CLARE Ries, all processed at winery in Adelaide Hills. Reds have become richer from '84 on, 88 and 90 are outstanding. Also: BRIDGEWATER MILL. Now owns TIM KNAPPSTEIN WINES. See also Croser.

Petersons Hunter Valley ★★→★★★ For a time, the most promising small HUNTER winery for exceptional Chard and vg Semillon; recently wobbly.

Piper's Brook Tasmania ★★★ (Ries) 79 82 84 85 89 91 92 93 (Chard) 82 84 86 87 88 91 92 Cool-area pioneer with vg Riesling and Pinot Noir, excellent Chard from the Tamar Valley nr Launceston. Lovely labels.

Pirramimma S Vales ★→★★ Big supply of good standard; reds best.

Plantagenet Mount Barker ★★→★★★ (Chard) 86 88 89 90 91 93 (Shiraz) 77 79 82 83 85 86 88 90 91 (Cab S) 77 79 81 83 85 86 87 89 90 The region's largest producer: wide range of varieties, especially rich Chardonnay, Shiraz and vibrant potent Cabernet Sauvignon.

Primo Estate Adelaide Plains ★★★ Successes incl vg botrytised Ries, tangy Colombard and rich Joseph Cab.

Quelltaler See Eaglehawk.

Redman Coonawarra ★→★★ (Cab S) 70 71 76 79 87 90 91 93 The most famous old name in COONAWARRA; makes two wines: 'Claret' and Cabernet. Quality reviving after a disappointing period.

Renmano Murray Valley ★→★★ Huge coop now part of Hardy BRL (see Hardy's). 'Chairman's Selections' value. Exceedingly voluptuous Chard.

Reynold's Yarraman Estate Upper Hunter Valley ★★ Former stone prison building promises well as winery of former HOUGHTON and WYNDHAM winemaker Jon Reynolds.

Rockford Barossa ★★→★★★ Small producer, wide range of thoroughly individual wines, often made from v old low-yielding v'yds. Sparkling Black Shiraz has super-cult status.

Rosemount Upper Hunter & Coonawarra ★★→★★★ Rich unctuous HUNTER 'Show' Chard is an international smash. This and COONAWARRA Cab lead the wide range, which gets better every year.

Rothbury Estate Hunter Valley ★★★→★★★★ (Cowra Chard) 81 86 90 91 92 (Shiraz) 73 75 79 80 81 83 89 91 A true estate with over 500 acres of v'yd. Now a public listed company under chairmanship of Len Evans. Traditional HUNTER Shiraz and Sems to keep for ever. Rich buttery COWRA Chard is vg and good value too. Hunter Chard now barrel-fermented. New: Chard and Sauv Bl v'yds in Marlborough, NZ. Also owns BAILEY'S and ST HUBERTS.

Rouge Homme Coonawarra ✴✴ (Shiraz-Cab S) 78 79 80 81 85 86 90 91 Separately branded and promoted arm of LINDEMANS with keenly priced Chard and Shiraz-Cab leaders.

Rymill Riddoch Run Coonawarra ✴✴→✴✴✴ Descendants of John Riddoch carrying on the good work of the founder of COONAWARRA. Strong dense Shiraz and Cab esp noteworthy.

St Hallett Barossa ✴✴✴ (Old Block) 80 82 83 84 86 88 90 91 Rejuvenated winery. 100-yr-old vines give splendid Old Block Shiraz. Rest of range is smooth and stylish.

St Huberts Yarra Valley ✴✴→✴✴✴ (Chard) 82 84 86 87 88 90 91 92 (Cab) 77 79 82 84 86 88 90 91 92 Acquired by ROTHBURY in late '92; accent on rich buttery Chard and smooth 'berry' Cab. Second label is Rowan.

St Leonards NE Vic ✴✴ Excellent varieties sold only 'cellar door' and by mailing list, incl exotics, eg Orange Muscat.

Saltram Barossa ✴→✴✴✴ Merged with ROTHBURY in late '93. Pinnacle Selection is the best label; also good are Mamre Brook wines.

Sandalford Swan Valley ✴→✴✴ Fine old winery with contrasting styles of red and white single-grape wines from SWAN and MARGARET RIVER areas. Wonderful old fortified Verdelho.

Schinus Molle See Dromana Estate.

Scotchman's Hill Geelong ✴✴ Newcomer making significant quantities of v stylish Pinot N, good Chard and Cab F at modest prices.

Seaview S Vales ✴✴→✴✴✴ Owned by PENFOLDS. Chard, Shiraz-Cab and Cab S frequently rise above their station in life, while sparkling wines are among Australia's best, now based on Pinot N and Chard.

Seppelt Barossa, Great Western, Keppoch, etc ✴→✴✴✴ (Hermitage) 70 78 81 84 85 86 89 90 91 (Salinger) 84 86 88 90 91 Far-flung producers of Australia's most popular sparkling (Great Western Brut); also good dessert and some vg private bin wines, incl Chard from GREAT WESTERN and Drumborg (in Victoria), PADTHAWAY and BAROSSA (in S Australia). Top sparkling is highly regarded 'Salinger'. Now linked with PENFOLDS/LINDEMANS/BURING, etc, to form Australia's biggest wine co.

Seville Estate Yarra Valley ✴✴→✴✴✴ (Chard) 82 86 87 90 91 92 (Shiraz) 85 86 88 90 91 92 Tiny winery with Chard, v late-picked Riesling, Shiraz, Pinot N and vg Cab.

Shaw & Smith S Vales ✴✴✴ Trendy new venture of flying winemaker Martin Shaw and Australia's first MW Michael Hill-Smith. Crisp Sauv Blanc and complex barrel-fermented Chardonnay are the two wines.

S Smith & Sons (alias Yalumba) Barossa ✴✴→✴✴✴ Big old family firm with considerable verve, using computers, juice evaluation, etc, to produce full spectrum of high-quality wines, incl HILL-SMITH ESTATE. HEGGIES and Yalumba Signature Reserve are best. Angas Brut, a good value sparkling wine, and Oxford Landing Chard are now world brands.

Stanley Bottled under Stanley-Leasingham label. See Leasingham.

Stanton & Killeen NE Vic ✴✴ Small old family firm. Rich Muscats, also strong Moodemere reds.

Stoniers Mornington Peninsula ✴✴✴ (Chard) 88 90 91 92 (Pinot N) 86 88 90 91 92 Seriously challenging DROMANA ESTATE for pride of place on the Peninsula. Chard, Pinot N are consistently vg; also Cab.

Taltarni Great Western/Avoca ✴✴✴ (Shiraz) 78 79 81 82 84 86 88 89 90 91 (Cab S) 79 81 82 84 86 88 89 90 91 Dominique Portet, brother of Bernard (Clos du Val, Napa), son of André (ex-Ch Lafite), makes huge but balanced reds for long ageing, good Sauv and adequate sparkling.

Tarrawarra Yarra Valley ✴✴✴ (Chard) 87 88 89 91 92 (Pinot N) 88 91 92 Multimillion dollar investment: limited quantities of idiosyncratic expensive Chard, robust long-lived Pinot N. Tunnel Hill is second label, Ryrie is third.

Taylors Wines Clare ✴→✴✴ Large unit: range of inexpensive table wines.

Terrace Vale Hunter Valley ✴✴ Small syndicate-owned winery with French winemaker. Good Sem and Chard.

Tim Knappstein Wines Clare *** Tim K, an exceptionally gifted winemaker, makes Ries, Fumé Bl, Gewürz, Cab. New Lenswood range from ADELAIDE HILLS produces flashy Sauv and Pinot N (see Petaluma).

Tisdall Wines Goulburn Valley **→*** Large winery at Echuca making local (Rosbercon) wines and finer ones from central Victorian ranges (Mt Helen Cab, Chard, and Ries), acquired by MILDARA BLASS in '93.

Tollana Barossa **→*** Old company once famous for brandy. Has latterly made some fine Cab, Chard, Ries. Acquired by PENFOLDS in '87.

Tolley Pedare Barossa ** Century-old family-run winery crushing 3,000 tonnes of grapes pa. Gewürz consistently among best in Australia; wooded Sem, Chard and Cab honest and reliable.

Tulloch Hunter Valley *→** Old name at Pokolbin for dry reds, Chard, Verdelho. Now part of PENFOLDS group but a shadow of its former self.

Tyrrell Hunter Valley **→*** (Sem Vat 1) 70 73 77 79 83 86 87 90 91 (Chard Vat 47) 72 73 77 79 82 84 85 89 90 92 (Shiraz Vats) 73 75 77 79 80 83 85 87 89 91 Some of best trad HUNTER wines, Hermitage and Sem. Pioneered Chard with big rich Vat 47. Also delicate Pinot.

Vasse Felix Margaret River **→*** (Cab S) 76 78 79 83 85 88 89 91 With CULLENS, pioneer of the MARGARET RIVER. Elegant Cabs, notable for midweight balance, bought by the late Robert Holmes à Court in '87.

Virgin Hills Bendigo/Ballarat **** 74 75 78 79 80 82 83 85 87 88 90 91 Tiny supplies of one blended red (Cab-Shiraz-Malbec) of legendary style and balance.

Wendouree Clare *** 83 86 89 90 91 Treasured maker (in tiny quantities) of some of Australia's most powerful and concentrated reds based on Shiraz, Cab S and Malbec.

Westfield Swan Valley *→** John Kosovich's Cab, Chard and Verdelho show particular finesse for a hot climate. Also good 'Port'.

Wirra Wirra S Vales **→*** (Ries) 76 79 81 84 86 89 91 92 93 (Chard) 82 84 88 90 91 92 (Cab S) 77 80 84 87 90 91 Under PETALUMA influence: high quality, beautifully-packaged whites and reds have made a big impact.

Woodleys Barossa ** Well-known for low-price Queen Adelaide label. Acquired by SEPPELT in '85.

Wyndham Estate Branxton (NSW) *→** Aggressive large HUNTER and MUDGEE group with brands: CRAIGMOOR, Hollydene, Hunter Estate, MONTROSE, Richmond Grove and Saxonvale. Acquired by ORLANDO in '90.

Wynns Coonawarra **→*** (Shiraz) 53 54 55 63 65 70 82 85 86 88 90 91 (Cab S) 57 58 59 60 62 82 85 86 88 90 91 Since its acquisition by PENFOLDS in '85 has produced even better wines: Ries, Chard, Shiraz and Cab – all very good, esp John Riddoch Cab.

Yalumba See S Smith & Sons.

Yarra Burn Yarra Valley ** Estate making Sem, Sauv, Chard, sparkling Pinot N, Cab; has found going tough, but perseveres.

Yarra Ridge Yarra Valley **→*** Expanding young winery, v successful Chard, Cab, Sauv Bl, Pinot, all with flavour and finesse at modest prices. Controlling interest acquired by MILDARA BLASS in '93.

Yarra Yering Yarra Valley ***→**** (Dry Reds) 78 79 80 81 82 83 84 85 87 90 91 Best-known Lilydale boutique winery. Esp racy powerful Pinot N, deep herby Cab (Dry Red No 1) and Shiraz (Dry Red No 2).

Yellowglen Bendigo/Ballarat *→** High-flying sparkling winemaker owned by MILDARA. Sales are more impressive than quality.

Yeringberg Yarra Valley *** (Marsanne) 83 84 86 88 90 91 92 (Cab S) 74 75 76 79 80 81 82 84 86 87 88 90 91 92 Dreamlike historic estate still in the hands of the founding family, now again producing v high quality Marsanne, Chard, Cab, Pinot N, in minute quantities.

For key to grape variety abbreviations, see pages 6–9.

New Zealand

Over the last decade New Zealand has made a world-wide name for table wines (mainly white) of startling quality, well able to compete with those of Australia or California. In 1982 it exported 12,000 cases; in 1992 some 403,000. Many now see it as the top cool-climate region among the world's newer wine countries.

White grapes predominate. Formerly dominant Müller-Thurgau is being rapidly overtaken by varieties in demand overseas: in 1993 Chardonnay supplanted it as number one. Next in line are Sauvignon Blanc, Cabernet Sauvignon and Pinot Noir respectively, with Riesling and Chenin Blanc gaining prestige.

Intensity of fruit flavours and crisp acidity are the hallmarks of New Zealand's wines. No region on earth can match the pungency of its best Sauvignon Blanc. Barrel fermentation and/or ageing add to their complexity (or at least flavour). Marlborough also makes very fine sweet Rieslings with botrytis. 1989 was perhaps the first vintage to produce really worthy reds. The principal areas and producers follow.

Allan Scott Blenheim Est '90. Chard, Ries and good Sauv Bl (first good vintage 92). Neighbour of famous CLOUDY BAY.

Ata Rangi Martinborough Est '80 primarily for reds. Vg Pinot N and Cab-Merlot-Petit Syrah (Célèbre). Now also excellent Chard.

Auckland (r) 89 90 91 92 93 (w) 89 91 92 93 Largest city in NZ. Location of head offices of major wineries; many medium and small in outskirts.

Babich Henderson (nr Auckland) Large old Auckland family firm, highly respected in NZ for consistent quality and value. Also uses MARLBOROUGH, GISBORNE and HAWKES BAY grapes. Good Chards (esp Irongate, Stopbank), Sauv Bl (92 is big medal-winner, vg and value), Sém-Chard, Gewürz, Cab S and Cab-Merlot. Pinot N still not so good.

Brajkovich See Kumeu River.

Brookfields Hawkes Bay One of the area's top v'yds: Chard, Sauv Bl, Cab S, Cab-Merlot (outstanding).

Cellier Le Brun Renwick, nr Blenheim Small winery est'd by son of Champagne family: some of NZ's best classic method sparkling incl vintage, NV, rosé (vg 89 90), Blanc de Blancs (90 exceptional).

Chifney Wines Martinborough Vg Cab S and good Chard.

Church Road Hawkes Bay Owned by MONTANA but run independently: top class Chard and Cab S, from old (McWilliams) estate.

Clearview Estate Hawkes Bay Small producer since '92. Already some good Chard and Cab S.

Cloudy Bay Blenheim Offshoot of W Australia's Cape Mentelle, both bought in '90 by Veuve Clicquot. Top name for Sauv Bl, Chard. Richly subtle Cab-Merlot 89 shows equal promise. New release Pelorus classic method sparkling is rich and dense (87 88 89).

Collard Henderson (nr Auckland) Small family winery using grapes from four main areas: top-award Chard from each. Also Sauv (esp Rothesay), Chenin, Ries, Cab-Merlot, Sém. Consistent quality (esp HAWKES BAY).

Cooks Hawkes Bay Large firm merged with CORBANS and McWilliams in '85. Good steady Chard (esp Winemakers Reserve). Also Cab-Merlot and late-harvest Sauv Bl-Sém. Value.

Coopers Creek Huapai Valley (NW of Auckland) Small winery augmenting own grapes with GISBORNE, HAWKES BAY and MARLBOROUGH fruit. Exporting good Chard, Sauv Bl, Ries, dry and late-harvest. Also Cab S-Merlot and popular blends: Coopers Dry (white), Coopers Red.

Corbans Henderson (nr Auckland) Old-established firm has grown to incorporate COOKS, McWilliams and (new premium brand) STONELEIGH (at MARLBOROUGH) and Longridge (HAWKES BAY). Vg Sauv, Chard, Ries, Cab. Corbans White Label collection is good low-priced. Additional premium wines: Robard & Butler label, classic method Amadeus sparkling.

Delegat's Henderson (nr Auckland) One of NZ's largest family-owned/ run wineries: v'yds in HAWKES BAY. Good Chard, Sauv Bl; Proprietor's Reserve Cabs, Merlots (89 90 91 93) outstanding. Also Chard and Sauv from MARLBOROUGH sold under successful Oyster Bay label.

De Redcliffe Mangatawhiri (SE of Auckland) Small comprehensive winery and resort 'Hotel du Vin'; good Chard, Ries, Sauv Bl, Sém, Cab-Merlot.

Deutz Auckland The Champagne firm in a pioneer joint venture with MONTANA. 'Classic method' is brisk, lively and vg.

Esk Valley Bayview (Hawkes Bay) Former large family firm, now merged with VILLA MARIA/VIDAL. Small range incl vg dry Chenin, and some of NZ's best reds, esp 90 91 Merlot and Merlot-Cab F, Cab-Merlot Private Bin.

Giesen Estate Burnham (S of Christchurch) and Canterbury (S Island) German family winery: good Chards (Reserve School Road), Sauv, botrytised Ries, Cab-Merlot from own and some MARLBOROUGH grapes.

Gisborne (r) 89' 90 91 92 (w) 89 90 91 Site of 3 large wineries, CORBANS, MONTANA and PENFOLDS, and centre of large viticultural area incl MATAWHERO and Tolaga Bay. Good for Müller-T, Chard, Sém and Gewürz.

Goldwater Waiheke Island Small v'yd at sea edge, esp for Cab-Merlot; also MARLBOROUGH Chard (outstanding own-grown 92 93 Delamore).

Grove Mill Blenheim Excellent new winery bursting onto the scene with 89 Chard; Lansdowne in '90 even better, also 91. Vg Blackbirch Cab S, Drylands botrytis Sauv Bl. Also Gewürz, Sauv Bl, Ries and Pinotage.

Hawkes Bay (r) 89 90 91' 92 (w) 89 91' 92 93 Large wine region on east coast of N Island. Known for high quality grapes, esp Chard and Cab.

Highfield Estate Marlborough Grower with award-winning Sauv Bl (oak-aged too), Chard, Ries, Merlot.

Hunters Marlborough Well-est'd small progressive winery using only MARLBOROUGH grapes. Highly reputed for outstanding Sauv Bl (oaky 'Fumé' style), and Chard. Ries since '89. Also Cab S and Pinot N.

Jackson Estate Blenheim Large private v'yd. First vintage 91: impressive Sauv (91 92), also Chard, Ries (sweet botrytis version one of NZ's best).

Kumeu River Kumeu (NW of Auckland) Family-run winery (son Michael is NZ's first MW). Outstanding Fumé-style Sauv, Chard, vg Cab-Merlot. Second label under family name, Brajkovich.

Landfall Wines Gisborne New organically-run winery with good Chard (Revington Vineyard, 89 90). Also vg Gewürz, Sauv Bl, Pinot N.

Lincoln Vineyards Henderson (nr Auckland) Medium-sized family winery; esp for Chard, Chenin Bl and Cab. 88, 90 show real promise. Other varietals: Sauv Bl, Ries, Müller-T, Merlot.

Marlborough (r) 89 91 (w) 89 91 92 Leading export (and now NZ's largest) wine region, at N end of South Island on stony plain formed by Wairau River. Well-suited to white varieties Chard, Sauv Bl and Ries, but also Cab S and promising Pinot N. Potential here for vg sparkling.

Martinborough (r) 89' 90 91 (w) 89' 90 91 New smallish appellation in S Wairarapa (North Island). Stony soils, similar to MARLBOROUGH.

Martinborough Vineyards Martinborough Largest of area's small estates, noted for Pinot N (89 91). Also Chard, 'Fumé' Sauv, Ries, Gewurz.

Matawhero nr Gisborne Small winery, esp Gewürz. Also concentrated aromatic Chard, Sauv Bl-Sém. Reds are Cab-Merlot, Pinot N, Syrah.

Matua Valley NW of Auckland One of NZ's best, most consistent wineries. Pioneer with new varieties. Own grapes supplemented by HAWKES BAY, GISBORNE & MARLBOROUGH fruit. Wide range incl Chard (from Ararimu & Judd Estate, Gisborne), Sauv Bl and Fumé Blanc. Top-class Cab S (v fine Ararimu). Vg wines under Shingle Peak label.

Merlen Wines Marlborough German-born Almuth Lorenz makes excellent Chard and Ries (90 91 92) with long life ahead. Also Sauv Bl, Gewürz.

Mills Reef Bay of Plenty Small-scale producer (since '89) of top quality stunning Chard, also Sauv Bl from HAWKES BAY grapes, Ries, Cab, Merlot.

Milton nr Gisborne Small organic producer. Good Chard (Clos de Ste-Anne 89 outstanding) and Ries (dry and late harvest, vg 91). Splendid barrel-fermented Chenin Bl (87 90) like fine Anjou.

Mission Greenmeadows (Hawkes Bay) Oldest continuing wine establishment in NZ, French mission-founded and still run by Society of Mary. Good Sém-Sauv Bl and Cab-Merlot; Reserve Cab-S is best wine by far.

Montana Auckland and Hawkes Bay NZ's largest wine enterprise: wineries in GISBORNE, MARLBOROUGH; incorporating Penfolds label (in NZ only). Pioneer v'yds in Marlborough, also uses Gisborne and HAWKES BAY grapes. Marlb'gh labels: Sauv, Chard (vg; outstanding Show Reserves), Ries, Cab, Pinot. Gisborne Chard also big-selling, sound. Original Lindauer sparkling joined by vg cuvée DEUTZ. An input of French know-how in recent Cordier joint venture should improve HAWKES BAY reds.

Morton Estate Tauranga (Bay of Plenty) Expanding winery bought by Mildara (of Australia) in '89: excellent Chard (range is best black label, white then yellow labels). Also Fumé Bl, Gewürz, Ries and good classic method sparkling (89 90 91).

Nautilus nr Auckland Owned by Australia's Yalumba, this young winery produces a vg Chard from MARLBOROUGH and Sauv Bl from HAWKES BAY fruit.

Neudorf Nelson Charming small-scale winery: award-winning meaty highly-scented Chard (89 90 91), good Ries, Sauv Bl and Pinot N.

Ngatarawa nr Hastings (Hawkes Bay) Boutique winery in old stables of est'd HAWKES BAY family. Good Glazebrook label Cab-Merlot. Also vg Chard (Alwyn) and good Sauv Bl.

Nobilo NW of Auckland NZ's largest family winery: own plus GISBORNE, HAWKES BAY, MARLBOROUGH fruit. Good Chard (Marlb'h and Dixon V'yd), vg pungent Sauv, Sém; long recognized for ageable red: eg Cab, Pinotage.

Oyster Bay See Delegats.

Palliser Estate Martinborough Ambitious new winery: first vintage 89. Good Chard, Sauv Bl, Ries; also v rich intense Pinot N.

Pask, C J Hawkes Bay Rising star of the area; outstanding Chard and Sauv Bl since 91. Also good Cab S, Pinot N and Cab-Merlot.

Robard & Butler See Corbans.

Rongapai Waikato (S of Auckland) German-influenced winery esp for botrytised Riesling and Chard. Now with Pinot N, Merlot, Cab S and Cab S-Merlot.

St Nesbit Karaka (S of Auckland) Expanding boutique winery for well-made barrique-matured red blend: Cab S-Cab F-Merlot (vg 91). Also rosé (when main vintage below standard).

Seifried Estate Upper Moutere (nr Nelson) Small winery started by Austrian: esp Chard, Sauv Bl, Ries (dry, late-harvest), Pinot.

Selak's Kumeu (NW of Auckland)   Small stylish family firm with export reputation for vg fresh sharpish Sauv, Chard (Founders Selection best), classic sparkling. Grapes: local, MARLBOROUGH, GISBORNE, HAWKES BAY.

Stoneleigh See Corbans.

Stonyridge Waiheke Island (nr Auckland)   Boutique winery concentrating on two reds in Bordeaux style: Larose is exceptional, one of NZ's best (esp 87 93, also good 91 92), Airfield is vg second label.

Te Kairanga Martinborough   Largest winery in region, with underground facilities. Chard, Sauv Bl, Pinot N, Cab S.

Te Mata Havelock North (Hawkes Bay)   Restored winery for good Chard (esp Elston) and Sauv Bl from nearby v'yds, plus one of NZ's v best Cab blends, 'Coleraine' Cab-Merlot (91 92) from proprietor's home v'yd.

Vavasour nr Blenheim   First vintage 89. 91 Chards top quality; Dashwood Chard also good. Vg Fumé Bl, Sauv, Cab S-Merlot, Cab S-Cab Fr.

Vidal Hastings (Hawkes Bay)   Top-class atmospheric old winery, merged with VILLA MARIA. Vg HAWKES BAY Chards (90 91), Cab, Cab-Merlot, Fumé Bl.

Villa Maria Mangere (S Auckland)   Large co incl VIDAL and ESK VALLEY. Ihumatao (nr Auckland airport), GISBORNE, HAWKES BAY grapes. Esp oak-fermented Chard, Sauv (and wooded 'Fumé'), Gewürz, Cab, Cab-Merlot.

Waipara Springs N Canterbury   Recent producer of model Sauv Bl, Chard and Pinot N (90 91 good). To follow (most is exported).

Wairau River Marlborough   Small winery, full-flavoured Sauv and Chard.

South Africa

Quality in South Africa's table wines began around 1975 when vineyard owners started to add to their plantings of Cabernet Sauvignon, already successful, the greater challenges of Chardonnay, Sauvignon Blanc and even Pinot Noir. New laws in 1973 defining Wines of Origin encouraged new small estates. The 1980s success of small new wineries encouraged others to buy oak barrels from France. Cellarmasters are now showing more care in harvesting and cellar treatment and standards are reaching those of eg Australia.

Allesverloren r *→** (Cab S) 86 87 89 91   Old 395-acre family estate, best known for 'Port' (86). Also hefty well-oaked but not always long-lived CAB and Shiraz (88 89) from hot wheatlands district of Malmesbury.

Alphen *   Gilbeys brand name for wines from STELLENBOSCH area.

Alto r **→*** (Cab) 86 87 89   Atlantic-facing mountain v'yds S of STELLENBOSCH. Solid CAB, Cab-Merlot, Shiraz. Best since mid-'80s (with new French oak).

Altydgedacht r w *→** (Cab S) 85 86 87 88 89   Durbanville estate, best for CAB; also gutsy Tintoretto blend of Barbera and Shiraz.

Avontuur r w ** (r) 87 89 90 91   200-acre ST'BOSCH v'yd, bottling since '87. Soft Bordeaux-style blend, Avon Rouge; CAB, Merlot, promising CHARD.

Backsberg r w **→*** (r) 84 88 87 89 91 92 (Merlot) 90 (Chard) 86 88 89 90 91 92   Prize-winning 395-acre PAARL estate. Pioneered oak-fermented CHARD in mid-'80s (with US advice. Delicious B'x blend Klein Babylonstoren is best; also vg oaked SAUV John Martin.

Bellingham r w *   Big-selling brand of DGB. Sound reds, popular whites, esp sweet, soft, CAPE RIES-based Johannisberger (exported as Cape Gold).

Bergkelder Big STELLENBOSCH co, member of Oude Meester group, making/distributing many brands (FLEUR DU CAP, GRUNBERGER), 17 estate wines. First to use French oak (now 10,000 barrels), top for fine oaked reds.

Bertrams r ** (Cab) 84 88 87 89 90 91 94 (Shiraz) 86 89   Gilbeys brand of varietals, esp Shiraz, PINOTAGE. Also Robert Fuller Res B'x-style blend.

Beyerskloof r *** (Cab S) 89 90 91   New small STELLENBOSCH property, devoted to vg tannic deep-flavoured CAB S.

Blaauwklippen r w ★★→★★★ (r) 84 86 87 88 89 90 91   STELLENBOSCH winery with some of the Cape's best bold reds, esp CAB Reserve. Also S Africa's top Zin (88 89); patchy but improving CHARD; good off-dry RIES.

Bloemendal r w ★→★★ (Cab) 88 89 91 (Chard) 90 91 92   Sea-cooled Durbanville estate. Fragrant light CAB; CHARD discontinued. Sparkling in preparation.

Boberg Controlled region for fortified wines comprising PAARL and TULBAGH.

NB This edition introduces a new short-cut vintage category. Vintages in colour are the ones you should choose first for drinking in 1995.

Bon Courage w sw ★→★★   ROBERTSON estate; vg dessert GEWURZ and CHARD.

Boplaas r w ★★   Estate in dry hot Karoo. Earthy deep 'Vintage Reserve Port' best since '87 (91), fortified Muscadels. Links with Grahams in Portugal.

Boschendal w sp ★★→★★★ (Chard) 89 91   617-acre estate in PAARL area. Good CHARD and METHODE CAP CLASSIQUE; also Cape's first 'blush' off-dry Blanc de Noirs. Now improving reds: Merlot (91), interesting full Pinot N.

Bouchard-Finlayson r w (★★★) (Chard) 91 93 (Pinot N) 93   First French-Cape partnership, between Paul Bouchard of Burgundy and Peter Finlayson at Hermanus, Walker Bay. Maiden release 91 esp PINOT N.

Breede River Valley Fortified and white wine region E of Drakenstein Mts.

Buitenverwachting r w sp ★★★ (Chard) 89 90 91   Exceptional, German-financed, recently replanted CONSTANTIA v'yds. Vg SAUV (plain, oaked Bl Fumé), CHARD, B'x blend (88 89), Merlot (91). Lively clean METHODE CAP CLASSIQUE (Pinots Gr and Bl). Restaurant worthy of a Michelin star.

Cabernet Sauvignon Most successful in COASTAL REGION. Range of styles: sturdy long-lived to elegant fruity. More use of new French oak since '82 giving great improvements. Best recent vintages: 82 84 86 87 89 91.

Cape Independent Winemakers Guild Young group of winemakers in the vanguard of quality. Holds an annual auction of progressive-style wines.

Cavendish Cape ★★   Range of remarkably good 'Sherries' from the KWV.

Chardonnay Fairly new in S Africa due to official restrictions. Recent release of good vines resulted in leap in quality and number. Great expectations. Now over 100 Chard labels; a decade ago, 3.

Chateau Libertas ★   Big-selling CAB s brand made by SFW.

Chenin Blanc Work-horse grape of the Cape; one vine in three. Adaptable, sometimes vg. KWV makes bulk good value example. See also Steen.

Cinsaut The principal bulk-producing French red grape in S Africa; formerly known as Hermitage. V seldom seen with varietal label.

Claridge r w ★★→★★★ (r) 91 (Chard) 91 92 93   Good barrel-fermented CHARD and CAB-Merlot from small new winery at Wellington nr PAARL.

Clos Malverne r w ★★ 89 90 91   Small STELLENBOSCH winery. Individual dense CAB s, PINOTAGE from own v'yds and purchased grapes.

Colombard French white grape, as popular in Cape as in California. Crisp lively flowery, usually short-lived wine; often in blends, or for brandy.

Constantia Once the world's most famous sweet Muscat-based wine (both red and white), from the Cape. See Klein Constantia.

De Wetshof w sw ★★→★★★ (Chard) 87 88 89 91 93   Pioneering ROBERTSON estate. Powerful CHARD (varying oakiness: Finesse lightly, Bataleur heavily) and fresh dry RHINE RIES. Also dessert GEWURZ, Rhine Ries under Danie de Wet label and own-brand Chards for British supermarkets.

Delaire Vineyards r w ★★ (Chard) 89 91 92 (r) 90 91   Full-flavoured CHARD, Bordeaux blend named Barrique, and elegant off-dry RHINE RIES, from young winery at Helshoogte Pass above STELLENBOSCH.

Delheim r w dr sw ★★→★★★ (r) 86 87 88 89 91   Big winery with mountain v'yds nr STELLENBOSCH. Elegant barrel-aged CAB s-Merlot-Cab F, Grand Reserve (88 91), PINOTAGE, Shiraz; variable PINOT N; improving CHARD, SAUV. Sweet wines: GEWURZ, outstanding botrytis STEEN.

Die Krans Estate ★   Karoo semi-desert v'yds making rich full Vintage Res 'Port'. Best is 91. Also traditional fortified sweet Muscadels.

Dieu Donné Vineyards r w ★★   Franschhoek estate. Good Chard 92.

Douglas Green ★→★★   Cape Town merchants marketing range of sound wines incl 'Sherries' and 'Ports' mostly from KWV.

Drostdy ★   Good range of 'Sherries' from BERGKELDER.

Drostyhof r w ★   Well-priced range incl CHARD made at TULBAGH cellars.

Edelkeur ★★★★   Excellent intensely sweet noble rot white by NEDERBURG.

Eikendal Vineyards r w ★★→★★ (red, Merlot) 87 88 90 91 93 (Chard) 91 92 93   Swiss-owned 100-acres v'yds and winery in STELLENBOSCH. Vg CHARD; CAB S-Merlot blend Classique. Fresh whites incl sweet-sweet CHENIN BL.

Estate wine Official term for wines grown and made on registered estates.

Fairview Estate r w dr sw ★★→★★★ (r) 88 90 91 (Chard) 90 91 92 93   Enterprising PAARL estate with wide range. Best are Reserve Merlot (89 91), Bordeaux blend Charles Gerard Reserve (90), Shiraz Reserve (90 91). Also lively Gamay, good CHARD, plus sweet CHENIN BL.

Fleur du Cap r w sw ★★→★★★ (r) 86 87 88 90 91 92   Value range from BERGKELDER at STELLENBOSCH: vg CAB (89) esp since '86. Also Merlot (90 92), Shiraz (86 88), improving CHARD (93), fine GEWURZ, botrytis CHENIN.

Gewürztraminer The famous spicy grape of Alsace, best at NEDERBURG and SIMONSIG. Naturally low acidity makes it difficult to handle at the Cape.

Glen Carlou r w ★★→★★★ (r) 89 90 91 (Chard) 90 91 92   PAARL property. Vg B'x blends Grande Classique (90 91), Les Trois, Merlot; gd CHARD (91 92).

Graça ★   Huge-selling slightly fizzy white blend in Portuguese-style bottle.

Graham Beck Winery w sp ★★   Avant-garde ROBERTSON winery (57 acres); first METHODE CAP CLASSIQUE Brut Royale NV and CHARD well-received.

Grand Cru (or Premier Grand Cru) Term for a totally dry white, with no quality implications. Generally to be avoided.

Groot Constantia r w ★★→★★★   Historic gov't-owned estate nr Cape Town. Superlative Muscat in early 19th C. Renaissance in progress; so far fine CAB (esp blend Gouverneur's Reserve 89), Shiraz (89), Merlot (90), Weiser (Rhine) Ries, Gewürz, Botrytis blend (92), decent Muscat.

Grünberger ✽   BERGKELDER brand: range of dry and semi-sweet STEEN whites.

Hamilton Russell Vineyards r w ★★★→★★★★ (Pinot N) 85 86 87 89 90 91 (Chard) 86 87 89 90 91 93   Cape's top PINOT 'Burgundy' v'yds and cellar. Small yields, French-inspired vinification in cool Walker Bay. Many awards. Priciest wines in S Africa. From '93 also Chard-Sauv Bl blend.

Hanepoot Local name for the sweet Muscat of Alexandria grape.

Hartenberg r w ★★   STELLENBOSCH estate, recently modernized; rich Shiraz.

J P Bredell ★★★ Stellenbosch v'yds. Rich, dark, deep Vintage Reserve 'Port' from Tinta Barocca and Souzão grapes.

Kanonkop r ★★★ (r) 84 86 89 90 91   Outstanding N STELLENBOSCH estate. Individual powerful CAB (89 91) and B'x-style blend Paul Sauer (86 89). Benchmark PINOTAGE (89 91), oak-finished since '89 (v improved).

Klein Constantia r w sw ★★★ (r) 86 87 88 89 (Chard) 90 91   Old subdivision of famous GROOT CONSTANTIA neighbour. Emphatic CHARD (91 92), SAUV, fine powerful CAB, Bordeaux-style blend Marlbrook first released in '88 (88 89), also Shiraz. A Muscat Frontignan 86, Vin de Constance, revives 18th-C Constantia legend. Top dry botrytis Sauv 'Blanc de Blancs' (87 93) is Cape's answer to Ygrec. Revamped since early '80s.

KWV The Kooperatieve Wijnbouwers Vereniging, S Africa's national wine coop created in 1917: vast premises in PAARL, a range of good wines, esp Cathedral Cellars reds, RIES, 'Sherries', sweet dessert wines. In '92 gave up widely criticized quotas, freeing growers to plant v'yds at will.

La Bri ★★   Coop whites from SAUV BL, RHINE RIES, Sém. Sauvage de la Bri is best.

La Motte r w ★★★ (r) 86 87 88 89 91   Lavish new Rupert family estate nr Franschhoek. Lean but stylish, intensely flavoured reds: CAB S (89 91), Shiraz (86 89), Merlot, B'x-style blend Millennium (90 91). Racy SAUV.

Laborie r w ★→★★   KWV-owned showpiece PAARL estate. White and red blends.

To decipher codes, please refer to symbols key at front of book, and to 'How to use this book' on page 5.

Landgoed Afrikaans for 'estate': on official seals and ESTATE WINE labels.

Landskroon r w *→*** Family estate owned by Paul and Hugo de Villiers. Good dry reds, esp Shiraz, CAB S, Cab F.

Late Harvest Term for a mildly sweet wine. 'Special Late Harvest' must be naturally sweet. 'Noble Late Harvest' is highest quality dessert wine.

Le Bonheur r w *** (r) 84 86 87   STELLENBOSCH estate often producing classic tannic minerally CAB; big-bodied SAUV BL. revived with 93.

Leroux, JC ★★ Old brand revived as BERGKELDER's sparkling wine house. SAUV (charmat), PINOT (top METHODE CAP CLASSIQUE is well-aged). Also CHARD.

Lievland r w **→*** (r) 87 89 90   STELLENBOSCH estate making top Cape Shiraz (89 90) and vg CAB S, Merlot. Also range of whites incl intense RIES, off-dry and promising Sauternes-style dessert wine.

L'Ormarins r w sw *** (r) 84 86 87 89 (Chard) 89 90   One of two Rupert family estates nr Franschhoek. CAB S (86 89) and vg claret-style Optima (87 89), also Shiraz (87). Fresh lemony CHARD, forward oaked SAUV BL, outstanding GEWURZ-Bukketraube botrytis dessert wine.

Louisvale w ** 90 91 92 93   STELLENBOSCH winery. Attractive CHARD only.

Meerlust r w *** (r) 84 86 87 89 90 91   Old family estate nr STELLENBOSCH; Cape's only Italian winemaker. Outstanding Rubicon (Médoc-style blend) (86 89), Cab (86 91), Merlot (87 89), PINOT N (87 89). CHARD still in pipeline.

Méthode Cap Classique Term for classic method sparkling wine in S Africa.

Middelvlei r ** (r) 89 90   STELLENBOSCH estate: good PINOTAGE (90), CAB (86 89).

Monis *→***   Well-known wine concern of PAARL, with fine 'Vintage Port'.

Morgenhof r w dr s/sw *   Fresh start at this expensively refurbished STELLENBOSCH estate. New French owner and change of winemaker (from '92). Improving reds; dry white (excellent 93 Sauv), s/sw whites; 'Port'.

Mulderbosch Vineyards w **→***   Enthusiastic reception for new penetrating impressive SAUV BL from mountain v'yds nr STELLENBOSCH, one oak-fermented, the other fresh, bold. 93 unoaked is exceptional.

Muratie Ancient STELLENBOSCH estate, esp 'Port'. Bright future expected.

Nederburg r w p dr sw s/sw sp **→**** (r) 82 84 86 87 89 91 (Chard) 89 90 91 92   Well-known large modern PAARL winery (650,000 cases pa, 50 wines). Bicentenary in '92. Own grapes and suppliers'. Sound CAB, Shiraz, CHARD, RIES, blends in regular range. Limited Vintages, Private Bins often outstanding. Fresh approach with late '80s top reds: richer fruitier flavour, barrel-ageing. '80s pioneer of botrytis dessert wines: CHENIN BL, GEWURZ, SAUV, Muscat, even Chard consistently good. Stages Cape's biggest annual wine event, the Nederburg Auction. See Edelkeur.

Neethlingshof r w sw **→*** (r) 87 89 90 91 (Chard) 91   Rising estate: replanted with classic grapes, cellar revamped at huge cost since '85. Run jointly with nearby Stellenzicht: 250,000-cases pa. Vg CAB S (89 90), Merlot, CHARD joining fresh SAUV BL, excellent GEWURZ (91 93) and blush Bl de Noir. National Champion dessert botrytis from RIES (92), Sauv Bl.

Neil Ellis Wines r w *** (r) 86 87 89 90 91 92 (Chard) 89 91 92 93   Good wines from Devon Valley nr STELLENBOSCH (16 widely spread coastal v'yds). Spicy structured CAB S; excellent Whitehall SAUV; full bold CHARD.

Nuy Cooperative Winery r w dr sw sp **   Small Worcester Coop, frequent local-award winner. Outstanding dessert wines; fortified Muscadels (91), regularly excellent Cape COLOMBARD. Good S African RIES.

Oak Valley Wines *   New export brand, blend of good coop cellar wines from STELLENBOSCH, incl CAB-Shiraz, SAUV BL-CHENIN BL blends.

Overgaauw r w ** (r) 84 86 87 89 90 91   Old family estate nr STELLENBOSCH; CHARD, CAB S, Merlot (90), and Bordeaux-style blend Tria Corda (88). Also 'Vintage Crusted Port' 85 from 5 Portuguese varieties.

Paarl Town 30 miles NE of Cape Town and the surrounding demarcated district, among the best in the country, particularly for 'Sherry'.

Paul Cluver w **   Label launched '92. Good SAUV BL, RHINE RIES: grapes from cool upland Elgin Coastal region. Wines made by NEDERBURG.

Pierre Jourdan sp ***   Fine NV METHODE CAP CLASSIQUE made at Clos Cabrière. Most notable: Brut Sauvage and Cuve Belle Rose (pure PINOT).

Pinot Noir Like counterparts in California and Australia, Cape producers struggle for fine, burgundy-like complexity. They are getting closer. Best are BLAAUWKLIPPEN, HAMILTON RUSSELL, MEERLUST, RUSTENBERG.

Pinotage S African red grape cross of PINOT N and CINSAUT, useful for high yields and hardiness. Can be delicious but overstated flamboyant esters often dominate. Experiments/oak-ageing show potential for finesse.

Plaisir de Merle r w *** New SFW-owned cellar nr PAARL producing its first reds from own v'yds in '93: Cab-Merlot is outstanding, supple. Paul Pontallier of Château Margaux is consultant.

Pongracz **→*** Successful good value NV METHODE CAP CLASSIQUE from PINOT N (75%) and CHARD, produced by the BERGKELDER, named after the exiled Hungarian ampelographer who upgraded many Cape v'yds.

Premier Grand Cru See Grand Cru.

Rheboksloof r w *→** (r) 90 (Chard) 92 200-acre estate behind PAARL mountain: sound small range. CAB is promising. Has the Cape's first American winemaker.

Rhine Riesling Produces full-flavoured dry and off-dry wines but reaches perfection when lusciously sweet as 'Noble LATE HARVEST'. Generally needs 2 yrs or more of bottle-age. Also called Weisser Riesling.

Riesling S African Ries (actually Crouchen Bl) is v different from RHINE RIES, providing neutral easy-drinking wines. Known locally as Cape Ries.

Rietvallei w sw ** ROBERTSON estate: excellent fortified Muscadel. Also CHARD.

Robertson District inland from Cape. Mainly dessert wines (notably Muscat); white table wines on increase. Few reds. Irrigated v'yds.

Roodeberg * Red blend from KWV: equal PINOTAGE-Shiraz-Tinta Barocca-CAB.

Rooiberg Cooperative Winery * Successful big-selling ROBERTSON range of more than 30 labels. Good CHENIN BL, COLOMBARD.

Rozendal r *** (r) 83 84 86 87 89 91 Small STELLENBOSCH v'yd cellar, making excellent CAB-Merlot blend.

Ruiterbosch ** Individual wines from outside traditional Cape vine area nr Indian Ocean. Striking SAUV BL, RHINE RIES. Made at BOPLAAS cellars.

Rust en Vrede r **→*** (r) 86 87 89 Well-known estate just E of STELLEN-BOSCH: red only. Gd CAB, Shiraz, vg Rust en Vrede blend (86 89).

Rustenberg r w ***→***** (red except Pinot N) 80 82 84 86 87 88 89 91 (Chard) 86 87 89 90 91 The most beautiful old STELLENBOSCH estate, founded 300 yrs ago, making wine for last 100. Grand reds, esp Rustenberg Gold CAB (86 89) and Médoc-style blend. Also lighter Cab-CINSAUT-Merlot and Cab (82 89). Variable PINOT (91). Individual CHARD.

Sauvignon Blanc Adapting well to warm conditions. Widely grown and marketed in both wooded and unwooded styles. Also v sweet.

Saxenburg Wines r w dr sw ** (r) 91 STELLENBOSCH v'yds and winery; recently prize-winning. Robust deep-flavoured PINOTAGE; Cab, Shiraz.

Simonsig r w sp sw **→*** (r) 84 86 87 89 90 91 (Chard) 88 89 90 91 92 Malan family STELLENBOSCH estate with a wide range: vg CAB, Shiraz (86 89), CHARD, PINOTAGE (89 92), dessert-style GEWURZ (90 92). First release in '92 of widely acclaimed Cab-Merlot Tiara (90 91). Also popular oak-matured white Vin Fumé and first Cape METHODE CAP CLASSIQUE (esp 91).

Simonsvlei r w p sw sp * One of S Africa's best-known coop cellars, just outside PAARL. A prize-winner with PINOTAGE.

Spier r w * Five-farm estate W of STELLENBOSCH. PINOTAGE probably best.

Steen S Africa's commonest white grape, said to be a clone of CHENIN BL. It gives strong tasty lively wine, sweet or dry: short-lived if dry, lasts better when off-dry or sweet. Normally better than S African RIES.

Stein Name often for commercial blends of s/sw white. Not to be despised.

Stellenbosch Town and demarcated district 30 miles E of Cape Town (oldest town in S Africa). Heart of wine industry, with the 3 largest companies. Most top estates, esp for red wine, are in the mountain foothills.

Stellenbosch Farmers' Winery (SFW) The world's fifth largest winery, S Africa's biggest after KWV: equivalent of 14 million cases pa. Range incls NEDERBURG; top is ZONNEBLOEM. Wide selection of mid-/low-price wines.

Stellenryck Collection r w ✯✯✯ Top quality BERGKELDER range. RHINE RIES, Fumé Blanc, CAB (87 89) among S Africa's best.

Swartland Cooperative r w dr s/sw sw sp ✱ Vast range from hot, dry wheatland: big-selling low-price wines, esp CHENIN and dry, off-dry or sweet, but (recently) penetrating SAUV, also big no-nonsense PINOTAGE.

Talana Hill r w ✯✯ (r) 88 89 (Chard) **89 90 91** 92 New STELLENBOSCH winery: good CHARD and Bordeaux-style blend Royale (91).

Tassenberg ✱ Popular PINOTAGE-based blend by SFW, known fondly as 'Tassies'. Traditional student party and braaivleis (barbecue) wine. Oom Tas, a dry Muscat, is white equivalent.

Thelema r w ✯✯✯ (Cab S) 89 **90 91** 92 (Chard) 88 89 **90 91 92 93** Outstanding v'yds and winery at Helshoogte, above STELLENBOSCH. Impressive minty CAB, B's blend (starting with vg 91), excellent CHARD, and unoaked SAUV.

Theuniskraal w ✱ TULBAGH estate: whites incl S Afrian RIES, GEWURZ.

Tulbagh Demarcated district N of PAARL best known for white THEUNISKRAAL, and dessert wines from DROSTDY. See also Boberg.

Twee Jongegezellen w sp ✯✯ Old TULBAGH estate, helped pioneer cold fermentation in '60s, night harvesting in '80s; still in Krone family (18th-C founder). Esp whites, best known: popular dry TJ89 (mélange of a dozen varieties), Schanderl off-dry Muscat-GEWURZ. Recently METHODE CAP CLASSIQUE Cuvée Krone Borealis Brut (CHARD, PINOT N).

Uiterwyk r w ✱ Old estate W of STELLENBOSCH. CAB, Merlot, pleasant whites.

Uitkyk r w ✯✯ (r) 86 87 89 Old estate (400 acres) W of STELLENBOSCH esp for Carlonet (big gutsy CAB, 87 89), Carlsheim (SAUV BL) white. Recently CHARD.

Van Loveren r w sw sp ✯✯ Go-ahead ROBERTSON estate: big range incl muscular CHARD (90 91), good Pinot Gr (92); scarcer Fernão Pires and Hárslevlü.

Vergelegen w ✯✯ One of Cape's oldest wine farms, founded 1700. Long neglected, now spectacularly restored. Les Enfants series marked '92 re-launch with wine from bought-in grapes; good CHARD (93), SAUV BL.

Vergenoegd r w sw ✯→✯✯ Old family estate in S STELLENBOSCH supplying vg 'Sherry' to KWV and bottling CAB S, Shiraz. New Bordeaux-style blend.

Villiera r w ✯✯✯ PAARL estate with popular NV METHODE CAP CLASSIQUE 'Tradition'. Top SAUV BL (93), good RHINE RIES, fine Bordeaux-style blend CAB-Merlot 'Cru Monro' (90 91). Recently exceptional Merlot (89 91).

Vredendal Cooperative r w dr sw S Africa's largest coop winery in hot Olifants River region. Big range: mostly white, reds incl Ruby Cab.

Vriesenhof r w ✯✯→✯✯✯ (Cab) **82 84 86 88 89** 91 (Chard) 88 **89 91** 92 Highly rated CAB and B's blend Kalista (89 91). Since '88, vg CHARD. Also Pinot Bl.

Warwick r w ✯✯→✯✯✯ (r) **86 87** 89 91 STELLENBOSCH estate run by one of Cape's few female winemakers. CAB and vg Médoc-style blend Trilogy (89 90), Cab Fr (89 90) and Chard (92).

Weisser Riesling See Rhine Riesling.

Welgemeend r ✯✯→✯✯✯ (r) **86 87** 89 Boutique PAARL estate: Médoc-style blends (87 90), delicate CAB, and Amadé (Grenache-Shiraz-PINOTAGE).

Weltevrede w dr sw ✯→✯✯ (Chard) **89 90** 91 Progressive ROBERTSON estate. Blended, white and fortified. Vg CHARD. Gewürz (93), White Muscadel (91).

Wine of Origin The Cape's appellation contrôlée, but without French crop yield restrictions. Demarcated regions are described on these pages.

Woolworths Wines Best S African supermarket wines, many specially blended. Top are CHARDS, young reds incl Merlot, Bordeaux-style blends.

Worcester Demarcated wine district round BREEDE and Hex river valleys, E of PAARL. Many coop cellars. Mainly dessert wines, brandy, dry whites.

Zandvliet r ✯→✯✯ (Shiraz) **86** 87 89 Estate in the ROBERTSON area making fine light Shiraz and recently a CAB S and Chard.

Zandwijk r w New estate in PAARL district producing quality kosher wine.

Zevenwacht r w ✯✯→✯✯✯ (Cab S) **84 86 87** 88 89 STELLENBOSCH wines only available via shareholders, restaurants. Impressive CAB, Rhine Ries (93).

Zonnebloem r w ✯✯ (Cab S) **82 84 86 87** 89 (Chard) **90 91** Good quality range from SFW incl CAB S, Merlot (88), Bordeaux-style blend Laureat (89) launched '92, Shiraz, PINOTAGE (87 91), SAUV BL, CHARD (91).

England and Wales

The English wine industry started again in the 1950s after a pause of some 400 years. Well over a million bottles a year are now being made from over 450 vineyards, amounting in total to some 2,700 acres. Almost all is white and generally Germanic or similar to Alsace in style (some more Loire-like), many from new German varieties designed to ripen well in cool weather. Acidity is often high, which means that good examples have a built-in ability (and need) to age. Four years is a good age for many, and up to eight for some. Experiments with both oak-ageing and bottle-fermented sparkling are promising; especially the latter. The English Vineyards Association (EVA) seal is worn by tested wines. Since 1991 non-hybrid English wines may be labelled as 'Quality Wine', taking them into the European Community ·quality bracket for the first time. But as the (excellent) hybrid Seyval Blanc is so important here, few growers apply. Beware 'British Wine', which is neither British nor indeed wine, and has nothing to do with the following.

Adgestone nr Sandown (Isle of Wight)   Prize-winning 8.5-acre v'yd on chalky hill site. Est'd '68. Wines with good structure and longevity.

Astley Stourport-on-Severn (Hereford and Worcester)   4.5 acres; some fair wines. Madeleine Angevine and Kerner are prize-winning.

Avalon Shepton Mallet (Somerset)   Organically grown grapes. 2.3 acres.

Bagborough Shepton Mallet (Somerset)   New v'yd to note. 3 acres.

Bardingley Staplehurst (Kent)   2.5-acres. Interesting red (some oak-aged).

Barkham Manor E Sussex   34 acres since '85. Wide range. Modern winery.

Barton Manor East Cowes (Isle of Wight)   15.5-acre v'yd: (trophy-winning) consistently interesting wines incl barrel-aged and bottle-fermented sparkling. Considerable recent investment. New owners since '91.

Bearstead Maidstone (Kent)   4 acres planted '86. Improving, esp Bacchus.

Beaulieu Abbey Brockenhurst (Hampshire)   4.6-acre organic v'yd, est '58 by Gore-Browne family on old monastic site. Good rosé.

Beenleigh Manor Totnes (Devon)   0.5 acres of esteemed Cab S and Merlot grown under polythene. Wine made at SHARPHAM. 90 is trophy winner.

Biddenden nr Tenterden (Kent)   20-acre v'yd planted '69: Wide range incl Ortega, Huxelrebe, Bacchus, bottle-fermented sparkling. Gd cider too.

Bookers Bolney (E Sussex)   4 acres of Müller-T; other varieties planted '92.

Boyton Stoke-by-Clare (Suffolk)   Small 2-acre v'yd: Huxelrebe (90), Müller-T.

Boze Down Whitchurch-on-Thames (Oxfordshire)   5.8 acres. Wide range; red and sweet now looking good. Worth watching.

Breaky Bottom Lewes (Sussex)   5.5-acre v'yd. Semi-cult following. Good dry wines, esp award-winning Seyval (89 90), Müller-T. Sparkling is next.

Brenchley Tonbridge (Kent)   17 acres of Seyval Bl, Schönburger, Huxelrebe, now with some style. One to watch.

Bruisyard Saxmundham (Suffolk)   10 acres of Müller-T. Since '76. Incl oak-aged and sparkling wine.

Cane End Reading (Berkshire)   12 acres; mixed vines. Good sweet late-harvest Bacchus in '90. Interesting style.

Carden Park Chester (Cheshire)   9-acre v'yd in large 'leisure park' nr Welsh Marches. Good Seyval Bl, some oak-aged. New sparkling in '94.

Carr Taylor Vineyards Sussex   21 acres, planted '73. Esp for Reichensteiner. Pioneer of classic method sparklers in UK: Kerner-Reichensteiner (vintage, NV), Pinot N rosé. Some lively, intense, balanced wines.

Chapel Down Winery Burgess Hill (W Sussex)   New winery venture, blending from bought-in grapes, esp classic-method sparkling. Barrel-fermented 'Epoch I' red is good, as are 'sur lie' still and sparkling.

Chiddingstone Edenbridge (Kent)   28-acre v'yd with stress on dry French-style wines. Some barrique-ageing.

Chilford Hundred Linton (Cambridge)   21 acres: fairly dry wines since '74.

Chiltern Valley Henley-on-Thames (Oxfordshire)   3 acres of own v'yds high up on chalk, plus neighbouring growers': incl prize-winning oak-aged unusual sweet late-harvest Noble Bacchus, Old Luxters Dry Reserve.

Crickley Windward Little Witcombe (Gloucestershire)   5.5 acres beginning to show well, esp 91 Schönburger Reserve.

Denbies Dorking (Surrey)   250-acre v'yd (England's biggest); first harvest '89. Impressive new winery, improving wines, esp 92 dessert Botrytis.

Elham Valley Canterbury (Kent)   Boutique winery/2 acre v'yd: impressive hand-crafted medium-dry Müller-T, and sparkling Kerner-Seyval Bl.

Elmham Park East Dereham (Norfolk)   4.5-acre v'yd, est '66. Makes light flowery wines, Madeleine-Angevine esp good. Also apple wine.

Fonthill Salisbury (Wiltshire)   9 acres. Incl good Seyval, Dornfelder rosé.

Hagley Court Hereford   7.5 acres planted '85, wines now worth watching.

Halfpenny Green W Midlands   28 v'yd-acres; esp good Madeleine Angevine.

Hambledon nr Petersfield (Hampshire)   The first modern English v'yd, planted in '51 on a chalk slope with advice from Champagne.

Headcorn Maidstone (Kent)   5-acre medal-winning v'yd: Seyval Bl, etc.

Helions Helion's Bumpstead, Haverhill (Suffolk)   One acre, 50:50 Müller-T and Reichensteiner; good dry wine (esp 90).

Hidden Spring Horam (E Sussex)   9 acres. Success esp with oak-aged Dry Reserve and Dark Fields red.

High Weald Winery Kent   No vines, but winemaker (proprietor Christopher Lindlar) for several growers. Buys in grapes for 'English Vineyard' blend.

Highfield Tiverton (Devon)   1.5 acres. Good wines, esp Siegerrebe.

La Mare Jersey (Channel Islands)   Only (but long-est'd) CI v'yd. Fair wines.

Lamberhurst (Kent)   England's top winery; 52 acres (4 in E Sussex) est'd '72. Consistent range: award winners (83 85 90), reds, sparkling, oak-aged. 91 Bacchus med-dry esp good. Winemaker for many other growers.

Leeford nr Battle (Sussex)   25-acre v'yd; more planned. Various labels: Saxon Valley, Battle, Conquest.

Llanerch S Glamorgan (Wales)   5.5 acres est'd '86. Wines sold under Cariad label. Individual style developing, worth its awards. Good rosé.

Loddiswell Kingsbridge (Devon)   6 acres plus one under plastic tunnels.

Manstree Exeter (Devon)   3-acres; esp sparkling: 'Essling' (90) is a winner.

Mersea Colchester (Essex)   Small v'yd. Wine quality gets better and better.

Monnow Valley Monmouth (Wales)   4 acres. Wines attracting increasing attention, esp 92 Huxelrebe-Seyval Bl.

Moorlynch Bridgwater (Somerset)   11 acres of an idyllic farm. Good wines: have been variable, now improving.

New Hall nr Maldon (Essex)   87 acres of mixed farm planted with Huxelrebe, Müller-T and Pinot N, etc. Some vinified elsewhere.

Northbrook Springs Bishops Waltham (Hampshire)   13 acres of young vines with improving range of wines.

Nutbourne Manor nr Pulborough (W Sussex)   18.5 acres: elegant and tasty Schönburger and Bacchus.

Oatley Bridgwater (Somerset)   4.5 acres of young vines now producing good wines. 92 Kernling worth trying.

Partridge Blandford (Dorset)   5 acres. 92 dry Bacchus is trophy-winning.

Penshurst Tunbridge Wells (Kent)   12 acres since '72, incl good Seyval Bl and Müller-T. Fine modern winery.

Pilton Manor Shepton Mallet (Somerset)   15-acre hillside v'yd (est'd '66). Wines regaining form, esp Westholme Late Harvest, a '92 prize-winner.

Plumpton Agricultural College nr Lewes (Sussex)   1-acre experimental v'yd at college for winemakers.

Priory Vineyards Little Dunmow (Essex)   10 acres; now some good wines.

Pulham Diss (Norfolk)   12.6-acre v'yd planted '73; Müller-T is top wine.

Queen Court Faversham (Kent)   Brewery-owned: esp Müller-T, Schönburger.

Rock Lodge nr Haywards Heath (Sussex) 8-acre v'yd since '65. Fumé (oak-aged Ortega-Müller-T blend) and Impresario sparkling recommended.

St-George's Waldron, Heathfield (E Sussex) 15 acres, planted '79. Müller-T etc and some Gewürz. Well-publicized; wide range, popular styles.

St-Nicholas Ash (Kent) 17 acres. Esp good for Schönburger.

Sandhurst Cranbrook (Kent) Mixed farm with 16 acres of vines, 80 of hops, plus apple orchards, sheep, etc. Wines improving, esp 91 Seyval Bl, 92 Bacchus (both oak-aged). Sparkling Pinot N-Seyval available from '94.

Scott's Hall Ashford (Kent) Boutique v'yd: oak-aged white, sparkling rosé.

Sharpham Totnes (Devon) 5 acres. Now own winery: getting interesting.

Shawsgate Framlingham (Suffolk) 17 acres incl Chard; Seyval Bl-Müller-T blends good. Wins awards.

Staple nr Canterbury (Kent) 7 acres planted '77. Excellent quality. Müller-T and Huxelrebe especially interesting.

Staplecombe Taunton (Somerset) 2.5 acres for some good wines.

Staverton (Woodbridge) Suffolk 1.5 acres of improving v'yds, esp Bacchus.

Tenterden (Kent) 12 acres, planted '79. Wines v dry to sweet, Müller-T, oak-aged Seyval (vg 81, 91 Trophy winner), rosé, sparkling.

Thames Valley Twyford (Berkshire) 25-acre v'yd: all styles of wine. Serious oak-matured white, red; classic method sparkling; also late harvest sweet: botrytis Clock Tower Selection won '92 Gore-Browne trophy.

Three Choirs Newent (Gloucestershire) 60 acres (more planned), est'd '74. Müller-T, Seyval Bl, Schönburger, Reichensteiner, and esp Bacchus Dry, Huxelrebe. Recent new £1M winery. English 'Nouveau' is popular.

Throwley Faversham (Kent) 4.5 acres. Excellent bottle-fermented sparkling from Pinot N and Chard. 91 Ortega also vg.

Wickham Shedfield (Hampshire) 9.5-acre v'yd (since '84): starting to show some style. Vintage Selection is worth trying, esp 91.

Wissett Halesworth (Suffolk) 10 acres beginning to show up well. Esp for Auxerrois-Pinot blends and Müller-T.

Wooldings Whitchurch (Hampshire) Young 7-acre v'yd. Vg Schönburger.

Wootton Shepton Mallet (Somerset) 6-acre v'yd of Schönburger, Müller-T, Seyval Bl, Auxerrois, etc. Consistently good fresh fruity wines since 71.

Wyken Bury-St-Edmunds (Suffolk) Range starting to look gd, esp Bacchus.

The current trend towards 'low-alcohol' wines and beers, from which most alcohol has been removed artificially, should be a golden opportunity for wines that are naturally lower in alcohol than the 12 or 13 degrees expected in most table wines. Germany is the prime exponent; England is another. Their best wines, with plenty of fruity acidity, do not need high alcohol to make an impact. Today's logical choice – at least at lunch-time.

Luxembourg

Luxembourg has 3,285 acres of vineyards on limestone soils on the Moselle's left bank. High-yielding Elbling and Rivaner (Müller-Thurgau) vines dominate, but there are also significant acreages of Riesling, Gewürztraminer and (usually best) Auxerrois, Pinot Blanc and Pinot Gris. These give light to medium-bodied (10.5–11.5°) dry Alsace-like wines.

The Vins Moselle coop makes 70% of the wines. Domaine et Tradition estates association, founded in 1988, is working to promote quality from noble varieties. The last five vintages were all good, 89, 90 and 92 outstanding. Best from: Aly Duhr et Fils, M Bastian, Caves Gales, Ch de Schengen, Clos Mon Vieux Moulin, 'Clos des Rochers' (Bernard-Massard), Sunnen-Hoffmann.

A little learning...

The jargon of laboratory analysis is often seen on the back-labels of New World wines. It has crept menacingly into newspapers and magazines. What does it mean? This hard-edged wine-talk, unsympathetic as it is to most lovers of wine, is very briefly explained below.

The most frequent technical references are to the ripeness of grapes at picking; the resultant alcohol and sugar content of the wine; various measures of its acidity; the amount of sulphur dioxide used as a preservative; and occasionally the amount of 'dry extract' – the sum of all the things that give wine its character.

The **sugar** in wine is mainly glucose and fructose, with traces of arabinose, xylose and other sugars that are not fermentable by yeast, but can be attacked by bacteria. Each country has its own system for measuring the sugar content or ripeness of grapes, known in English as the '**must weight**'. The chart below relates the three principal ones (German, French and American) to each other, to specific gravity, and to the potential alcohol of the wine if all the sugar is fermented.

Sugar to alcohol: potential strength

Specific Gravity	°Oechsle	Baumé	Brix	% Potential Alcohol v/v
1.065	65	8.8	15.8	8.1
1.070	70	9.4	17.0	8.8
1.075	75	10.1	18.1	9.4
1.080	80	10.7	19.3	10.0
1.085	85	11.3	20.4	10.6
1.090	90	11.9	21.5	12.1
1.095	95	12.5	22.5	13.0
1.100	100	13.1	23.7	13.6
1.105	105	13.7	24.8	14.3
1.110	110	14.3	25.8	15.1
1.115	115	14.9	26.9	15.7
1.120	120	15.5	28.0	16.4

Residual sugar is the sugar left after fermentation has finished or been artificially stopped, measured in grams per litre.

Alcohol content (mainly ethyl alcohol) is expressed in percent by volume of the total liquid. (Also known as 'degrees'.)

Acidity is both fixed and volatile. **Fixed acidity** consists principally of tartaric, malic and citric acids which are all found in the grape, and lactic and succinic acids which are produced during fermentation. **Volatile acidity** consists mainly of acetic acid, which is rapidly formed by bacteria in the presence of oxygen. A small amount of volatile acidity is inevitable and even attractive. With a larger amount the wine becomes 'pricked' – starts to turn to vinegar.

Total acidity is fixed and volatile acidity combined. As a rule of thumb for a well-balanced wine it should be in the region of one gram per thousand for each 10°Oechsle (see above).

pH is a measure of the strength of the acidity, rather than its volume. The lower the figure the more acid. Wine normally ranges in pH from 2.8 to 3.8. Winemakers in hot climates can have problems getting the pH low enough. Lower pH gives better colour, helps prevent bacterial spoilage and allows more of the SO_2 to be free and active as a preservative.

Sulphur dioxide (SO_2) is added to prevent oxidation and other accidents in winemaking. Some of it combines with sugars etc and is known as '**bound**'. Only the '**free**' SO_2 that remains in the wine is effective as a preservative. **Total SO_2** is controlled by law according to the level of residual sugar: the more sugar, the more SO_2 needed.

A few words about words

In the shorthand essential for this little book (and often in bigger books and magazines as well) wines are often described by adjectives that can seem irrelevant, inane – or just silly. What do 'fat', 'round', 'full', 'lean' and so on mean when used about wine? Some of the more irritatingly vague are expanded in this list:

Attack	The first impression of the wine in your mouth. It should 'strike' positively, if not necessarily with force. Without attack it is feeble or too bland.
Attractive	Means 'I like it, anyway'. A slight put-down for expensive wines; encouragement for juniors. At least refreshing.
Balance	See Well-balanced.
Big	Concerns the whole flavour, including the alcohol content. Sometimes implies clumsiness, the opposite of elegance. Generally positive, but big is easy in California and less usual in, say, Bordeaux. So the context matters.
Charming	Rather patronizing when said of wines that should have more impressive qualities. Implies lightness and possibly slight sweetness. A standard comment regarding Loire wines.
Crisp	With pronounced but pleasing acidity; fresh and eager.
Deep/depth	This wine is worth tasting with attention. There is more to it than the first impression; it fills your mouth with developing flavours as though it had an extra dimension. (Deep colour simply means hard to see through.) All really fine wines have depth.
Easy	Used in the sense of 'easy come, easy go'. An easy wine makes no demand on your palate (or intellect). The implication is that it drinks smoothly, doesn't need maturing, and all you remember is a pleasant drink.
Elegant	A professional taster's favourite term when he or she is stuck to describe a wine whose proportions (of strength, flavour, aroma), whose attack, middle and finish, whose texture and whose overall qualities call for comparison with other forms of natural beauty.
Fat	With flavour and texture that fills your mouth, but without aggression. Obviously inappropriate in eg a light Moselle, but what you pay your money for in Sauternes.
Finish	See Length.
Firm	Flavour that strikes the palate fairly hard, with fairly high acidity or tannic astringency giving the impression that the wine is in youthful vigour and will age to gentler things. An excellent quality with high-flavoured foods, and almost always positive.
Flesh	Refers to both substance and texture. A fleshy wine is fatter than a 'meaty' wine, more unctuous if less vigorous. The term is often used of good Pomerols, whose texture is notably smooth.
Flowery	Often used as though synonymous with fruity, but really means floral, like the fragrance of flowers. Roses, violets, etc are sometimes specified.
Fresh	Implies a good degree of fruity acidity, even a little nip of sharpness, as well as the zip and zing of youth. All young whites should be fresh: the alternative is flatness, staleness. . . ugh.
Fruity	Used for almost any quality, but really refers to the body and richness of wine made from good ripe grapes. A fruity aroma is not the same as a flavoury one. Fruitiness

213

	usually implies at least a slight degree of sweetness. Attempts at specifying *which* fruit the wine resembles can be helpful. Eg grapefruit, lemon, plum, lychee. On the other hand writers' imaginations frequently run riot, flinging basketfuls of fruit and flowers at wines which could well be more modestly described.
Full	Interchangeable with full-bodied. Lots of 'vinosity' or wineyness: the mouth-filling flavours of alcohol and 'extract' (all the flavouring components) combined.
Hollow	Lacking a satisfying middle flavour. Something seems to be missing between first flavour and last. A characteristic of wines from greedy proprietors who let their vines produce too many grapes. A very hollow wine is 'empty'.
Lean	More flesh would be an improvement. Lack of mouth-filling flavours; often astringent as well. Occasionally a term of appreciation of a distinct and enjoyable style.
Length	The flavours and aromas that linger after swallowing. In principle the greater the length the better the wine. One second of flavour after swallowing = one 'caudalie'. Ten caudalies is good; 20 terrific.
Light	With relatively little alcohol and body, as in most German wines. A very desirable quality in the right wines.
Meaty	Savoury in effect with enough substance to chew. The inference is lean meat; leaner than in 'fleshy'.
Oaky	Smelling or tasting of fresh-sawn oak, eg a new barrel. Appropriate in a fine wine destined for ageing in bottle, but currently often wildly overdone by winemakers to persuade a gullible public that a simple wine is something more grandiose. Over-oaky wines are both boring and tiring to drink.
Plump	The diminutive of fat, implying a degree of charm as well.
Rich	Not necessarily sweet, but giving an opulent impression.
Robust	In good heart, vigorous, and on a fairly big scale.
Rough	Flavour and texture give no pleasure. Acidity and/or tannin are dominant and coarse.
Round	Almost the same as fat, but with more approval.
Structure	The 'plan' of the flavour, as it were. Without structure wine is bland, dull, and won't last.
Stylish	Style is bold and definite; wears its cap on its ear.
Supple	Often used of young red wines which might be expected to be more aggressive. More lively than an 'easy' wine, with implications of good quality.
Well-balanced	Contains all the desirable elements (acid, alcohol, flavours, etc) in appropriate and pleasing proportions.

Masters of Wine

The Institute of Masters of Wine was founded in London in 1953 to provide an exacting standard of qualification for the British wine trade. A small minority pass its very stiff examinations, even after rigorous training, both theoretical and practical. (They must be able to identify wines 'blind', know how they are made, and also know the relevant EC and Customs regulations.) In all, only 178 people have qualified to become Masters of Wine. Twenty-seven 'Masters' are women.

In 1988 the Institute, aided by a grant from the Madame Bollinger Foundation, opened its examinations for the first time to non-British candidates. The first to pass was a New Zealander (see Kumeu River, page 201). 'Master of Wine' (MW) should eventually become the equivalent of a Bachelor of Arts degree in the worldwide wine trade.

What to drink in an ideal world

Wines approaching their peak in 1995

Red Bordeaux
Top growths of 87, 85, 83, 81,
79, 78, 75, 70, 66, 62, 61, 59
Other crus classés of 87, 86 (St-
Emilion/Pomerol), 85, 83, 82
(St-Emilion/Pomerol), 81, 79,
78, 75, 70, 66, 61
Petits châteaux of 90, 89, 88, 86,
85, 83, 82

Red Burgundy
Top growths of 89, 87, 85, 83,
82, 80, 79, 78, 76, 72, 71, 69,
66, 64
Premiers Crus of 89, 88, 87, 85,
83, 78, 76, 71
Village wines of 92, 91, 90, 89,
88, 85

White Burgundy
Top growths of 90, 89, 88, 86,
85, 83, 79, 78...
Premiers Crus of 92, 91, 90, 89,
88, 86, 85, 83, 78...
Village wines of 93, 92, 90, 89,
88, 86

Champagne
Top wines of 86, 85, 83, 82, 81,
79, 78, 76, 75...

Sauternes
Top growths of 85, 83, 82, 81,
79, 78, 76, 75, 71, 70, 67...
Other wines of 89, 88, 86, 85, 83,
82, 81, 79, 76, 75...

Sweet Loire wines
Top growths (Anjou/Vouvray) of
90, 88, 86, 85, 78, 76, 75,
71, 64...

Alsace
Grands Crus and late-harvest
wines of 89, 88, 86, 85, 83, 81,
78, 76, 67...
Standard wines of 93, 92, 91, 90,
89, 88, 85...

Rhône reds
Hermitage/top northern Rhône
reds of 88, 86, 85, 83, 82, 79,
78, 71, 70, 69...
Châteauneuf-du-Pape of 91, 89,
88, 86, 85, 83, 82, 81

German wines
Great sweet wines of 89, 88, 86,
85, 83, 76, 71, 67...
Auslesen of 90, 89, 88, 86, 85,
83, 79, 76, 71...
Spätlesen of 91, 90, 89, 88, 86,
85, 83, 79, 76...
Kabinett and QbA wines of 92,
91, 90, 89, 88, 85, 83...

Italian wines
Top Tuscan reds 90, 88, 86, 85,
82, 79, 78
Top Piedmont reds 88, 87, 86,
85, 83, 82, 79, 78, 74, 71...

California wines
Top Cabernets/Zinfandels of 90,
88, 86, 85, 84, 82, 81, 80, 79,
78, 77, 76, 75, 74, 70
Most Cabernets etc of 92, 90, 89,
88, 87, 86, 85...
Top Chardonnays of 91, 90, 89,
88, 87, 86, 85, 83, 81...
Most Chardonnays of 93, 92, 91,
90, 89, 88...

Australian wines
Top Cabernets and Shiraz of 89,
88, 86, 84, 82, 80, 79, 75...
Most Cabernets etc of 91, 90, 89,
88, 87, 86...
Top Chardonnays of 92, 90, 89,
88, 87, 86
Most Chardonnays of 93, 92, 91...
Top Sémillons and Rieslings of
92, 91, 90, 88, 86, 82, 79...

Vintage Port
83, 82, 80, 75, 70, 66, 63, 60,
55, 48, 45...

QUICK REFERENCE VINTAGE CHARTS

These charts give a picture of the range of qualities made in the principal areas (every year has its relative successes and failures) and a guide to whether the wine is ready to drink or should be kept.

I	drink now	—	needs keeping
/	can be drunk with pleasure now, but the better wines will continue to improve	ㅈ	avoid
		0 no good	10 the best

FRANCE

	RED BORDEAUX MEDOC/GRAVES	POM/ST-EM	WHITE BORDEAUX SAUTERNES & SW	GRAVES & DRY	ALSACE	
93	4-7 ↙	4-8 ∠	2-5 /	6-8 ↙	6-8 ↙	93
92	3-6 ↙	3-6 ↙	3-6 —	4-8 ↙	7-9 ↙	92
91	5-8 ∠	2-4 ↘	2-5 /	6-9 ↙	5-8 ↙	91
90	7-10 ↙	8-10 ∠	7-9 ∠	7-8 ↘	7-9 ↘	90
89	6-9 ↙	7-9 ↘	7-9 ∠	6-8 ↘	7-10 ↘	89
88	6-9 ∠	7-9 ↘	6-10 ↙	7-9 ↘	8-10 ↘	88
87	3-6 I	3-6 I	2-5 ㅈ	7-10 ↘	7-8 I	87
86	6-9 ↙	5-8 ↘	7-10 ↙	7-9 I	7-8 I	86
85	7-9 ↘	7-9 ↙	6-8 ↘	5-8 I	7-10 ↘	85
84	3-5 I	2-5 ㅈ	4-6 ㅈ	5-7 ↘	4-6 ㅈ	84
83	5-8 ↘	6-9 I	6-10 ↙	7-9 I	8-10 I	83
82	8-10 ↘	7-9 ↙	3-7 ↘	7-8 I	6-8 I	82
81	5-8 ↘	6-9 I	5-8 ↘	7-8 I	7-8 I	81
80	4-7 I	3-5 ↘	5-9 I	5-7 ㅈ	3-5 ㅈ	80
79	5-8 ↘	5-7 I	6-8 ↘	4-6 ㅈ	7-8 I	79
78	6-9 ↘	6-8 I	4-6 I	7-9 I	6-8 I	78
77	3-5 ㅈ	2-5 ㅈ	2-4 ㅈ	6-7 ㅈ		77
76	6-8 I	7-8 I	7-9 ↘	4-8 ㅈ		76

	BURGUNDY COTE D'OR RED	COTE D'OR WHITE	CHABLIS	RHONE RHONE (N)	RHONE (S)	
93	4-8 ∠	4-6 ↘	4-7 ↘	3-6 ↘	4-7 ∠	93
92	4-7 ∠	6-8 ∠	5-8 ↘	4-8 ∠	3-6 ∠	92
91	5-7 ↙	4-6 ↘	4-6 ↘	6-9 ↙	4-5 ↘	91
90	7-10 ↙	7-9 ↙	6-9 ↘	6-9 ∠	7-9 ∠	90
89	6-9 ↙	6-9 ↘	7-10 ↘	6-8 ∠	6-8 ↙	89
88	7-10 ↙	7-9 ↘	7-9 ↘	7-9 ↙	5-8 ↘	88
87	6-8 ↘	4-7 I	5-7 I	3-6 ↘	3-5 I	87
86	5-8 ↘	7-10 ↘	7-9 I	5-8 ↘	4-7 ↘	86
85	7-10 ↘	5-8 ↘	6-9 I	6-8 ↘	6-9 ↘	85
84	3-6 ㅈ	4-7 ↘	4-7 ㅈ	5-7 I	4-6 ㅈ	84
83	5-8 ↘	6-9 I	7-9 I	7-10 ↙	7-9 I	83
82	4-7 I	6-8 I	6-7 I	5-8 I	5-8 I	82
81	3-6 I	4-8 I	6-9 I	5-7 I	4-7 I	81

Beaujolais 93 Crus will keep, 92 was vg, 91 superb. **Mâcon-Villages** (white) Drink 93, 92, 91 and 90 now. **Loire** (Sweet Anjou and Touraine) best recent vintages: 93, 90, 89, 88, 85, 84, 83, 82, 79, 78, 76. **Upper Loire** (Sancerre and Pouilly Fumé): 93, 90, 89, 88 are good now. **Muscadet** DYA.

GERMANY   ITALY   USA

	RHINE	MOSELLE	TUSCAN REDS	CALIFORNIA CABS	CALIFORNIA CHARDS	
93	5-8 ↙	6-9 ↙	7-9 ↘	6-8 —	5-8 ↙	93
92	5-9 ↙	5-9 ↙	3-6 ↘	7-9 ∠	6-8 ↙	92
91	5-7 ↙	5-7 ↙	4-6 ↘	8-10 ∠	5-7 ↘	91
90	8-10 ↙	8-10 ↙	7-10 ↙	8-9 ∠	6-9 ↘	90
89	7-10 ↘	8-10 ↘	5-8 ↘	6-9 ∠	5-8 I	89
88	6-8 ↘	7-9 ↘	6-9 I	6-8 ↘	6-8 I	88
87	4-8 I	5-7 I	4-7 I	7-10 ↙	7-9 I	87
86	4-8 ↘	5-8 ↘	5-8 I	7-9 ↙	7-9 I	86
85	6-8 ↘	6-9 ↘	7-10 ↘	7-9 ↙	7-9 I	85
84	3-6 ㅈ	4-6 ㅈ	0-4 ㅈ	5-7 I	4-6 ㅈ	84
83	6-9 I	7-10 ↘	5-7 I	4-8 ↘	7-8 I	83
82	4-6 ㅈ	4-7 ㅈ	5-8 I	5-8 ↘	5-6 I	82
81	5-8 ㅈ	4-8 I	4-7 I	4-7 I	6-8 ㅈ	81